Equity and Trusts

Pearson

At Pearson, we have a simple mission: to help people make more of their lives through learning.

We combine innovative learning technology with trusted content and educational expertise to provide engaging and effective learning experience that serve people wherever and whenever they are learning.

We enable our customers to access a wide and expanding range of market-leading content from world-renowned authors and develop their own tailor-made book. From classroom to boardroom, our curriculum materials, digital learning tools and testing programmes help to educate millions of people worldwide — more than any other private enterprise.

Every day our work helps learning flourish, and wherever learning flourishes, so do people.

To learn more, please visit us at: www.pearson.com/uk

Selected chapters from:

Blueprints: Equity and Trusts
John Duddington

Equity and Trusts
Third edition
Sukhninder Panesar

Blueprints: Land Law
Elliot Schatzberger

Harlow, England • London • New York • Boston • San Francisco • Toronto • Sydney • Dubai • Singapore • Hong Kong
Tokyo • Seoul • Taipei • New Dehli • Cape Town • São Paulo • Mexico City • Madrid • Amsterdam • Munich • Paris • Milan

Pearson
KAO Two
KAO Park
Harlow
Essex CM17 9NA

And associated companies throughout the world

Visit us on the World Wide Web at:
www.pearson.com/uk

Compiled from:

Blueprints: Equity and Trusts
John Duddington
ISBN 978-1-4082-7729-4
© Pearson Education Limited 2014

Equity and Trusts
Third edition
Sukhninder Panesar
ISBN 978-1-292-08579-1
© Pearson Education Limited 2017

Blueprints: Land Law
Elliot Schatzberger
ISBN 978-1-4479-0494-6
© Pearson Education Limited 2014

ISBN 978-1-83961-167-4

Printed and bound in Great Britain by Ashford Colour Press, Gosport, Hampshire.

CONTENTS

Tables of cases and statutes

CASES

STATUTES

How to use this guide

Blueprints was created for students searching for a smarter introductory guide to their legal studies

This guide will serve as a primer for deeper study of the law – enabling you to get the most out of your lectures and studies by giving you a way in to the subject which is more substantial than a revision guide, but more succinct than your course textbook. The series is designed to give you an overview of the law, so you can see the structure of the subject and understand how the topics you will study throughout your course fit together in the big picture. It will help you keep your bearings as you move through your course study.

Blueprints recognises that students want to succeed in their course modules

This requires more than a basic grasp of key legislation; you will need knowledge of the historical and social context of the law, recognition of the key debates, an ability to think critically and to draw connections among topics.

Blueprints addresses the various aspects of legal study, using assorted text features and visual tools

Each Blueprints guide begins with an **Introduction**, outlining the parameters of the subject and the challenges you might face in your studies. This includes a **map** of the subject highlighting the major areas of study.

Each **Part** of the guide also begins with an Introduction and a map of the main topics you need to grasp and how they fit together.

Each guide includes advice on the specific **study skills** you will need to do well in the subject.

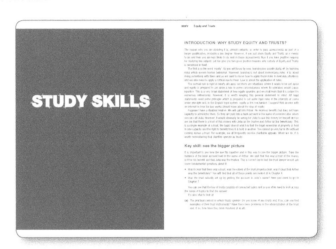

Each chapter starts with a **Blueprint** of the topic area to provide a visual overview of the fundamental buildings blocks of each topic, and the academic questions and the various outside influences that converge in the study of law.

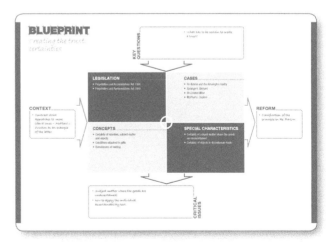

A number of text features have been included in each chapter to help you better understand the law and push you further in your appreciation of the subtleties and debates:

Setting the scene illustrates why it is important to study each topic.

Setting the scene

You have been promised by your friend Pam that, to celebrate her 21st birthday, she will take you with her on a trip to Paris. You are naturally very excited about this but then Pam suddenly tells you that she has changed her mind and will not be going after all. Relations between you and Pam deteriorate as you not unnaturally feel that Pam should have kept her promise.

Let's change the scenario a bit. Pam has now told you that she intends to set up a trust fund with £50,000 which she has won on the lottery and that Sheila will be the trustee and that you will be one of the beneficiaries. Sheila confirms that this is true and Pam has told her that this is what she will do.

You then wait . . . and wait . . . and wait . . . and nothing happens. Once again Pam has not kept her word. Pam, as the settlor, has failed to constitute the trust as she has not transferred the £50,000

Cornerstone highlights the fundamental building blocks of the law.

CORNERSTONE

Methods of constitution

The fundamental rules for how a trust can be constituted were set out by Turner LJ in *Milroy* v. *Lord*. Note that this leads to two methods of constitution of a trust:

(a) the settlor has vested the legal title to the trust property in the trustee(s) (Method One); *or*

(b) the settlor has declared that he now holds the property as trustee (Method Two).

Application shows how the law applies in the real world.

APPLICATION

Amanda says to her sister, Dawn: 'I am thinking of making a will but I really haven't the time or money to see a solicitor about it. As you are my only relative you will get everything on my death but I want you to hold my property on trust for the following friends of mine, each of whom is to have an equal share.' Amanda then tells Dawn the names of the friends who are to benefit. Dawn agrees to this. On Amanda's death her estate will vest in Dawn as administrator.

Intersection shows you connections and relationships with other areas of the law.

INTERSECTION

Company law

Although company law is a specialist area which you may not study it is important to be aware of what company law says about situations where a director has an interest which conflicts, or possibly may conflict, with the interests of the company.

Section 175(4)(b) of the Companies Act 2006 now provides that a director must avoid acting in situations where he has an interest which conflicts, or possibly may conflict, with the interests of the company. Section 175(4)(b) provides that this duty is not infringed if the matter has been authorised by the directors. This seems to reflect the dissenting speech of Lord Upjohn in *Boardman*.

Reflection helps you think critically about the law, introducing you to the various complexities that give rise to debate and controversy.

The dilemma of the courts

Before we come to look at how the law has developed since *Lloyds Bank* v. *Rosset* it is a good idea to pause and remind ourselves of the dilemma faced by the courts. On the one hand one can have rules such as those laid down in the cases stemming from *Gissing* v. *Gissing* with the consequent danger that in some cases a party will fall outside them, as in *Burns* v. *Burns*, and what seems to many as grave injustice will be done. On the other hand if the courts are left with too much discretion all may depend on the whim of each judge. In *Aspden* v. *Elvy* (2012) Judge Behrens put it this way:

> The Court has a discretion as to how the equity is to be satisfied in any particular case. It has been said that this is an area where equity is displayed at its most flexible; however it has also been said that the court must take a principled approach and cannot exercise a completely unfettered discretion according to the individual judge's notion of what is fair in any particular case.

REFLECTION

Context fills in some of the historical and cultural background knowledge that will help you understand and appreciate the legal issues of today.

Take note offers advice that can save you time and trouble in your studies.

(b) **Animals.** Trusts for the care of specific animals are valid as in *Re Dean* (1889) where money was left for the maintenance of the testator's horses and hounds. A trust for the maintenance of animals in general can be charitable (see Chapter 6). However, trusts to not only maintain but also *to breed from* the testator's animal would be invalid.

(c) **Miscellaneous.** A trust for the saying of masses was originally void as being for 'superstitious uses' but in *Bourne* v. *Keane* (1919) they were upheld but without consideration of the beneficiary issue, possibly on the assumption that they would be said in public. Trusts for the saying of masses in public would be charitable (*Re Hetherington* (1989) and see Chapter 6). It would be strange if the gift specifically

Take note

It is sometimes said that in *Re Thompson* (1934) the court held that a trust for the promotion of fox hunting was valid. In fact, the case concerned a gift to be applied to the promotion of fox hunting with a gift of residue to Trinity Hall, Cambridge. The issue was

Key points lists the main things to know about each topic.

KEY POINTS

There are detailed rules in statute governing the appointment, retirement and removal of trustees.

A trustee may delegate in certain cases. If so, then the trustee may be liable for the delegate's acts on certain conditions.

There is a fundamental distinction between duties (mandatory) and powers (permissive) of trustees.

The right to seek disclosure of trust documents is part of the jurisdiction of the court to supervise

Core cases and statutes summarises the major case law and legislation in the topic.

CORE CASES AND STATUTES

Case	About	Importance
Bray v. *Ford* (1896)	Trustee should not put herself in a position where her duty and interest conflict.	States a fundamental fiduciary principle; but is it a 'counsel of prudence rather than a rule of equity'?
Pitt v. *Holt* (2013)	Sets the rule in *Re Hastings-Bass* in the context of general principles governing control by the courts of discretionary decisions of trustees.	Limits the extent to which trustees who had relied on incorrect tax advice and its effect can undo the transaction

Further reading directs you to select primary and secondary sources as a springboard to further studies.

FURTHER READING

Cottrell, R. (1971) **'Re Remnant's Settlement Trusts' 34 MLR 98.**
This is one of the more important cases on the Variation of Trusts Act and you will find this article most helpful.

Harris, J.W. (1975) *Variation of Trusts* (Sweet & Maxwell).
This is most useful on the background to the passage of the Variation of Trusts Act. It also

This is still useful on powers of maintenance and advancement as the basic principles have not really changed.

Luxton, P. (1997) **'Variations of trusts: settlor's intentions and the consent principle in *Saunders* v. *Vautier*' 60 MLR 719.**
This article looks at the decision in *Goulding* v. *James* (1997) and, more widely, at whether

What is a Blueprint?

Blueprints provide a unique plan for studying the law, giving you a visual overview of the fundamental buildings blocks of each topic, and the academic questions and the various outside influences that converge in the study of law.

At the centre are the 'black-letter' elements, the fundamental building blocks that make up what the law says and how it works.

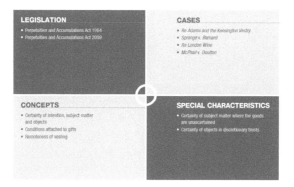

As a law student you will need to learn what questions or problems the law attempts to address, and what sort of issues arise from the way it does this that require critical reflection.

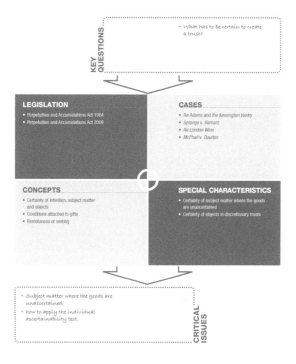

To gain a more complete understanding of the role of law in society you will need to know what influencing factors have shaped the law in the past, and how the law may develop in the near future.

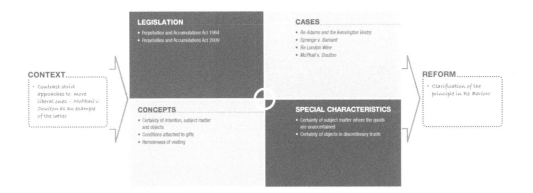

You can use the Blueprint for each topic as a framework for building your knowledge in the subject.

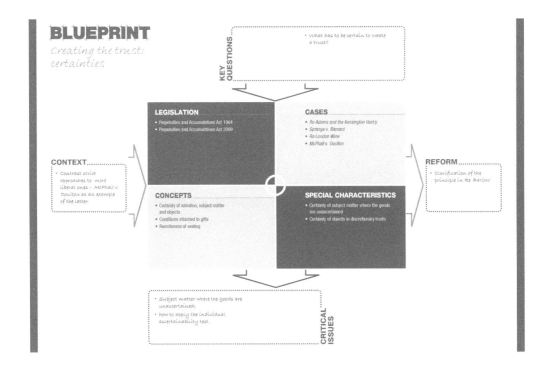

Introduction

Are you interested in the practical application of the law? How it relates to everyday life and helps us all to live a better, fuller and more satisfying existence? If so, then equity and trusts is for you. But why is this so? Surely equity and trusts has the reputation of being dry and dull? Let's look at it from the other side as it were: not from the point of view of the student but from that of a person, who is in fact all of us, who needs the law to help them to solve a problem.

Let's say that I have a young family aged 8, 10 and 12. I think that I will go on living for a while yet and my doctor tells me that I am in good health. However, I own a house and have some investments. I go abroad a lot on business and I wonder what would happen if I died early and left a family of children all well under age. My wife could sort things out, I suppose, and the house would be hers, but it would be unfair on her not to make some arrangements.

So I go to see my solicitor who suggests that I set up a trust. What is this? We shall see in more detail in this book but briefly it is a legal device where the legal ownership of property and what we can call the right to benefit from that property are split. One person, or preferably two, owns the property but unlike in most situations where a person is the owner, in this case they do not have the right to benefit from that property as instead my children are the beneficiaries. It may be my brother or sister together with my wife who act as owners in law and are known as the trustees.

So now if I die soon my investments, or some of them, are placed in the trust fund to benefit my three children when they come of age.

Of course this is only an outline but I hope that you can see how useful a trust can be in planning ahead and how often trusts can be used in this type of situation and many others.

Or perhaps you are another type of person, or perhaps you are the same person as in the previous example but with other interests. At all events you are interested in the great questions of life: how we can achieve a just society for instance and how the law can achieve fairness. Here too we have something for you, as the very idea of equity implies fairness; indeed at the very heart of equity is the idea that although we do need a degree of certainty in the law and in our lives we must guard against over-rigidity and must strive for what we can now call equity in individual cases. Equity is a difficult notion to pin down but if we equate it with fairness for the moment we won't go far wrong.

So you come to study this subject. What is the key to success?

Equity and trusts exams have a mixture of questions ranging from very technical questions on areas such as constitution of trusts to questions dealing with theoretical areas such as the nature of a resulting trust. Sometimes you may wonder how to navigate your way through it all. Here is an idea: first locate the central ideas that underpin each topic and keep these in mind throughout your study of it. For an example, the two themes that underpin the whole of equity are a willingness to see *behind* a rule and if need be to set it aside in the interests of justice, and a concern for conscience.

You will not go far, however, before you discover that many areas are controversial. One example is the extent to which equitable remedies are discretionary. A poor answer will simply say: 'Equitable remedies are discretionary.' A good answer will first ask: 'What is meant by discretion?' So another message is to avoid bland over-definite statements and instead ask questions as you go along.

You must also remember that equity needs to be seen in contrast to the common law and so just because you are studying equity does not mean that you should leave behind your knowledge of, for example, contract and tort. Questions in an equity exam may ask about the relationship between equity and the common law, one instance being the extent to which flexibility in the application of the law is unique to equity. If you can illustrate your answer by reference, for example, to the common law of negligence then this will immediately improve your marks.

Above all, make up your mind to really enjoy your study of equity, ask questions, put your book down and *think* about the subject, and be adventurous in your reasoning.

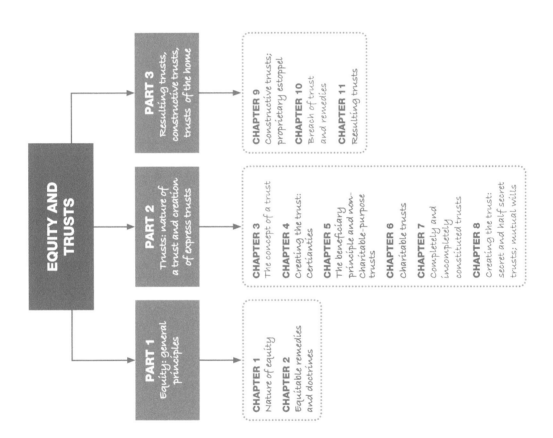

STUDY SKILLS

INTRODUCTION: WHY STUDY EQUITY AND TRUSTS?

The reason why you are studying it is, almost certainly, in order to pass assessments as part of a larger qualification, probably a law degree. However, if you just study Equity and Trusts as a means to an end then you are less likely to do well in those assessments than if you have positive reasons for studying this subject. Let me give you two good positive reasons why a study of Equity and Trusts is beneficial in itself.

The first is in the word 'equity'. As you will know by now, learning law usually starts off by learning rules which govern human behaviour. However, learning is not about memorising rules: it is about doing something with them and so we need to know how to apply those rules in everyday situations and we also need to apply a critical eye to them. Law is about the application of rules.

The normal rule is right in nearly all cases but there are situations where it needs to be set aside and equity is prepared to set aside a rule in some circumstances where its operation would cause injustice. This is a very broad statement of how equity operates and we shall learn that it is subject to numerous refinements. However, it is worth keeping this general statement in mind. All legal statements need some principle which is prepared to set aside rigid rules in the interests of some wider principle and, in the English legal system, equity is the mechanism. I suggest that anyone with an interest in how the law works should know about the idea of equity.

Suppose I have a disabled relative. We will call him Arthur. He receives benefits but does not have capacity to administer them. So they are paid into a bank account in the name of someone else whom we can call Julia. However, it would obviously be wrong for Julia to use this money for herself and so we say that there is a trust of this money with Julia as the trustee and Arthur as the beneficiary. This is a simple example of a trust, the basic idea of which is that the legal ownership of property is held in one capacity and the right to benefit from it is held in another. You cannot go very far in life without coming across a trust. For example, we all frequently receive charitable appeals. When we do, it is worth remembering that charities operate as trusts.

Key skill: see the bigger picture

It is important to see how the law fits together and in this way to see the bigger picture. Take the instance of the bank account held in the name of Arthur. We said that this was a trust of the money in it for his benefit and that Julia was the trustee. This is correct but in fact the trust lawyer would ask some fundamental questions about it:

- Was it clear that there was a trust; was the extent of the trust property clear; was it clear that Arthur was the beneficiary? You will find that all of these points are looked at in Chapter 4.

- Was the trust actually set up by putting the account in Julia's name? Here you need to go to Chapter 7.

You can see that the law of trusts consists of connected topics and so you often need to look across the range of topics to find the answer.

It's also vital to look at:

(a) The practical context in which trusts operate. Look especially at Chapter 10 which deal with the working of trusts and contain examples of clauses found in trust instruments. Do you know of any trusts and, if so, can you find examples of their trust instruments? Have there been problems in the administration of the trust and, if so, how have they been resolved (if at all).

(b) The social and economic context. Some chapters obviously lend themselves to this more than others. Good examples of where you can add value to your answers are:

- Trusts of the family home, where you could ask why the law on trusts of the family home become far more important than it was say in 1960.
- Charitable trusts (Chapter 6), where you could ask, for instance, why people set up charitable trusts? Why indeed do people give to charity at all?

Putting what you have learnt into practice

Keep in touch with the news to see how what you have learnt is applied in practice. Here is an example from the *Daily Telegraph* of 10 June 2013. The story concerned what was said to be an attempt by 'manufacturing tycoon' John Barry Wild to avoid inheritance tax that led to a court battle over his legacy which, the paper said, 'would have made him turn in his grave'.

Rather than making a traditional will, Mr Wild set up a discretionary family trust to ensure his wealth was passed to his wife Susan, 79, daughter Julia, 47, and son Ian 54, in the most tax efficient manner possible. But the plan backfired when his son and his widow – Ian's mother – fell out over Ian's belief that she had cut him out of *her* own will with the result that Ian blocked a payment of £500,000 to his mother from the trust and also blocked attempts by the other trustees to pay this money out.

The court removed Ian as a trustee and Arnold J said: 'I consider that Ian has allowed himself to become unduly influenced by his concern over Susan's will. Ian has allowed his judgement as a trustee to become clouded by matters which are not relevant to the exercise of his duties as a trustee. The proper course for this court is to remove him.'

This case really brings to life the areas of:

- Discretionary trusts – see Chapter 4.

SPECIFIC STUDY SKILLS

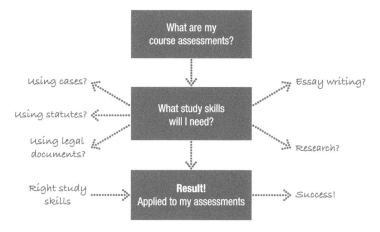

When you study equity and trusts you are first and foremost learning about this subject. However, at the same time you should take this opportunity to use your study of it to develop your study skills as you will find that this will help you to improve your performance not only in assessments in this subject but in other subjects, both in your academic studies of the law and in any vocational studies which you may go on to undertake.

This chapter contains a number of examples of how to enhance your study skills, based on material which we will cover. Look through it carefully and then use the skills you have acquired in this chapter in other areas of equity and trusts and in other areas of the law too.

Study skill: when it comes to writing an essay on equity

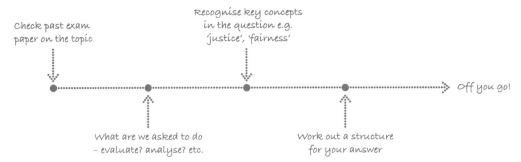

You are far more likely to get an essay question on the nature of equity than a problem as this topic lends itself to essays, although the equity exam taken as a whole is likely to have a mixture of problems and essays.

In fact equity, perhaps more than other areas such as land law, does lend itself very much to essays as there are so many broad themes, e.g. the nature of equity, the relationship between equity and the common law and the fiduciary principle. Check past exam papers at your institution and see if essays are set on the nature of equity. If so, look through them and see what study skills you will require to gain a good mark.

Take this example:

'Equity is a word with many meanings. In a wide sense, it means that which is fair and just, moral and ethical; but its legal meaning is much narrower'.

(Hanbury Modern Equity, 18th edition, p. 1)

Critically consider what this statement tells us about modern equity.

What study skills does this question need?

First we need to be clear about what we are asked to do. The question asks us to be **critical**, which does not necessarily mean to criticise but to exercise your critical faculties. So you need to think about the question: what does it mean, do we agree with the assumptions behind it? What we are not asked to do is simply give out information. Remember that critical analysis includes, where relevant, discussion of dissenting judgments, especially in House of Lords (now Supreme Court) cases; it also includes academic analysis of relevant areas.

Next, note exactly what the question says. We will see that it asks about modern equity, which is generally taken to mean equity following the Judicature Acts 1873–75. So an account of the history of equity will earn at best only minimal marks.

When you turn to the quotation this will enable you to **analyse** exactly what the question is about. If you do not analyse the question you will just see the one word 'equity' and then proceed to write all about the nature of equity, in effect giving a potted version of this chapter.

Analysing the question means **recognising** the key words and concepts in it. So here we have:

- Equity as a concept.
- Equity in a wider sense – fairness, justice, morality, ethical.
- Equity in a narrower sense – legal meaning.

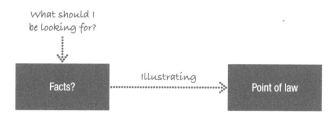

This leads us at once to a **structure** for our answer, as we can see that the question is asking us to look at the concept of equity but in doing so to contrast two meanings of equity.

We then need to plan an **introduction**, setting the scene, and then **structure** the answer around the two areas which we need to **contrast**.

When we are writing the essay we need to keep coming back to the word **'critical'** and so throughout we should aim to **contrast** the two ideas in the question. In order to do this you need to be able to **select** relevant points to illustrate your answer. For example, you may decide to choose trusts of the family home. You then need to **distinguish** between one approach which says that the courts should base their approach simply on what is fair whereas other judges would say that the basis is the search for the common intention of the parties. Come back to the question though: even when the judges use the word 'fair' this is still used in a legal sense and contrasts with general ideas of fairness.

Finally, you must have a conclusion which comes back to the question. Do not summarise what you have said but engage with the question and be critical here as in the rest of your answer.

Study skills feature: When it comes to using cases in assessments

How would you use cases in assessments?

The basic point, which applies to all law assessments but which cannot be repeated too often, is that you must bring out the point(s) of law considered by the case and only use the facts to illustrate the law. Remember that facts of cases generally are not necessary unless they are fundamental to the question that you are answering.

How do we do this in the context of these chapters?

Take *McPhail* v. *Doulton* in Chapter 4 at pages 80–81. This is of course one of the seminal cases in trusts law and above all you need to use it as an authority for the rule on certainty of objects in discretionary trusts as stated by Lord Wilberforce in the House of Lords. Having done this you can use the facts of the case to illustrate this point. Why not go further and consider the majority and minority speeches. Why did the majority change the test for certainty of objects? What was the reasoning of the minority in seeking to retain the complete list test? It is this type of detailed research that really makes an answer stand out.

If you dig deeper in your research you will find, as pointed out on pages 81–82 that when this test came to be applied by the High Court and the Court of Appeal in *Re Badens's Deed Trusts (No. 2)* there was considerable debate among the judges as to how it should be applied. You should see in particular the judgments of LJJ Stamp, Sachs and Megaw.

McPhail v. *Doulton* is an example of a case which really merits detailed research. Other cases need a different treatment. For instance, *Re Ralli's Will Trusts* (see Chapter 7 at page 159) has very complicated facts and you really need to just concentrate on understanding the point of law it makes. Another example is *Re Keen*, which lays down complex rules on communication of secret trusts where there is more than one intended trustee (see Chapter 8 at page 187). Here the vital point is to master the rules and there is no need to go into the facts of the case.

Re Keen concerned the position where the details of a secret trust are communicated by a sealed envelope. The Court of Appeal held that, had the rules on communication been complied with in other ways, the fact that the envelope was not opened until after the testator's death would not have made communication of the trust invalid.

You could leave the case at this point but you would lose marks. This is because the Court of Appeal then went on to consider the rules on communication of half secret trusts and, as you can see on page 187, they left the law in a confused state by indicating that there could be two different rules for the communication of half secret trusts.

You then need to research the subsequent cases to see how the courts have dealt with this apparent confusion. Examples are *Re Spence* and *Re Bateman*.

Study skill: when it comes to distinguishing cases in assessments

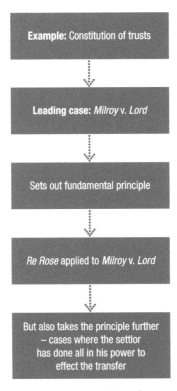

Often, when you are using cases, you come across a line of cases all on the same general topic but which are in fact slightly different.

What you must not do is give the facts and decisions in more than one case and then say lamely at the end: 'So all these cases make the same point'. This gets you nowhere. Each case that you mention needs to bring out a slightly different point and thus add to your marks. You need to learn how to distinguish between cases and so trace a line of cases showing how the law has developed from one case to another.

Take some cases on constitution of a trust (dealt with in Chapter 7), an area which students always find difficult.

One area is the principle in *Re Rose* (1952) that in certain cases a trust can be completely constituted when the settlor has done everything which is in his power to do to transfer the property even though the transfer is not complete until some other person has done a particular act. A frequent example is a transfer of shares. The principle was applied to land registration in *Mascall* v. *Mascall* (1985) but you may decide that this is just a straightforward example of the application of *Re Rose* and decide not to spend too much time on it.

Instead, go back to the main case on constitution of trusts, *Milroy* v. *Lord* (1862), and see how *Re Rose* distinguishes it. Look at the judgment of Evershed MR in *Re Rose* and see how he sets out the rationale behind *Milroy* v. *Lord*, explaining that: 'if a man purporting to transfer property executes documents which are not apt to effect that purpose, the court cannot then extract from those documents some quite different transaction and say that they were intended merely to operate as a declaration of trust'. However, having said this, he then goes on to explain that Turner LJ, who gave the leading judgment in *Milroy* v. *Lord*, cannot have meant 'that, as a result, either during some limited period or otherwise, a trust may not arise, for the purpose of giving effect to the transfer'.

Here we have the precise point of departure: Evershed MR agrees with the judgment of Turner LJ in *Milroy* v. *Lord* that an ineffective transfer cannot be rescued by the imposition of a trust. However, and this is where *Re Rose* strikes out on its own, Evershed MR holds that a trust may come into operation for a limited period simply to effect the transfer. Thus he finds that where the settlor has done all in his power to transfer the property, such as making a share transfer, then pending registration of the transferee as owner of the shares, the settlor will hold those shares on trust for the transferee.

You can follow this up by looking at the major recent case which has considered *Re Rose*, *Pennington* v. *Waine* (2002), and identify the exact point at which the court developed the law. You will find that in *Pennington* v. *Waine* Arden LJ and Clarke LJ gave slightly different reasons for their decision although they concurred in the result. I suggest that you look at Arden LJ's judgment first.

Clearly there is much more that you could say here: for example you could say that *Pennington* v. *Waine* has now been distinguished and not followed in the recent Court of Appeal case of *Zeital* v. *Kaye*. At least this example should have given you some ideas on how to start! Remember that it is vital to identify inconsistencies when discussing relevant cases – why do you think cases reach court? If everything was so clear-cut there would be no need for judges or lawyers!

Study skills feature: when it comes to using statutes in assessments

Equity and Trusts is not a statute-based subject as, for example, employment law very largely is, but there is a substantial amount of statutory material. How should you use it to the best advantage in assessments?

Take the law on formalities in the creation of trusts which are contained in two paragraphs of s. 53(1) of the LPA 1925: the law on creation of trusts of land (s. 53(1)(b)) and the law on the disposition of equitable interests under trusts (s. 53(1)(c)).

The fundamental statutory provisions are simple enough: trusts of land require written evidence and dispositions of equitable interests require written evidence. This is fundamental. You then need to go further and explain exactly what these paragraphs of s. 53(1) require: the best way is to make a list of the main points of each rather than try to learn the exact words of the statute off by heart.

You then need to go further and ask if there have been any cases on the interpretation of these paragraphs. In this instance there have been of course but the problem is that the facts of them are complex, in particular those involving the *Vandervell* litigation.

Here you could easily get completely lost in the intricacies of the cases and you need to concentrate on exactly what the statutes say (see above) and link your discussion of the cases to this.

Example

Take *Vandervell* v. *IRC* (1967). First, you need to be clear about which statutory provision this case illustrates. Here it is s. 53(1)(c) and so the issue to concentrate on is whether a disposition required writing. The next stage is to point out that writing will be required if it is a disposition of a subsisting equitable interest and so your explanation of the facts must concentrate on this one point. So you need to read the case carefully and then strip down the facts to the bare essentials, as we have done on page 103. From this you will be able to point out that there was no disposition of an equitable interest but instead a disposition of the entire legal and beneficial interest.

Moreover, you can often isolate vital words and then stress these in an exam.

Example

Section 31(1) of the Trustee Act 1925:

> Where any property is held by trustees in trust for any person for any interest whatsoever, whether vested or contingent, then, subject to any prior interests or charges affecting that property –
>
> **(i)** during the infancy of any such person, if his interest so long continues, the trustees may, at their sole discretion, pay to his parent or guardian, if any, or otherwise apply for or towards his maintenance, education, or benefit, the whole or such part, if any, of the income of that property as may, in all the circumstances, be reasonable, whether or not there is –
>
> > **(a)** any other fund applicable to the same purpose; or
> >
> > **(b)** any person bound by law to provide for his maintenance or education.

This, frankly, seems absolutely dreadful to the average law student! How do you disentangle it when you are studying it?

It is always better to look at complex legal wording in the context of an actual situation, so assume that you need to use it in an exam question:

> Helen's father, who has died, left her a gift by will of £500,000 provided that she reaches the age of 25. Helen is now aged 16 and is a promising ballet dancer. She wishes the trustees, Teresa and Richard, to pay £1,000 a year for her ballet lessons.

Take these steps:

(a) How did we know that this section was relevant at all? This gave us a starting point: s. 31(1) is relevant if the trustees wish to exercise a power of maintenance and here we are told that Helen wishes the trustees to pay £1,000 a year for her ballet lessons. Helen is 16 and so the power is exercisable as she is a minor. The Act did indeed use the word 'infancy' but now 'minority' or 'minor' is used.

(b) How did we identify that there was a power and not a duty so that trustees are not obliged to make maintenance payments? The clue is first in the heading, which says 'power', but this is not enough: where does this appear in s. 31? Look at paragraph (i), where you will see that it says: 'trustees may, at their sole discretion . . .'. The word 'may' is enough to indicate a power but in addition we are told that they have 'sole discretion'. Whenever you are studying a statute which allows a person(s) to take certain actions look for whether there is a power (indicated by 'may') or a duty (indicated by 'shall' or 'must').

(c) Check if there is a prior life interest – e.g. the question may say that Helen's father, who has died, left a gift by will of £500,000 to his wife Suzi for life and then to his daughter Helen. Suzi has a prior interest as she is a life tenant. If so, your answer will change as the entitlement of the beneficiary (Helen) to income will only come into effect when the life tenant (Suzi) dies.

(d) Now note that the gift is to Helen provided that she reaches the age of 25. This means that it is a contingent gift. Does s. 31 apply? Yes, as the opening words state that s. 31 applies if trustees hold property 'in trust for any person for any interest whatsoever'.

(e) Now read on in the question: 'Helen is now aged 16 and is a promising ballet dancer. She wishes the trustees to pay £1,000 a year for her ballet lessons'. We can now look at s. 31 of the Trustee Act (TA) 1925 and see that trustees may pay the income from the trust for the maintenance, education, or benefit of beneficiaries, so here again we have identified some vital words. In principle ballet lessons are for Helen's education.

So, if we go back to s. 31(1) of the TA we can annotate it as follows:

Where any property is held by trustees in trust for any person for any interest whatsoever, whether vested or contingent, then, subject to any prior interests or charges affecting that property –

(i) during the infancy of any such person, if his interest so long continues, the trustees may, at their sole discretion, pay to his parent or guardian, if any, or otherwise apply for or towards his maintenance, education, or benefit, the whole or such part, if any, of the income of that property as may, in all the circumstances, be reasonable, whether or not there is –

(a) any other fund applicable to the same purpose; or

(b) any person bound by law to provide for his maintenance or education.

Note that the heading also refers to 'accumulate surplus income during a minority'. This is contained in s. 31(2) which you can study and apply to the question!

Study skills feature: when it comes to using legal documents in assessments

Take this example of a clause which often appears in wills:

I DECLARE that in the application to the trusts of this my Will or any Codicil hereto the statutory power of maintenance given to my Trustees by Section 31 of the Trustee Act 1925 as amended the proviso in sub-section (1) of that section shall not apply and shall be deemed to be omitted and that clause (i) of sub-section (1) of the said section shall be read as if the words 'as the trustees think fit' were substituted for the words 'as may, in all the circumstances, be reasonable'.

You will see that in fact it relates to s. 31 of the Trustee Act 1925 which we have just looked at in the study skill feature above.

What is it doing? You can see that it relates to a will, and look at the words in line three: 'shall not apply'. What the will is doing is providing that part of s. 31 of the Trustee Act 1925 shall not apply and so the will is overriding the Act. Do not always assume that it is possible for a legal document to override either a statute or case law. For example, a trustee exclusion clause cannot always do so: see Chapter 10.

What does this clause do?

First it excludes the 'proviso' in sub-section (1) as it says that the proviso of that section 'shall not apply and shall be deemed to be omitted'. So we need to look at the proviso to s. 31. Note that we did not consider this proviso when we looked at s. 31 in the study skills section above.

> Provided that, in deciding whether the whole or any part of the income of the property is during a minority to be paid or applied for the purposes aforesaid, the trustees shall have regard to the age of the infant and his requirements and generally to the circumstances of the case, and in particular to what other income, if any, is applicable for the same purposes; and where trustees have notice that the income of more than one fund is applicable for those purposes, then, so far as practicable, unless the entire income of the funds is paid or applied as aforesaid or the court otherwise directs, a proportionate part only of the income of each fund shall be so paid or applied.

How did we know that it was a 'proviso'? This is easy: it opens with the words 'Provided that'. What does the proviso say though? Again we need to look carefully at the actual words and you will see that the vital ones are 'the trustees shall have regard to'. How do we know that they are the vital words? This is because they tell the trustees what to do.

So, what the proviso says is that when exercising their power of maintenance the trustees shall have regard to certain factors which are set out further on. These are, as you can see, such matters as 'the age of the infant and his requirements'.

We can now interpret the will as saying that, as the proviso does not apply, the trustees will not be bound to have regard to certain particular factors and so their discretion on whether to pay maintenance is widened.

There is more, too: the will also says that 'clause (i) of sub-section (1) of the said section shall be read as if the words "as the trustees think fit" were substituted for the words "as may, in all the circumstances, be reasonable"'. If we go back to s. 31 and what it says, we can see that the omission of the words 'reasonable' and substitution of 'as the trustees think fit' does give the trustees a much wider discretion as there is no room for any decision of theirs to be challenged on the ground that it is not 'reasonable'.

This particular clause is in fact commonly found in wills and in 2011 the Law Commission published a report, 'Intestacy and Family Provision on Death', which proposed reforming powers of maintenance and advancement to make them accord with current practice. One result would be to change s. 31 to make it accord with what is in this clause. This, of course, is an example of you using your research study skill (see below) to supplement your skill in analysing legal documents.

Study skills feature: when it comes to researching a topic for an assessment

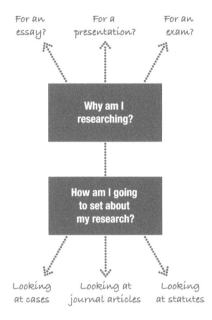

You will need to research topics in equity and trusts for various reasons: it may be preparation for an exam or an assignment or possibly a presentation. Researching topics in equity and trusts involves the same basic study skills as in other areas which you study but it is helpful to see how these can be applied to equity and trusts. Here is an example:

Suppose that you are researching the question of what is a fiduciary? First be clear about exactly what you want to research. Is it just the meaning of this term or are you really trying to find out what it means in certain contexts, for example whether a company director is a fiduciary? So remember, right at the start, to refine and clarify your research question.

This area is contained in case law and so you need to look for a fairly recent discussion of exactly who is a fiduciary is, preferably in a decision of the Court of Appeal, House of Lords or Supreme Court. Recent decisions have the advantage over earlier ones that they will usually refer to the earlier ones and so give you a trail for your research.

A quick search in a text book will show you that one often quoted case is *Bristol and West Building Society* v. *Mothew* (1998), where Millet LJ said that a 'fiduciary is someone who has undertaken to act for or on behalf of another in circumstances which give rise to a relationship of trust and confidence'.

Now that you have a start you need to follow the trail. Have a look at one of the most recent cases. A good example is *Sinclair Investments (UK) Ltd* v. *Versailles Trade Finance Ltd* (2011). This decision was of great importance on the issue of claims by a beneficiary, to whom a fiduciary owed duties, to a proprietary interest, but do not get led astray! You are researching the concept of a fiduciary and not this topic. Look at the leading judgment, that of Neuberger MR, and search for any reference to *Bristol and West Building Society* v. *Mothew* (1998). You will find it at para. 35.

If you then look further down this judgment you will see, as we mentioned earlier, that as it is a recent case it will refer you to earlier ones and in fact Neuberger MR in the next paragraph (36) refers to *Regal (Hastings) Ltd* v. *Gulliver* (1967). If you go to this case you will find references to *Boardman* v.

Phipps and *Keech* v. *Sandford*, both leading cases in this area. However, although this trail is now promising, do not be sidetracked: if your search is for what the courts said about a fiduciary then keep to this! However, if you do come across something else interesting then make a note of this and you can come back to it later.

When you research a case which has gone on appeal you should also research the decision in the court(s) below. Here you will see that at para. 33 Neuberger MR referred to the judgment of Lewison J in the High Court, with which, in fact, he agreed.

Finally you do need to research the opinions of authors of journal articles and textbooks! Judges increasingly refer to these and in his decision in *Sinclair Investments (UK) Ltd* v. *Versailles Trade Finance Ltd* Neuberger MR referred at para. 58 to one by Andrew Hicks, '*The Remedial Principle in Keech* v. *Sandford Reconsidered*' (2010) *Cambridge Law Journal* 287. Clearly this would be useful to look at and again it will have leads to other articles.

The trail will be endless and you will then need to decide whether you have enough material to weld into a coherent whole. Remember as well that it is in the nature of equity that many of the concepts are fluid and so you are not necessarily going to arrive at a very final and certain answer to your research question.

Useful websites

You should keep an eye on the Charity Commission website for developments in charity law. It is an indispensable resource. A lot is going on in the world of charities at the moment and this is the place to begin.	**www.charity-commission.gov.uk**
Many changes in the law in the law since 1966 have come about through the activities of the Law Commission which was established in that year. Examples from the law of trusts are the Trustee Act 2000 and the Perpetuities and Accumulations Act 2009. Have a look through Law Commission Consultation Papers and Reports. In addition to containing proposals for law reform they provide excellent explanations of the law.	**http://lawcommission.justice.gov.uk/**
There is often a link between trusts and land law and so you should familiarise yourself with the land registry website. You will find the land registry guides very helpful. One example is where there is a beneficial interest in property and you can refer to Public Guide 18 – Joint property ownership.	**www.landregistry.gov.uk/**
The Chancery Bar Association is, as its name suggests, the professional association for barristers who practise in chancery matters, which of course includes trusts law. Although their website is orientated towards practice issues it is still worth keeping an eye on it as, for example, you can find texts of the annual lectures to the Chancery Bar Association. The one by Lord Neuberger in 2008 is especially useful.	**www.chba.org.uk/**

➔

Useful websites	
The *Guardian* newspaper has a free online section on law. It is regularly updated and will have links to important legal developments, opinion pieces and speeches by important persons such as judges.	**www.guardian.co.uk/law**
The British and Irish Legal Information Institute. This website contains the transcript of all new cases and many older cases.	**www.bailii.org/**

SUMMARY

Please remember:

- Why studying equity and trusts is valuable in itself.
- How it applies in practice.
- Why seeing the bigger picture adds value to your studies.
- The advice on using specific study skills to enhance your performance in equity assessments when writing essays, using cases, statutes and legal documents and undertaking research.
- The useful websites – and these are only a start!

PART 1

Equity: general principles

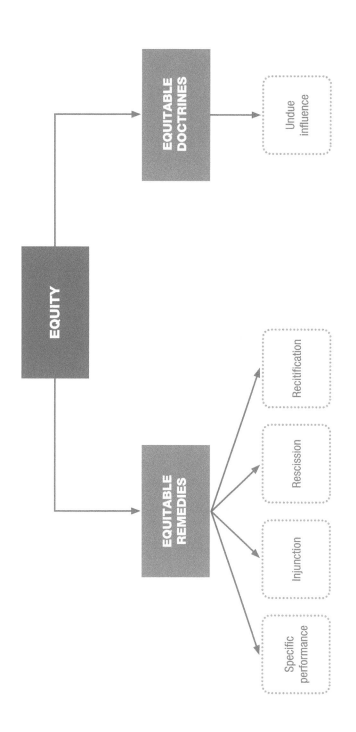

PART 1 INTRODUCTION

The focus of this part is on equity in general, rather than on the trust, which is the major creation of equity. As such it looks at the general nature of equity and its remedies and doctrines.

You may find the following story useful when you are trying to recall exactly what the nature of equity is.

When I was writing this chapter I took a relative, who happens to be disabled, to a supermarket café. The food which they could eat was not sold in the café and the café has a rule that only food bought in the café can be consumed there. However, the food was available round the corner in the actual supermarket. I asked the assistant if I could buy it from the supermarket and give it to my relative. He agreed.

In a sense he applied the rule of equity. The normal rule is right in nearly all cases but there are situations where it needs to be set aside and this was one of them. The extra dimension which equity adds to this familiar kind of situation is that when equity acts in this way it does so on grounds of conscience. As you will see, equity does not always operate in this way; sometimes it applies rigid rules, but we can say that one of the aims of equity is to look beyond the letter of the law. As Watt (2009, p. 35) puts it: 'According to equitable discourse, the rule is not the law; it is merely, as Bacon wrote: "the magnetic needle" which "points to the law".' Incidentally Francis Bacon was a well-known Elizabethan philosopher and lawyer who was Lord Chancellor from 1618 to 1621.

CHAPTER 1
Nature of equity

BLUEPRINT
Nature of equity

LEGISLATION

- Judicature Acts 1873–1875

CONTEXT

- What is the place of equity in a legal system?

CONCEPTS

- Meaning of equity
- What is equity about?
- Historical development of equity
- Relationship between equity and common law
- Fusion of common law and equity

- What part should the concept of unconscionability play in the development of equity?

- What do we mean by equity?

CASES

- *Patel* v. *Ali*
- *Walsh* v. *Lonsdale*

SPECIAL CHARACTERISTICS

- Relationship between equity and common law
- Meaning of discretion in equity
- Role of conscience in equity

REFORM

- Further integration of equity and common law?

CRITICAL ISSUES

Setting the scene

A discussion of the nature of equity can be somewhat abstract so at the start we ought to ground it in a real-life situation.

John orally agrees to sell some land to Teresa. Teresa's intention was to start a small farm on the land. There are all the elements for a valid contract in place but in addition contracts for the sale of land have to comply with the formalities set out in s. 2 of the Law of Property (Miscellaneous Provisions) Act 1989 and in particular they must be in writing. (You will find further details of this in Chapter 9.)

The result is that according to the rules of this statute the contract between John and Teresa cannot be enforced. If Teresa wishes John to go ahead and transfer the land to her John is quite within his rights to refuse. In most cases this will be right. The requirement of certain formalities is there to protect both sides. Land is usually the most valuable asset we can own and so there must be clarity about whether there has been an agreement at all to transfer it and what that agreement contains.

Now let's bring in another dimension. Suppose that following their oral agreement Teresa had said to John 'Shouldn't this be in writing?' and John had replied: 'Yes I'll see to this.' Teresa then says to John: 'Meanwhile do you mind if I start putting up some farm buildings?' John says: 'No, fine, go ahead'. Teresa spends a considerable sum of money erecting a pig sty and a barn and she asks John what he thinks. John says: 'That looks great.' John did intend to write to his solicitor about getting the agreement put in writing but he forgot. So later on he told Teresa that she must vacate the land as she has no legal rights there.

We are, I think, instinctively on Teresa's side here: she will suffer an injustice if she has to leave. But that is not how equity looks at the matter. First, as in the above example of my friend in the café, equity notes that there is a rule and in fact in most cases equity will enforce that rule. However, there is another element: Teresa has acted on the basis that her agreement to buy the land was binding and has acted on the basis that it is valid and enforceable. We could say that it would be against conscience to allow John to turn her out and for John to then take the benefit of the pig sty and barn that Teresa has erected. This may well be the view of equity and so it may enforce the agreement for the sale of the land by John to Teresa. (Note, by the way, that we do not say 'Equity *will* enforce the agreement' because, as we shall see, there is a strong element of discretion in equity).

From this example we can see the two strands of equity: its insistence that the actual rule is not always the law combined with an emphasis on conscience. The operation of these principles is not an exact science, which is why a court, when applying equity, will often have a degree of discretion, a term which we shall look at more closely later on.

WHAT DOES EQUITY DO?

CORNERSTONE

What is equity about?

The distinguishing characteristics of equity are a willingness to see *behind* a rule and a concern for conscience.

A definition of equity could be that it consists of the body of rules which, before the Judicature Act 1873, was administered in the Court of Chancery and not in the common law courts. Later on in this chapter you will find out about the Court of Chancery and the Judicature Act but for now I suggest that you think about the two central strands of equity, mentioned above. These strands mean that, put very briefly, equity does two things:

(a) It recognises that, in some cases, if a strict rule of law applied in a particular situation it would result in greater injustice than would result if that rule of law was not applied. So equity may be prepared to set that rule aside.

(b) It applies a kind of yardstick based on conscience to assess whether it should intervene. If conduct is found to be against conscience and thus to be unconscionable then equity may either grant or withhold an equitable remedy.

The above are really themes running right throughout equity. Keep them in mind throughout your studies. Remember that this book aims to navigate you through your studies in equity. Use these two themes as stars to help you to navigate. Everything you learn in equity can be referred back to them.

HOW AND WHY DID EQUITY DEVELOP?

There is no need to learn a vast amount of history here but it is vital to know how and why equity developed in order to understand how it operates today.

We need to go back briefly to medieval times, roughly some 800 years ago and some years after the Norman Conquest. England was a strong central state with a vigorous legal system but there were two defects:

(a) In some cases the law was applied too rigidly.

(b) In some cases the procedure was too technical.

Equity arose in response to these problems but here we have to answer an important question: Why did the common law not just reform itself?

The answer lies in the ancient office of Chancellor, or Lord Chancellor as he was known. One famous Chancellor of whom you may have heard was Thomas Becket, who famously fell out with King Henry II and was murdered in Canterbury Cathedral in 1170.

The Chancery was the royal secretariat and its clerks issued the writs referred to above. As such it constituted a permanent body of trained personnel headed by the Chancellor, who was generally a lawyer and also an ecclesiastic as well as being one of the chief ministers of the Crown. It was therefore a natural process to pass petitions complaining about the common law to the Chancery. Originally the Chancery saw its function as assisting the common law courts in dispensing justice but from around 1350 onwards the Chancery began to deal with cases itself and by 1390 petitions were directed to the Chancellor directly rather than to the King in Council.

The advantages of the Chancellor over the common law courts were that:

(a) The Chancery was able to deal with the case without a jury.

(b) The Bill procedure did not require any particular form and so the bar which the common law courts applied on new types of actions being brought disappeared if the action was begun in Chancery.

(c) The relative informality of procedure at this early date meant that the services of a lawyer were not always needed.

(d) The Chancellor acted *in personam*. This famous phrase, one of the great characteristics of equity, meant that the Chancellor acted against a person rather than against his land, and so he could be ordered to carry out an obligation by a decree of specific performance or do, or refrain from doing, an act by an injunction. However, it should be pointed out that the early common law courts also acted *in personam* but their jurisdiction withered away. Note the emphasis on equitable remedies, which are considered in detail in Chapter 2. They, along with the trust (see below) are the distinctive contributions of equity to the legal system today.

(e) The fact that the Chancellor recognised and enforced trusts. This topic is dealt with in more detail in Chapter 3 but, briefly, the essential feature of a trust is that the ownership of the property in law and the rights over it in equity are split. The trustee is the owner in law but others may have rights over it in equity.

> It is wrong to overstate the contrast between equity and the common law and say that equity looked at broad notions of justice and the common law courts were rule bound. The early courts of common law, when applying the law, were willing to disapply it when otherwise injustice would be done. Allen (1964, p. 402) mentions a case of 1309 when a man had promised to hand over a document by a certain day and to pay a penalty if he did not do so. He was, however, unable to so as he was overseas at the time and pointed out that the creditor had suffered no damage by the delay. The court took the point and told the creditor that he would have to wait seven years in this case for the money.
>
> **REFLECTION**

Once fairly launched the development of equity was rapid under a succession of vigorous Chancellors and reached a peak under Wolsey, who held office from 1515 to 1529. He was followed by Thomas More (1529–1532) and the growth of Chancery jurisdiction can be judged by the fact that he heard 2,356 cases in the 31 months when he held office. The type of cases dealt with by the Chancellor have been analysed by Guy (1980) as follows: 47% concerned real property, 15% mercantile and the rest were a mixed bag consisting of e.g. fraud, forgery, defamation and false imprisonment. It is this last part of the Chancellor's jurisdiction which has very largely died away.

Equity was originally seen as a court of conscience and indeed Klinck (2010) observes that in the Middle Ages the term 'Court of Conscience' would have been used rather than 'Court of Equity'. Nicholas St Germain, in his influential work *Doctor and Student* published around 1530, emphasised the importance of the principle of conscience both from a moral standpoint and also as a corrector of strict legal rules which should be applied according to their intention and not necessarily their strict meaning and it is here that we see the development of the two themes of equity to which we referred at the start of this chapter.

Conscience in equity

We often come across the term 'conscience' in equity and, especially in more recent cases, the term 'unconscionability'. We have already noted that if you had asked the Court of Chancery in the medieval period how to describe its guiding principle it would have answered 'conscience' and not 'equity'. Later on, in the seventeenth century, the terms 'conscience' and 'equity' were taken to mean much the same thing. Now it is time to examine what conscience means.

The word 'conscience' is often misunderstood. People frequently use the term 'conscience' in what is essentially a subjective sense: 'I could not say that, it would be

CONTEXT →

against my conscience.' Note the emphasis on '*my* conscience'. However, conscience means something deeper. Conscience comes from the Latin '*conscientia*' and means 'knowledge in oneself'. The objective term 'conscience' was one used in Roman Catholic moral teaching and so in the Middle Ages conscience was not understood in a subjective sense but in an objective one as springing from a set of principles which governed the behaviour of us all. It is this meaning of the term conscience which would have been applied in the Court of Chancery in the Middle Ages.

After the Reformation in the sixteenth century, when Protestantism became the established religion of England, the idea of conscience slowly became, under the influence of Protestant theology, one which emphasised the individual responsibility of each individual before God and thus was understood in a more subjective sense. However, this was a very gradual development. Lord Nottingham in *Cook* v. *Fountain* (1676) distinguished between 'political' and 'internal' conscience. This is, in fact, an expression of the medieval idea of conscience: the conscience of each individual ('internal') and what Francis Bacon called 'the general conscience of the realm, which is Chancery' (see Klinck 2010, p. 225).

Equity from the seventeenth century onwards

CORNERSTONE

Later development of equity

Equity very gradually hardened into a body of rules, not unlike the common law, although always with an equitable flavour.

After the era of Wolsey and More there was a gradual hardening of equitable jurisdiction and a move towards definite principles and rules. In one way this was surprising, given that, as we have just seen, the idea of conscience was now seen as a vital feature of equity. In effect equity began to turn in on itself, becoming stagnant; this phase lasted until the middle of the nineteenth century.

In the time of Lord Nottingham C (1673–1682) (see also the Context box 'Conscience in equity') the equitable maxims began to be formulated and this was one of the reasons why equity changed from being based on the general notion of conscience to a more formal and predictable system. The maxims describe some of the main principles that guide equitable intervention but their importance should not be over-stressed. They consist of brief, pithy phrases which remain easily in the mind but in fact judges today do not use them so often. You will find references to them throughout this book but here are some examples

- The maxim 'delay defeats equities' is shown by the doctrine of laches under which undue delay can bar an equitable remedy (see Chapter 2).

- The maxim 'equity does not assist a volunteer' is important in connection with the enforcement of promises to transfer property to be held on trust (see Chapter 7).

- The maxim 'equity will not allow a statute to be used as an instrument of fraud' means that equity will sometimes prevent a party from relying on the provisions of a statute where this would result in fraud (see Chapter 9).

Nevertheless it is vital not to overstress the significance of the maxims and some judges have preferred to ignore them. As Lord Esher MR said in *Yarmouth* v. *France* (1887):

> I need hardly repeat that I detest the attempt to fetter the law by maxims. They are almost invariably misleading: they are for the most part so large and general in their language that they always include something which really is not intended to be included in them.

In the early nineteenth century, especially under the leadership of Lord Eldon, the Court of Chancery became a byword for delay, and in Charles Dickens' *Bleak House* the practices of the old Court of Chancery are mercilessly exposed. Miss Flite, the perpetual suitor, observes, with considerable understatement, that 'Chancery justice is so very difficult to follow'. As it happened, by the time *Bleak House* was published in 1852, one of the first steps had been taken to reform the procedures of the Court with the passage of the Chancery Amendment Act. This was part of a series of measures culminating in the Judicature Acts of 1873 and 1875.

CORNERSTONE

Judicature Acts

The Judicature Acts marked the end of equity as a completely separate system of law and overhauled and modernised the structure of the courts.

The old Court of Chancery was abolished along with the old common law courts of Kings Bench, Common Pleas and Exchequer. In their place a new High Court was established which also incorporated the old courts of Probate, Divorce and Admiralty. Much of the work of the Court of Chancery was assigned to the new Chancery Division of the High Court but the vital point was that equity jurisdiction could be exercised by any of the divisions of the High Court and this is the case today. The effect was that equity was no longer administered separately from the common law; instead they are both now administered side by side in all courts.

Finally you should note that by the Constitutional Reform Act 2005 the ancient office of Lord Chancellor was unexpectedly and, in the view of many, quite unnecessarily altered and its judicial functions were transferred to the Lord Chief Justice with the result that the Lord Chancellor need not be a lawyer. The actual office of Lord Chancellor remains, shorn of much of its historic significance, and the present holder is also the Minister of Justice.

Figure 1.1 The court system before and after the Judicature Acts

What is important is that as the new Court of Appeal heard appeals from all three divisions of the High Court the old separation between common law and equity was inevitably broken down.

CORNERSTONE

Equitable remedies are discretionary

The fact that equitable remedies are discretionary is a significant feature of equity but it is vital to be clear on what equity means.

To what extent is equity based on discretion and what does discretion mean? Although a court, when awarding equitable remedies, has some discretion, it is not a *complete* discretion. The court, when applying equity, does not start with a blank sheet of a paper. It cannot simply do what it feels to be just in the circumstances and it must be emphasised that the fact that equity is a discretionary system should not lead you to the idea the equity is all about vagueness. It has been said that 'there is a real danger in simply assuming that equity stands for flexibility and vagueness. Equity needs to be principled and equity needs to be clear' (Virgo 2003). Indeed, in many areas, as we shall see, there is no more discretion in equity than there is in the common law. A good example is the rules on constitution of a trust in Chapter 7. Furthermore, there are many areas of the common law where the courts exercise discretion, such as judicial review and the imposition of a duty of care in negligence.

REFLECTION

EQUITY AND COMMON LAW

CORNERSTONE

Relationship between equity and common law

Equity and the common law are interdependent systems.

Although, as we shall see below, equity and the common law are administered separately, they are still separate systems of law. It is in fact often said that the great difference between equity and the common law is that equity is not a complete system whereas the common law is. Thus, as the law of contract is based on common law, it would be possible to write a book about the law of contract, for example, and not mention the equitable remedies. On the other hand, one could not write a book about equity without mentioning the common law. For example, if one wrote on the way in which equitable remedies (see Chapter 2) work in the law of contract one would have to mention common law as the law of contract *is* mainly common law.

Although there is something in all this, it really does not take us very far, if at all, because in fact it is impossible to understand something about the law of contract by looking solely at the rules laid down by the common law courts, ignoring equitable interventions. Not only would nothing be said about equitable remedies but also nothing about such doctrines as promissory estoppel.

Moreover, it is also impossible to understand contract law without knowing something about statute law which is so important in such areas as exclusion clauses.

The truth is that in the modern legal system all parts, common law, statute law and equity, are interdependent and no one can be understood without the others. You will see throughout this book how equity meshes with common law. Take for example Chapter 7 on constitution of trusts where you will find that the common law doctrine of consideration is adopted by equity which then adds to it with some ideas of its own.

The poet Rudyard Kipling (1865–1936) once wrote: 'What do they know of England who only England know?' The same could be applied to common law, statute law and of course to equity.

To what extent are equity and the common law fused?

CORNERSTONE

Fusion debate

The administration of law and equity are fused but there is a continuing debate about the extent to which the actual principles of common law and equity are fused and whether they should be.

Take note

Equity is often contrasted with the common law but it can be misleading to use this term in relation to modern equity. This term is often taken to mean law made by the courts under common law principles such as the law of contract and tort as distinct from law made by the courts under equitable principles. However, if we just contrast equity with common law in this way we are leaving out all of the areas where equity contrasts with statute law. Thus although examination questions often ask you to contrast equity with common law you should point out at the start of your answer that in fact the contrast is with both common law and statute law.

The administration of equity and the common law are fused by the Judicature Acts but are equity and the common law themselves fused so that it is no longer correct to speak of equity and the common law as distinct systems? This question has been much debated. Did fusion occur with the Judicature Acts, has it occurred since and, if not, should it occur now? The general view is that they have not. This was expressed in a well-known metaphor by Ashburner (1902) that 'the two streams of jurisdiction, though they run in the same channel, run side by side and do not mix their waters'. This view has been contradicted, most notably by Lord Diplock in *United Scientific Holdings* v. *Burnley Borough Council* (1978), who said that this 'fluvial metaphor' is 'mischievous and deceptive' and that the two systems of law, common law and equity, were indeed fused by the Judicature Acts. The truth is, however, that they have not, as any glance at the areas covered in this book will show. Equitable and common law remedies operate together but are not governed by the same principles, as shown by *Patel* v. *Ali* (see later in this chapter). Another example is *Walsh* v. *Lonsdale* (below).

The fusion debate has been revived from another angle by Worthington (2006), who suggests that it is time that equity and the common law were fully integrated. This approach goes beyond the somewhat sterile discussion as to the effect of the Judicature Acts and argues that, in any event, there is now no reason why integration should not be pursued. She points out that it is untrue to say that it is only equity which permits the exercise of discretion; so does the common law. She instances, for example, the discretionary element in deciding if a duty of care exists in tort or if a consumer contract contains unfair terms. At times, on the other hand, equity has no discretion at all, for example in deciding if equitable proprietary remedies should be awarded or not. She makes the telling point that, if there were discretion here, the law of insolvency would turn into a farce. Moreover, she rightly draws attention to the increased willingness of the common law to adjudicate according to the standard of reasonableness. This is true, as in the above examples, but one could say that there is an undoubted flavour of equity which could be lost if it were simply taken under the umbrella of the common law. Moreover, the common law standard of reasonableness is not the same as some equitable principles which have a specifically ethical dimension to them that is not necessarily present in the standard of reasonableness.

Section 25(11) of the Judicature Act 1873 (the rule is now in s. 49 of the Senior Courts Act 1981) provided that where the rules of equity and common law conflict then equity shall prevail. The effect of this can be exaggerated as in many cases there is no conflict. In the administration of the law of trusts equity holds undisputed sway and in the case of remedies equity and the common law work alongside each other so the court may award the appropriate remedy, whether it is equitable or common law. An instance is *Patel* v. *Ali* (below) where it was felt that the equitable remedy of specific performance was inappropriate and so common law damages were awarded. However, in some cases there is the possibility of conflict and so s. 25(11) comes into play.

INTERSECTION

Another means by which some areas of common law and equity could be fused is if unjust enrichment was accepted as the remedial basis where a defendant had been unjustly enriched at the claimant's expense where the basis of that claim was common law or equitable. (This is considered further in Chapter 9.)

CORNERSTONE

Walsh v. Lonsdale

Walsh v. *Lonsdale* illustrates the extent to which equity and the common law were regarded as fused in the period immediately after the Judicature Acts.

In *Walsh* v. *Lonsdale* (1882) the parties had agreed on a lease of a mill for seven years. Rent was payable quarterly in arrears but the landlord was entitled to demand a year's rent in advance. However, the agreement was not contained in a deed as required to make it binding in law (this requirement is now in s. 52(1) of the Law of Property Act 1925). The result was that the lease was void in law.

Nevertheless the tenant entered into possession and paid rent in accordance with the lease for 18 months. The landlord then demanded a year's rent in advance and when the tenant refused to pay the issue was whether the terms of the agreement for a lease could be relied on. At common law the landlord could not have demanded a year's rent in advance as the lease was void and the yearly periodic tenancy which arose when the tenant went into possession excluded a right to claim payment of rent in advance. However, equity could be applied and here the maxim 'equity looks on that as done which ought to be done' meant that, as the parties had *agreed* on a lease, equity would then act on the principle that the agreement had now been given effect to by a deed as this was what the parties ought to have done. When the agreement was applied it was seen that it allowed the landlord to claim payment of rent in advance and so the landlord's claim succeeded.

Common Law	Equity
No deed – agreement ineffective – landlord had no rights under it.	Lack of a deed did not matter – agreement could be enforced – including landlord's rights under it

Figure 1.2 Summary

Common law and equity in operation today: a contrast

The truth is that equity and the common law still approach matters from quite different standpoints. Watt (2009) draws a distinction between how the common law and equity would have provided a remedy in the case of *Donoghue* v. *Stevenson* (1932) where, as he puts it: 'a decomposed snail is supposed to have been accidentally served to café customers in an opaque bottle of ginger beer (the facts were never firmly established)'. As is well known, the remedy of the common law was to impose a general duty of care based on the neighbour principle. How might equity have reacted? Watt (p. 80) suggests that it would not have established any positive duty, as that is not how equity operates. Instead it could have provided that a contracting party (i.e. here the manufacturer) was prevented from unconscionably denying a duty of care to a non-contracting party (i.e. here the consumer) in certain types of case rather than a general duty of care. Watt suggests that this piece by piece approach would have been preferable as it would have prevented the vast increase in litigation today based on the general duty of care in negligence and instead focused on particular cases.

REFLECTION

EQUITY TODAY

CORNERSTONE

Patel v. *Ali* illustrating how equity operates today

The decision in *Patel* v. *Ali* illustrates how equity operates today.

As you will see from this book, equity enjoyed something of a renaissance in the last century and is still capable of developing new concepts such as the remedial constructive trust, and existing doctrines are also being developed: for example, the doctrine of estoppel. Both of these are considered in Chapter 9 and Chapter 11 looks at the *Quistclose* trust, which has had such vitality in commercial transactions.

This section looks at equity today in more detail through a detailed consideration of the decision in *Patel* v. *Ali* and a discussion of unconscionability in the modern context.

The decision in *Patel* v. *Ali*

In 1979 Suriya Ali and Nazir Ahmed, who were joint owners of a house, contracted to sell it to Mr and Mrs Patel. In May 1979 Mr Ali, Suriya Ali's husband, was adjudged bankrupt and within a week his

trustee in bankruptcy had obtained an **injunction** preventing a sale. The reason was to preserve the house, as a claimed asset of Mr Ali, for his creditors.

In January 1980 the court allowed the sale of the house to proceed on the basis that the trustee's claim would be met out of the proceeds of sale. In August 1980 the Patels brought a claim for **specific performance** of the 1979 contract but had difficulty in serving the claim on Mr Ahmed as he had left the country and who, indeed, plays no further part in the story. At about that time Mrs Ali became seriously ill with bone cancer. In July 1980 she became pregnant and had a leg amputated. As a result she needed help with household duties and shopping. A month later she gave birth to their second child. In 1981–1982 Mr Ali was in prison and in August 1983 Mrs Ali gave birth to their third child. By this time she was very much dependent on her family and close friends nearby for help. An additional factor was that she spoke virtually no English.

The facts above are those of *Patel* v. *Ali* (1984). Did the court grant the remedy of specific performance which was sought? The answer depends on an examination of some fundamental principles of equity.

There was undoubtedly a breach of the contract made in 1979. Mrs Ali and Mr Ahmed had not given the Patels possession of the house as agreed. Therefore at **common law** the Patels had a right to damages for breach of contract. However, damages were not the appropriate remedy. The Patels, having contracted for the purchase of a particular house, wanted that house and not money instead. This is where we reach equity, since the remedy sought, specific performance, is an equitable one that compels a party to perform their contractual obligations. In this case, that meant giving up possession of their house.

However, as we shall see in more detail later, equity has a discretion in whether to grant its remedies. Indeed the very word 'equity' implies a desire to be fair and just. In this case the court had to balance the position of Mrs Ali, who needed to remain where she was, against that of the Patels, who not unreasonably wanted what they had contracted for, the house.

The court held that, if the defendants were forced to complete the sale and Mrs Ali had to move out, there would be 'hardship amounting to injustice', in the words of Goulding J. The fact that a person would suffer hardship in having to complete a sale was not in itself enough to justify the court in refusing an order for specific performance. Hardship would, said the court, only justify the refusal of an order in an exceptional case. This was one.

That was not the end of the matter, though. The court also had to be satisfied that the remedy at common law, in this case, **damages**, would be effective. Otherwise the Patels would have no remedy at all. Here it was felt that it would be and there was evidence that the Muslim community would pay the damages awarded against Mrs Ali and Mr Ahmed.

The following points emerge from this case:

(a) The discretion of the court is guided by principles. Thus here the court did not have a complete discretion whether or not to grant specific performance. Instead it considered whether hardship would be caused if it did grant the remedy and not only hardship but also 'hardship amounting to injustice'. In addition it had to be satisfied that the common law remedy would be effective. The extent to which equity exercises discretion is considered in Chapter 2.

(b) Common law remedies (damages here) are considered first. Only if they are not adequate will equitable remedies be considered.

(c) The equitable remedy of specific performance is directed against particular persons rather than their money, like the common law remedy of damages.

(d) In some cases equity is not discretionary at all and the common law at times exercises what amounts to a discretion, a point to which we shall return at the end of this chapter.

The notion of unconscionability in equity today

CORNERSTONE

Unconscionability

The concept of unconscionability plays a major role in equity today but we need to be clear on exactly what unconscionability can mean.

As you go through this book, you find frequent references to the term 'unconscionability'. This is a good place to examine the role of unconscionability in equity today. The term 'unconscionability' has been increasingly used, especially in Commonwealth jurisdictions, from where much of the current thought on equity comes, and it has played a major part in the development of equity. As Morris (1996, p. 293) has said: 'The point has now been reached in Australia that equity now recognises a general principle pursuant to which transactions may be set aside on the ground of a party's unconscionable conduct.' We have not reached this stage in England but the passage does emphasise the part played by the notion of unconscionability in modern equity. As Lord Browne-Wilkinson observed (in the context of trusts) in *Westdeustsche Landesbank* v. *Islington LBC* (1996): 'Equity operates on the conscience of the owner of the legal interest.' Moreover, in the decision of the Court of Appeal in *Pennington* v. *Waine* (2002), which may have liberalised the law on incompletely constituted trusts, Arden LJ expressly based her decision on unconscionability (see Chapter 7).

If it is true that conscience is now a mainspring of equity then the question is: what do we mean by unconscionability? Lord Nicholls in *Royal Brunei Airlines Sdn Bhd* v. *Tan Kok Ming* (1995) observed that 'if unconscionability is to be the touchstone for liability . . . it is essential to be clear on what . . . unconscionable means'. Watt (2009, p.108) suggests the touchstone of conduct which is 'not routine' in the sense that it is 'non-routine reliance on a routine reading of law'. He gives as an example the situation where a landowner evicts a non-owner from his land. In routine cases this would be perfectly fair, as where the non-owner is simply a trespasser. Suppose though that the non-owner has built a house on this land in reliance on the landowner's promise to allow the non-owner to occupy the house for life (see, for example, *Inwards* v. *Baker* (1965) in Chapter 9). One could argue that the owner's conduct was 'non-routine'; it would be 'unreasonable or oppressive to an extent that affronts ordinary minimum standards of fair dealing'. Thus it brings the familiar equitable concept of estoppel into play. The question is ultimately whether unconscionability is only valuable as a general pointer to the direction which equity should take or whether it has value as a practical tool in the application of equitable principles.

> **Take note**
>
> You will find it useful to refer to this section as you go through this book and you come across instances of the possible application of the notion of unconscionability'.

KEY POINTS

- Equity is not a system of law in itself: it intervenes where the strict rules of the law have failed to do justice.
- There is another strand of equity: the idea that its jurisdiction is based on conscience.
- The result is that there is more emphasis on discretion in the application of equitable rules than there is with common law rules.
- The administration of equity and the common law is fused but the general view is that the actual rules of equity and the common law are not fused and are distinct.

CORE CASES AND STATUTES

Case	Concerning	Application
Patel v. *Ali* (1984)	Refusal by the court to grant specific performance of a contract for the sale of land.	Extent to which the courts have discretion in the grant of equitable remedies.
Walsh v. *Lonsdale* (1882)	Agreement for a lease was enforceable in equity although not in a deed as required by statute law.	Distinction between approaches of equity and the common law. Also shows the effect of the Judicature Act 1873 (see below).

Statute	Concerning	Application
Section 25(11) of the Judicature Act 1873 (the rule is now in s. 49 of the Supreme Court Act 1981)	Where the rules of equity and common law conflict then equity shall prevail.	Cases e.g. *Walsh* v. *Lonsdale* where the rules of equity and common law give different answers to a legal problem.

FURTHER READING

Allen, C.K. (1964) *Law in the Making*, 7th ed. (Oxford University Press).

Ashburner, W. (1902) *Principles of Equity* (Butterworths).

Baker, J. (2002) *Introduction to English Legal History*, 4th ed. (Oxford University Press).
The above three standard works provide extra detail on the early development of equity and on its principles.

Birks, P. (1996) 'Equity in the modern law: an exercise in taxonomy' 26 *University of Western Australia Law Review* 1 at 16–17.
This presents the argument that unconscionability is not valuable as a legal tool and so reading this gives you a different slant on this topic.

Brundage, J. (1995) *Medieval Canon Law* (Longman).
Useful on the relationship between canon law (i.e. the law of the church) and equity.

Delaney, H. and Ryan, D. (2008) 'Unconscionability: a unifying theme in equity' 72(5) *Conveyancer and Property Lawyer* 401.
This looks at the capacity of unconscionability to act as a unifying theme in equitable developments with the focus primarily in the years since the turn of the twenty-first century. Its views are a useful contrast to those of Birks (above).

Dickens, C. *Bleak House*.
The early chapters, especially Chapter 1, give a flavour of equity before the reforms culminating in the Judicature Acts.

Guy, J. (1980) *The Public Career of Sir Thomas More* (Harvester Press).
This throws light not only on the work of Thomas More as Lord Chancellor but also that of the Court of Chancery at that period.

Klinck, D. (2010) *Conscience, Equity and the Court of Chancery in Early Modern England* (Ashgate).
This valuable study traces the development of the notion of conscience in equity and argues that how conscience was understood changed.

Morris, A. (1996) 'Equity's reaction to modern domestic relationships' in A.J. Oakley (ed.) *Trends in Contemporary Trust Law* (Oxford University Press).

Plucknett, T.F.T. (1948) *A Concise History of the Common Law*, 4th ed. (Butterworths).
Despite its title this book is also useful in giving an account of the early development of equity, although its approach is now a bit dated.

Virgo, G. (2003) 'Restitution through the Looking Glass' in J. Getzler (ed.) *Rationalising Property, Equity and Trusts, Essays in Honour of Edward Burn* (Butterworths).

Watt, G. (2009) *Equity Stirring: the Story of Justice Beyond Law* (Hart Publishing).
This is really valuable in giving you some excellent ideas to consider on the nature unconscionability. See especially pages 104–113.

Worthington, S. (2006) *Equity*, 2nd ed. (Oxford University Press).
(See especially Chapter 10.) She suggests that it is time for cohesive substantive integration of equity and the common law.

CHAPTER 2

Equitable remedies and doctrines

BLUEPRINT

Equitable remedies and doctrines

LEGISLATION

- Senior Courts Act 1981, s. 50
- Trade Union and Labour Relations (Consolidation) Act 1992, s. 236

CONTEXT

- Why are equitable remedies needed?

CONCEPTS

- Injunctions
- Specific performance
- Rescission
- Rectification
- Equitable damages
- Doctrine of undue influence

- Should the remedy of specific performance be more readily available?

- What do we mean by equitable
  remedies and how do they differ
  from other remedies?

CASES

- *Mareva etc.* v. *International Bulk Carriers SA*
- *Anton Piller KG* v. *Manufacturing Processes Ltd*
- *Co-operative Insurance Society* v. *Argyll Stores*
- *Royal Bank of Scotland Plc* v. *Etridge* (No. 2)

REFORM

- Development of principles
  on which freezing and
  search orders granted.

SPECIAL CHARACTERISTICS

- Discretion in equity
- Equity acts in personam
- Equitable remedies granted where common law
  remedy of damages would be inadequate

CRITICAL ISSUES

Setting the scene

John runs a small printing business. He is expanding the business having secured a lucrative contract to print law textbooks. As a result he has decided to acquire larger premises. He has agreed to buy premises from Alex and contracts have been exchanged. He has also agreed terms with Jim, who is a very experienced printer, to join the firm and he has agreed to buy new printing machinery from Baker Ltd with delivery agreed in one month's time.

However, Alex has now told John that he cannot complete the contract for the sale of the premises as Alex has himself decided to expand his own business and needs the extra space. Jim has told John that he is not going to join him as he has received a more lucrative offer from another firm and Baker Ltd tell John that the machinery will not be ready for delivery for two months.

John's solicitor tells him that he can seek damages from Alex, Jim and Baker Ltd for breach of contract but John is desperate to make sure that his contract to print the law books actually goes ahead as he thinks that this could make or break his business.

This means that he needs to compel Alex, Jim and Baker Ltd to keep to their contracts as agreed. Can equitable remedies assist John?

Take note

Do not think that discretion means that a judge hearing an equity case can decide it how he wishes. The court cannot simply do what it feels to be just in the circumstances and it must be emphasised that the fact that equity is a discretionary system should not lead to the idea the equity is all about vagueness. In *Vercoe and others v Rutland Fund Management Ltd and others* (2010) it was said that: 'Although in a certain sense the courts' decisions about these matters might be described as discretionary, in truth I think the courts are now seeking to articulate underlying principles which will govern the choices to be made as to the remedy or remedies available in any given case.'

MAIN PRINCIPLES ON WHICH EQUITABLE REMEDIES ARE GRANTED AND WITHHELD

CORNERSTONE

Characteristics of equitable remedies

There are three characteristics of equitable remedies: they are discretionary, they act *in personam* and they are granted where common law damages would be inadequate.

When you study equitable remedies you need to bear in mind that the following principles apply to them generally:

(a) They are discretionary, whereas the common law remedy of damages is available as of right. This does not, however, mean that everything is left to the discretion of the court in each case. We saw in Chapter 1 in relation to the decision in *Patel* v. *Ali* that there are clear principles governing the grant of equitable remedies and we will come across further examples here.

(b) They are granted where the common law remedies, e.g. damages, would be inadequate or where the common law remedies are not available because the right is exclusively equitable, e.g. a right of a beneficiary under a trust.

(c) They act *in personam*, i.e. against the defendant personally. Thus failure to comply with an order giving effect to an equitable remedy is contempt of court punishable either by imprisonment or, where the order can be enforced without a personal restraint on the defendant, then an order against his property can be made, such as an order of sequestration. Under this order the court can appoint sequestrators to take possession of the defendant's property until he has complied with the original order.

APPLICATION

Egbert has applied for planning permission to extend his house but the local authority, Barset Council, has refused this. Egbert is well aware that he needs permission but he decides to go ahead anyway and commences building. Barset Council uses planning law procedures in an effort to get him to stop but he continues with the extension. Eventually Barset Council decides to obtain an injunction, which, as you know, is an equitable remedy, against Egbert to compel him to cease building and to demolish what he has already built.

If we refer to the characteristics of equitable remedies above we can note that:

(a) The court will have discretion whether to grant the remedy. However, there seems no reason why it should not do so as Egbert deliberately defied the law.

(b) The common law remedy of damages would be of no use to Barset Council as this would only make Egbert pay compensation to them when what is needed is for the building to stop.

(c) As an injunction acts *in personam* then if Egbert disobeys it this will be contempt of court and so he could be punished by imprisonment.

INJUNCTIONS

CORNERSTONE

Injunctions

An injunction is a court order requiring a party either to do or not to do a particular act.

An injunction can be sought by anyone who alleges that a legal or equitable right of theirs has been infringed. An example of where such a right was held not to exist is *Paton* v. *Trustees of the British Pregnancy Advisory Service* (1979) where the claimant was refused an injunction to prevent his wife from having an abortion. The Abortion Act 1967 gave the father no right to be consulted about the termination of a pregnancy.

Examples of the use of injunctions

(a) To restrain a breach of contract or tort.

(b) To restrain a breach of confidence.

(c) To restrain a breach of trust. Thus in *Buttle* v. *Saunders* (1950) an injunction was used to restrain a trustee from selling trust property at a price below that offered by a prospective purchaser.

(d) In matrimonial and family matters. The Family Law Act 1996 gives the courts extensive powers to grant injunctions in divorce proceedings, other matrimonial proceedings and where the parties are cohabitees. Injunctions can require the respondent for instance to refrain from assaulting, molesting or otherwise interfering with the other party to the marriage, or a cohabitee, and their children.

(e) In disputes between members of unincorporated associations. An injunction can be granted to restrain a member from being expelled from the association in breach of the rules (*Lee* v. *Showmen's Guild of Great Britain* (1952)).

(f) In public law matters. An old example is *A-G* v. *Fulham Corporation* (1921) where an injunction was obtained to prevent a local authority from acting *ultra vires* by running a municipal laundry.

INTERSECTION

Injunctions in public matters form part of constitutional and administrative law.

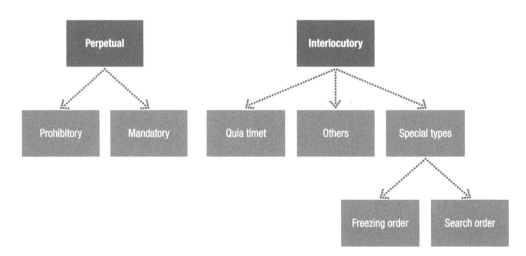

Figure 2.1 Types of injunctions

Perpetual injunctions

These are known as perpetual injunctions in contrast to interlocutory and *quia timet* injunctions which by their nature will only last for a certain time. Perpetual injunctions will not necessarily last forever but they are final in that they will finally resolve the issue between the parties. There are two types:

(a) Prohibitory. This restrains a person from doing some particular act, e.g. breaking a contract.

(b) Mandatory. This commands a person to perform some positive act. It is less frequently granted than a prohibitory injunction and, because it is similar to an order of specific performance, it is subject to similar restrictions as to when it may be granted, e.g. where supervision would be difficult. A mandatory injunction is rarely granted in industrial disputes although it was granted in *Parker* v. *Camden LBC* (1986) to require the turning on of a boiler when a strike of boilermen meant that tenants of council houses had no heating or hot water.

Suspension of injunctions

Where it would be difficult for the defendant to comply with an injunction immediately or where it would cause him/her undue hardship the court may grant the injunction but suspend its operation for a specified time. In *Pride of Derby Angling Association* v. *British Celanese* (1953) an injunction restraining a local authority from polluting a river by discharging sewage into it was suspended to give the local authority time to make other arrangements.

Public interest

The court, in deciding whether or not to grant an injunction, may sometimes take the wider public interest into account. In *Miller* v. *Jackson* (1977) the court refused to grant an injunction restraining a ground from being used for the playing of cricket because of cricket balls landing in the claimants' garden. The public interest in being able to enjoy the playing of cricket outweighed the claimants' need for protection, although they were awarded damages.

Interlocutory injunctions

The object of an interlocutory injunction is to preserve the status quo until the trial of an action. They have been granted, for example, to prevent a dismissal alleged to be in breach of agreed procedures (*Irani* v. *Southampton and South-West Hampshire Health Authority* (1985)) and to restrain an association from holding a meeting without allowing certain members to attend (*Woodford* v. *Smith* (1970)). Important instances are Freezing and Search orders – see below.

Interlocutory injunctions may be prohibitory, mandatory or *quia timet* (see below) and normally remain in force until the trial although a shorter period may be specified.

When will an interlocutory injunction be granted?

In *American Cyanamid Co.* v *Ethicon Ltd* (1975) Lord Diplock laid down the following rules:

(a) Is there a serious question to be tried? The claimant must show that his claim is not frivolous and he must adduce sufficient evidence to satisfy the court that his claim has a real prospect of success at the trial. If the defendant has no arguable defence at all then an injunction will be granted and points (b) and (c) below do not arise (*Official Custodian for Charities* v. *Mackey* (1985)). Otherwise the court will consider the following points:

(b) If there is a serious issue, will damages be an adequate remedy so that an injunction will not be needed? This must be looked at from the point of view of:

    (i) The claimant, i.e. would damages be adequate compensation for loss caused to him by acts of the defendant before the trial?

(ii) The defendant, i.e. if the claimant loses at the trial then could any loss to him be compensated by the claimant giving an undertaking in damages? (See below.)

In *Hubbard* v. *Pitt* (1976) picketing by the defendants of the claimant's estate agents premises was held to be likely to result in serious damage to the business and there was also doubt about whether the defendants could pay damages. Thus an injunction was granted.

(c) If damages would be inadequate, then should an injunction be granted taking into account the balance of convenience to each party? In *Hubbard* v. *Pitt* it was held that the disadvantage of lost trade suffered by the claimants was greater than the disadvantage suffered by the defendants, who were complaining of certain local housing developments, in having to argue their case elsewhere.

(d) There may be other special factors to be considered as in the *American Cyanamid* case (1975) itself, where an interlocutory injunction was granted to prevent infringement of a patent for a pharmaceutical product and partly because of the argument that if the defendant's product had been used prior to the trial, and the claimant then obtained a permanent injunction against its further marketing, the claimants would themselves lose goodwill. Accordingly the interlocutory injunction prevented the defendants from marketing the product at all.

A claimant who is granted an interlocutory injunction is almost always required to undertake that if he does not succeed at the trial he will compensate the defendant for any damage suffered because the injunction was granted. The undertaking is given to the court and so a failure to comply with it is contempt of court.

Quia timet injunctions

These are granted to restrain a threatened apprehended injury to the claimant's rights even though no injury has yet occurred. The claimant must show 'a strong case of probability that the intended mischief will in fact arise' (Chitty J in *A-G* v. *Manchester Corporation* (1893)). Thus just to say '*timeo*' (I am afraid) is not enough. In *Torquay Hotel Co. Ltd* v. *Cousins* (1969) the defendants, members of a trade union, intended to picket the claimant's hotel to prevent the delivery of fuel oil which would interfere with the execution of contracts which the claimant had made for the supply of fuel oil. A *quia timet* injunction was granted.

Defences to a claim for a perpetual or interlocutory injunction

(a) Delay (*laches*). See for an example *Gafford* v. *Graham* (1999) – below.

(b) Acquiescence. In *Gafford* v. *Graham* (1999) injunctions were sought to demolish a building erected in breach of covenant and to restrain an unlawful use of the land. Relief in respect of the breach of covenant by building was refused as the defendants had acquiesced in this. They had known of it for more than three years before taking action. In the case of unlawful use, although here there was no acquiescence, there was sufficient inactivity to make the award of an injunction unconscionable, but the claimants were still awarded equitable damages (see later in this chapter).

(c) The claimant's conduct. A claimant who has failed to 'come to equity with clean hands' may not be granted an injunction. Thus in *Goddard* v. *Midland Railway* (1891) it was held that a claimant who has not complied with a restrictive covenant may not be able to enforce it against another.

(d) Hardship to the defendant. This is especially relevant in considering whether to grant an interlocutory injunction and a perpetual mandatory injunction. Hardship can sometimes be mitigated by suspending the operation of an injunction (see above).

FREEZING ORDERS

CORNERSTONE

Freezing order

This is an interlocutory injunction designed to prevent the defendant from disposing of assets which would otherwise be available to meet the claimant's claim or removing them from the courts' jurisdiction. It originated with the *Mareva* case.

APPLICATION

Giles owns a business supplying office machinery. He supplied a large order costing £50,000 to a firm, Hanbury Ltd, with which he had often done business in the past and which had always paid him regularly. This time, however, Giles is not paid and he then learns that Hanbury is in financial difficulties. Giles wishes to try to reclaim the money and has details of Hanbury Ltd's bank account. Giles comes to you for advice. At this point you might consider the use of a freezing order which could operate against Hanbury Ltd's bank account. This could be taken out even before proceedings are issued and will freeze the sum of £50,000 in Hanbury Ltd's bank account pending the outcome of any court action to recover the debt.

What a freezing order achieves

Since its introduction in 1975 (in *Mareva Compania Naviera* v. *International Bulk Carriers*) freezing orders have become widely used, especially because of the ease with which assets can now be moved from one country to another with modern systems of banking and finance. The injunction is normally granted without notice to the other side (the old term was *ex parte*) because of the need for speed. The practice is now governed by the Civil Procedure Rules 1999 (see Practice Direction CPR 25, para. 6 which contains an example).

> **Take note**
>
> The Practice Direction on freezing orders contains an example of a freezing order – you may find it useful to look at this to give your studies a practical slant.

The general principles laid down in the *American Cyanimid* case (above) apply in deciding whether a freezing order should be granted together with the following points:

(a) The claimant must have a good arguable case. The court will therefore need to form a provisional view on the final outcome of the case on the evidence before it and where there are substantial disputes of fact the requirement of a 'good arguable case' will be difficult to meet (see Kerr LJ in *The Niederesachen* (1984)).

(b) The claimant should make full and frank disclosure of all material matters (*Brinks-MAT* v. *Elcombe* (1989)) together with full particulars of his claim and its amount and should state fairly the points made against it by the defendant.

(c) The claimant should normally give grounds for believing that the defendants have assets in the jurisdiction. All assets are within the scope of a freezing order which has thus been ordered in relation to, for example, bank accounts (the most frequent situation), motor vehicles, jewellery and goodwill. A limit is normally specified on the amount to which the injunction applies.

(d) Territorial extent of freezing orders. In *Republic of Haiti* v. *Duvalier* (1989) an injunction was granted in respect of worldwide assets alleged to have been embezzled by Jean-Claude Duvalier, the former President of the Republic. Worldwide freezing orders are an essential weapon here as so often fraud crosses national borders. Guidelines on the grant of a worldwide freezing order were set out in *Dadourian Group* v. *Simms* (2006) where it was emphasised that the court will need to have evidence on the applicable law and practice in courts of countries where the assets are believed to be held as of course their co-operation will be needed.

(e) The claimant should normally give grounds for believing either that the assets will be removed from the jurisdiction before the claim is satisfied or that in some way they might be dissipated.

SEARCH ORDERS

CORNERSTONE

Search order

This is an interlocutory injunction allowing entrance of premises to, for example, allow the inspection of documents and to remove them into the custody of the claimant's solicitors. It originated with the *Anton Piller* case.

APPLICATION

Mark, the managing director of a small but active research and development company telephones you one morning. He has just found that Eric, one of his leading research scientists, has left and cleared his desk and has taken his laptop. All of the details of the projects on which he was working are missing. This includes customer details and pricing structures. However, a careful search of the office waste paper bin has discovered the contact details of a competitor in Germany with whom Eric may now be in touch. Mark has also been told by one of Eric's colleagues that he overheard Eric telling someone that he was hoping to work from home in future. Mark wants action to be taken urgently to prevent Eric from using this information. This is where you need to consider the use of a search order.

These orders owe their origin to the decision in *Anton Piller KG* v. *Manufacturing Processes Ltd* (1975). In contrast to freezing orders, where the claimant has the evidence for commencing proceedings but is concerned about enforcement, here the claimant may lack even the evidence to begin. It is especially useful in cases of e.g. alleged video pirating or cases of passing off where, once proceedings have been served, the defendant may destroy evidence. The order allows the search of the defendant's premises and seizure of articles, making lists, taking photographs etc. It does not allow forcible entry.

In *Anton Piller* Ovmerod LJ laid down the following conditions which must be satisfied by the claimant for the grant of the order:

(a) an extremely strong *prima facie* case;

(b) actual or potential damage of a very serious nature;

(c) clear evidence that the defendant has incriminating documents or things and a real possibility of their destruction before an application without notice can be made.

The idea of making orders which can have serious consequences when the other party has not had the chance to put his case led judges to emphasise the need for caution in making them, especially as there was evidence that in the early days they had been made too readily. In *Columbia Pictures Ltd* v *Robinson* (1987), Scott J pointed out that the usual result of the order was to close down the defendant's business and then said: 'It is a fundamental principle of civil jurisprudence in this country that citizens are not to be deprived of their property by judicial or quasi-judicial order without a fair hearing . . . What is to be said of the Anton Piller procedure which, on a regular and institutionalised basis, is depriving citizens of their property and closing down their businesses by orders made *ex parte,* on applications of which they know nothing and at which they cannot be heard, by orders which they are forced, on pain of committal to obey, even if wrongly made?'

As a result of this and other criticisms (see Dockray and Laddie 1990), in *Universal Thermosensors* v. *Hibben* (1992) conditions were imposed on their use which have now been incorporated into the standard form and the practice is now governed by the Civil Procedure Rules 1999.

Practice Direction CPR 25, para. 7.4 sets out conditions that must be observed when a search order is served, e.g.:

- Service of a search order must be supervised by an independent solicitor (the supervising solicitor).
- Where the supervising solicitor is a man and the respondent is likely to be an unaccompanied woman, at least one other person named in the order must be a woman and must accompany the supervising solicitor.
- The order may only be served between 9.30 a.m. and 5.30 p.m. Monday to Friday unless the court otherwise orders.

INTERSECTION

Freezing and search orders are excellent examples of the fact that equity is still able to be creative and, in this case, adapt the old remedy of an injunction to new situations. Thus you can use these orders as instances of the nature and development of equity as explained in Chapter 1.

SPECIFIC PERFORMANCE

CORNERSTONE

Specific performance

A decree of specific performance is positive, in that it requires a party to perform his contractual obligations.

A decree of specific performance orders the defendant to perform his contractual obligations, i.e. to do what he promised to do. The grant of a prohibitory injunction can have the same effect as in *Sky Petroleum* v. *VIP Petroleum* (1974) (see below).

The grant of specific performance in certain situations

Contracts for the sale of land

Here SP is often granted in cases where the seller of land, having exchanged contracts, then refuses to complete the sale, as each piece of land is regarded as unique. In *Matila Ltd* v. *Lisheen Properties Ltd* (2010) the purchaser of two apartments had lost its bank funding partly through the downturn in the property market and used this as the reason for being unable to complete the sale. However, the court granted SP and held that it was only in extraordinary cases that hardship can be a reason not to grant SP. Although inability to perform a contract for financial reasons could raise the defence of impossibility (see *North East Lincolnshire BC* v. *Millennium Park (Grimsby) Ltd* (2002) there was no evidence here that it was impossible to obtain the necessary finance to complete the purchase.

Covenants in leases

CORNERSTONE

Co-operative Insurance v. *Argyll Stores*

Co-operative Insurance v. *Argyll Stores* is one of the major decisions on the availability of specific performance.

In *Co-operative Insurance Society Ltd* v. *Argyll Stores (Holdings) Ltd* (1998) specific performance was refused of an undertaking to keep a supermarket open during the usual hours of business in a lease which had still 19 years to run. The supermarket was an 'anchor store' in a shopping centre and its closure would badly affect the viability of the rest of the centre. However, the House of Lords, overruling the Court of Appeal, considered that if the store was ordered to be kept open the loss to the tenant would exceed that which would be suffered by the landlord if the supermarket closed. In addition, the principle that the court would need to supervise any order of SP (see below) remained important. It is fair to say that this decision was regarded as a setback by those who favour an extension of this remedy.

REFLECTION

It is easy to just say: 'Why shouldn't the store owners have been made to do what they promised and keep it open?' However, commercial realities are different. The decision of the Court of Appeal to grant SP of the lease alarmed the commercial property market as it was feared that tenants who could not assign the lease to someone else or sub-let might be compelled to continue trading at a loss, which might ultimately drive them into insolvency.

Dowling (2011) points out that in these cases the effect of refusal of the claimant's application for specific performance is not that the defendant escapes liability to the claimant, but that the claimant is left to his remedy in damages. Thus the court is exercising its discretion to award the remedy of SP or to withhold it on the basis that the defendant can set up a defence making it inequitable for the court to compel performance of the defendant's obligations, and instead to leave the claimant to seek compensation from the defendant.

Contracts where an order of specific performance would require constant supervision

In *Ryan* v. *Mutual Tontine Association* (1893), specific performance of a contractual obligation to provide a porter constantly in attendance at a service flat was refused but in *Posner* v. *Scott-Lewis* (1987) specific performance of a covenant to employ a resident porter for certain duties, although not to be constantly in attendance, was granted. The court felt that enforcing compliance would not involve it in an unacceptable degree of supervision.

Contracts for the sale of chattels which are especially rare, beautiful or of particular value to the claimant

Although s. 52 of the Sale of Goods Act 1979 empowers the court to grant specific performance of a contract for the sale of specific or ascertained goods, this does not seem to have extended the grounds on which equity will grant specific performance. Thus in *Cohen* v. *Roche* (1927) specific performance was refused of a contract to sell Hepplewhite chairs. A less restrictive attitude was taken in *Sky Petroleum* v. *VIP Petroleum* (1974), where an injunction was granted restraining the defendants from withholding supplies of petrol which they had contracted to supply to the claimants. There was a petrol shortage at the time and so if only damages had been awarded to the claimants they would have been unlikely to obtain supplies elsewhere. The effect of the injunction was to compel the defendants to continue to supply the petrol and so it was in effect an order of specific performance. Although this contract concerned unascertained goods, which are not covered by s. 52 of the Sale of Goods Act, the court was still able to make the order.

Contracts for personal services

CORNERSTONE

Enforcement of contracts for personal services

Cases on equity's attitude to the enforcement of contracts for personal services must be read subject to s. 236 of the Trade Union and Labour Relations (Consolidation) Act 1992.

Equity traditionally refuses to grant specific performance here for various reasons: the difficulty of supervision, the undesirability of one person being compelled to submit to the orders of another and the difficulty of deciding whether an employee was actually performing his contract. Section 236 of the Trade Union and Labour Relations (Consolidation) Act 1992 prohibits the courts from enforcing performance of contracts of employment either by specific performance or injunction but equitable principles are still important in three areas:

(i)   Where the contract is not covered by the Act, e.g. a contract for services made with an independent contractor. Such a contract was specifically enforced in *Posner* v. *Scott-Lewis* (1987) (above).

(ii) Where the remedy is sought by an employee against an employer to compel the employer to continue to employ him. In *Irani* v. *Southampton and South West Hampshire Health Authority* (1985) the injunction restrained implementation of a dismissal notice until a disputes procedure had been complied with. However there was the special factor that the grant of an injunction would enable the claimant to seek some other remedy as Irani would be able, as an employee, to use the disputes procedures.

Equity's traditional reluctance to order specific performance against an employer was shown in *Page One Records* v. *Britton* (1968), where the claimant who had been dismissed as manager of 'The Troggs' pop group sought an injunction to restrain the group from engaging anyone else as manager. This was refused as its effect would be to compel 'The Troggs' to continue to employ the claimant because it would need a manager.

INTERSECTION

Under the Employment Rights Act 1996 an employment tribunal may order the reinstatement or re-engagement of an unfairly dismissed employee but the employer cannot be compelled to take the employee back; if the employer fails to comply with the order he is simply ordered to pay extra compensation to the employee.

(iii) Where the grant of an injunction to restrain the breach of a contract for personal services would amount to indirect specific performance of the contract.

APPLICATION

Anita, an actress, has a contract under which she agrees to work only for Mollywood film-makers for a period of five years. Anita leaves the employment of Mollywood. Mollywood cannot obtain an injunction preventing Anita from working for someone else because the practical effect of this would be to compel Anita to work for Mollywood in order to earn a living.

Suppose that Anita's contract stated only that she would not *act* for any other employer during that time. This was the situation in *Warner Bros* v. *Nelson* (1937) where the court granted the injunction (the actress being Bette Davis) on the ground that Miss Davis could earn a living doing other work. See also *Warren* v. *Mendy* (1989).

Defences to an action for specific performance

(a) Where the contract was obtained by unfair means, e.g. undue influence or taking advantage of another's mistake. In *Webster* v. *Cecil* (1861) the defendant offered to sell land to the claimant for £1,250. The claimant accepted although, as his own offer to buy at £2,000 had been rejected by the defendant, he must have known that the defendant had meant £2,250. Therefore specific performance was refused to the claimant.

(b) Where to grant the remedy would cause undue hardship. An excellent example is *Patel* v. *Ali* (1984) which is dealt with in Chapter 1.

(c) Where the claimant has been guilty of undue delay (doctrine of *laches*). This will depend on the circumstances. In *Lazard Brothers* v. *Fairfield Properties* (1977) specific performance was granted where there had been over two years' delay and Megarry V-C disapproved of the idea that specific performance was a prize to be awarded to the zealous and denied to the indolent.

(d) The claimant's conduct. The claimant must show that he has either performed his part of the contract or has tendered performance and is willing to perform any further obligations under the contract (*Chappell* v. *Times Newspapers* (1975)).

EQUITABLE DAMAGES

When they can be awarded

> ### Take note
>
> Note that this is different from equitable compensation awarded for a breach of trust which is dealt with in Chapter 10.

CORNERSTONE

Equitable damages

The statute law on when equitable damages can be awarded is s. 50 of the Senior Courts Act 1981.

Section 2 of Lord Cairns Act (Chancery Amendment Act) 1858 gave the Court of Chancery power to award damages either in addition to, or in substitution for, an injunction or specific performance. These provisions are now found in s. 50 of the Senior Courts Act 1981. The object of this provision was to give the court power to award damages where they would not be available at common law, as in *Wrotham Park Estate* v. *Parkside Homes Ltd* (1974) where damages were awarded for breach of a restrictive covenant. However, no jurisdiction exists to award damages here unless there is jurisdiction to grant one of the equitable remedies. In *Surrey CC* v. *Bredero Homes* (1992) a developer exceeded the number of houses which he was allowed to build by a restrictive covenant but, by the time the action was brought on the covenant, he had sold all the houses. Thus no injunction could have been granted under Lord Cairns' Act and so damages in equity were not available either (contrast with *Wakeham* v. *Wood* (1981)).

Basis on which equitable damages are awarded

In *Johnson* v. *Agnew* (1980) Lord Wilberforce held that the principles under which damages would be assessed were the same in equity as at common law. This view has been disputed for example by Millett LJ in *Jaggard* v. *Sawyer* (1995), who said that this statement was limited to cases where the damages were recoverable in the same cause of action. The common law action could compensate only for existing breaches, whereas, where the breach was a continuing one, damages under Lord Cairns' Act could compensate for losses resulting from anticipated future breaches made possible because of the withholding of the equitable remedy. An example of a different basis from that at common law is provided by the earlier case of *Wroth* v. *Tyler* (1974) where damages for breach of contract for the sale of land were assessed by Megarry J on the basis that they must be a substitute for specific performance. The normal rule is that damages for breach of a contract for the sale of land are measured by the difference between the contract price and the market price at the time of completion (i.e. the date of the breach) but he held that damages here could be assessed as at the market price at the date of judgment. The result was that while damages applying the common law rule would have been £1,500, in fact £5,500 was awarded.

RESCISSION

CORNERSTONE

Rescission

Rescission sets the contract aside and restores the parties to their pre-contract positions.

Rescission often occurs without the intervention of the courts, e.g. John buys a car from Fred as a result of a misrepresentation made by Fred. John, on learning that he has been deceived, returns the car to Fred who gives him his money back. The effect is that the parties are restored to their positions before the contract was made.

Rescission applies in situations such as this where the contract is voidable because of some vitiating factor, e.g. mistake, misrepresentation or undue influence. The word rescission is sometimes also applied to the situation where there is a serious breach of contract and the innocent party is said to have a right to rescind the contract and so is relieved from performing his part although he can sue the party in breach for damages. In *Photo Production* v. *Securicor* (1980) Lord Wilberforce disapproved of the word rescission in this context and in any event it is not an area in which equity plays a part.

RECTIFICATION

CORNERSTONE

Rectification

Rectification sets the contract aside and restores the parties to their pre-contract positions.

This remedy is used where a written instrument does not accord with the intentions of the parties and so it is rectified to make it do so. It is available for contracts, deeds, and by s. 20 of the Administration of Justice Act 1982 it is also available for wills. In *Craddock Bros* v. *Hunt* (1923) a written agreement for the sale of a house included its adjoining yard which had not been intended. The court rectified the written agreement to exclude the yard and ordered specific performance of the rectified agreement.

EQUITABLE DOCTRINE: UNDUE INFLUENCE

There are many equitable doctrines but some of the traditional ones, such as election and satisfaction, are best studied as part of the law of succession and more modern ones, such as the developing law on breach of confidence, may not be considered part of equity at all. However, it is important to appreciate that there are doctrines of equity other than those related to trusts and an examination of the doctrine of undue influence is offered here as an illustration of an equitable doctrine in a contemporary context.

CORNERSTONE

Undue influence

Undue influence is an equitable doctrine which, although impossible to define precisely, in essence aims to prevent the vulnerable from exploitation. It is really directed at the manner in which a transaction is entered into.

What is meant by undue influence?

It is difficult to pin down this doctrine in a general statement but easier to appreciate what it means when looking at an actual situation.

APPLICATION

A wealthy elderly lady, Florence, has become a recluse and relies for advice on her accountant, Tom, who is the only person she sees regularly apart from her carers. She tells the accountant that she intends to make a will but has no one to leave her property to. Tom says that he will give the matter some thought and, in the course of many conversations, gradually persuades her to leave a substantial part of her property to him. Here there is no actual duress and indeed there may have been no wrongdoing at all. However, it looks as though Tom was placed in a position where he was able to use his existing influence over Florence to persuade her to make the gift in her will to him. This could be a case of undue influence. By its nature it is more subtle and more difficult to pin down than duress (see below), partly because usually, but not always, it consists of conduct over a period of time.

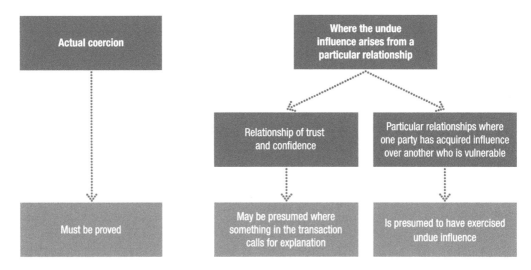

Figure 2.2 Types of undue influence

Source: from the speech of Lord Nicholls in *Royal Bank of Scotland* v. *Etridge*

⊙ CORNERSTONE

Royal Bank of Scotland v. *Etridge*

Royal Bank of Scotland v. *Etridge (No. 2)* is now the leading case on undue influence itself and on when third parties can be affected by it.

Take note

It is vital to stress the significance of deciding whether the particular type of undue influence falls into which category. This does not decide if there has been undue influence or not but how it is proved. In cases of actual coercion undue influence must be proved; in case (b) (i) above it will be presumed where something in the transaction calls for explanation and in (b) (ii) it is presumed and must be disproved by the party against whom undue influence is alleged.

In *Royal Bank of Scotland plc* v. *Etridge (No. 2)* (2001) Lord Nicholls held that there is a distinction between:

(a) Cases of actual coercion

(b) Cases where the undue influence arises from a particular relationship.

In (b) there is a subdivision between:

(i) Cases where there is a relationship of trust and confidence between two people. If it is established that there has been a transaction which calls for some explanation then the burden shifts to the person seeking to uphold the transaction to produce evidence to counter the inference of undue influence.

(ii) Certain types of relationship where one party has acquired influence over another who is vulnerable and dependent and by whom substantial gifts are not normally to be expected (e.g. parent and child, trustee and beneficiary and medical adviser and patient). In these cases there is a presumption of undue influence by the stronger party over the weaker.

CONTEXT

The doctrine of undue influence originated in the eighteenth century (the first reported case seems to be *Norton* v. *Relly* (1764)) and was developed by the Court of Chancery through the nineteenth century. Ridge (2006) points out that its development coincides with the growth in religious diversity, following on from greater religious toleration, and consequently religious giving. The undue influence cases on *inter vivos* religious gifts treated strong religious faith as a disability affecting the donor's autonomy and warranting the law's vigilance. The other side of this coin was that spiritual influence held over a donor by a religious body was viewed as dangerous and potentially coercive. However, these concerns did not apply to religious giving in general but were largely confined to *inter vivos* gifts by women to non-mainstream religious groups. The classic example is *Allcard* v. *Skinner* (1887) (below). Perhaps this reflects the traditional English suspicion of religious enthusiasm?

In more recent times this concern has been replaced by another: that of coercion used by one owner of property(X) on a co-owner(Y) to induce Y to guarantee X's debts.

Cases of actual coercion

In *Royal Bank of Scotland* v. *Etridge (No. 2)* Lord Hobhouse said that actual undue influence

> is an equitable wrong committed by the dominant party against the other which makes it unconscionable for the dominant party to enforce his legal rights against the other. It is typically some express conduct overbearing the other party's will . . . Actual undue influence does not depend upon some pre-existing relationship between the two parties though it is most commonly associated with and derives from such a relationship. He who alleges actual undue influence must prove it.

Presumed undue influence

Here the claimant must establish a relationship of trust and confidence between him and the wrong-doer together with the existence of a transaction that appeared to result in some unfair advantage to the alleged wrongdoer. This then brings the presumption into play so that it is up to the alleged wrongdoer to prove that there was no undue influence.

Lord Browne-Wilkinson in *CIBC Mortgages plc* v. *Pitt* (1994) held that in a case of actual undue influence, the victim's right to have the transaction set aside will not depend upon the disadvantageous quality of the transaction. The undue influence is enough. However, if it is a case where undue influence has to be proved then the type of transaction will be material. For instance, as he said: 'Some transactions will be obviously innocuous and innocent. A moderate gift as a Christmas or birthday present would be an example.' Thus, he said, we need to look at 'the combination of relationship and the nature of the transaction that gives rise to the presumption'.

INTERSECTION ....

Where undue influence is alleged in the making of a will a different test applies: whether the testator was coerced. In *Hubbard* v. *Scott* (2011) it was emphasised that as there was no presumption of undue influence in probate actions, the test to be applied was more stringent than that laid down in *Royal Bank of Scotland plc* v. *Etridge (No. 2)*.

Independent advice

The fact that a party has received independent advice before entering into the transaction is a factor in deciding whether there has been undue influence but it is not decisive. As Lord Nicholls pointed out in *Royal Bank of Scotland* v. *Etridge* 'a person may understand fully the implications of a proposed transaction . . . and yet still be acting under the undue influence of another'. In *Allcard* v. *Skinner* (1887) Miss Allcard entered into a convent and three days later made a will bequeathing all her property to Miss Skinner, the lady superior. She then claimed the money back after she left the sisterhood and it was held that she would have been able to recover such of the property as remained in the hands of the sisterhood, one vital factor being the lack of independent advice given to her on whether she should make the gift. However, in the event her claim was barred by laches (delay).

Undue influence and third parties

This area has become of great importance in recent years especially since the decision of the House of Lords in *Barclays Bank* v. *O'Brien* (1994). This case has really led to a new area of equitable intervention and can be seen as one example of the modern renaissance of equity.

APPLICATION

John persuades Claud, his partner, to enter into a second mortgage of their jointly owned home to the Viper Bank in order to secure some business debts of John. It is clear that John exercised undue influence over Claud to persuade him to sign. The question is whether the Viper Bank is affected by what John has done. If it is not, then, although John may be liable to Claud, the actual mortgage is unaffected.

Figure 2.3 VIPER BANK: is the bank bound by John's undue influence/misrepresentation?

The House of Lords in *Royal Bank of Scotland* v. *Etridge* then clarified the steps which the creditor should reasonably be expected to take in satisfying itself that the security has been properly obtained:

(a) The lender must contact the surety and request that they nominate a solicitor.

(b) The surety must reply nominating a solicitor.

(c) The lender must, with the consent of the surety, disclose to the solicitor all relevant information – both the debtor's financial position and the details of the proposed loan.

(d) The solicitor must advise the surety in a face-to-face meeting at which the debtor is not present. The advice must cover an explanation of the documentation, the risks to the surety in signing and emphasise that the surety must decide whether to proceed.

(e) The solicitor must, if satisfied that the surety wishes to proceed, send written confirmation to the lender that the solicitor has explained the nature of the documents and their implications for the surety.

In *National Westminster Bank plc* v. *Amin* (2002) it was held that the solicitor must be expressly instructed to advise the surety on the nature and effect of the transaction and clearly this had not happened here.

Finally there has been some discussion as to whether the surety should still be liable for the amount to which she consented. In *TSB* v. *Camfield* (1995) a husband misrepresented that the security was limited to £15,000 but in fact it was unlimited. It was held that the wife had no liability even for the £15,000 because the mortgage so far as the wife as surety was concerned should be entirely set aside.

> **Take note**
>
> You must put this in the correct order. First decide if the lender is put on enquiry and only if it is do you need to consider the steps which it should take to satisfy itself that the security has been properly obtained.

> **Take note**
>
> Note that liability can arise in these situations not only where there has been undue influence but also in cases of misrepresentation and so you need to revise your definition of this.

INTERSECTION

The common law doctrine of duress is often dealt with in the law of contract where it is one of the vitiating factors which can make a contract void.

REFLECTION

Duress at common law is often linked with undue influence but it can be argued that with duress the situation is different: it is that the unlawful conduct, such as actual violence or the threat of it, or economic duress, results in a person entering into a transaction which they did not intend to enter into. Where there is undue influence the person may act freely but, as explained above, it is the way in which their intention is procured which may lead the court to set the transaction aside. Worthington (2006) looks at the matter slightly differently: she argues that in cases of both duress and undue influence, although consent has apparently been given, in reality there has been no genuine consent. What has happened is that a person has entered into a transaction as a result of being pressurised into doing so and the law has to determine which types of pressure are legitimate and which are not.

KEY POINTS

- Equitable remedies are discretionary.
- Equitable remedies act *in personam.*
- An injunction is an order requiring a party either to do or not to do a particular act.
- A order of specific performance orders defendants to perform their contractual obligations.
- Rescission sets the contract aside and restores the parties to their pre-contract positions.
- Rectification is used where a written instrument does not accord with the intentions of the parties and so the instrument is rectified to make it do so.
- Damages may be awarded in equity in addition to or in substitution for an injunction or specific performance.
- Undue influence is an equitable doctrine which, although impossible to define precisely, in essence aims to prevent the vulnerable from exploitation.

CORE CASES AND STATUTES

Case	Concerning	Application
Mareva Compania Naviera v. *International Bulk Carriers SA* (1975)	Grant of an interlocutory injunction to freeze assets often in advance of the issue of proceedings.	Cases where a debt is claimed and there is the possibility that the defendant may dissipate assets.
Anton Piller KG v. *Manufacturing Processes Ltd* (1975)	Grant of an interlocutory injunction to search for possible evidence often in advance of proceedings.	Cases of e.g. suspected breach of copyright and it is suspected that a potential defendant may destroy evidence.
Co-operative Insurance Society Ltd v. *Argyll Stores (Holdings) Ltd* (1998)	Whether specific performance should be granted of a covenant in a lease.	Factors that the court will consider in exercising its discretion in deciding whether to grant specific performance.
Warner Bros v. *Nelson* (1937)	Possible grant of an injunction to restrain breach of an employment contract.	The courts will not grant such an injunction where it would have the effect of enforcing the contract.
Royal Bank of Scotland plc v. *Etridge (No. 2)* (2001)	Possible liability of third parties (e.g. lenders) for undue influence or misrepresentation.	Cases where one co-owner (X) uses undue influence/ misrepresentation over another (Y) to make Y stand as surety for debts owed by X to a lender (Z) and the steps that Z should take to ensure that he is not affected by the undue influence/misrepresentation.

Statute	Concerning	Application
Lord Cairns Act (Chancery Amendment Act) 1858. Now s. 50 of the Supreme Court Act 1981	Courts have power to award damages in addition to, or in substitution for, specific performance or injunction.	Situations where damages are a more appropriate remedy than specific performance or injunction.
Section 236 of the Trade Union and Labour Relations (Consolidation) Act 1992	Prohibits the courts from enforcing performance of contracts of employment either by specific performance or injunction.	Cases where an order is sought actually compelling an employee to carry out his contract of employment.

FURTHER READING

Andrews, G. (2002) 'Undue influence – where's the disadvantage?' 66 *Conveyancer and Property Lawyer* 456.
This gives a clear analysis of the decision in *Royal Bank of Scotland* v. *Etridge (No. 2)*.

Dockray, M. and Laddie, H. (1990) 'Piller problems' 106 *LQR* 601.
This article demonstrated the problems which had arisen with the grant of what were then called Anton Piller orders and made a strong case for restrictions to be placed on their use.

Dowling, A. (2011) 'Vendors' application for specific performance' 3 *Conveyancer* 208–228.
This article looks at a series of decisions, including *Matila Ltd* v. *Lisheen Properties Ltd* (above) where the courts have established principles to be applied in determining whether an order for specific performance should be made. It is especially valuable in looking at similar cases in other jurisdictions.

Luxton, P. (1998) 'Are you being served? Enforcing keep-open covenants in a lease' *Conveyancer* (Sept/Oct) 396–406.
This looks in detail at the practical implications of the decision in *Co-operative Insurance Society* v. *Argyll Stores*.

Ridge, P. (2006) 'Legal regulation of religious giving' 157 *Law and Justice, the Christian Law Review* 17.
This article not only looks at undue influence in the context of gifts to religious bodies but also at religious giving more generally and so is valuable in the context of trusts for religious purposes (see Chapter 11).

Suen, Henry and Cheung, Sai On (2007) 'Mareva injunctions: evolving principles and practices revisited' 23(2) *Const. L.J.* 117–136.
This is a valuable account of how the law has developed and also gives light of the practice in Hong Kong in granting these orders.

Thompson, M. (2003) 'Mortgages and undue influence' in E. Cooke (ed.) *Modern Studies in Property Law*, Vol. 2 (Hart Publishing).
This sets the decision in *Royal Bank of Scotland* v. *Etridge (No. 2)* in its context.

Worthington, S. (2006) *Equity*, 2nd ed. (Oxford University Press).
See Chapter 7 for the discussion of duress and undue influence referred to in the text.

PART 2

Trusts: nature of a trust and creation of express trusts

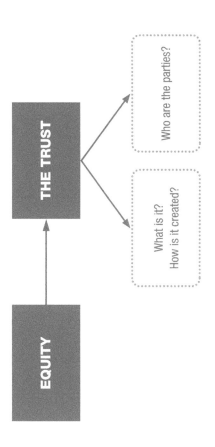

PART 2 INTRODUCTION

This part looks at the concept of a trust (Chapter 3) and then at the essential requirements in the creation of a trust. The best way is to look at a simple example.

Suppose that Bert wishes to set up a trust of £100,000 to benefit his friend Amy and that Sean is to be the trustee. We need to be clear about the terms of the trust: is there a trust, what is it of and who is it for? Then we must ask whether there are any formal requirements (i.e. of writing) needed to prove the trust. All this is dealt with in Chapter 4.

Then the £100,000 needs to be transferred to Sean and here we come to what is known as constitution of a trust (Chapter 7). Finally, many trusts are set up by will and in fact this one might be. If so, Chapter 8 looks at trusts and testamentary formalities.

First, however, we need to be clear on what a trust actually is and so we come to Chapter 3.

CHAPTER 3
The concept of a trust

BLUEPRINT

The concept of a trust

LEGISLATION

CONTEXT

- Tax avoidance – trusts developed as a means of achieving this

CONCEPTS

- Parties to a trust
- Equitable proprietary interest
- Trusts and contracts
- Types of trusts

- Relationship between trust and contract.

- What is a trust and what are its main features?

CASES

- *Barclays Bank Ltd* v. *Quistclose*
- *Kingsnorth Finance* v. *Tizard*
- *Turner* v. *Turner*

REFORM

- Will there be greater use of the trust concept in other jurisdictions?

SPECIAL CHARACTERISTICS

- Versatility of trusts
- Meaning of notice in equity

CRITICAL ISSUES

Setting the scene

Carl owns a house. It belongs to him and he lives in it. This means that he has the legal ownership of the house and also the right to benefit from it. Benefit comes first from being able to live in it but there are also specific legal advantages: Carl can sell it or can grant a lease over it; if Carl sells it then he has the right to receive the proceeds of sale. Alternatively he can stay in the house until he dies and then leave it to someone in his will. The point is that as the owner Carl can do these things without asking permission from anyone.

Take another example. Eileen is the legal owner of a house, 'The Gables'. She has a disabled son, Michael, who lives with her in 'The Gables' and she wishes him to continue to live in the house after her death. However, Michael, because of his disability, would not have the legal capacity to have the property transferred into his name. This means that Eileen has to find someone to hold the legal title for Michael and Eileen's friend Anne agrees to do so. If a trust is created during Eileen's lifetime then she will be the settlor, and if she creates it in her will then she will be the testator (or, more correctly, the testatrix which is the feminine form).

Anne is the trustee and here we see the difference between her and Carl in the above example. If Anne wishes to sell it or to grant a lease over it then she can do so as she is the legal owner but she must observe the duties of a trustee. To take one example: suppose that Carl has been offered a very highly paid job abroad and wants to leave soon. So he sells the house to the first buyer who comes along even though the price is far below the market value. Anne as trustee cannot do this as she is under a duty to obtain the best possible price. Again, if the house is sold then Anne cannot keep the proceeds of sale. Instead the trust will continue and they will be held on trust for Michael. All the time, as you can see, the focus is on the beneficiary, Michael. The trust is for his benefit and not that of Anne or indeed Eileen.

WHAT IS A TRUST?

> ### Take note
>
> The states of ownership are legal (held by the trustee) and beneficial (held by the beneficiary).

The essential idea behind a trust is that the right of legal ownership over property and the right to enjoy that property is split between two persons. In the above situation it was split between Anne as the trustee and Michael as the beneficiary. Watt (2009, p.118) puts it this way: 'The trust is not so much a *state of* ownership as a dramatic tension maintained between *states of* ownership' (my italics).

A precise definition of a trust is difficult because the trust concept has been adapted to so many different ends. Underhill's definition is one commonly given: 'A trust is an equitable obligation, binding a person (who is called a trustee) to deal with property over which he has control (which is called trust property) for the benefit of persons (who are called **beneficiaries** or ***cestuis que* trust)** of whom he himself may be one and any one of whom may enforce the obligation.' Even so, this definition does not cover charitable trusts, which are not enforceable by the beneficiaries but by the Attorney-General or the Charity Commissioners (see Chapter 6), or those trusts for non-charitable purposes which are recognised as valid despite the absence of beneficiaries who can enforce them (see Chapter 5).

ESSENTIAL CHARACTERISTICS OF A TRUST

CORNERSTONE

Parties to a trust

The parties to a trust are the settlor/testator (the creators of the trust), the trustees (who hold the legal title to the trust property and are subject to fiduciary and other duties) and the beneficiaries (who have the equitable interest in the trust property).

- The legal ownership of the trust property is held by the trustee(s).
- In equity the beneficiaries are the owners.
- It is the beneficiaries who enforce the trust and so private trusts (i.e. trusts for the benefit of individuals) must have beneficiaries who can enforce them. Charitable trusts are enforced by the Attorney-General (see Chapter 6) and there are also exceptional cases of trusts for non-charitable purposes (see Chapter 5).
- Trustees may also be beneficiaries. In the example given above in 'Setting the Scene', Anne could also have been a beneficiary under the trust of 'The Gables' although as she is a sole trustee and Michael is under a disability this would not be wise. (In practice it is best to have at least two trustees.)
- The creator of the trust is the **settlor** if the trust is created by a living person and is the **testator** if it is created by will.
- The trustee is bound to exercise his duties and powers as a trustee for the benefit of the beneficiaries.
- A trust may be set up to benefit either individuals or purposes.

The settlor and the trust

Once Eileen has created the trust in the example in 'Setting the Scene' then, if she is the settlor and so still alive, she must, unless she is named as a trustee, let go of the property and cannot give directions to the trustees and in effect still control the trust.

CORNERSTONE

Turner v. Turner

Turner v. *Turner* illustrates the fundamental principle that once the trust has been set up (a process dealt with in Chapters 4 and 7) the settlor, unless also a trustee, must let go of the trust.

This happened in *Turner* v. *Turner* (1984). That was a case in which a farmer set up a discretionary trust which he did not understand, and appointed as trustees family friends who never realised that they had any responsibility at all except to do as the settlor asked and so they simply did what they were told. They thought that it would be intruding into the settlor's affairs if they were to read the documents that they were asked to sign, where the settlor set up a trust for the benefit of members of his family. The court held that their decisions would be set aside.

The position of the trustee

Anne is the trustee in 'Setting the Scene' and is the legal owner of 'The Gables' with the same rights and duties as any other owner of property. For example, she can be liable for the (common law) tort of nuisance if there is unreasonable use of the property. In addition, though, she owes duties in equity to the beneficiaries. At this stage you should be aware of the fundamental equitable principle that a trustee 'is not, unless otherwise expressly provided, entitled to make a profit; he is not allowed to put himself in a position where his interest and his duty conflict' (Lord Herschell in *Bray* v. *Ford* (1896)). For example, suppose that Anne sold 'The Gables' to John and then disappeared with the proceeds of sale. Anne is quite entitled legally to sell the property as it belongs in law to her and not to Michael. However, equity regards the trust imposed on Anne as binding on her in conscience and so she could be made to repay the proceeds of sale to Michael. Michael also has the right to trace the proceeds of sale into other assets which Anne has, a topic to which we shall return in Chapter 10.

The position of the beneficiary

Michael is the beneficiary under the trust in 'Setting the Scene'; he is not the owner of the house in law and so, for example, the Land Registry will only mention Anne as the owner. However, he does have rights in equity to have the trust administered according to its terms and to compel Anne to observe the duties of a trustee. In addition, he is said to have an equitable proprietary interest in the trust property ('The Gables'), which is why he has the right to trace the proceeds of sale and he may also be able to argue that John, the buyer, holds the house on trust for him, as we shall see below.

ORIGIN OF THE TRUST

The trust originated in medieval times when it was known as a 'use', i.e. the trustee held property to 'the use' of a beneficiary. (The word 'use' bore no relation to the modern verb 'to use' but was derived from the Latin *ad opus* 'to the use or benefit of'.) Beneficiaries were referred to as *cestui que* use and indeed today they are still some times called '*cestui que* trust'.

Uses were found in very early times in English law. Simpson (1986) points out that instances of them can be found at the time of Doomsday Book (1086). They were always of land and various reasons have been put forward for their use. It is instructive to look at some of these and see how today trusts are still used for the same reasons:

(a) *To assist in a fraud.* Simpson observes that when someone was proposing to engage in some treasonable enterprise, which could lead to his lands being forfeited to the Crown if he was caught and punished, he might put his lands in the ownership of a 'blameless confederate' who would then hold them to his use.

(b) *To enable property to be used for the benefit of causes.* The Franciscan friars were not allowed to own property, either individually or as an Order, in imitation of the poverty of Christ. Thus any houses and land of theirs had to be owned by others for their use. In effect it was held for the Order rather than individual friars.

(c) *To avoid or minimise tax.* The main reason for the emergence of 'the use' was the desire to escape from the rigidity of the feudal system. Once caught in it, what we would now call various taxes could be demanded from the landowner and the object of the use was to escape these. The cornerstone of the feudal system was the relationship between the tenant who held land from his lord and from whom the lord was entitled to demand various services and from which there were various incidental consequences for the lord (incidents). For example, a 'relief' had to be paid to the lord when a tenant succeeded to land by descent from the previous tenant. A way to avoid this was for a tenant (Alf) to grant the land on trust to some friends (Tim and Tom), who in turn were to grant the land to a named beneficiary (Will) after the tenant's death. As the land did not now pass by descent the payment of a relief was avoided. The effect was to allow land to be devised by will although wills of land, as such, were not allowed. Suppose that Tim and Tom in the above example refused to carry out Alf's wishes and instead conveyed the land to a stranger? (We saw the same situation in 'Setting the Scene' above.) The common law refused to recognise the trust as it was unable to devise procedures which would protect someone who had a beneficial interest in land but not legal ownership. Thus it would not allow any claim by Will, the beneficiary. The Chancellor, however, held that the trustees had obligations imposed on them in conscience and so would enforce the rights of beneficiaries such as Will.

By 1500 most land in England was held under a use (the modern trust) and so the King was deprived of almost all of his feudal revenue. King Henry VIII (he of the six wives) tried to reverse this trend by the Statute of Uses (1535) which provided, in effect, that where property was left by say Tom to Ted as trustee for Simon until Simon comes of age then Simon simply became the absolute owner and as such was liable to feudal dues. This brilliantly simple device did not work as Chancery lawyers found means to evade it and so the loss of feudal revenue to the King continued.

This had important political consequences: as the King had lost his revenue from feudalism he had to summon Parliament more frequently to vote him sums of money. Parliament in return demanded a greater say in how this was spent. Conflict between the two led ultimately to the Civil War (1642–1651) and to the eventual curbing of royal powers and the supremacy of Parliament. And uses started it all!

As a footnote to this Henry VIII did, as a kind of compromise following the Statute of Uses, allow land to be devised by will by the Statute of Wills (1540).

The trust, in medieval times, was seen as an essentially static institution designed to achieve a particular purpose. However, the versatility of the trust meant that it came to be used increasingly as a means to achieve a framework for future action. Thus trustees were no longer concerned only with land but with investments in stocks, shares, mortgages and other securities which needed to be bought and sold whereas the object of a trust of land was simply to retain it.

MAIN USES TO WHICH TRUSTS ARE PUT TODAY

CORNERSTONE

Uses of trusts

The trust is a versatile instrument which facilitates many different activities in society.

The trust enables many things, often those we take for granted, to be achieved in our society today. Take the situations shown in Figures 3.1 and 3.2.

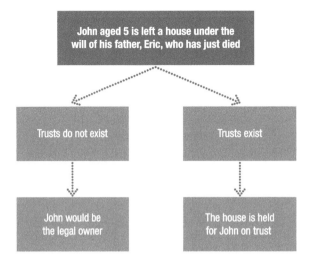

Figure 3.1 Situation One

As we can see from Figure 3.1, if the concept of a trust did not exist we would be faced with the impossible situation of a child of five being faced with the burdens of land ownership. However, because we have a trust, the house can be held for John on trust, until he comes of age at 18. It is worth noting that land law does not permit a minor to hold land (s. 1(6) of the LPA 1925) and so the trust is essential.

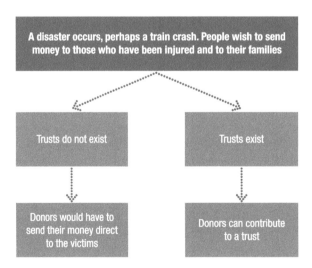

Figure 3.2 Situation Two

Again we can see from Figure 3.2 the practical value of the trust: in most cases we do not know who the victims are and cannot send them money directly. By using a trust we can contribute easily.

Here are some other uses of trusts. In each case try to work out yourself what the consequences would be if the trust solution was not available.

(a) Tax-saving. The original reason for the emergence of the modern trust, the avoidance of feudal dues, was to save tax and this is still one of the principal uses of the trust.

.... **APPLICATION**

If Miranda has an income of £100,000 a year from investments she will pay tax on the dividends received on the shares. She could set up a trust under which some of the shares are held for her two children, Poppy and Rupert. Although the Revenue taxes the beneficial owner of property, in this case Poppy and Rupert, they may have no other income and so will not be liable to tax on the dividends.

In addition, favourable tax treatment is given to various types of trust such as accumulation and maintenance trusts established for the benefit of minors and the creation of a discretionary trust (see Chapter 4) can be an effective way of avoiding or reducing Inheritance Tax.

(b) To enable investments to be made through unit trusts where trustees buy holdings in companies and then invite members of the public to buy 'units' or shares in the trust fund.

(c) To hold pension funds for employees. Most occupational pension schemes are held under a trust.

(d) To enable two or more persons to own land. Land held by more than one person has to be held on a trust of land (ss. 34–36 of the LPA 1925) and as married couples normally have the matrimonial home vested in their joint names it will be held on a trust of land. These are governed by the Trusts of Land and Appointment of Trustees Act (TLATA) 1996.

INTERSECTION ....

Trusts of the home are explored and you should refer to your Land Law materials for details of the Trusts of Land and Appointment of Trustees Act.

(e) To decide disputes relating to the ownership of property by the use of either a **resulting trust** (see e.g. *Barclays Bank* v. *Quistclose* in Chapter 11 and below) or a **constructive trust** (see Chapter 9).

(f) Other uses, for instance the establishment under the National Health Service and Community Care Act 1990 of self-governing trusts to run NHS hospitals and other bodies.

In *Selected Essays* (1936, p. 129) Maitland made what is now a celebrated statement: 'If we were asked what is the greatest and most distinctive achievement performed by Englishmen in the field of jurisprudence I cannot think that we should have any better answer to give than this, namely the development from century to century of the trust idea.' Maitland's point is that, as we saw above, the trust is an endlessly versatile instrument.

CONTEXT

In fact the idea of the trust has not been taken up in Continental legal systems but in 'Developing the law of trusts for the 21st century' (1990) David Hayton pointed out that after the First World War, when Germany was ordered to meet the cost of the war by reparations, there was a need to find some body which would hold the money paid by Germany before it was distributed. So the Bank of

International Settlements was set up to act as trustee for the German payments, illustrating the useful-ness of the trust. Hayton then quotes a French lawyer, Pierre Lepaulle, who wrote: 'Thus from the settlement of the greatest of wars down to the simplest inheritance on death, from the most audacious Wall Street Scheme down to the protection of grandchildren, the trust can see marching before it the motley procession of the whole of human endeavour'. He ends: 'The trust is the guardian angel of the Anglo-Saxon, accompanying him everywhere, impassively, from the cradle to the grave.'

Note that under the Hague Convention on the Law Applicable to Trusts and on their Recognition, which was given force in the UK by the Recognition of Trusts Act, there is a mechanism by which the courts of countries where the trust is unknown can deal with trust matters.

THE CONCEPT OF EQUITABLE OWNERSHIP

In *Westdeutsche Landesbank Girozentrale* v. *Islington LBC* (1996) Lord Browne-Wilkinson set out the essential character of equitable ownership in the following passage, which is recognised as an authoritative statement of the law:

> Once a trust is established, as from the date of its establishment the beneficiary has, in equity, a proprietary interest in the trust property, which proprietary interest will be enforceable in equity against any subsequent holder of the property (whether the original property or sub-stituted property into which it can be traced) other than a purchaser for value of the legal estate without notice.

This passage sets out two vital concepts which you need to be clear about before you study the law of trusts in detail:

(a) The beneficiaries acquire a *proprietary* interest in the trust property. They do not acquire only a personal right to claim damages as for a breach of contract or tort but instead they acquire rights in the trust property itself.

(b) This proprietary interest is not only binding on the trustee but also on third parties into whose hands the trust property comes, with the one exception of a purchaser for value of the legal estate which comprises the trust property without notice of the beneficiaries' proprietary interest.

THE EQUITABLE PROPRIETARY INTEREST

CORNERSTONE

Equitable proprietary interest

There are two fundamental points to keep in mind:

(a) What is meant by a proprietary interest?

(b) Assuming that the interest is a proprietary one, what is the significance of it being an equit-able one?

The idea of a proprietary interest

There is a fundamental difference between the rights of beneficiaries under a trust and the rights of parties to a contract. A contract creates personal rights which bind the parties but, apart from special cases, as where the Contracts (Rights of Third Parties) Act 1999 applies, it does not confer either rights or obligations on third parties. The significance of this is seen when the trustees, for example, wrongfully part with the trust property to others.

The consequences of an equitable proprietary interest

APPLICATION

John contracts to sell his guitar to Sue. Sue pays John £100.00 for it and John promises to deliver it to Sue's house the next day. That evening John sells the guitar to Peter for £100.00. This is a breach of contract.

Sue can of course sue John for breach of contract and recover her £100.00. However she cannot claim the guitar from him or Peter as John's obligation to sell the guitar to Sue is personal. In traditional language, Sue's rights against John are *in personam*: against the person.

Suppose that John had created a trust of the guitar for Sue. John is the trustee (and the settlor) and Sue is the beneficiary. The trust property is the guitar. John parts with the guitar to Peter. This, as we have seen, is a breach of trust. This time Sue can in principle claim the guitar back from Peter. This is because John's obligations under the trust related to the trust property, the guitar, unlike in contract where they related to him personally. Thus, because John broke his obligations in selling the guitar to Peter, the transfer to him was a breach of trust and Sue can claim that the guitar is still hers and must be restored to the trust. Here Sue's rights are *in rem*: against the thing itself.

Do note the words 'Sue can *in principle* claim the guitar back from Peter'. For now the principle is important but later we shall see, especially in Chapter 10, that in some cases Sue may not be able to recover the guitar from Peter.

The significance of the proprietary interest being equitable

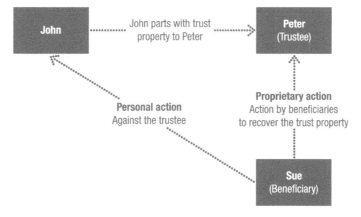

Figure 3.3 The equitable proprietary interest

CORNERSTONE

Equitable proprietary interests are property rights

The fact that a trust creates a proprietary interest means that the beneficiaries have an actual property right in whatever is the subject matter of the trust.

> ### Take note
>
> The vital point is that you cannot say that someone who receives property subject to an equitable proprietary interest is definitely bound by it or is not bound by it. Instead you must ask if they are a purchaser for value without notice of it.

In equity the position is different. The rule is that an equitable proprietary interest may be lost if the legal estate is acquired **by a purchaser in good faith for value without notice of the equitable interest**. This is a fundamental rule of equity and must be mastered at the outset of studying the subject.

Thus, if in the above example John transfers the guitar to Peter who knows nothing of the trust, then although Sue will have a personal claim against John for breach of trust this will be useless if John is insolvent or cannot be traced. Will Sue have a claim against Peter for the guitar? This will depend on the following:

- Is Peter a purchaser for value of the guitar? If it was a gift from John to him then Sue's rights will prevail.

- Assuming that Peter was a purchaser for value, was he in good faith without notice of Sue's equitable rights? If Peter was not then again Sue's rights will prevail. If, however, Peter had no notice of Sue's rights then his rights will prevail against those of Sue.

> ### Take note
>
> Do not confuse notice with knowledge. It is not necessarily the same.

The central issue is: what is meant by notice? (The words 'good faith' by themselves mean little.) If a purchaser has notice of an equitable interest then she is bound by it. If not, she is not bound. Notice means more than just knowledge and can be:

(a) *Actual notice.* This is knowledge by the purchaser.

(b) *Constructive notice.* This is where the purchaser does not have actual knowledge but she would have had actual knowledge had she made the reasonable inquiries which a prudent purchaser would have made. In effect, the purchaser ought to have known of the interest.

(c) *Imputed notice* is where the agent of the purchaser has actual or constructive notice. This is then imputed to the purchaser.

The doctrine of notice is one of the fundamental principles of equity and, at this stage, it is useful to have some idea of how it works in practice. An example of actual notice is provided by *Barclays Bank* v. *Quistclose* (below). Barclays Bank was bound by the trusts in favour of the creditors and then in favour of Quistclose as it had actual notice of them. The letter stating that the loan was only to be used to meet the dividend was sent to Barclays and, as this gave rise to the trust, Barclays clearly had notice of it.

CORNERSTONE

Kingsnorth Finance v. *Tizard and the doctrine of notice*

Kingsnorth Finance v. *Tizard* illustrates the doctrine of notice in equity, especially constructive and imputed notice.

Constructive and imputed notice is illustrated by *Kingsnorth Finance Ltd* v. *Tizard* (1986). Mr Tizard was the sole legal owner of the matrimonial home but held it on trust for himself and his wife. They had separated but she visited the house every day. Mr Tizard decided to mortgage the house to Kingsnorth Finance and a surveyor from them came to inspect it. The visit was on a Sunday afternoon, when Mr Tizard knew that his wife would not be there. Mr Tizard told the surveyor that he and his wife had recently separated and that she had no interest in the house. The mortgage was granted but Mr Tizard then absconded with the mortgage money. Kingsnorth Finance sought to sell the house but the wife resisted the claim on the ground that she had an equitable interest in it.

The question was therefore whether Kingsnorth was bound by this interest and it was held that it was. Although Kingsnorth was a purchaser (a lender on mortgage – a mortgagee – is a purchaser) and had given value (the mortgage advance) they did have notice of Mrs Tizard's equitable interest. This was because:

(a) The surveyor had constructive notice. Knowing that the Tizards had recently separated he should not have simply accepted at face value Mr Tizard's statement that his wife had no interest in the house but should have made further inquiries.

(b) Given that the surveyor had constructive notice and was employed by Kingsnorth to carry out the survey, Kingsnorth had imputed notice of his constructive notice.

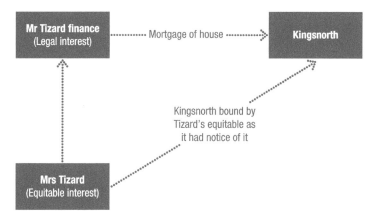

Figure 3.4 Constructive and imputed notice

INTERSECTION ....

This case is also an excellent illustration of how equitable interests are protected in unregistered land. If you have studied land law then do check your land law materials to make sure that you are clear on the distinction between registered and unregistered land. If you have not yet studied land law then store this case away to use again when you do.

TRUSTS AND CONTRACTS

CORNERSTONE

Trusts and contracts – *Barclays Bank* v. *Quistclose*

Although trusts and contracts are different concepts it is possible for a trust and a contract to arise from the same set of facts. The difference between the two is illustrated by *Barclays Bank* v. *Quistclose*.

It may be that both a contract and a trust may exist side by side. A good example is *Barclays Bank* v. *Quistclose Investments Ltd* (1970). Rolls Razor was in great financial difficulties. It declared a dividend on its shares but did not have the money to pay it and so Quistclose made a contract to make it a loan for the express purpose of enabling it to pay this dividend. The money was paid into a separate account at Barclays Bank and it was agreed with the bank that the account would 'only be used to meet the dividend due on July 24th 1964'. Before the dividend was paid Rolls Razor went into liquidation and the question was whether Barclays Bank could set the sum in the account off against Rolls Razor's overdraft or whether they held it on trust for Quistclose.

The House of Lords held that there was a trust for Quistclose as the letter clearly indicated that the money was to be used to pay the dividend and for no other purpose. It followed that if for any reason the money could not be used for this purpose then it had to be returned to Quistclose. Accordingly it was held by Rolls Razor on trust for Quistclose.

The significance of the decision was first that if all had gone well and the loan had achieved its purpose of enabling the dividend to be paid then the relationship would have been simply one of debt and Rolls Razor would have been liable to repay the loan. If it had not done so, a personal action for breach of contract could have been brought. In addition, if the court had held on the facts that there was no trust then the loan arrangement would have applied and Quistclose would have had to join the queue of creditors against Rolls Razor and would probably have had very little chance of ever seeing their money again.

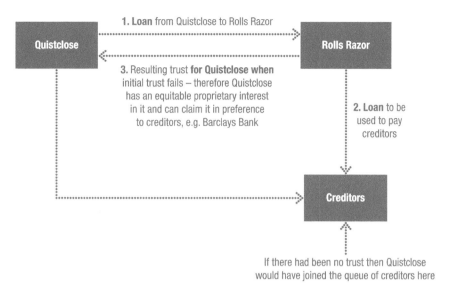

Figure 3.5 *Barclays Bank* v. *Quistclose*

This is the first case which we meet where there is the classic contest: Trust = rights of beneficiaries take precedence; Contract only = creditors will come first. This will include those who would have been beneficiaries had there been a trust but they will have to take their place in the queue, whereas as beneficiaries they, in effect, by-pass the queue of creditors altogether. Given that we just saw in Chapter 1 that conscience is a distinguishing feature of equitable jurisdiction, is equity being used in the right way here? All that is happening is that a trust is being imposed to give one person or group of persons a greater right to get their money back than others when the debtor is insolvent. This point is considered again in Chapter 11 when we look at the *Quistclose* trust in more detail.

What happened, however, was that a relationship of trust was imposed on the existing loan arrangement. Thus, as the money was held on trust for Quistclose, it had an equitable proprietary interest in it which took precedence over any personal claim in the law of debt. Quite simply, in equity the money was theirs.

> **Take note**
>
> This case held that there was a resulting trust and it raised a number of issues, some of which are controversial. These are considered in Chapter 11 which considers resulting trusts in full. You should, for the moment, use this case simply as an illustration of the relationship between personal rights, created here by contract, and equitable proprietary rights.

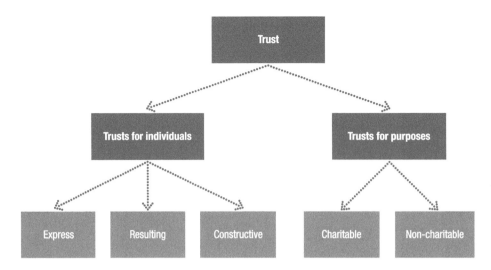

Figure 3.6 Main types of trust

INTERSECTION

Look at *R* v. *Clowes* in Chapter 4 for another good example of the relationship between trust and contract.

CORNERSTONE

Types of trusts

The list below is just a brief statement of what the main types of trusts are. Treat it as a snapshot and use it for reference throughout this book. However, do remember that all of the statements below will be elaborated when we look in detail at each type of trust.

The precise circumstances in which certain trusts, especially resulting and constructive trusts, can arise is a matter of debate, but the following is a brief description of the main ideas behind each type of trust.

(a) *Express private trusts.* These are expressly created whether by the settlor or the testator to benefit a particular person or persons. You will find references to them throughout this text but the rules for their creation are in Chapter 4.

(b) *Resulting trusts.* These arise where property has been transferred from one person to another but the beneficial interest results back to the transferor. A resulting trust can arise from the presumed intention of the transferor but this does not explain all cases of resulting trusts. Chapter 11 deals with them specifically and you will also find that they play a part in trusts of the family home.

(c) *Constructive trusts.* These arise by operation of law. Equity says that in certain instances a person will be compelled to hold it on trust for others. Constructive trusts are increasingly important in practice and are often used to prevent fraud or unjust enrichment by one person at the expense of another. Chapter 9 has the details and, as with resulting trusts, they play a part in trusts of the family home.

(d) *Charitable (public) trusts.* These are designed to benefit either society, or a section of it, as distinct from particular persons, as in the case of private trusts. They are therefore more concerned with purposes than with persons. Charitable trusts are dealt with in Chapter 6.

(e) *Non-charitable-purpose trusts.* These, like charitable trusts, are concerned with purposes and are considered in Chapter 5.

Trusts are also classified, not according to their function as above, but in other ways such as completely and incompletely constituted trusts (see Chapter 7). One particular type of trust which it is useful to be aware of at this stage is a **bare trust**. This is where the trustee holds property on trust for an adult beneficiary who is absolutely entitled to the property. It may be, for example, that a person finds it convenient to put property in the hands of a trustee as she is going abroad and in these cases the trustee is often known as the nominee. In such cases the trustee may have no duties to perform other than to hold the property to the order of the beneficiary.

KEY POINTS

- Trusts have three parties: first the creator of the trust (the settlor, who creates an *inter vivos* trust or the testator where the trust is created by will), second the trustee(s) who hold(s) the legal title to the trust property and third the beneficiaries who have the beneficial interest.
- Trustees can be beneficiaries and the settlor can be a trustee.
- Trusts developed in medieval times and were known as 'uses'.
- Trusts are extremely versatile instruments.
- The beneficiaries acquire an equitable proprietary interest in the trust property.
- An equitable proprietary interest may be lost if the legal estate is acquired by a purchaser in good faith for value without notice of the equitable interest.
- Rights under a trust and rights under a contract can exist on the same set of facts.
- A bare trust is where the trustee holds property on trust for an adult beneficiary who is absolutely entitled to the property. In such cases the trustee may have no duties to perform other than to hold the property to the order of the beneficiary.

CORE CASES AND STATUTES

Case	Concerning	Application
Turner v. *Turner* (1984)	Where trustees simply did what the settlor told them to do the court held that these acts would be set aside.	Trustees must exercise an independent judgment of their own and not act as the settlor tells them to.
Barclays Bank Ltd v. *Quistclose Investments Ltd* (1970)	Money lent to a company for the specific purpose of paying dividends was held for the lender on a resulting trust when the dividends could not be paid as the company went into liquidation.	Where property is given for a specific purpose which then cannot be carried out a resulting trust may be used to return that property to the person who gave it.
Kingsnorth Finance Co. Ltd v. *Tizard* (1986)	A mortgage lender was bound by the equitable interest of a person under a trust as it had constructive notice of it.	The extent to which equitable interests are binding on persons with notice and the different types of notice.

FURTHER READING

Hayton, D. (1990) 'Developing the law of trusts for the 21st century' 106 *LQR* 87.

Jones, N. (1997) 'Uses, trusts and a path to privity' 56 *CLJ* 175.
This is useful in illuminating the transition from uses to trusts.

Maitland, F. (1909) *Essays in Equity*, 2nd ed. 1936 (reissued 2011 Cambridge University Press).
You will find that Lectures I–XII, which deal with equity and the trust, are most useful. The style, as these were delivered as actual lectures, is most readable.

Simpson, A. (1986) *A History of the Land Law* (Oxford University Press).
Although the title of this book might lead you to think that it is for land lawyers it does contain a very valuable account of the development of the use and then the trust in Chapter VIII.

Watt, G. (2009) *Equity Stirring: The Story of Justice Beyond Law* (Hart Publishing).
This has an excellent and stimulating discussion of the nature and development of the trust on pages 117–128.

CHAPTER 4

Creating the trust: certainties

BLUEPRINT

Creating the trust: certainties

KEY QUESTIONS

LEGISLATION

- Perpetuities and Accumulations Act 1964
- Perpetuities and Accumulations Act 2009

CONTEXT

- Contrast strict approaches to more liberal ones – *McPhail* v. *Doulton* as an example of the latter.

CONCEPTS

- Certainty of intention, subject matter and objects
- Conditions attached to gifts
- Remoteness of vesting

- Subject matter where the goods are unascertained;
- how to apply the individual ascertainability test.

- What has to be certain to create a trust?

CASES

- *Re Adams and the Kensington Vestry*
- *Sprange* v. *Barnard*
- *Re London Wine*
- *McPhail* v. *Doulton*

REFORM

- Clarification of the principle in *Re Barlow*.

SPECIAL CHARACTERISTICS

- Certainty of subject matter where the goods are unascertained
- Certainty of objects in discretionary trusts

CRITICAL ISSUES

Setting the scene

Suppose that Jack wants to provide for some of his grandchildren after he has died. He says to his friend Sue: 'Can you make sure that some of my grandchildren have part of my money so that it can be used for their education after I have gone?' Sue says: 'Yes of course, anything to help. Don't worry any more about it.' After Jack has died Sue remembers the conversation but the following points strike her.

Has Jack told her that this is something that she must do or can she only do it if she wishes? If she does decide to carry out this project of Jack's then she realises that she does not know how much is available. She also realises that Jack did not specify which of the grandchildren were to benefit. The reason for these problems is that it seems as if Jack wished to create a trust with Sue as the trustee but he did not comply with what are known as the three certainties which are needed to create a valid trust.

In the introduction to this part we mentioned that we need to be clear about the terms of the trust: is there a trust, what is it of and who is it for? These are, in essence, the three certainties. They are not mere technicalities but are needed to answer the questions Sue has asked. To take them in order: the reason why Sue is uncertain if she has to do this or not is because Jack has not shown any **certainty of intention to create a trust**. The problem that Sue has over the amount available is because there is no **certainty of subject matter**. The fact that Sue does not know which of the grandchildren is to benefit is because Jack has not specified the objects of the trust, which means the beneficiaries. Thus there is no **certainty of objects**. There is another reason for requiring certainties: as a trust creates legal obligations which can be enforced by the courts, the courts will not uphold a trust when it creates obligations which they cannot enforce because, for example, they are insufficiently clear. This would apply in the above example.

INTRODUCTION

CORNERSTONE

The three certainties

The three certainties are the essential building blocks of a private trust. They are certainty of intention, certainty of subject matter and certainty of objects. If you are tackling any problem question on trusts you must check first that these three certainties are present.

If a trust is a public trust then certainty of objects is not required. This is because public trusts are charitable trusts and their objects will be general ones such as 'the advancement of education'.

INTERSECTION

The terms private and public trusts are explained in Chapter 3. Charitable trusts are explained in detail in Chapter 6.

It is vital that you always find a home for the property. If there is no certainty of intention then there is no trust and the person who would otherwise have been a trustee (Sue in the above example) will not be one. Instead we use the language of gifts and say that Sue will be the donee of the gift, which means that she can keep it unless some other legal relationship arises such as a contract.

CERTAINTY OF INTENTION: IS THERE A TRUST?

Certainty of intention – general principles

There are two approaches to the question of intention:

(a) In *Re Hamilton* (1895) Lindley LJ said that the courts must look at all the words used by the testator or settlor to see if, on their true construction, in the context of the particular gift, a trust was intended. This might involve holding in one case that particular words did not create a trust even though in previous cases similar words have been held to create one.

APPLICATION

In *Re Johnson* (1939) the court held that the words: 'I request that' did not create a trust. Suppose that the wording went like this: 'I request John to hold the property for the benefit of my nieces and nephews.' Here the use of the words 'hold' and 'for the benefit of' is likely to mean that there would be a trust. The message is not to concentrate too much on individual words but to look at the wording as a whole.

(b) In Re *Steele's WT* (1948) it was held that a trust was created because the draftsman had used words very similar to those used in *Shelley* v. *Shelley* (1868) which had been held to create a trust and thus this showed the requisite intention. In both cases the will directed that property should descend through the family passing to the eldest son in each generation and that each eldest son should do everything possible to give effect to this wish.

Although this approach is just a particular method of finding intention it is generally considered that it places too much importance on the precise words used, and indeed it can be seen that the effect of using this rule was that in *Re Steele* the court imposed a trust despite the use of the word 'wish'. It is suggested that the approach of Lindley LJ in *Re Hamilton* is to be preferred and that you should use this when answering questions on this area.

Subjective test

The test of intention is subjective in that it asks what the actual intentions of the person were, looking at the words as a whole, rather than concentrating only on particular words.

Use of the word 'trust'

When you are looking at certainty of intention you should not place too much emphasis on the use of the word 'trust' as this does not *necessarily* mean that a trust was intended. In *Tito* v. *Waddell (No. 2)* (1977) phosphate was mined on Ocean Island by a British Company under licences from the Crown but in 1920 these licences were vested in Commissioners appointed by the UK, Australian and New Zealand governments. It was provided that where land was compulsorily acquired by the Commissioners for mining purposes any royalties or compensation were to be held 'on trust' for the former owners.

It was held that this did not create a trust in what Megarry VC called the 'lower sense' (i.e. an enforceable obligation) but did create one in the 'higher sense' of a moral obligation, in this case owed by the governments. Thus there was no enforceable trust. As Lord O'Hagan put it in *Kinloch* v. *Secretary of State for India* (1882): 'There is no magic in the word "trust"'.

An interesting modern example is *Duggan* v. *Governor of Full Sutton Prison* (2004) where a prisoner claimed that money of his which was taken from him when he entered the prison and placed in an account under the control of the governor was held in trust for him. It was held that it was clear that under rule 43 of the Prison Rules 1999 both ownership and possession of the money passed to the governor and so there was no room for the imposition of a trust as there was clearly no intent to create one.

Two types of case

Cases involving wills

CORNERSTONE

Re Adams and the Kensington Vestry

Re Adams and the Kensington Vestry is the classic case on certainty of intention in this area.

In cases dating mainly from the early to middle nineteenth century 'precatory words', i.e. words indicating hope or request, were held to create a trust. In *Palmer* v. *Simmonds* (1854), for instance, the words 'full confidence' were held to show sufficient intention. From about this time, however, the attitude of the courts changed and it was increasingly held that words were needed which clearly put the intended trustee under an obligation rather than making a request. This can be seen in contrasting *Palmer* v. *Simmonds* with *Re Adams and the Kensington Vestry* (1884). Here a testator left his property to his wife absolutely 'in full confidence that she will do what is right as to the disposal thereof between my children . . .'. It was held that no trust was created but there was only a moral obligation on her to provide for the children. Such a case is often known as gift with a motive.

This case is often contrasted with *Comiskey* v. *Bowring-Hanbury* (1905) because in both cases the words 'in full confidence' were used but in fact a closer examination of the actual words shows that in *Comiskey* the language was entirely different. Here a testator also left his property to his wife 'in full confidence that she will make such use of it as I would myself and that at my death she will devise it to such one or more of the nieces as she may think fit and in default of any disposition by her thereof by will or testament I hereby direct that that all my estate and property acquired by her under this my will shall at her death be divided among my said nieces'. The language is clearly intended to create a binding obligation. As Halsbury LC observed, one significant phrase is 'I hereby direct' and the effect was that the widow would take all the property subject to an obligation at her death to leave it to the nieces but that if she did not then the property was to be divided among them anyway.

> ### Take note
> You will find it helpful to remember straightforward instances of where a trust has not been created e.g. *Re Diggles* (1888) ('it is my desire') and *Re Johnson* (1939) ('I request that') but, as said above, concentration on individual words can give a misleading impression.

Cases other than those arising by will, where the question is usually whether there is an inter vivos gift or a trust

A good example is *Paul* v. *Constance* (1977) where the question was whether money in a bank account in the name of Paul was held in trust for Constance, with whom he cohabited. The account was in his name only because of the social embarrassment caused by having an account in two different names and damages received by Paul from an injury at work together with joint bingo winnings were paid into it. Paul had said that he wanted Constance to be able to draw on the money and had also said on various occasions that the money belonged to Constance as much as to him. It was held that this was sufficient to create an express trust in her favour.

INTERSECTION

The decision in *Paul* v. *Constance* is also important in connection with constitution of trusts dealt with in Chapter 7.

An interesting example of intention, which also shows the interplay of the concepts of contract and trust, is *R* v. *Clowes (No. 2)* (1994). Investors were persuaded by Clowes to part with money apparently for offshore investments but which was in reality taken by Clowes himself to fund an extravagant lifestyle. The question was whether the money was held on trust by him for the investors or if the relationship between him and them was only one of contract?

If it was a trust, then the investors, as beneficiaries, would have a proprietary interest in it as they would own in equity. Therefore by appropriating it Clowes would be guilty of dishonest appropriation of it contrary to s. 5 of the Theft Act 1968. If the relationship was merely one of contract then this would not apply as the investors would not acquire any proprietary interest in it and so there would be no property belonging to another to appropriate. It was held that there was a trust mainly because of the words used in the brochure inviting investments: 'All moneys received are held in a designated clients' account and the clients are the beneficial owners of all securities purchased on their behalf.'

The relationship between contract and trust in this case can be expressed as follows:

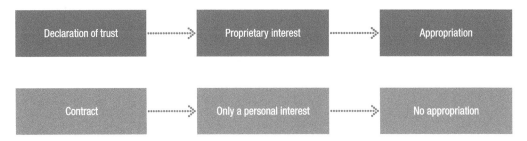

Figure 4.1 The relationship between contract and trust in *R* v. *Clowes (No. 2)*

Effect of a lack of certainty of intention

Where the gift was in a will the donee will take beneficially because no trust was intended (Rule in *Lassence* v. *Tierney* (1849)). In other cases, although there may be no trust there may be a contract or some other legal relationship instead.

...............APPLICATION

Teresa leaves £1,000 to Richard 'in the hope that he will remember' her two friends, Anita and John. The words 'in the hope that he will remember' do not show sufficient certainty of intention and so Richard can take the money beneficially, which means that it is his to keep. He is the donee of a gift and not the trustee of a trust.

CERTAINTY OF SUBJECT MATTER: IF THERE IS AN INTENTION TO CREATE A TRUST, THEN WHAT IS IT OF?

When you are clear on certainty of intention you should move on to certainty of subject matter. Any property can form the subject matter of a trust, whether it is a chattel, a chose in action, or even a milk quota under EC rules as in *Swift* v. *Dairywise Farms* (2000), a decision which is worth reading for its analysis of equitable doctrines in the light of modern commercial practices.

CORNERSTONE

Sprange v. *Barnard*

The decision in *Sprange* v. *Barnard* illustrates not only the need for certainty of subject matter but also the situation where there is a trust where the subject matter is uncertain and an absolute gift.

You will find it helpful to consider the topic of certainty of subject matter under four headings:

(a) **There must be certainty as to the actual property left on trust**. In *Anthony* v. *Donges* (1998) a widow was left 'such minimal part of (the) estate as she might be entitled to . . . for maintenance purposes'. This was held to be too uncertain as no such minimal entitlement exists.

(b) **There must be certainty as to how much is left on trust and how much is an outright gift**. If not, the donee will take the property absolutely. This happened in *Sprange* v. *Barnard* (1789) where the will gave property to the testatrix's husband 'for his sole use' and then provided that 'the remaining part of what is left, that he does not want . . . to be divided between' members of his family. As the term 'remaining part' was uncertain the husband took absolutely and so the others got nothing.

(c) **Where the property to be held on trust forms part of a larger whole**. Here there must be certainty as to how much is to form part of the trust. An example is *Curtis* v. *Rippon* (below).

(d) **Where the beneficial shares are uncertain**. An example is *Boyce* v. *Boyce* (1849), a testator devised two houses to trustees to convey one to Maria, whichever she should select, and the other to Charlotte. Maria died before making a choice and so the trust in favour of Charlotte failed. The consequence was that, as Maria could obviously not make a choice, both houses were held on a resulting trust for the testator's grandson, who was entitled to the property on the testator's death.

INTERSECTION

You may recall that we met the basic idea of a resulting trust in Chapter 3 and the whole subject of resulting trusts will be considered in Chapter 11. You will find that resulting trusts apply in exactly the same way where the trust fails due to lack of certainty of objects.

You also need to note two final points:

(a) Where the subject matter of the trust does not yet exist (i.e. it is future property) then there is no certainty of subject matter. In *Williams* v. *Commissioner of Inland Revenue* (1965) an attempt to assign 'the first £500 of the net income which shall accrue to the assignor' on trust failed on this ground.

(b) Where the trustees are given a discretion this may sometimes enable the court to declare that there is certainty of subject matter. This seems to be the explanation of *Re Golay* (1965) where the testator directed that a Mrs Bridgewater should 'enjoy one of my flats during her lifetime' and 'receive a reasonable income from my other properties'. It was held that the word 'reasonable' provided a sufficiently objective standard to enable the court if necessary to quantify the amount. You should be careful about how you use this case as it must be regarded as borderline since there was no further assistance given in the will to guide the trustees or the court.

Certainty of subject matter where the goods are not yet ascertained

CORNERSTONE

Re London Wine as illustrating the problem where goods are unascertained

There are special problems where the subject matter of the trust is not yet ascertained, e.g. 50 bottles of wine out of a store of 1,000. One of the first cases to consider this, and one which is still a leading authority, is *Re London Wine*.

APPLICATION

Clare owes a total of £50,000 to a range of creditors and declares that she holds £5,000 of this in trust for Guy. The problem is: which £5,000? Does it matter? No, because all money is the same. Suppose that Clare spends all her money except for £5,000. She has many creditors and the question is whether the money belongs to Guy or to them. If there is a trust then Guy's claim will succeed as he has a proprietary interest unlike the creditors, who have merely a personal one under a contract (see Chapter 3). If there is no trust then the creditors will succeed as Guy will be only the donee of a promised gift.

Take another situation: Clare is a wine merchant and has contracted with Guy to sell him 50 bottles of Hanbury 1947 wine out of her stock of 1,000 bottles. Clare's company then goes into liquidation. Guy claims his 50 bottles but which are his? Not all wine is the same. Even if they are all the same vintage, individual bottles differ in quality.

INTERSECTION

Many of the problems here have been caused by failing to observe the relationship between the requirements of certainty and those of constitution of a trust which are dealt with in Chapter 7. If the actual £5,000 had been placed in an account specifically set aside for the trust then there would be no problem. It is the failure to set it aside by constituting the trust that brings difficulties. In addition, it should be noted that, as in the above example, the contest is often between the intended beneficiary under a trust and creditors.

The first of the modern cases on certainty of subject matter where the goods are not yet ascertained is *Re London Wine Ltd* (1976). Wine was sold to customers but it often remained at the warehouse of the company. It was held that no trust of the wine for the customers had been created even though they did receive a certificate of titles describing them as beneficial owners of particular wine. Nothing had been done to appropriate the wine to individual customers by setting actual wine apart for individuals exclusively and the existence of the certificates proved little, as in some cases they were issued before the wine had even been ordered by the company.

This was followed by *Re Goldcorp Exchange Ltd (in receivership)* (1995). The claimants had purchased bullion for future delivery from Goldcorp but, although they received a certificate of ownership, no bullion was set aside for them, nor indeed was this intended as the aim of the transaction was to enable the owners to sell it when the price had increased. The claim was the same as in *Re London Wine* were the claimants beneficiaries under a trust so that they had an equitable proprietary interest and therefore had priority over the unsecured creditors? The answer, said the court, was no because, under the law of contract, title to it could not pass because the gold bullion was unidentified and so there was no certainty of subject matter. Thus it could not be the subject of a private trust. Another decision in this area to look at is *MacJordan Construction Ltd* v. *Brookmount Erostin Ltd* (1992).

INTERSECTION

As you can see the claim failed as it was held that there was only a contract. Once again we see the relationship between trust and contract as demonstrated by *Barclays Bank Ltd* v. *Quistclose Investments* (1970) which is dealt with in Chapters 3 and 11.

INTERSECTION

You should note how the concept of 'appropriation' is important in these cases. You should compare how this terms is used in the criminal law in the law of theft with how it is used in the law of trusts.

THE APPROACH IN *HUNTER V. MOSS*

> ### Take note
>
> You can break down the reasoning behind all of these decisions into two linked elements:
>
> (a) How can the obligations of a trustee attach to property which is unidentified?
>
> (b) How can the suggested beneficiaries claim in equity against property which is unidentified?

The decision in *Hunter* v. *Moss* (1994) shows a different approach. The defendant, Moss, who was the registered owner of 950 shares in a company, executed a declaration that he held 50 of them on trust for the claimant, Hunter, who was also an employee of that company. The court upheld the trust even though the shares, which were the subject of the trust, could not be identified.

The decision is usually explained on the basis that the court applied a different rule to trusts of intangible assets such as shares, as in this case, and trusts of tangible assets such as wine and bullion, as in the cases such as *London Wine* (above), although in fact the court simply referred to a distinction between trusts of chattels and shares. In addition the court relied on an analogy with gifts of shares in a will. Such a gift is valid even though the shares are part of a larger whole, e.g. 100 shares out of 1,000 shares of mine in the Hanbury Bank. The problem is that this analogy is false as there is no trust in this case. Instead of the shares being held by the executors as trustees they are held as personal representatives until administration of the estate has been completed (*Commissioner of Stamp Duties* v. *Livingston* (1964)). The result is that the beneficiaries in this situation do not have rights as holders of a proprietary interest in the property and so the problems set out above do not apply.

Was the decision in *Hunter* v. *Moss* correct?

Arguments against the decision. *Hunter* v. *Moss* has been criticised on the basis that the distinction between shares (or intangible property) and chattels (or tangible property) is a distinction without a difference. Even if there is likely to be less difference between individual shares than there is between individual bottles of wine, the question is whether this is a satisfactory basis on which to ground a distinction between which trusts are valid and which are not.

Arguments for the decision. In support of the decision it has been said that the problem of precisely which shares are subject to the trust can be solved by applying the duty of trustees to safeguard the trust property. This means in this context that the trustee is under an immediate duty once the trust is declared to separate those shares which are subject to the trust from the rest of them. If a trustee fails to do this then he/she has mixed trust property with other assets and would be liable under the tracing rules (see Chapter 10). It could be argued, however, that this confuses two distinct issues: the rules on establishing a trust, with which we are concerned here, and the rules which apply once a trust has been established, such as the duties of trustees.

Effect of a lack of certainty of subject matter

If the subject matter of the trust is uncertain then there can of course be no trust of that property and so you must deal with the consequences of this. You need to distinguish carefully between three different situations:

(i)   If a settlor has failed to specify the trust property at all then there can be no trust. One example is *Anthony* v. *Donges* where there could not be a trust of a 'minimal part'.

(ii) There is a different situation where the settlor has given all the beneficial interest to one beneficiary, subject to a trust in favour of others of an uncertain amount, then that beneficiary receives all the property as a gift. In *Curtis* v. *Rippon* (1820) a testator left all his property to his wife but asked her to make such use of it as should be for the 'spiritual and temporal good' of her children and asked her to remember 'the Church of God and the poor'. As the shares to be taken by the children, the Church and the poor were uncertain, the wife took absolutely. Similarly in *Sprange* v. *Barnard* the husband took absolutely as the words 'the remaining part' did not show sufficient certainty of subject matter.

(iii) If the settlor has failed to specify the shares which different beneficiaries will take, as in *Boyce* v. *Boyce*, there will be a resulting trust for the settlor or his estate.

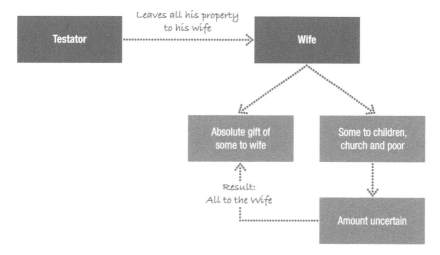

Figure 4.2 *Curtis* v. *Rippon* as an example of where the settlor has given all the beneficial interest to one beneficiary, subject to a trust in favour of others of an uncertain amount

Certainty of objects (beneficiaries): if there is an intention to create a trust and we know what it is of, then who is it for?

It will help you in studying this subject if you keep in mind that there are two reasons why some degree of certainty of objects is required:

(a) The practical one is that unless the trustees know who the beneficiaries are they cannot distribute the trust property. However, the trustees may from their own knowledge be quite clear who the beneficiaries are but the actual words of the trust may be unclear. For example John may leave all his property to 'my old drinking pals'. His trustee, Bert, knows perfectly well who these are but this is not enough because of (b).

(b) The court needs to be able to control the trust. If, for example, the trustees come to the court asking for directions as to who the beneficiaries are then the court needs to be able to give them. This principle derives from the judgments in *Morice* v. *Bishop of Durham* (1804) where, as Sir William Grant put it: 'There can be no trust over the exercise of which this court will not assume control; for an uncontrollable power of disposition would be ownership, and not trust.'

Take note

Even though there may be certainty of intention to create a trust and the subject matter is certain, a private trust will still fail if its objects are not certain. This means that it must be possible to identify who the beneficiaries of the trust are, although the exact degree to which they have to be identified will depend on the type of trust, as we shall see.

CERTAINTY OF OBJECTS AND TRUSTS

CORNERSTONE

Distinction between fixed and discretionary trusts

The central issue here is the distinction between certainty of objects in fixed and discretionary trusts as different rules apply to each.

Certainty of objects in fixed trusts

A fixed trust is a fixed interest trust. This means that it arises where the share or interest to be taken by each beneficiary is specified in the trust instrument. An example would be where there is a gift by will of 'all my property to my children in equal shares'.

In cases of fixed trusts the rule for certainty of objects is almost certainly that each beneficiary must be ascertained, i.e. known (*IRC* v. *Broadway Cottages Trust* (1955)). This point is often expressed by saying that it must be possible to draw up a list of all the beneficiaries. The reason is simple: unless the trustee, or the court, knows who the beneficiaries are they cannot carry out their duty of dividing the property. Thus in the above example it is impossible to distribute the property amongst the children until we know exactly how many there are. If a list cannot be made then the trust will fail.

Certainty of objects in discretionary trusts

CORNERSTONE

McPhail v. Doulton and the individual ascertainability test

The leading case in this area is *McPhail* v. *Doulton* that set out the individual ascertainability test which is the starting point of the law in this area.

APPLICATION

If there is a gift by will to my trustees of 'all my property to be distributed by my trustees amongst my children in such shares as my trustees shall in their absolute discretion decide' then this is a discretionary trust. The key point is that discretionary trusts are more flexible as they allow trustees to decide how much individual beneficiaries shall receive. It may be, for example, that one child develops an illness as a result of which they need continuing care. The trustees may therefore give that child a larger share of the property. This could not have happened with a fixed trust.

In *McPhail* v. *Doulton* the trustees were directed to apply the net income of a fund in making at their absolute discretion grants to the following beneficiaries: the officers and employees or ex-officers or ex-employees of a company or their relatives or dependants. Under the list principle the trust would have failed as although a list of the officers and employees of the company could doubtless be drawn up, it would not be possible to do so in the case of relatives and dependants. Should this cause the trust to fail?

The court held that it could be valid and laid down the modern test for certainty of objects in discretionary trusts. Lord Wilberforce in the House of Lords said that it was. 'Can it be said with certainty that any given individual is or is not a member of the class?' (Often known as the *individual ascertainability test.*)

The case was then remitted to the Chancery Division to decide if the test was satisfied in this case. The High Court and the Court of Appeal held that it was: *Re Baden's Deed Trusts (No. 2)* (1973).

You should note that the House of Lords, in this case, over-ruled *IRC* v. *Broadway Cottages Trust* (1955) which had applied the same test to discretionary trusts as applies to fixed trusts (the list principle). In *McPhail* v. *Doulton* the House of Lords held instead that the test for discretionary trusts was the same as that which applies to powers, as laid down in *Re Gulbenkian's Settlement Trusts* (1970) (see below).

How to apply the decision in McPhail v. Doulton

The problem has been to find a way of reconciling the need for a more relaxed test in discretionary trusts than the 'list' test in fixed trusts, given that discretionary trusts by their nature are more flexible, with the need for a test which gives the courts a reasonable yardstick with which to exercise control if need be. The issue with *McPhail* is simple: the actual wording of the test: 'Can it be said with certainty that any given individual is or is not a member of the class?' Take the facts of *McPhail* v. *Doulton*. Suppose that in the *McPhail* situation a brother of an employee came to the trustees and said that they were a relative. It could doubtless be proved that they were or were not. But suppose that James came was and said that he was a second cousin twice removed? How could it be said with certainty that he was not a relative? He might be able to show that he probably *was* a relative but how could it be proved that he *was not*?

REFLECTION

In *Re Baden* the views of the three judges in the Court of Appeal differed.

Sachs LJ took a straightforward view: if a person is not proved to be within the class then he is not within it. Thus in the above example if James could not prove that he was a second cousin twice removed and thus a relative then it would be assumed that he was not a relative and so unable to claim under the trust. This, with respect, avoids the issue: the test requires proof of a negative: that James was not within the specified class. The fact that James cannot be proved to be actually in the class does not mean that he is not, in fact, within it. Proof of a negative does not follow from lack of proof of a positive.

Megaw LJ said that the individual ascertainability test was satisfied if 'as regards a substantial number of objects, it can be said with certainty that they fall within the trust' even though it cannot be proved whether others fall within it or not. This test has merit, but it is not the individual ascertainability test of Lord Wilberforce. It is not clear how James would fare under this test as it does not focus on individual claimants.

Stamp LJ sought the aid of the principle in *Re Benjamin* (1902) (see also Chapter 10) where the trustees, having done their best to find the beneficiaries, can apply to the court to be allowed to distribute the estate to those of whom they have knowledge. Thus if trustees find some people who are within the specified class, e.g. relatives, they can apply to distribute the money to them even though there may turn out to be other claimants that the trustees are not aware of. The problem with this is that it does not answer the problem in the case of James as the problem in his case is not that the trustees do not know of his existence. Instead the problem is that they do not know if James is a second cousin. A *Benjamin* Order is essentially an administrative device, which is not appropriate where, as here, the problem is essentially conceptual.

The root of the trouble with the individual ascertainability test seems to be the words 'is not'. Why not omit them and the test would then simply be 'can there be certainty that any given individual is a member of the class?' The negative requirement did not appear in *Re Gestetner*, which began the modern development of this branch of equity, and it first appeared in the speech of Lord Upjohn in *Re Gulbenkian*. The problem is that if we omit them we then arrive at the one-person test proposed by Denning MR in *Re Gulbenkian's Settlement Trusts* (1970) and rejected by the House of Lords: is it sufficient if it can be said with certainty that any *one* person is a member of the class? This is considered, in the case of trusts for classes, to be too narrow as there might only be one certain member of the class and it has led to other problems, as discussed below.

The truth is that we do not have a satisfactory test for deciding the objects of a discretionary trust and so we are left with the *McPhail* one, and must now turn to the other issues raised by it.

The discretionary trust was initially used as part of what is known as a protective trust. This is used where the settlor thinks that the beneficiary should not be trusted with the money and so he was given a 'protective life interest' which ended if he tried to mortgage his interest or went bankrupt. In that event a discretionary trust sprang up and so whether the beneficiary received anything depended on the discretion of the trustees.

In more recent times discretionary trusts have been used both to increase the flexibility of the trust and as a device to save tax (see for example pages 56–57 in Chapter 3). Their use became much more common following the decision in *McPhail* v. *Doulton* which, as we have seen, liberalised the law on certainty of objects in discretionary trusts.

CONTEXT

The distinction between conceptual uncertainty and evidential uncertainty

(a) Conceptual uncertainty is where the words used by the trust to define the beneficiaries lack certainty and so the trust fails. One example is a trust 'to persons to whom I am under a moral obligation'. It is impossible to pin down the term 'moral obligation' with any certainty and so the trust fails.

(b) Evidential uncertainty. This is where the actual class of beneficiaries may be defined with certainty (e.g. 'my employees and ex-employees') but there is a difficulty in finding the evidence as to who the ex-employees are. This does not affect the validity of the trust as on the basis of the individual ascertainability test it is still possible for someone to come forward and prove that they are indeed an ex-employee.

REFLECTION

The decision in *McPhail* v. *Doulton* can be seen as an example of a trend by the courts from a strict and rather dogmatic approach to a more liberal one. The dogmatic approach resulted in trusts being held invalid if they did not meet certain requirements. Examples are *Leahy* v. *A-G for New South Wales* (1959) (see Chapter 5) and *IRC* v. *Broadway Cottages Trust* (1955) (see above).

In addition to this case and *Re Barlow* (1979) (see below), *Re Denley's Trust Deed* (1969) and *Re Lipinski's WT* (1976) (see Chapter 5) both show a different approach from that in *Leahy* v. *A-G for New South Wales*. The hallmark of the more liberal and pragmatic approach is that the judges are more inclined to uphold trusts where possible.

How should trustees apply the test in *McPhail* v. *Doulton*?

Given that the *McPhail* test, with all its problems, represents the law, how should it be applied in practice by trustees?

APPLICATION

The beneficiaries of a discretionary trust set up by Debbie are 'all residents of my home town'. Here there is evidential uncertainty: what is the hometown of the testator? Assuming that this is identified, the trustees must not simply hand out the money, for example, to the first ten residents to come forward. They must find out how many residents there are and, perhaps, devise a scheme for advertising for claims.

Lord Wilberforce in *McPhail* v. *Doulton* pointed out that trustees should not approach their duties in a narrow way. Instead they 'ought to make such a survey of the range of objects or possible beneficiaries as will enable them to carry out their fiduciary duty'. In *Re Hay's ST* (1982) Megarry V-C said that a trustee should first appreciate the 'width of the field' and the 'size of the problem' before considering whether a grant was appropriate in individual cases. The point is that trustees in the above example must not just hand out the money to the first claimants but must first ask just how many possible claimants there might be from Debbie's hometown.

Administrative unworkability

When considering certainty of objects in discretionary trusts you also need to consider the question of administrative unworkability. In *McPhail* v. *Doulton* Lord Wilberforce said that even though a description of beneficiaries complied with the individual ascertainability test he had laid down it might be 'so hopelessly wide as not to form anything like a class', and gave as an example 'all the residents of Greater London'. This principle was applied in *R* v. *District Auditor, ex parte West Yorkshire Metropolitan County Council* (1986) where a trust was set up for the inhabitants of the County of West Yorkshire, of which there were about 2.5 million, which was held void for administrative unworkability. Although the court accepted that the word 'inhabitants' could be sufficiently certain, without deciding the point, Lloyd LJ held that 'A trust with as many as $2^1/2$ million potential beneficiaries is . . . quite simply unworkable'. Unfortunately he did not explore this issue further. In *Re Beatty* (1990) Hoffmann J was content to uphold a clause requiring trustees to distribute chattels and money 'among such persons or persons . . . as they think fit' because everyone was an object. The administrative unworkability issue was not discussed and you should not regard this requirement as a settled principle of the law.

INTERSECTION ....

The West Yorkshire decision is a good example of the inter-relationship between different areas of trust law. The trust was not a valid private trust as it was administratively unworkable and so it could only be valid if it took effect as a trust for charitable purposes, where, as we shall see in Chapter 6, the test for certainty is much more relaxed. However, it was not contended that it could be charitable and so it fell into the category of non-charitable-purpose trusts, which are normally invalid, as was the case here. This topic is dealt with in more detail in Chapter 5.

Capricious trusts and certainty of objects

In *Re Manisty's Settlement* (1974), which concerned a power, Templeman J took a different view and observed that the phrase 'all the residents of Greater London' was capricious because it negated 'any sensible intention on the part of the settlor', but in the *West Yorkshire* case Lloyd LJ held that there was nothing capricious about the trust as it was perfectly sensible for the local authority to want to benefit the inhabitants of its area. In addition, he indicated that the capriciousness point only applied to a power (see below).

CERTAINTY OF OBJECTS AND POWERS OF APPOINTMENT

CORNERSTONE

Powers of appointment

The test for certainty of objects where there is a power of appointment or a condition attached to a gift differs from where there is a trust.

You now need to look at the requirements of certainty in the context of powers of appointment. A power of appointment is not a trust, there is no trustee and the place of a trustee is taken by the donee of the power. However, powers of appointment are often found in trusts.

APPLICATION

Barbara wishes to leave her property to her brother Aidan on trust for her children Lucy and Peter. However, she cannot decide the proportion in which her property should be divided among them. She therefore gives a power of appointment to Aidan. Barbara is the donor of the power and Aidan is the donee and Aidan is given power to appoint her property among her children Lucy and Peter with a provision that if no appointment is made they shall take in equal shares. This is known as a gift over in default of appointment.

Unlike a trust, Aidan is not obliged to exercise this power, hence the gift over if he does not. Powers are discretionary, whereas trusts are obligatory in that the trustees must carry out the trust.

There are two types of powers:

(a) Special, where the donee can only exercise the power in favour of either specified individuals or a specified class, as in the above example.

(b) General, where the donee can exercise the power in favour of anyone, including him/herself. Thus in the above example had there been a general power Aidan would have been able to appoint himself as the object of the power and so in effect give the property to himself.

In *Re Gestetner's Settlement* (1953) it was held that in the case of powers the test for certainty of objects was whether it could be said with certainty that particular persons were objects of the power. (*McPhail* v. *Doulton* later applied the same test for discretionary trusts.) Thus in the above example Lucy and Peter will take equally if Aidan does not exercise the power of appointment.

Test where a condition is attached to a gift

APPLICATION

Alice by will leaves £100 to her niece Mary 'provided that she shall pass her examinations in Equity and Trusts'. This is clearly a different situation than those which we have been considering as there is no trust. The property is not held on trust for Mary, nor is it held on a discretionary trust for a number of possible claimants and so there is the need to make a selection between them. There is one possible claimant and the question is whether she satisfies this condition.

In *Re Allen* (1953) the gift was to 'the eldest of the sons of A who shall be a member of the Church of England and an adherent to the doctrine of that church'. The Court of Appeal held that this was valid. All that the claimant had to do was to establish that he satisfied the condition.

This straightforward principle has, most unfortunately, been extended from situations as above where there is just a question of whether a particular person satisfies a condition to those where there is a question of ascertaining the identity of the persons who can satisfy the condition.

CORNERSTONE

Conditions attached to gifts

The test for certainty of objects where there is a condition attached to a gift differs from where there is a trust.

You may find it helpful to use the way in which Emery (1982) distinguishes between:

- a gift to the eldest son of A *if that son* shall be a member of the Church of England and an adherent to the doctrine of that church, as in *Re Allen* (we can call this Situation A); and
- a gift to the eldest son of A *who shall* be a member of the Church of England and an adherent etc. (we can call this Situation B).

In the first case the gift can only go to the eldest son of A. The test is simply whether he fulfils the condition and this is the same situation as in the above example of the gift to Mary. In the second case there is a different situation: it is a gift to the eldest son who fulfils the condition. The court will then have to decide what the term 'doctrine of the Church of England' means in order to decide who will receive the gift. We are then back to the familiar issues of certainty, as in *McPhail* v. *Doulton*.

It is the distinction between Situation A and Situation B which the court failed to recognise in *Re Barlow* (1979), although the fault line may be traced to Denning MR who, in *Re Gulkbenkian*, stated that *Re Allen* was authority for saying that where there is a condition attached to a gift, even where this is uncertain or imprecise, it is still valid so long as at least one beneficiary comes within it.

In *Re Barlow* a testatrix directed her executor 'to allow any member of my family and any friends of mine who wish to do so' to purchase paintings belonging to her. This is a Situation B case but the court held that the trust was valid, even though the words 'family' and, more particularly, 'friends' may have been uncertain. The reasoning was that this was not a discretionary trust, where trustees had to 'survey the field' but merely a case of conditions being attached to individual gifts. Thus a gift to a person who did come within the meaning of 'family' or 'friend' would not be invalidated by uncertainty as to whether another person does come within these terms.

It may, however, be objected that this begs the question: the issue remains that the word 'friends' is uncertain. This was not a case of a gift to one person but a class gift. Suppose that the executors thought that the testator had few friends and so allowed the first three claimants to have all the paintings. It then turned out that the testator had many other friends who were therefore deprived of the chance of acquiring any paintings. Surely the trustees should 'survey the field' and, if so, what would their yardstick be?

Take note

A trust may contain a power to cure uncertainty, especially certainty of objects, but any yardstick laid down should itself be measurable.

Power to cure uncertainty

Where the objects of the trust do not satisfy the tests for certainty of objects then there may be a clause in a trust where trustees, or a third party, may be given a power to decide whether a particular individual is a beneficiary.

APPLICATION

John leaves £10,000 in his will to be held on trust by his wife Anne to be distributed at her discretion amongst 'my old friends'. This is a discretionary trust and so the individual ascertainability test applies: 'Can it be said with certainty that any given individual is or is not a member of the class?' You will almost certainly decide that it does not as the term 'old friends' is conceptually uncertain. This means that the £10,000 will be held by Anne on a resulting trust for John's estate.

Suppose though that John had included in his will the phrase: 'In case of doubt Anne knows who my old friends are'. Will this make a difference?

Is the question one of fact? If so then a power to cure uncertainty may work. In *Re Tuck's Settlement Trusts* (1978) any dispute as to whether a person was of the Jewish faith was to be determined by a chief rabbi and that was held to validate the trust. However, this may help only where the problem is one of evidential uncertainty. Where there is conceptual uncertainty then it is submitted that the defect is incurable and the gift would fail. Thus the gift to 'my old friends' in the example would probably not be saved by allowing trustees to decide who they were. Nor would it help if the gift stated that 'in case of doubt my wife Anne knows who they are'. Anne may indeed know but how could the court measure her actions if a person alleged that she was a friend but that Anne had excluded her? The result is that in the above example the clause allowing Anne to decide would not save the gift and so the £10,000 would still go on a resulting trust to John's estate.

INTERSECTION

It is probable, although not decided, that the test in *McPhail* v. *Doulton* will apply also to objects in purpose trusts of the kind held valid in *Re Denley's Trust Deed* (1972) (see Chapter 5).

REFLECTION

This chapter has taken the view that the beneficiaries need to be defined with at least reasonable precision in order for the court to be able to control the trust and this is the generally accepted view.

However, it is not the only view. Gardner (2011) points out that the courts have increasingly tried to uphold the facilitative aspect of the law of trusts. This means that, wherever possible, their role is to uphold the wishes of the settlor as expressed in the trust, and he gives as instances of this approach both *Re Tuck* (above) and *Re Tepper's Will Trusts* (1987). In line with this view Gardner has no difficulty with *Re Barlow* holding that, as long as a description has a recognisable core meaning, it is valid. 'Old friends', he feels, has a large grey area but also a core meaning and, on this basis, the term is sufficiently certain.

Effect of uncertainty of objects

The property will be held on a resulting trust for the settlor or his estate.

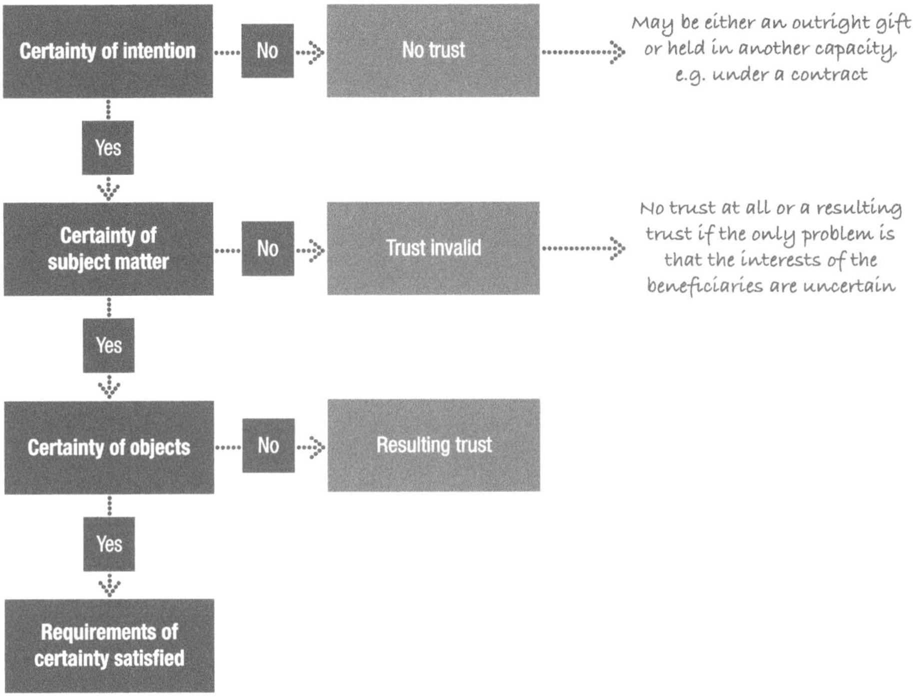

Figure 4.3 Summary of the three certainties

TRUSTS AND THE RULES CONCERNING REMOTENESS OF VESTING

When questions of certainty of objects arise it is also important to ask if the trust will meet the requirements of the law on remoteness of vesting in the objects.

> The law has always taken the view that property should not be tied up for too long a time. This has led to the following rules which not only apply to interests under trusts but also to other interests in land. As the Law Commission points out (Report No. 251, 1999), the justification for these rules is 'the need to place some restriction on how far one generation can control the devolution of property at the expense of generations to follow'.

The rule against remoteness of vesting

CORNERSTONE

Remoteness of vesting

The rule against remoteness of vesting is directed at the tying up of property for too long a time.

(a) **The common law rule**. A general statement of the rule is that 'an interest must vest, if it vests at all, within some life or lives in being or twenty-one years thereafter'. The following examples show the operation of the rule:

APPLICATION

Property is left on trust for Kate if she qualifies as a barrister. This is valid because, if Kate is to qualify, she must do so within a life in being (her own here).

APPLICATION

Property is left on trust for the first child of Kate to qualify as a barrister. This is void under the common law rule because Kate may have a child born after the date of the execution of the trust instrument who may qualify as a barrister more than 21 years after the date of Kate's death, Kate being the life in being. This may be highly improbable, but the point is that it is possible.

As you can see, these rules were highly restrictive and they have been modified. Unfortunately the statutes which have modified them are not retrospective and so you need to learn them both.

CORNERSTONE

Remoteness of vesting – statutory provisions

There are two statutes, either of which can apply to cases involving remoteness of vesting: the Perpetuities and Accumulations Act 1964 and the Perpetuities and Accumulations Act 2009.

(b) **The effect of the Perpetuities and Accumulations Act 1964**. This Act only applies to dispositions coming into effect *after 15 July 1964*. In the case of such a disposition one must first look at the common law rule (see (a) above). If the disposition is void under the common law rule then one considers whether it can be saved by the application of the rules in this Act.

   (i) Section 1 of the Act allows a settlor to specify a perpetuity period of a maximum of 80 years rather than the common law period.

   (ii) Section 3(1) of the Act provides that where a disposition is void under the common law rule then rather than declaring it void one must 'wait and see' whether in fact the interest does vest outside the common law rule perpetuity period. If so, it will of course be void; if not, it will be valid.

The effect of this Act is shown by the following example which should be contrasted with the examples in the Application boxes above showing the operation of the common law rule.

APPLICATION

Property is left on trust to the first child of Kate to qualify as a barrister. Under the 1964 Act one must wait and see whether in fact a child of Kate does become a barrister within the perpetuity period rather than simply declaring the gift void because of the perhaps remote possibility that it might not do so. Alternatively the settlor could have specified a period of 80 years in which case one would have simply waited 80 years. If so then after 80 years if a child of Kate has not qualified as a barrister the gift will fail.

(c) **The effect of section 5 of the Perpetuities and Accumulations Act 2009**. This provides for a period of 125 years which overrides any different provision in the trust instrument. The Act applies to instruments such as trusts which take effect on or after the commencement day of the Act, which was 6 April 2010. Where a will is executed before that day the Act will not apply even though the testator dies and so the will comes into force after this date. Here the former rule will apply which provided that a period of 80 years could be specified.

Take note

Do remember the date 6 April 2010 as this will decide which law is applicable to ascertain if the trust satisfies the rule on remoteness of vesting.

Also remember this tip: people trusts must comply with the rule on remoteness of vesting; purpose trusts must comply with the rule against inalienability.

APPLICATION

Let us return to our familiar example where property is left on trust to the first child of Kate to qualify as a barrister. Under the 1964 Act the settlor could have specified a period of 80 years in which case one would have simply waited 80 years. This is now 125 years provided that the will was executed on or after 6 April 2010. The difference between the two Acts is not only in the longer period but also that the 2009 Act overrides any other period specified in the trust instrument. The 1964 Act allowed the settlor to specify a period of *up to* 80 years.

INTERSECTION

Note that there is another rule, the rule against inalienability, which is designed to prevent the tying up of capital and income for an excessive time. It applies to non-charitable trusts and you can find details in Chapter 5. These two rules are together known as the rules against perpetuities.

KEY POINTS

- There must be certainty of intention to create a private trust, the trust property (subject matter) must be certain and the objects (beneficiaries) must be certain.
  - Where there is a fixed trust then it must be possible to list all the beneficiaries.
  - Where there is a discretionary trust then the individual ascertainability test applies: 'Can it be said with certainty that any given individual is or is not a member of the class?'
- Conditions attached to gifts
- Power to cure uncertainty

CORE CASES AND STATUTES

Case	About	Importance
Re Adams and the Kensington Vestry (1884)	A testator left his property to his wife absolutely 'in full confidence that she will do what is right as to the disposal thereof between my children . . .'. Held: The words 'in full confidence' did not show sufficient intention taken in the context of the rest of the words.	Certainty of intention to create a trust.
Sprange v. *Barnard* (1789)	The will gave property to the testatrix's husband 'for his sole use' and then provided that 'the remaining part of what is left, that he does not want . . . to be divided between' members of his family. Held: 'The remaining part of what is left' did not identify the trust property with sufficient certainty.	Certainty of subject matter in the creation of a trust.
Re London Wine Ltd (1986)	There was no trust of wine that had been sold to customers but remained at a warehouse as it had not been set apart for individual customers.	Certainty of subject matter where the goods are not ascertained.
McPhail v. *Doulton* (1971)	The trustees were directed to apply the net income of a fund in making at their absolute discretion grants to the following beneficiaries: 'the officers and employees or ex-officers or ex-employees of a company or their relatives or dependants'. Held: The words 'officers and employees or ex-officers or ex-employees of a company or their relatives or dependants' satisfied the test of certainty of objects in discretionary trusts.	Certainty of objects in the creation of a trust.

Statute	About	Importance
Perpetuities and Accumulations Act 1964	Gifts which may be void as offending the rule against perpetuities.	Applies to dispositions coming into effect on or after 15 July 1964 and allows a settlor to specify a perpetuity period of a maximum of 80 years rather than the common law period. Also introduces a 'wait and see' period.
Perpetuities and Accumulations Act 2009	Gifts which may be void as offending the rule against perpetuities.	This provides for a period of 125 years which overrides any different provision in the trust instrument. However the new period will not apply to a will (but will apply to other documents) executed before the 2009 Act comes into force. This was on 6 April 2010.

FURTHER READING

Emery, C. (1982) 'The most hallowed principle' 98 *LQR* 551.
This is a clear analysis of the law on conditions attached to gifts. This is a difficult area and a clear knowledge of the law will improve your marks.

Gardner, S. (2011) *Introduction to the Law of Trusts*, 3rd ed. (Oxford University Press).

Harris, J. (1971) 'Trust, power and duty' 87 *LQR* 31.
This analyses the decision in *McPhail* v. *Doulton*.

Hayton, D. (1994) 'Uncertainty of subject matter of trusts' 110 *LQR* 335.
This subjects the decision in *Hunter* v. *Moss* to critical analysis. This should be read in conjunction with Parkinson's article (below) as it gives a different perspective on *Hunter* v. *Moss*.

Parkinson P. (2002) 'Reconceptualising the express trust' 61(3) *Cambridge Law Journal* 657–683, especially pages 663–676.
This should be read in conjunction with Hayton's article (above) as it gives a different perspective on *Hunter* v. *Moss* which the author considers to be a sensible and workable decision.

CHAPTER 5

The beneficiary principle and non-charitable-purpose trusts

BLUEPRINT

*The beneficiary principle
and non-charitable-purpose
trusts*

KEY
QUESTIONS

LEGISLATION

- LPA 1925, s. 53(1)(c)

CONTEXT

- Problems when gifts are
  made to, for example, a
  favourite animal or a
  political party.

CONCEPTS

- Non-charitable-purpose trusts are generally
  invalid but some exceptions
- Gifts to unincorporated associations and
  distribution of any surplus funds of these
  associations

- Unincorporated associations have
  no real legal status – leads to
  problems with gifts to them and
  disposal of their assets.

- Why are gifts for non-charitable-purposes generally invalid?

CASES

- *Re Astor*
- *Re Denley*
- *Re Recher*
- *Re Grant*

REFORM

- Recognition of these types of trusts as valid.

SPECIAL CHARACTERISTICS

- Attempts to make gifts for purposes valid, e.g. holding that they are gifts for individuals
- Rule against inalienability

CRITICAL ISSUES

Setting the scene

Imagine that as a hobby you breed a rare type of cat. You are well known as a cat breeder and now you are making your will in which you wish to leave the sum of £20,000 to your friend, Felix, another cat breeder, so that he can look after the cats and breed from them.

You may be surprised to know that a clause such as this in a will is not valid. Why not? There is nothing illegal in what you are doing but the bequest will not be enforceable. The reason is first that you have created a trust under which Felix will be the trustee and the cats the beneficiaries. Suppose, though, that Felix broke the terms of the trust and did not spend the money on the cats but instead on a weekend trip to Paris. The cats would doubtless be annoyed but by themselves they would be unable to instigate any legal action. Thus the trust is unenforceable.

Is there any way round this?

One way, which would go beyond the scope of the law of trusts, would be to set up a company to carry on the business of cat breeding and so take the matter out of the ambit of trust law altogether. However, cat breeding has only ever been a hobby of yours.

Another way would be to limit the gift in the will to one to just care for the existing cats and not to breed from them. This would not be what you want, but at least the cats would be cared for. The law allows such gifts in wills even though here the trust is also enforceable, but this is an anomaly.

You could try to make this into a charitable trust but that would require you to satisfy s. 3(1)(k) of the Charities Act 2011 which provides that a charitable purpose is 'the advancement of animal welfare'. In addition, to be charitable a trust must have an element of public benefit. However, this is not an animal welfare charity and so, although it is not illegal to make this bequest to Felix there will be nothing to stop him ignoring it.

This is all very unsatisfactory! Isn't it possible for the law of trusts to find a way of making gifts of this kind valid? In this chapter we will not only be setting out the present law but also looking at how it might be changed to allow gifts of the kind that you wish to make.

INTRODUCTION

Gifts to be held on trusts which are for purposes, rather than for individuals, and which are not for charitable purposes, are, as a general rule, held to be void and thus unenforceable. In this chapter we will look at the rationale for this rule, then at how it is applied, noting exceptions to the rule, and finally at possible ways in which the law can move forward to hold that, in some cases at least, these trusts can be upheld.

Example One

John transfers property to Pam for her to hold as trustee for Ray. This is a straightforward private trust where property is to be held on trust for a particular beneficiary and it is of course valid.

Example Two

John transfers property to Pam for her to hold as trustee for charitable purposes. This is not a trust for particular persons and is therefore not a private trust. Instead it is a trust for purposes and see Chapter 6, because those purposes are charitable, the trust is valid even though there are no identifiable beneficiaries.

Example Three

John transfers property to Pam for her to hold 'for the maintenance of good relations between nations . . . the preservation of the independence of the newspapers and similar purposes'. This is also a trust for purposes rather than persons but here the purposes are not charitable and so the trust is invalid.

Table 5.1 Can this be a valid trust?

Trust for individuals – private trust?	Yes
Trust for charitable purposes	Yes
Trust for non-charitable purposes	No – except in certain special cases

WHY ARE TRUSTS FOR NON-CHARITABLE PURPOSES GENERALLY HELD TO BE VOID?

CORNERSTONE

Trusts for non-charitable purposes generally void

The general rule is that trusts for non-charitable purposes are invalid is illustrated by *Re Astor*, which is usually taken as having established this principle in modern equity.

The origin of the rule that trusts for non-charitable purposes are generally void is sometimes said to be the dictum of Grant MR, who said in *Morice* v. *Bishop of Durham* (1804) 'there must be somebody in whose favour the court can decree performance'. In fact, however, this was a trust which failed through lack of certainty of objects. It is more accurate to say that the basis of the rule is found in the beneficiary principle: a trust must have a beneficiary who can enforce it. As Harman J said in *Re Wood* (1949): 'a gift on trust must have a *cestui que trust*'.

The problem is really one of control. If there is no one who can take action in the case of, for example, maladministration of trust funds, then there is not really a trust at all but an absolute gift to the supposed trustee. The point was made by Roxburgh J in *Re Astor's ST* (1952): 'it is not possible to contemplate with equanimity the creation of large funds devoted to non charitable purposes which no court and no department of state can control or, in case of maladministration, reform'.

Charitable trusts can be enforced by the Attorney-General rather than by a beneficiary (see Chapter 6) and so are subject to control. A trust for non-charitable purposes, rather than persons, has no beneficiary who can enforce it and the settlor will not be allowed to do so. These trusts are sometimes known as trusts of imperfect obligation because of this lack of beneficiaries who can enforce them. Examples are *Re Astor's ST* (1952), of which the terms were given in Example Three above, and *Leahy*

v. *A-G for New South Wales* (1959), where a testator left a sheep station on trust for 'such order of nuns of the Catholic Church or the Christian Brothers as my executors and trust shall select'. It would therefore have been held an invalid purpose trust had it not been saved by a New South Wales statute which allowed trusts with a charitable and non-charitable element to be applied only in favour of the charitable element.

INTERSECTION

The reason why the gift was not charitable was because of the lack of public benefit as some of the orders of nuns were contemplative. See *Gilmour* v. *Coats* (1949) in Chapter 6 for another example of this.

Despite this apparently fundamental objection to trusts for non-charitable purposes the law did not become finally settled until *Re Astor* in 1952. Until then it was arguable that there was no absolute principle that these trusts were void and, in particular, that these trusts were not subject to the inalienability rules (see below).

Valid non-charitable-purpose trusts

CORNERSTONE

Valid non-charitable-purpose trusts

There are certain exceptional cases where trusts for non-charitable purposes have been held valid.

In the following exceptional cases trusts for non-charitable purposes have been held valid but in *Re Endacott* (1960) Evershed MR said that these categories should not be extended. Another theory is that these are not anomalous cases at all but existed before the general principle that trusts for non-charitable purposes were invalid was developed.

(a) *Tombs and monuments.* A trust for the building or maintenance of a tomb or monument has been held valid, as in *Re Hooper* (1932) where a testator made a gift for the care of some family graves and monuments and a tablet in a church window. Such trusts can be charitable and therefore valid where they are for a tomb which can be regarded as part of the fabric of the church (*Hoare* v. *Osborne* (1866)) or for the maintenance of the churchyard as distinct from a particular tomb (*Re Vaughan* (1886)). However, in all cases the trust must comply with the requirement of certainty of objects (see Chapter 4). This requirement was not met in *Re Endacott* (1960) where a testator left money to a parish council to 'provide some useful memorial to myself' which was held much too wide and uncertain. Although the court in *Re Endacott* did not doubt any of the earlier cases it is clear that it does represent the stricter approach indicated in *Re Astor*.

(b) *Animals.* Trusts for the care of specific animals are valid as in *Re Dean* (1889) where money was left for the maintenance of the testator's horses and hounds. A trust for the maintenance of animals in general can be charitable (see Chapter 6). However, trusts to not only maintain but also *to breed from* the testator's animal would be invalid.

(c) *Miscellaneous.* A trust for the saying of masses was originally void as being for 'superstitious uses' but in *Bourne* v. *Keane* (1919) they were upheld but without consideration of the beneficiary issue, possibly on the assumption that they would be said in public. Trusts for the saying of masses in public would be charitable (*Re Hetherington* (1989) and see Chapter 6). It would be strange if the gift specifically provided that the masses were only to be said in private but if they were actually said in private then the trust would probably also be valid. This would be on the basis that the gift for the saying of masses provided stipends for the priests saying them and so assisted in the endowment of the priesthood (Browne-Wilkinson V-C in *Re Hetherington* (1989)). In *Re Khoo Cheng Teow* (1932) a trust for the performance of non-Christian private ceremonies was upheld to be extended.

> ## Take note
>
> It is sometimes said that in *Re Thompson* (1934) the court held that a trust for the promotion of fox hunting was valid. In fact, the case concerned a gift to be applied to the promotion of fox hunting with a gift of residue to Trinity Hall, Cambridge. The issue was whether the trust was void as there was no beneficiary but the court held that it was not as the purpose was sufficiently certain. A trust for the promotion of fox hunting would now be void anyway in view of the Hunting Act 2004.

CONTEXT

Sir Arthur Underhill, in his law *Law of Trusts* (10th edn, p. 97) did not think much of these exceptional cases: he called them 'concessions to human weakness and sentimentality'. You may be tempted to agree with him and think: isn't this just a lot of old-fashioned stuff that modern lawyers like me can just forget about? Well, you would be wrong! In a fascinating article in *The Conveyancer* in 2007 James Brown published the results of a national survey which he had conducted amongst probate departments in solicitors' firms across England and Wales during April 2006 about the extent to which they use these types of trusts. You should read this in full yourself but, in brief, 53% stated that they had been contacted about making provision in wills to leave money/property on trust(s) for the purpose of maintaining a particular animal; 37.25% had been approached by clients wishing to leave money by will and on trust for the erection of tombs, gravestones and/or sepulchral monuments (and for their maintenance); and 7.8% had been contacted about leaving a gift for the saying of prayers or other religious ceremony or rituals in private. Not surprisingly, no request for money to be left for the promotion and furtherance of fox-hunting (see below) was disclosed in the replies! James Brown suggests that the current problems with enforcing these trusts could be met by a promise given by a nominated person (probably the trustee) and contained in a 'deed of commitment and enforcement'. The trustee would ordinarily be given a yearly/regular fee, on condition that he applied the trust monies towards the fulfilment of the relevant purpose (e.g. the maintenance of an animal/tomb, etc.).

VALID NON-CHARITABLE-PURPOSE TRUSTS AND THE RULE AGAINST INALIENABILITY

CORNERSTONE

Rule against inalienability

If the trust is valid in principle then it must still satisfy the rule against inalienability which provides that the trust will be invalid unless from the outset it is certain that persons will be absolutely entitled (and so the trust has ended) by the end of the perpetuity period. This period is defined as any relevant lives in being plus 21 years.

The trusts in the above cases must comply with the rules against inalienability. This is concerned with the tying up of money for an excessive time. A general statement of the rule is that 'an interest must vest, if it vests at all, within some life or lives in being or twenty-one years thereafter'.

APPLICATION

John sets up a trust fund of £500,000 to be used to 'erect a suitable memorial to myself and to maintain it for ever afterwards'. The effect is that some of this fund must be kept indefinitely as the monument is to be maintained for ever. It is a general policy of the law that this is undesirable.

The rule against inalienability is applicable to non-charitable-purpose trusts which could tie up a fund to be used, for example, 'to maintain and breed from the testator's cats', indefinitely. The effect is that such a trust will be void unless from the beginning it is certain that persons will have become absolutely entitled by the end of a period of time. It should be noted that the 'wait and see' provisions of the Perpetuities and Accumulations Act 1964 do not apply to purpose trusts (see s. 15(4)).

The question is then: in what period of time must this occur? The general view is that the 80-year period does not apply to non-charitable-purpose trusts and the period is 21 years plus any relevant lives in being. Often there will be none, as in the case of gifts to animals, and so the period will be 21 years. In the Irish case of *Re Kelly* (1932) it was held that 'there can be no doubt that lives means lives of human beings, not of animals or trees in California'.

The courts within these limits have tried to see that otherwise valid purpose trusts do not fail on the ground of falling foul of the perpetuity rules. A striking illustration is *Re Haines* (1952), where judicial notice was taken of the doubtful proposition that a cat cannot live for more than 21 years. The courts assume that monuments will be erected within the perpetuity period (*Mussett* v. *Bingle* (1876)) and trusts which are to continue 'for so long as the law allows' will be construed as lasting for 21 years (*Pirbright* v. *Salwey* (1896)). In *Re Dean* (1889) a gift of an annual sum for 50 years if any of the testator's horses and hounds should live so long was held valid and the perpetuity point was ignored.

> ### Take note
>
> Section 18 of the Perpetuities and Accumulations Act 2009 provides that it does not affect the rule of law which limits the duration of non-charitable-purpose trusts, i.e. the rule against inalienability. It only applies to the rule against remoteness of vesting – see Chapter 4.

TRUSTS EXPRESSED FOR A PURPOSE BUT WHICH ARE REALLY FOR THE BENEFIT OF INDIVIDUALS

CORNERSTONE

Re Denley principle

Re Denley established the principle that it may be possible to save what seems to be an invalid purpose trust by holding that it is a trust for individuals.

Given that, apart from the above cases, English law appeared to set its face against recognising non-charitable-purpose trusts, the bold decision of Goff J in *Re Denley's Trust Deed* (1969) appeared to offer a way forward. Here he was able to construe what appeared to be a trust for purposes as one for individuals. A plot of land was conveyed to trustees 'for the purpose of a recreation or sports ground primarily for the benefit of the employees of the company' and also for the benefit of such other persons as the trustees might allow. This was held valid as a trust for the employees because they were entitled to the use of the land. The reasoning in this case was approved in *Re Lipinski* (see p. 105).

INTERSECTION

If it is the case that the trust can take effect as a private trust then it must satisfy the requirements of certainty of objects and, in particular, the 'individual ascertainability test' in *McPhail* v. *Doulton* where it is a discretionary trust (see Chapter 4).

The decision in *Re Denley* has, however, been difficult to classify. Was the trust one for individuals, in which case there is no problem, or is it a kind of hybrid trust, being partly private and partly for purposes?

In *Re Grant's Will Trusts* (1979) Vinelott J had no difficulty in holding that the *Denley*-type trust was a private trust. He saw no distinction in principle between a 'trust to permit a class defined by reference to employment to use and enjoy land' and 'a trust to distribute income at the discretion of trustees among a class'. The problem is that this is not how Goff J saw the position in his judgment in *Re Denley*. His judgment expressly distinguished between two kinds of purpose trust:

(a) those where the benefit 'is so indirect or intangible' that no individual who may benefit has the right to apply to the court to enforce it, and

(b) those where, as here, there are individuals who can apply.

It has been said that Goff J concentrated too much on the fact of benefit rather than whether particular persons were beneficiaries and that this has muddied the waters (see Matthews 1996). Could the rule in *Saunders* v. *Vautier* (1841) apply to allow the beneficiaries (if they could be identified) to end the trust and claim the trust property? If they could, then the purpose of the trust is defeated and this brings us back to the point that this seems to be a trust for purposes as well as individuals.

In addition, Goff J himself acknowledged the difficulty which could arise where there were differences between the beneficiaries over the purposes for which the sports club could be used. Could the court settle a scheme? He felt that it could not, as this was not a charitable trust. One could say that this comparison with a charitable trust is precisely the point: it was a trust for purposes but these were not charitable. Also, who could bring an action for breach of trust? Certainly the employees could, but the trust envisaged others as being beneficiaries. The truth is probably that, although *Re Denley* is suspect from the theoretical point of view, it made good sense on the facts.

GIFTS TO UNINCORPORATED ASSOCIATIONS

CORNERSTONE

Gifts to unincorporated associations

Gifts to unincorporated associations pose a number of problems all based on the fundamental problem that strictly these associations do not exist in law: what if the gift takes effect as a trust; does the gift offend the rule against inalienability?

Definition of an unincorporated association

In *Conservative and Unionist Central Office* v. *Burrell* (1982) Lawton LJ said that an unincorporated association exists where two or more persons are

> bound together for one or more common purposes, not being business purposes, by mutual undertakings, each having mutual duties and obligations, in an organisation which has rules which identify in whom control of it and its funds rests and upon what terms and which can be joined or left at will. The bond of union between the members . . . has to be contractual.

There are many examples of unincorporated associations, such as local clubs and societies, where there is no point in forming a company as the formalities would be too burdensome. Even larger bodies, such as county cricket clubs and football clubs are sometimes unincorporated, with any property such as the club ground being held by trustees, although the trend is towards incorporation. The problem is that English law has never developed a consistent theory of how these bodies should be regarded in law and, in particular, how they should hold property.

The problem with gifts to these associations

With the exception of a trade union (see s. 2 of the Trade Union and Labour Relations (Consolidation) Act 1992) an unincorporated association cannot hold property and so a gift cannot be made to it. Thus the position is different from where a gift is made to a corporation (e.g. a company): here the gift is made to the body itself. But as an unincorporated association the gift must be held for its purposes. If those purposes are charitable then there is no problem but what if they are not?

·· APPLICATION

You make a gift of £100 by will to the Campaign for a Hanbury By-Pass. This is not a corporation (e.g. a company as, although it technically could be, the formalities would make this not worth-while and company status may not be appropriate) and so the gift cannot be to the campaign itself. It is not charitable as it is for political purposes (see Chapter 6) and so the gift is for the association and not for its purposes and these purposes are not charitable.

If the gift is instead for the association's purposes there are two problems:

(a) Unless these purposes are charitable, the gift may be held a non-charitable-purpose trust as in *Leahy* v. *A-G for New South Wales* (1959) (see above).

(b) The gift may contravene the inalienability rule if the capital comprised in it must be maintained for longer than the period of 21 years plus any relevant lives in being.

The consequence is that what appears to be a straightforward everyday situation, the making of a gift to an unincorporated association, is fraught with legal difficulties. The only way to avoid the problems outlined above seems to be to hold that any gift is simply an outright one to the members, to be divided between them equally. Yet this is not what the donee usually intends. A gift to, for example, a local club, is not meant to be immediately divided up by the members but to be used for the benefit of the club. Yet this requires some form of holding of the property, which brings us back to the trust.

Possible solutions to the problem

CORNERSTONE

Possible solutions to the problem of gifts to unincorporated associations

The courts have tried to deal with the problem that gifts to unincorporated associations may be void by means of two devices: those of trust and of contract.

In both the trust and contract cases the application of the law may seem artificial but the alternative is that the gift would be void and this would defeat the intention of the donor. *Re Denley's Trust Deed* (above) is an example of the trust approach and *Re Recher* (below) the contract approach.

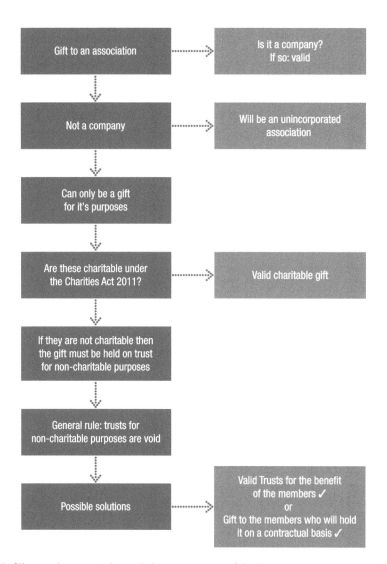

Figure 5.1 Gifts to unincorporated associations: a summary of the law

Trust for the benefit of the members

The courts have sometimes been able to hold that a gift is construed as a gift to the association's members and so a private trust is created. This was the approach in *Re Denley's Trust Deed* (1969) (see above) and an earlier example is *Re Drummond* (1914) (see above). The reasoning is that as the gift is made to the association the members can claim it by winding up the association and dividing its assets among themselves and so they have a beneficial interest.

The trust will still be void, however, this time for infringing the rule against inalienability, if it is impracticable or impossible for the members to wind up the association. The gift then becomes one for future as well as present members. In *Carne* v. *Long* (1860) a testator left his house to the trustees of the Penzance Public Library to be ever for the maintenance and support of the library. The court held that this was not a gift to the present members but instead to the library, which was intended to be a perpetual institution and so the gift was void. In *Re Denley's Trust Deed* (1969) the gift was expressly limited to the perpetuity period and in *Re Drummond* (1914) the inalienability point was not fully considered.

Problem where the association cannot wind itself up

CORNERSTONE

Re Grant

Re Grant is an example of a gift to an unincorporated association which offended the rule against inalienability.

In *Re Grant's WT* (1979) a gift was made to the Chertsey Labour Party. In this case the members could not change the rules and divide the gift between themselves because the rules were subject to control by the National Executive Committee of the Labour Party. Thus they could not, even if they wished, divide the funds between themselves and accordingly the gift was for future members as well and was void for inalienability.

This decision has been criticised by Matthews (1996) on the basis that in law the local party could, at a later date, have agreed to change its own rules without reference to the National Executive. In this way the local party could have gained access to the funds. Be that as it may, the Australian courts have come to the same conclusion as in *Bacon* v. *Pianta* (1966) where a legacy to 'the Communist Party of Australia for its sole use and benefit' was held void as a gift to both present and future members.

REFLECTION

Gift to the members who will hold it on a contractual basis

CORNERSTONE

Re Recher

Re Recher is an example of the contract approach to gifts to unincorporated associations.

In *Re Recher's Will Trust* (1972) the court held that where there is a gift to an unincorporated association there is a presumption that it is a gift to the members subject to the rules of the association. This presumption can be rebutted where the gift is for the association's purposes or, as in *Re Grant* (above), the association cannot wind itself up. Thus here a gift made to the London and Provincial Anti-Vivisection Society was held to be a beneficial gift to the members, not so as to entitle each of them to an immediate share but as an addition to the funds of the association subject to the contract between the members as set out in the rules.

This approach was followed in *Re Lipinski's Will Trusts* (1976) where a testator bequeathed half of his residuary estate in trust to an association to be used solely in constructing or maintaining the association's buildings. This was held valid as a gift to the members subject to the contract between them as members even though the word 'solely' might have indicated that a trust was intended for the purpose specified. The result is that where the gift specifies a purpose for it to be held then this will not rebut the presumption of a gift for the members. The position would be different if it expressly said that the gift was to be held on trust.

Re Horley Town Football Club; Hunt v. *McLaren* (2006) concerned a surplus arising on a sale of land held in trust as an endowment for an unincorporated association. It was held that the beneficial interest vested in the current full members and was held on a bare trust for them. This entitled them to call in a general meeting for the assets to be transferred to them as individuals. This decision follows the line of authority in *Re Recher* in basing the solution on contract but the device of a trust is used to solve the problem of exactly where the legal ownership of the property lies pending any distribution between the members.

The contract approach has the advantage over the trust approach in that the trust cases are open to attack as being inconsistent with *Leahy* v. *A-G for New South Wales* (1959) (above). However, the contract approach, like the trust approach, will not validate a gift in circumstances like those in *Re Grant* (1979) where the members do not control the association's property, because the members do not have complete control over the association's rules and so cannot end the association and divide the gift among themselves. It should be noted that the application of either the trust approach or the contract approach can have the same result and this was recognised by Oliver J in *Re Lipinski* (1976), who held that the gift would also have been valid on the trust approach.

Where the body is not an unincorporated association neither the trust nor the contract solution is appropriate (see *Conservative and Unionist Central Office* v. *Burrell*). In this case the Conservative Party had no rules which enabled the members to gain control and so they could not divide the gift among themselves. The court held that the basis of the gift was that of mandate. A contributor gives funds to an official of the body, in this case the treasurer of the Conservative Party, with a mandate to use them in a certain way. An agency relationship thus arises and, apart from the fiduciary relationship inherent in this, there is no question of any trust.

A '*Quistclose* trust'?

It has been argued that a possible solution to the problems outlined above lies in adopting the model utilised in *Barclays Bank* v. *Quistclose Investments Ltd* (1970).

INTERSECTION

Refer to Chapter 11 for a detailed explanation of what a *Quistclose* trust is.

Refer (see Chapter 11) that the trust arose on payment of money to be used for a specific purpose. When that purpose could not be carried out a resulting trust arose under which the property was held for the lender. The point here, however, is that until that time there was a trust for a purpose and Chambers (1997, p. 63) points out that the 'presence of an identifiable class of intended payees is irrelevant to the validity of the *Quistclose* trust'.

DISPOSAL OF SURPLUS FUNDS OF UNINCORPORATED ASSOCIATIONS

CORNERSTONE

Distribution of surplus funds of unincorporated associations

The courts have evolved several possible solutions to deciding where any surplus funds should go when an unincorporated association ceases to exist.

We are not concerned now with whether a gift to an unincorporated association is valid but with what happens to the gift when the association ends and some funds remain. If the funds are for charitable purpose there is no problem: they can be applied *cy-près*; the construction in *Re Finger's WT* (1972) may be used (see Chapter 6). If the purpose is not charitable then another solution must be found.

The '*Gillingham* solution'

Re Gillingham Bus Disaster Fund (1958), although not concerned itself with an unincorporated association, provides a useful starting point. The facts were given in detail in Chapter 11 but, briefly, a surplus remained from a fund established in memory of Royal Marines cadets killed and injured in an accident. Some of the money was in identifiable sums from individuals but most was from street collections and other non-identifiable sources. The fund was held not to be charitable because funeral expenses and care of the boys did not come within relief of poverty. The solution therefore was to hold that the money was to be held on a resulting trust for the donors because, as Harman J said, 'the donor did not part with his money out and out absolutely' but only to the extent that his wishes as declared by the trust could be carried into effect. Thus when 'this has been done any surplus still belongs to him'.

INTERSECTION

At this point you really do need to make sure that you are clear on what a resulting trust is. See Chapter 11.

The '*West Sussex Constabulary* solution'

In *Re West Sussex Constabulary's Benevolent Fund Trust* (1971) a fund had been established to provide benefits to widows and dependants of deceased members. The income came from members' subscriptions, proceeds of entertainments, sweepstakes, raffles, collecting boxes and various donations and legacies. When the constabulary was amalgamated with other police forces the question of the distribution of the fund arose.

(a) *The members' subscriptions.* The court held that the surviving members had no claim to these based on a resulting trust. They had received all that they had contracted for either because their widows and dependants had received benefits or because they had no widows or dependants. The members had no right themselves to the fund because it was not established for their benefit. Accordingly this part of the fund went to the Crown as *bona vacantia* with the possibility of a successful claim by the members based on frustration of contract or total failure of consideration being met by the Crown giving an indemnity to the trustees.

(b) *Identifiable donations and legacies.* These were to be held on a resulting trust for the donors.

(c) *Proceeds of entertainments, raffles, sweepstakes and collecting boxes.* These were to go to the Crown as *bona vacantia.* Contributors must be taken to have parted with their money out and out. The relationship was one of contract not trust: those who paid for the entertainment, etc. had had their entertainment and so no longer had any claim to the money. Accordingly the resulting trust solution in *Re Gillingham* (1958) was rejected.

> ### Take note
>
> The decision in West Sussex was given before the decision in Re Recher (above) that members could hold a gift on the basis of contract between themselves. Had it been after Re Recher the decision in West Sussex might have applied the Re Recher approach.

Although this decision was a welcome advance on that in *Re Gillingham*, point (c) above has been criticised by Chambers (1997) on the basis that Goff J 'did not address the question of who owned the fund prior to dissolution or how it became ownerless afterwards'. On Chambers' argument, the payments, having been made either for valuable consideration or as gifts, should have become the beneficial property of the recipients and so held on a resulting trust for them.

The '*Bucks Constabulary* solution'

The facts in *Re Bucks Constabulary Fund (No. 2)* (1979) were similar to those in *Re West Sussex* (1971): the fund was established to provide benefits for widows and dependants of deceased members and the fund was wound up on the amalgamation of the force with other forces. Here the court decided that the fund belonged to the members and the court did not follow that part of the decision in *Re West Sussex* (1971). It was held that the funds had belonged to the surviving members all the time because they could at any time have altered the rules and obtained the funds. The fact that the fund was not established for the benefit of the members did not alter the fact that the members controlled it. (There were no other contributions in this case and so the other parts of the *West Sussex* decision were not considered.)

Hanchett-Stamford v. *Attorney-General* (2008) dealt with the position where there was one surviving member of the association. Could they claim the funds? The court held that they could. The claimant was, on her husband's death, the last surviving member of the Performing and Captive Animals Defence League, which was an unincorporated non-charitable association. She wished the assets to be held on trust to select a charity with similar objects to which the funds could be given. Lewison J could not see the logic in saying that 'if there are two members of an association which has assets of, say, £2m, they can by agreement divide those assets between them and pocket £1m each, but if one of them dies before they have divided the assets, the whole pot goes to the Crown as bona vacantia'. In addition he took account of Article 1 of the First Protocol of the European Convention on Human Rights. This provides that no one is to be deprived of their possessions except in the public interest and subject to the conditions provided by law.

What do you think of this decision? Through the accident that she was the last member alive Mrs Hanchett Stamford acquired a large property known as 'Sid Abbey' in Sidmouth, Devon, which was the principal wing of a nineteenth-century Gothic house. In addition there were stocks and shares valued at £1.77 million.

However, she did not wish to keep these but to give all the property to The Born Free Foundation, a registered charity devoted to animal welfare. However, there was nothing to stop her from keeping all the money. Had this been a registered charity then the assets could have been applied *cy-près*.

Does this decision tell us that the law on the disposal of assets of an unincorporated association is wrong and, if so, what result do you think would have been just?

REFLECTION

Method of distribution among members

In *Re Hobourn Aero Components Air Raid Distress Fund* (1946) it was held that assets should be distributed among both present and past members in shares proportionate to their contributions. However, inclusion of past members indicates a resulting trust approach. The contractual approach under which only present members benefit, as in *Re Bucks Constabulary Fund*, is more likely to be followed. The basis of distribution will normally be on a per capita basis in equal shares as in *Re Bucks* (1979), rather than in proportion to contributions made, unless the rules provide otherwise. In *Re Sick Funeral Society of St John's Sunday School, Golcar* (1972), where there were two classes of members, adults and children, distribution was on a per capita basis, but the children received only a half share.

Surplus funds of pension fund trusts

The rules governing surplus funds of unincorporated associations have also been applied to surpluses of pension fund trusts (*Davis* v. *Richard and Wallington Industries* (1990)).

When does an unincorporated association end?

In the *West Sussex* (1971) and *Bucks* (1979) cases there was no doubt about the date when the association ceased to exist but matters may not always be so straightforward. In Re *G.K.N. Bolts and Nuts Ltd and Social Club* (1982) the club had been in financial difficulties for some time and during 1975 membership cards ceased to be issued, the steward was dismissed and the stock of drinks was sold. On 18 December 1975 the club resolved to sell its sports ground but this was not sold until August 1978. The court held that although inactivity was not enough to dissolve an association, it might be the inactivity was such that the only reasonable inference was that here the club had ceased to exist. On the facts this took place on 18 December 1975.

The effect of s. 53(1)(c) of the LPA 1925

CORNERSTONE

Section 53(1)(c) of the LPA 1925

Section 53(1)(c) of the LPA 1925 may be relevant when deciding on the distribution of surplus funds of an unincorporated association.

It has been urged that the effect of s. 53(1)(c) has been overlooked in the cases above where it has been held that the members gain some interest in the property, as in *Re Bucks Constabulary*. If they do have an interest then it must be an equitable one and so, if at any time they resign or are expelled and their interest passes to other members, then there is a disposition of an equitable interest and so under s. 53(1)(c) this must be in writing. Yet there is no evidence that the courts have ever considered this point.

The future for non-charitable-purpose trusts

The present position is widely considered to be unsatisfactory but the solution is far from clear. There are the following possible ways forward:

(a) To hold that these trusts could take effect as mere powers. This would have the advantage that the enforceability point did not matter: a power is discretionary anyway and does not have to be carried out (see Chapter 4). Although this avenue was closed by *IRC* v. *Broadway Cottages Trust* (1955), which held that an invalid purpose trust cannot take effect as a power, such a solution has been adopted in other jurisdictions, for example by s. 16 of the Ontario Perpetuities Act 1966, and the American Restatement of the Law of Trusts, Second (1959) endorses this solution.

(b) That there should be an 'interested adversary principle'. Given that the initial problem is that these trusts have no beneficiary who can enforce them, it has been suggested that this should be an alternative instead to the 'beneficiary principle' and under it persons or institutions might be identified as being watchdogs to act in enforcing the trust (see Ford 1985). Legislation would probably be needed for this and one possibility is that the Attorney-General might undertake this role. This idea is similar to that of an 'enforcer', an office that exists in many trusts set up in Jersey, the Isle of Man and the Cayman Islands. Here legislation has been passed in order to make trusts for non-charitable purposes attractive for business purposes such as estate planning and it is suggested that there is no reason why the same should not apply in the United Kingdom. The only other express requirement would be that the trust was limited to the perpetuity period, but a particular period could be stated for this type of trust (see Hayton (2001) for an illuminating discussion of this whole topic).

KEY POINTS

- Trusts for non-charitable purposes are generally void.
- This is because of a lack of a beneficiary to enforce them.
- In certain exceptional cases trusts of this type are enforceable, e.g. trusts for animals and monuments.
- Trusts for non-charitable purposes are subject to the rule against inalienability.
- Gifts to unincorporated associations have to be for their purposes as the association does not exist and if these purposes are not charitable then the gift may be void.
- The courts have found two ways of holding gifts for non-charitable purposes valid: a trust for the members and an immediate gift to the members who will hold it on the basis of the contract between them.
- There have been various attempts by the courts to find a solution to the problem of what to do with the surplus assets of an unincorporated association when it is dissolved: a resulting trust for donors, that they should go to the Crown as *bona vacantia*, and that they should go to the surviving members.

CORE CASES AND STATUTES

Case	About	Importance
Re Astor's Settlement Trusts (1952)	Trust 'for the maintenance of good relations between nations . . . and preservation of the independence of the newspapers and similar purposes' – held void.	Established the general principle that trusts for non-charitable purposes are void.
Re Denley's Trust Deed (1969)	Gift of a plot of land to trustees 'for the purpose of a recreation or sports ground primarily for the benefit of the employees of the company' – held valid as a trust for the employees.	May be possible to hold that what appears to be a trust for purposes can be construed as a trust for individuals.
Re Recher's Will Trusts (1972)	A gift to the London and Provincial Anti-Vivisection Society was held to be a beneficial gift to the members.	A gift to an unincorporated association may be valid on the basis of a contract between the members.
Re Grant's WT (1979)	A gift was made to the Chertsey Labour Party. The members could not change the rules and divide the gift between themselves because the rules were subject to control by the National Executive Committee of the Labour Party.	The application of the inalienability rule made the gift void.
Hanchett-Stamford v. *Attorney-General* (2008)	There was one surviving member of the association. Could they claim the funds?	Yes: where there is only one surviving member of an unincorporated association which is not charitable then they can claim the funds.

Statute	About	Importance
Section 53(1)(c) of the LPA 1925.	Disposition of an equitable interest must be in writing.	Possible application where the equitable (beneficial) interest of members of an unincorporated association in its property passes to other members.

FURTHER READING

Brown, J. (2007) 'What are we to do with testamentary trusts of imperfect obligation?' 71 *Conv*. 148.
This article, which is referred to in the text, contains some really useful material on the extent to which these trusts are actually used.

Chambers, R. (1997) *Resulting Trusts* (Oxford University Press).
There is a valuable discussion of the topic of disposal of surplus funds at pages 61–67.

Ford, H. (1985) 'Dispositions for purposes' in P. Finn (ed.) *Essays in Equity* (The Law Book Company).

The Australian perspective makes this especially useful.

Hayton, D. (2001) 'Developing the obligation characteristic of the trust' 117 *LQR* 96.
This considers how this area can be developed in a more satisfactory way.

Matthews, P. (1996) 'The new trust: obligations without rights?' in A.J. Oakley (ed.) *Trends in Contemporary Trust Law* (Oxford University Press).
This is another attempt at charting the way forward.

CHAPTER 6

charitable trusts

BLUEPRINT
Charitable trusts

KEY
QUESTIONS

LEGISLATION

- Charities Act 2011

CONTEXT

- Importance of charities today.
- Role of charities vis-à-vis the state.

CONCEPTS

- Requirements for charitable status: charitable purposes; public benefit; must be exclusively charitable
- Political trusts
- Failure of charitable gifts and *cy-près* doctrine

- Role of charities in society.
- Extent to which public benefit is required.
- Should political purposes be charitable?
- Disaster appeals and charitable status.

- Why are charitable trusts important in society and what does the law mean by a charitable trust?

CASES

- *Re Coulthurst*
- *Re Shaw*
- *Thornton* v. *Howe*
- *Dingle* v. *Turner*
- *Oppenheim* v. *Tobacco Securities*
- *Gilmour* v. *Coats*
- *McGovern* v. *Attorney-General*

REFORM

- Clarification of when public benefit is required.

SPECIAL CHARACTERISTICS

- Types of charitable organisations
- Article 9 of ECHR and trusts for religion
- Charity Commission and its role

CRITICAL ISSUES

Setting the scene

You are a keen conservationist and you have spotted an area of woodland for sale. You feel that it could be developed as a countryside centre with a building housing an exhibition and information centre and a café. You would manage the centre and receive a salary. When you discuss the idea with friends it becomes obvious that you will need to consider forming a charity. This can give you various tax advantages; for instance, if you set up a membership scheme then membership fees can be gift aided. Charitable status will also help you when you apply for grants from different bodies.

You download the details of how to apply from the website of the charity commission (www.charity-commission.gov.uk) and you see that in order to qualify for charitable status your organisation must have certain purposes recognised by the Charities Act 2011. You look through these and you feel that your proposed charity should satisfy purpose (i) 'advancement of environmental protection or improvement' and possibly others such as the advancement of education.

You also see that a charity must exist for the public benefit and you look through the guidelines which are available on the Charity Commission website on what constitutes this. Although you will be receiving a benefit personally as you will be the manager and be paid a salary this does not prevent the charity existing for the public benefit. After all, many charities employ paid staff. What is vital is that the actual activities must benefit the public or a section of the public. This is satisfied as the woodland will be open to anyone and so will the centre and the café. This all looks most promising but you also need to cross a big hurdle: finding suitable trustees. You can be a trustee, although you will need to declare your financial interest (your salary) at each meeting, but you need others and they need to be aware of the fiduciary nature of trusteeship. Thus, if you are a trustee you must not make any profits from the charity. It would be a breach of trust if, for example, you made a loan to the charity at a much higher rate of interest than the charity could have obtained elsewhere and, as a trustee, persuaded the other trustees to agree to it.

Assuming that you can find suitable trustees and you submit the application correctly then the Charity Commission will register you as a charity.

This is not the end, though: the charity will need to comply with the requirements of the Charity Commission regarding the submission of annual returns and other matters. This chapter explores the legal requirements for charitable status and then at the position where a charity comes to an end and there are surplus assets. What is to be done with them?

Take note

You should keep an eye on the Charity Commission website for developments in the charity law: www.charity-commission.gov.uk. It is an indispensable resource. A lot is going on in the world of charities at the moment.

You will find here details of how the Commission regulates charities, a topic not dealt with in detail in this book. An example is the investigation announced in August 2013 into the alleged disposal by the Trustees of the Spiritualist Association of Great Britain of assets for £6 million, which appeared to be significantly less than their market value, especially as shortly after the disposal they were sold on for £21 million. Both the original buyer of the assets and the subsequent buyer were companies registered in the British Virgin Islands.

You should also look at the review of charity legislation 'Trusted and Independent: Giving Charity back to Charities' (2012) available at www.gov.uk/government/ . . . /charities-act-2006-review. The Public Administration Select Committee (PASC) also undertook an inquiry into the regulation of charities and its report is considered below.

INTRODUCTION

As the Report 'Trusted and independent: Giving Charity back to Charities, a Review of the Charities Act 2006' (2012) points out (at para. 1.1):

> Charities have a long history in this country. The oldest charity in England is believed to be the King's School Canterbury, which was established in 597 and, despite some gaps in its history, still exists today.

It then points out (at para. 1.2) that:

> There are many aspects of the sector which have stood the test of time; for example, the Hospital of St Cross in Winchester was set up in 1136 by William the Conqueror's grandson, Bishop Henry deBlois, and to this day provides accommodation for the elderly and bread and ale to passing travellers who ask for it.

The Report of the Public Administration Select Committee (2013) points out that 'The charitable sector is at the heart of UK society, with £9.3 billion received in donations from the public in 2011/2012, and around 25 new applications for charitable status received by the Charity Commission every working day.' The Committee made various detailed proposals, some of which are considered below.

CONTEXT

Today there are over 163,000 charities employing around 600,000 paid staff.

Why do we give to charities and how much do we give?

We give to charities either directly, by making a donation, or indirectly. I buy a dress from a charity shop; I pay the admission fee to a National Trust property; in both cases I am donating to charity. My motives may be mixed too. I may just want to be generous and help others or I may be mainly concerned with reducing my tax bill.

CONTEXT

According to figures from the UK Giving Report, produced by the National Council of Voluntary Organisations, in 2009/10 around 55% of us donated to charity in any month, equivalent to 28% of all adults, and each of us typically gave £10, giving a grand total of £9.3 billion, and numbers have been over 50% for several years (see also the review of charity legislation 'Trusted and Independent: Giving Charity back to Charities' (2012) at para. 2.14).

CORNERSTONE

Charities Act 2011

The present law on charities is contained in the Charities Act 2011.

Although the present law on charities is contained in the Charities Act 2011 this is only a consolidating statute which consolidated a number of statutes including the Charities Act 2006, which is therefore no longer in force. However, it was the Charities Act 2006 which brought the first major change in the statute law on this subject since the Statute of Charitable Uses Act 1601 and so exam questions often refer to changes made by the Charities Act 2006.

Why have charitable status?

(a) ***Charities benefit from the actions of society in various ways.*** For example, charitable status facilitates the winning of contracts or grants and registration with HMRC, which opens the way to Gift Aid. Charities benefit from other tax reliefs and exemptions, or reductions in the level of Council Tax payable. Moreover, registration as a charity opens the door to working with the statutory sector in delivering services. The very fact of being able to call oneself a charity opens the door to public support.

(b) ***There are also significant legal advantages.*** The objects of a charitable trust need not be certain. Thus, as we saw in Chapter 4, while the objects of a private trust must be certain, and thus a gift for 'benevolent purposes' would fail, a gift for 'charitable purposes' would be valid. In cases such as this, the courts may establish a scheme for the application of the funds to particular charitable objects, and the Charity Commissioners have similar powers, which are considered later in this chapter. Moreover, although charitable trusts are trusts for purposes rather than individuals, the absence of ascertainable beneficiaries who can enforce them does not affect their validity because it is the Attorney-General who enforces charitable trusts. Under s. 115 of the Charities Act 2011 charity proceedings can be brought by the charity or the Attorney-General, or 'by any person interested' which, in *Richmond-upon-Thames LBC* v. *Rogers* (1988), was held to include a local authority in the case of a local charity.

Charities and the rule against perpetuities

Charitable trusts are subject to the rule against remoteness of vesting, in that a gift to a charity must vest within the perpetuity period which is now 125 years (Perpetuities and Accumulations Act 2009). Therefore, if there is a gift to an individual followed by a gift (a gift over) to a charity, the gift to the charity will fail if it vests or might vest outside the perpetuity period. However, a gift to one charity with a gift over to another charity is valid even though the gift to the second charity may take place outside the perpetuity period (*Christ's Hospital* v. *Grainger* (1849)).

....**APPLICATION**

Jack by will leaves all his estate to his daughter, Mary, with a proviso that on her death any remaining funds will go to the Hanbury School, a registered charity. This gift is subject to the perpetuity rules but will be valid as clearly Mary will die within the next 125 years.

Suppose that instead Jack had left his estate to the Hanbury School but provided that if the school shall ever cease to exist then any remaining funds from the estate not used shall go to the Hospital of St John, another registered charity. Clearly this may take place long beyond the new 125-year perpetuity period. Even so, the gift is valid as the perpetuity rules do not apply.

TYPES OF CHARITABLE ORGANISATIONS

CORNERSTONE

Types of charitable organisations

The main ways in which charitable organisations can exist are as trusts, companies and unincorporated associations.

Charities do not need to exist under the form of a trust, although many of them do. They can exist in other forms as follows:

(a) *Charitable corporations.* The corporation will almost invariably be a company limited by guarantee, and the advantage of corporate status is that the company, as a legal person, will have legal rights and liabilities rather than the trustees. On the other hand, it may well be felt in the case of small trusts that the expense and trouble of complying with the statutory formalities outweighs this advantage. The Charities Act 2006 introduced a new form of organisation, a Charitable Incorporated Organisation, which will avoid dual regulation under both charity and company law. It became available to charities from 10 December 2012.

(b) *Unincorporated associations.* These will normally be run by a chairman and committee and their basis, as with all unincorporated associations, is that of a contract between their members. Such an organisation has the advantage of flexibility and may be suitable for small charities.

(c) *Other types of organisations,* e.g. societies registered under the Friendly Societies Act.

All forms of charitable organisation, whether or not they are trusts, are, in general, governed by the same rules. Thus references to charitable trusts in this chapter should, unless otherwise indicated, be taken to include other forms of charitable organisations.

REFLECTION

Charities are known as the 'third sector' and play a vital part in delivering services. They are increasingly recognised as partners by central and local government and other public bodies. For instance, Barnardo's works with local authorities across the UK to provide a broad range of fostering and adoption services, including placements for children with extra needs. If you have been involved in volunteering, possibly through work abroad or at home, perhaps through advocacy services or legal advice centres, you will probably find that they have been run by charities.

REGISTRATION AS A CHARITY

Most charities are required, whatever form the charity takes, to register with the Charity Commissioners, although certain charities are exempt (see later in this chapter). The advantage of registration as a charity is that the organisation is conclusively presumed to be a charity (s. 37 of the Charities Act 2011) and so the privileges of charitable status outlined above can be claimed.

The fact that an organisation is not included on the register of charities does not mean that it is not a charity but it does mean that in order to claim the above privileges it will have to prove to the relevant authorities, such as HM Revenue & Customs, that it *is* a charity.

CORNERSTONE

Requirements for charitable status

Three requirements must be satisfied for an organisation to have charitable status:

(a) Does it exist for charitable purposes as laid down in the Charities Act 2011?

(b) Is there an element of public benefit?

(c) Are the purposes for which it exists exclusively charitable?

CHARITABLE PURPOSES RECOGNISED UNDER THE CHARITIES ACT 2011

CORNERSTONE

Charitable purposes

An organisation, in order to be charitable, must exist for one or more of the following purposes set out in the Charities Act 2011.

The list of charitable purposes is set out in s. 3(1) of the Charities Act 2011:

A purpose falls within this subsection if it falls within any of the following descriptions of purposes –

(a) the prevention or relief of poverty;

(b) the advancement of education;

(c) the advancement of religion;

(d) the advancement of health or the saving of lives;

(e) the advancement of citizenship or community development;

(f) the advancement of the arts, culture, heritage or science;

(g) the advancement of amateur sport;

(h) the advancement of human rights, conflict resolution or reconciliation or the promotion of religious or racial harmony or equality and diversity;

(i) the advancement of environmental protection or improvement;

(j) the relief of those in need because of youth, age, ill-health, disability, financial hardship or other disadvantage;

(k) the advancement of animal welfare;

(l) the promotion of the efficiency of the armed forces of the Crown or of the efficiency of the police, fire and rescue services or ambulance services;

(m) any other purposes –

  (i) that are not within paragraphs (a) to (l) but are recognised as charitable purposes by virtue of section 5 (recreational and similar trusts, etc.) or under the old law,

  (ii) that may reasonably be regarded as analogous to, or within the spirit of, any purposes falling within any of paragraphs (a) to (l) or sub-paragraph (i), or

  (iii) that may reasonably be regarded as analogous to, or within the spirit of, any purposes which have been recognised, under the law relating to charities in England and Wales, as falling within sub-paragraph (ii) or this sub-paragraph.

> ### Take note
> This is a good time to remind you, before we plunge into the details of charity law, of the importance of the guidance issued by the Charity Commission under s. 17 of the Charities Act 2011. When you are faced with a question on charitable status, you must look at this as well as at the case law.

CHARITABLE PURPOSES UNDER THE CHARITIES ACT 2011 IN DETAIL

(a) Trusts for the relief of poverty

CORNERSTONE

Re Coulthurst

Re Coulthurst is a leading example of a trust for the relief of poverty.

In *Re Coulthurst* (1951) Evershed MR explained that 'poverty does not mean destitution, . . . it may not unfairly be paraphrased for present purposes as meaning persons who have to ' "go short" in the ordinary acceptation of that term'. On this basis a gift for the widows and orphans of deceased employees of a bank was upheld as charitable. Nor is there any objection to poverty being defined in terms of minimum income qualification, provided, of course, that the qualifying level is appropriate.

There are difficult decisions: in *Re Sanders WT* (1954) a gift to provide 'dwellings for the working and their families' was not held to be charitable because the expression 'working classes' did not denote poor persons. See also *Re Niyazi's* (1978).

(b) Trusts for the advancement of education

CORNERSTONE

Re Shaw

Re Shaw explains what is meant by advancement of education in the context of charity law.

Education includes the provision of schools, universities and other similar institutions, together with ancillary purposes, such as the payment of teachers and administrative staff (*Case of Christ's College, Cambridge* (1757)). However, education includes much more than this. In *Royal Choral Society* v. *IRC* (1943) Lord Greene MR rejected the argument that education meant only teaching a class. It did not, he said, mean only the teaching of painters and the training of musicians but, as in this case, the 'purpose of raising the artistic taste of the country' by the performance of choral works. However, where the purpose is propaganda, rather than education, then it will not be charitable. Thus in *Re Shaw* (1952) a gift in George Bernard Shaw's will for research into a new phonetic alphabet was not charitable partly because one object was to persuade the public that a phonetic alphabet would be a good thing. Another reason why the gift failed was that it aimed merely at the increase of knowledge, which is not necessarily by itself education.

In *Re Besterman's WT* (1980) Slade J likewise emphasised that a trust for research will only be charitable if, in addition to the subject of that research being useful, there is the intention to disseminate it. In *Re Hopkins' WT* (1964) a gift to be applied towards finding the Bacon–Shakespeare manuscripts was held charitable because the result of any discovery was intended to be published and the research was in itself valuable as being designed to improve the literary heritage.

> **Take note**
>
> Do remember that a gift may be valid under one or more heads of charity or, alternatively, it may not be valid under one head but may be under another. In the case of the gift in *Re Pinion* you might like to consider if the gift could be valid under s. 3(1)(f): the advancement of the arts, culture, heritage or science. However, the court would still need to decide if the contents were of artistic value.

You will see that in many of these cases the courts are called on to make judgments on what is of educational value. Clearly such judgments must be objective and assisted by expert evidence. In *Re Pinion* (1965) the judges relied on expert evidence that, for example, 'in particular the pictures and china are quite worthless and the suggestion that they should be shown in public in London or anywhere else does not bear serious consideration'. There was worse to come: the expert inspected the silver and said: ' "It is a perfect example of the tastelessness and ugliness of Victorian silver of this date" ', which in fact was 1895.

Today we do actually rate Victorian objects more highly then was the case in the 1960s but the judges can only act on the evidence of the expert opinion of their time. However, we can still ask if the judges were, even unconsciously, influenced by their own views.

(c) Trusts for the advancement of religion

The term 'religion' includes not only Christianity but other religions such as Judaism (*Straus* v. *Goldsmid* (1837)) and, although there is no authority on other religions such as Islam and Buddhism, regulations which were made under the Charities Act 1960 assumed that religions other than Christian were charitable. In any event these will now be charitable under s. 3(2) of the Charities Act 2011 (above). The Unification Church has been registered but the Church of Scientology has not.

> ### Take note
>
> Section 3(2) of the Charities Act 2011 provides that
>
> ' "religion" includes –
> (i) a religion which involves belief in more than one god, and
> (ii) a religion which does not involve belief in a god.'
>
> Most of the cases on the meaning of religion were decided before this provision came into force and you should bear this in mind.

The question of what is a religion was addressed by the Charity Commissioners in *Church of Scientology's Application for Registration as a Charity* (1999), where it was considered Scientology did not qualify as a religion principally as there was no element of worship. It was found that the one element of scientology, auditing, 'appears in essence very much akin to counselling, conducted on a one to one basis, in private, and addressed to the needs of the individual receiving auditing'. The other element, training in Scientology, involving the detailed study of the works of L. Ron Hubbard according to particular sets formulae or methods of study, similarly lacked the elements of reverence or veneration necessary to constitute worship. Look also at *Hansard*, 3 February and 10 February 1988, which details debates on the decision to refuse registration as a charity to the Unification Church (The Moonies).

The Supreme Court in *Hodkin* v. *Registrar-General of Births, Deaths and Marriages* [2013] has decided that Scientology is to be regarded as a religion and that its chapters can be registered under the *Places of Worship Registration* Act 1855. This indicates a changing attitude to Scientology.

CORNERSTONE

Thornton v. Howe

Thornton v. *Howe* is a leading example of what is meant by advancement of religion in the context of charity law.

Moreover, charitable status is accorded to sects which are small and may be considered eccentric. The leading case here is *Thornton* v. *Howe* (1862) where a trust for the publication of the works of Joanna Southcote, who styled herself as the mother of the second Messiah, was held charitable even though the judge considered them foolish.

The Charity Commission, in its *Commentary on the Descriptions of Charitable Purposes in the Charities Act 2006* (2008) stated (at para. 22) that the characteristics of a religious belief include:

- belief in a god (or gods) or goddess (or goddesses), or supreme being, or divine or transcendental being or entity or spiritual principle ('supreme being or entity') which is the object or focus of the religion;
- a relationship between the believer and the supreme being or entity by showing worship of, reverence for or veneration of the supreme being or entity;
- a degree of cogency, cohesion, seriousness and importance;
- an identifiable positive, beneficial, moral or ethical framework.

The law does insist on some form of theistic belief. In *Re South Place Ethical Society* (1980) the Society's objects were the 'study and dissemination of ethical principles and the cultivation of a rational religious sentiment'. Dillon J held that these were not concerned with the advancement of religion because 'Religion as I see it is concerned with man's relations with God, and ethics are concerned with man's relations with man'. However, he did hold that the objects were educational and thus charitable.

CORNERSTONE

Article 9 of the European Convention on Human Rights

Article 9 of the European Convention on Human Rights must be considered when deciding if a body qualifies for charitable status on the ground that it is for the advancement of religion.

Article 9 of the European Convention on Human Rights, which of course is now incorporated into UK law by the Human Rights Act 1998, provides that

Everyone has the right to freedom of thought, conscience and religion; this right includes freedom to change his religion or belief and freedom, either alone or in community with others and in public or private, to manifest his religion or belief, in worship, teaching, practice and observance.

You should also note that the right is qualified in Article 9(2).

The application of Article 9 was considered in *Church of Scientology's Application for Registration as a Charity* (1999) (above) and it will also be relevant in future cases involving claims to charitable status on the ground of religion.

(d) Advancement of health or the saving of lives (including the prevention of sickness, disease, or human suffering)

In *Re Resch* (1969) a private hospital was held charitable even though, although it did not operate for profit, its charges were not low. Gifts for ancillary purposes, such as the training of doctors and nurses or the provision of extra facilities for patients, will also be charitable, as will gifts for the treatment and/or investigation of particular diseases or conditions such as drug addiction (*Re Banfield* (1968)) or blindness (*Re Lewis* (1955)).

(e) Advancement of citizenship or community development (including rural or urban regeneration, promotion of civic responsibility, volunteering, the voluntary sector or the effectiveness or efficiency of charities)

Examples here are scouts and guides.

(f) Advancement of the arts, culture, heritage or science

··· APPLICATION

Suppose that I wish to establish a music festival. This would be charitable on this ground and so would a museum.

(g) Advancement of amateur sport

By s. 3(2)(d) sport means sports or games which promote health by involving physical or mental skill or exertion.

··· APPLICATION

Physical exertion seems clear enough but what about mental exertion? In *Re Dupree's Deed Trusts* (1945) the playing of chess was held charitable as chess involves mental exertion but clubs where the activity is games of chance would not be charitable. However, some games involve both an element of chance and also mental skill, such as bridge. Would a bridge club be charitable?

(h) Advancement of human rights, conflict resolution or reconciliation or the promotion of religious or racial harmony or equality or diversity

As the Amnesty case (*McGovern* v. *Attorney-General* (1982) – see below) shows, activities of this kind can easily come within the definition of political trusts and so lose their charitable status. Presumably these trusts, in order to remain charitable, will need to concentrate on research and activities such as the actual promotion of mediation and conciliation.

The research paper published by the Charity Commission in 2007 (RS16 – 'Charities Working in the Field of Human Rights') found that there were many ways in which charities promoted human rights on a practical level, for example:

- monitoring abuses of human rights;
- obtaining redress for the victims of human rights abuse;
- relieving need among the victims of human rights abuse;
- research into human rights issues;
- educating the public about human rights.

(i) Advancement of environmental protection or improvement

The National Trust was recognised as charitable in 1916 by the decision in *Re Verrall* and in *Attorney-General (NSW)* v. *Sawtell* (1978) a bequest to preserve native wildlife was upheld as charitable.

(j) Relief of those in need by reason of youth, age, ill-health, disability, financial hardship or other disadvantage, including the provision of accommodation or care to these persons

A specific example here is the charity 'Motability', which provides transport for the disabled and, more generally, charities for the young, the old, the disabled and for the other purposes mentioned above. The relief of suffering caused by disasters (*Re North Devon and West Somerset Relief Fund Trusts* (1953)), which can include not only relief from factors such as damage to property, which might otherwise cause poverty, but also relief from bereavement and personal injury will be included.

Disaster funds: should a disaster fund have charitable status?

An article in the Law Society's *Gazette* (8 January 1986) examined the problems. It pointed out that too often appeals are launched almost immediately following a disaster, under-standably, sponsored by the mayor or some such person. 'The terms of the appeal may not be very carefully thought out. A charity may be established, wittingly or unwittingly. A charity is seemingly very desirable.'

However, it points out that, as the appeal fund launched after the Aberfan disaster in 1966 showed, there may be considerable disadvantages because if the fund is charitable then 'distribution can only be according to need but a means test will often seem unacceptable'. In this disaster a huge slag heap slid from a hill above Pantglas junior school in South Wales, killing 116 children and 28 adults.

It is possible to have a non-charitable appeal fund such as happened in the case of the Penlee lifeboat disaster in 1981. The Penlee Lifeboat went to the aid of the ship *Union Star* after its engines failed in heavy seas. After the lifeboat had managed to rescue four people both vessels were lost and sixteen people died including eight volunteer lifeboatmen. This was a private trust which raised £3 million and distributed about £375,000 each to some eight bereaved families. The article says that: 'No-one would wish to belittle the loss to a family of a brave husband and father. But £375,000 is a very substantial sum, yielding presumably some £40,000 a year. Riches can destroy both people and communities, it has been said. And what would the donors have said if they had known how things in fact turned out?'

One suggestion is to have a national disaster fund, permanently in being. But this would not tug the heart-strings as an appeal launched just after a specific disaster. The website of the Charity Commission contains guidance on disaster appeals.

Finally have a look at the Charity Commission publication (CC40) on starting, running and supporting charitable disaster appeals which sets out the Attorney-General's Guidelines.

CONTEXT

(k) Advancement of animal welfare

Gifts for animal welfare have always been charitable as in *Re Murawski's WT* (1971) an animal sanctuary of a more usual kind, providing care and shelter, was held charitable. A difficult decision is *Re Wedgwood* (1915), where a gift to be applied to ensure that animals were humanely slaughtered was held charitable. Lord Cozens-Hardy held that the gift 'tended to promote public morality by checking the innate tendency to cruelty'.

(l) Promotion of the efficiency of the armed forces of the Crown

This is already recognised as charitable, for example, the promotion of the efficiency of the armed services (e.g. *Re Stephens* (1892) – teaching of shooting in the Army).

(m) Any other purposes that

(i) are not listed but are currently charitable under charity law,

(ii) any purposes analogous to any purpose currently charitable or listed above, and

(iii) any purpose analogous to a purpose recognised as charitable

Some examples from the previous law which do not seem to fit into any of the above examples are: gifts to the fire service (*Re Wokingham Fire Brigade Trusts* (1951)) and the police (*IRC* v. *City of Glasgow Police Athletic Association* (1953)) and gifts to localities. In *Goodman* v. *Saltash Corporation* (1882) Selborne LC held that a gift 'for the benefit of the inhabitants of a parish or town or of any particular class' of them is charitable.

Recreational charities

CORNERSTONE

Recreational charities

Recreational charities can have charitable status.

Recreational charities are dealt with by s. 5 of the 2011 Act which provides that it is charitable to provide, or assist in the provision of, facilities for recreation or other leisure-time occupation if the facilities are provided in the interests of social welfare, provided that what are called the 'basic conditions' are met.

These are:

(a) that the facilities are provided with the object of improving the conditions of life for the persons for whom the facilities are primarily intended, and

(b) that:

(i) those persons have need of the facilities because of their youth, age, infirmity or disability, poverty, or social and economic circumstances, or

(ii) the facilities are to be available to members of the public at large or to male, or to female, members of the public at large.

Section 5(4) provides that in particular the provision of facilities at village halls, community centres and women's institutes, and the provision and maintenance of grounds and buildings to be used for purposes of recreation or leisure-time occupation shall be charitable if the facilities are provided in the interests of social welfare.

What is meant by social welfare?

In *IRC* v. *McMullen* (1981) Walton J in the High Court said that the term 'social welfare' connoted some element of relief from deprivation especially because of the words in s. 1(2)(a), 'improving the conditions of life', but Bridge LJ in the Court of Appeal disagreed. Social welfare need not be limited to the deprived: 'Hyde Park improves the conditions of life for residents in Mayfair as much as for those in Pimlico or the Portobello Road.' In *Guild* v. *IRC* (1992) the House of Lords agreed with the view of Bridge LJ and held that a gift of residue to a sports centre was charitable.

THE REQUIREMENT THAT CHARITIES MUST BE FOR THE PUBLIC BENEFIT

CORNERSTONE

Public benefit

A body cannot have charitable status unless there is an element of public benefit.

Section 2(1)(b) of the Charities Act 2011 provides that any charitable purpose must be for the public benefit and s. 4 of the Charities Act 2011 sets out the ' "public benefit" ' test.

Introduction

> **Take note**
>
> The law on public benefit is at present in a state of flux. The Charity Commission issued Guidance under the Charities Act 2006 on what constituted public benefit but this was challenged in two cases which are dealt with below.

The result is that the Public Administration Committee in its report (see above) said that: 'We have concluded that, while the Act has been broadly welcomed by the charitable sector, it is critically flawed on the issue of public benefit.'

There is a fundamental issue which will probably have to be resolved by legislation: to what extent do the objects of charities have to demonstrate public benefit? Do keep an eye on developments here.

The background to the law

Prior to the Charities Act 2006 there was said to be a presumption (but see the 'Reflection' below) that charities for three purposes (poverty, education and religion) were charitable and in other cases public benefit had to be proved. Section 4(2) of the Charities Act 2011 appeared to remove this presumption and so it was argued that public benefit must be proved in all cases. However, this was confused by s. 4(3), which provides that 'any reference to the public benefit is a reference to the public benefit as that term is understood for the purposes of the law relating to charities in England and Wales'. The effect of this was to preserve the case law which existed before the 2006 Charities Act, a good deal of which was on the basis that there *was* a presumption of public benefit in certain cases. The matter has now been clarified by the following case.

The decision in *Attorney-General* v. *Charity Commission for England and Wales* (2012)

The case involved a number of charities concerned with the relief of poverty but the Upper Chamber took the opportunity to re-state the law on public benefit. It held, in a decision of great importance, that public benefit is part of the nature of each charitable purpose. Thus education is by itself charitable and so is the relief of poverty. There could of course be cases where this was not so, one example often given being a school for pickpockets, but that does not affect the general principle. That

being so, there is no question of any presumption of public benefit: that benefit is intrinsic to the charitable purpose. However, those who may benefit from the carrying out of the purpose must be sufficiently numerous, and identified in such a manner, as to constitute what is described in the authorities as 'a section of the public'. Thus, whether or not an institution satisfies the public benefit requirement must be assessed by reference to the criteria which are relevant to its purposes. What is or is not a sufficient section of the public to satisfy the second aspect of public benefit varies depending on the nature of the charity. However, trusts for the relief of poverty are subject to a unique test of public benefit (see below).

> **Take note**
>
> There are two aspects of public benefit:
>
> (i) the benefit aspect – is the purpose beneficial?
> (ii) the public aspect – does the purpose benefit the public or a section of it?

REFLECTION

Jeffrey Hackney (2008) argues that the law on public benefit was not altered by the Charities Act 2006. He says that the answer is that the 'law has always been that those seeking to establish a charity have had to prove that it was of a public character: this has not been presumed in any way nor was it a matter for dogmatic assumption'. His argument is that the distinction between the first three heads of charity and the others was *not* that public benefit was presumed in the first three cases but that as there was no doubt that they were charitable there was no need to prove that. For instance, the argument was that education was by itself beneficial and thus charitable. On the other hand when other purposes were gradually recognised as charitable by the courts it was necessary in the first instance to establish that they were beneficial and thus charitable.

In effect this argument has been accepted by the Upper Chamber in this case.

Charity Commission guidance

Section 17 of the Charities Act 2011 obliges the Charity Commission to issue guidance on the meaning of public benefit and by s. 17(5) charity trustees must have regard to this although it is clear that this will now have to be revised in the light of the above decision.

The Charity Commission has revised its guidance for public benefit in the light of recent decisions by the courts, and you should go to the Commission website for the up-to-date version.

The guidance also mentioned that benefit must not be unreasonably restricted by ability to pay any fees charged but this section was successfully challenged in *The Independent Schools Council* v. *The Charity Commission and others* (2011) where the Upper Chamber considered the Charity Commission's public benefit guidance in relation to independent schools. It held that the use of the word 'unreasonable' in the guidance was wrong as charity law (see e.g. *Re Resch* (above)) had never imposed such a requirement and it pointed out that 'a wholly capricious restriction – nothing to do with an ability to pay – unrelated to the objects of the charity might not be valid even if the restricted class was numerically very large'. There was a duty on educational charities to make provision for the poor and this must be more than minimal or tokenistic. Beyond that, the level of provision to be made for those unable to pay the full fees was to be decided by the trustees in the context of their charity's circumstances. There were no objective benchmarks about what is appropriate.

Requirement of public benefit in particular cases

Poverty cases

CORNERSTONE

Dingle v. *Turner*

Dingle v. *Turner* illustrates the point that the public benefit test in poverty cases is narrower than in others.

Take note

Virtually all of the cases below were decided before the law on public benefit was changed by the Charities Act 2006. As pointed out above, the Charities Act 2006 introduced the requirements that public benefit will need to be proved in all cases. Although by s. 4(3) of the Act existing case law is preserved, you might care to consider if the decisions in any of these cases would now be different especially in the light of the revised guidance published by the Charity Commission.

It has long been recognised that the test of public benefit in these types of trusts is narrower than in other cases. In *Dingle* v. *Turner* (1972) a trust fund to pay pensions to poor employees of a certain company was held charitable. The House of Lords recognised the poverty exception/anomaly and rejected the submission that the test in *Re Compton* (1945) (below) applied to these trusts. However, it is wrong to say that in trusts for the relief of poverty there is *no* requirement of public benefit: the point is that the line is drawn differently than in other cases. In *Dingle* v. *Turner* the House approved the statement of Lord Cross in *Re Scarisbrick* (1951) that a distinction is drawn between 'whether the gift was for the relief of poverty amongst a particular description of poor people or was merely a gift to particular poor persons, the relief of poverty among them being the motive of the gift'. In the latter case it would not be charitable. It may be that, as in *Dingle* v. *Turner*, that group is defined by reference to a personal connection (here, employment by a particular firm) but it is still a group.

Education cases

CORNERSTONE

Oppenheim v. Tobacco Securities

Oppenheim v. *Tobacco Securities* is a leading example of what is meant by public benefit in the context of advancement of education in charity law.

A clear example of where this requirement was not met is *Re Compton* (1945) where a trust for the education of the children of three named families was held not to be charitable. In *Oppenheim* v. *Tobacco Securities Trust Co. Ltd* (1951) a trust was held not charitable where it was to provide for 'the education of children of employees or former employees of the British American Tobacco Co. Ltd or any of its subsidiary or allied companies' even though the number of employees exceeded 110,000. Lord Simonds held that the fact that the group was large did not make the trust charitable if the connection between its members was based on some personal tie, whether it was membership of a particular family as in *Re Compton* (1945) or employment by a particular employee or employees, as here. Lord MacDermott dissented, holding that there was the intention to benefit a class of substantial size and importance in such a way that the interests of the class as a whole were advanced. He felt that the question should always be one of degree, depending on the facts of each case, and pointed to the difficulties of applying the rule laid down by Lord Simonds: was a distinction to be drawn between those employed in a particular industry, with a number of firms, before it was nationalised (presumably the public) and those employed when it was nationalised (presumably not the public because the relationship depended on the connection with one employer)? In *Dingle* v. *Turner* (1972) (see above) Lord Cross (with whom all the other Law Lords concurred) agreed with Lord MacDermott, although this was *obiter*.

The decision in *Oppenheim* has been criticised, especially given that the company had more than 100,000 employees and so the potential beneficiaries were a very large number. The actual decision may have been correct but should have rested on a different basis: trusts of the *Oppenheim* kind are essentially attempts to provide tax-free fringe benefits for employees. Why should they be charitable at all?

CONTEXT

In *Re Koettgen's WT* (1954) the trust was for the promotion of commercial education for those who could not afford to pay for it themselves with a preference to be given of up to 75% of income to employees of a particular firm. This was held charitable because the gift to the primary class contained the necessary element of public benefit. If a particular group had had an absolute right to part of the money, or if the trust had been phrased the other way round, so that there was a preference for the public in the absence of qualified applicants from employees of the firm, then it would not have been charitable.

> ### Take note
>
> *Re Koettgen* often comes up in problem questions and you should be familiar with the facts, as the problem will have slightly different ones. It is likely that a trust which provided that a greater proportion of the income than in this case would go to the preferential class (e.g. 85%) would not be valid.

In *IRC* v. *Educational Grants Association Ltd* (1967) Pennycuick J found 'considerable difficulty' with *Re Koettgen* (1954) and thought that a trust for the public with a preference for a private class was a trust for both charitable and non-charitable objects. In this case the defendant was a corporation established for the advancement of education which was financially supported by payments made by the Metal Box Co. Ltd and some of its employees. In one year between 75% and 85% of income had been paid towards the education of children connected with this company and the court held that, although it was conceded that the trust was established for charitable purposes, these payments were not charitable. The fact was, as Pennycuick J put it, that between 75% and 85% of income had been spent for the benefit of children by virtue of a private characteristic: their connection with the Metal Box Co. Ltd.

> ### Take note
>
> Do make sure that you use the current guidance on public benefit issued by the Charity Commission. Much of the original guidance has been withdrawn but it is still on some websites.

REFLECTION

The court was, in effect, applying the *Oppenheim* decision here but the difficulty with that decision remains: suppose that 50% or 25% of the funds had been applied solely for their children? Would the payments then have been charitable? A better course might be to say that trusts such as those in the above cases are not charitable because their purposes are not charitable since they are essentially trusts for the purposes of a particular organisation, rather than basing the decision on the requirement of public benefit.

Religion cases

CORNERSTONE

Gilmour v. *Coats*

Gilmour v. *Coats* is a leading example of what is meant by public benefit in the context of advancement of religion in charity law.

It appears that the public benefit requirement can be met in one of two ways:

(i) By providing religious activities which are available to the public. It is on this basis that a trust for the provision of church buildings will be of public benefit and also a trust for other religious activities such as the publication of literature or missionary work. In *Re Hetherington* (1989) it was held (following *Re Caus* (1934)) that a trust for the celebration of masses was charitable because 'the public celebration of a religious rite edifies and improves those who attend it'. The fact that the masses could be said in private was not a bar to charitable status as there was, in effect, one purpose, the saying of masses, capable of implementation in two different ways. One, public masses, is charitable, the other, private masses, is not. The court applied the principle that where a gift has a single purpose which could be performed by either charitable or non-charitable means, it should be construed as a gift to be performed by charitable means. However, in *Gilmour* v. *Coates* (1949) a gift to a community of strictly cloistered and enclosed nuns was not held charitable because the benefit conferred on the public by their prayers was, per Lord Simonds, 'manifestly not susceptible of proof'. In addition, the possibility that the public might have been edified by the nuns' example of self-denial was too vague and intangible. Yet it will be recalled that in *Re Watson* (1973) (above) works of no intrinsic religious value were held charitable, the element of public benefit presumably being satisfied on the basis that the books had been distributed. The contrast between the cases is strange.

(ii) By the presence among the public of persons who have been edified by attendance at a place of worship. In *Neville Estates* v. *Madden* (1962) a trust for the advancement of religion among members of the Catford Synagogue was held charitable on this basis even though the services at the synagogue were only open to those on its list of members. Had the services at the convent in *Gilmour* v. *Coats* (1949) been open to the public then that part of their activities might have been charitable, although even so the gift might have failed on the ground that their activities were not exclusively charitable.

A recent example of the operation of the public benefit requirement was the decision by the Charity Commission to refuse to grant charitable status to the Preston Down Trust, which runs meeting halls for the Exclusive Brethren in Torquay, Paignton and Newton Abbot, because the Commission was not satisfied that it had been established for the advancement of religion for public benefit. The Commission said that its decision took into account such matters as the nature of Christian religion embraced by the trust and the means through which this was promoted, including the public access to its services and the potential for its beneficial impact on the wider community. However, on hearing the evidence the Commission did register the Trust as a Charity.

This case has been seen by some as an attempt by the Charity Commission to use the notion of public benefit to advance a left-wing, secularist anti-religion agenda especially in the light of the rejection of the Commission's guidance on fee paying by independent schools – see above. The Charity Commission would make the point that as the Charities Acts 2006 and 2011 oblige it to issue guidance on what constitutes public benefit this inevitably brings the Commission into the public arena more than in the past.

Have a look too at Luxton and Evans (2011), who analyse two recent decisions of the Charity Commission on registration as a religious charity: *Re Gnostic Centre* (2009) where it was held that the trust was not charitable and *Re Druid Network* (2010) where it was held that it was.

REFLECTION

POLITICAL TRUSTS

CORNERSTONE

Political trusts

A trust where the main object is to achieve a political purpose is not charitable but where political activities, e.g. campaigning, are ancillary to the main activities of the trust and support them then they can be charitable. The leading case is *McGovern* v. *Attorney-General.*

Meaning of 'political purpose'

Slade J in *McGovern* v. *Attorney-General* (1982) said that it included trusts to:

(i)   further the interests of a particular political party;

(ii) to procure changes in the laws of either the United Kingdom or a foreign country;

(iii) to procure a reversal of government policy or of particular decisions of governmental authorities whether in the United Kingdom or in a foreign country.

However, the Charity Commission (in 'Speaking Out: Guidance on Campaigning and Political Activity by Charities (CC9)', March 2008) has explained that a charity can carry out political activity for a change in the law if it supports its own charitable purpose. In the same document the Charity Commission emphasised the key point that 'any charity can become involved in campaigning and in political activity which further or support its charitable purposes, unless its governing document prohibits it'.

APPLICATION

The Charity Commission has given three examples of possible political purposes:

Example one: An organisation set up to oppose a new runway at an airport applies for charity registration. The Charity Commission would reject the application as having a political purpose, as it would oppose the government's policy on airports.

Example two: An organisation set up to protect the environment applies for charity registration. The organisation carries out a range of activities, including some political activity aimed at securing a change in the government's policy on airports. The Charity Commission would accept the application if it was clear that securing a change in government policy was not the continuing and sole activity of the charity, but part of a wider range of activities aimed at furthering its charitable purposes.

Example three: An organisation which has been established to protect life and property by the prevention of all abortions applies for charity registration. Since the purpose can only be achieved through a change in law, the Charity Commission would reject the application as having a political purpose.

INTERSECTION......

Consider Article 10 of the European Convention on Human Rights which provides for freedom of expression. Could the restriction on the 'political activities' of charities be an infringement of the rights of organisations under Article 10?

Examples of possible political purposes

Furthering the interests of a particular political party

In *Re Hopkinson* (1949) a testator gave the residue of his estate to found an educational fund to advance adult education with particular reference to a programme of education put forward by the Labour Party. Vaisey J held that this gift was for political propaganda and thus not charitable. Similar decisions have been reached on trusts for the support of the Conservative Party (*Bonar Law Memorial Trust* v. *IRC* (1933)) and the Liberal Party (*Re Ogden* (1933)), although here the trust was upheld on other grounds.

Political activities by students' unions

A university or college students' union is a charitable body, as it is connected with the advancement of education. Accordingly a students' union must not use its funds for political purposes, as in *Baldry* v. *Feintuck* (1972) where the use of union funds to campaign for free school milk to be restored was held to be political. In *Webb* v. *O'Doherty* (1991) an injunction was granted to restrain a students' union from spending money in support of a campaign against the Gulf War. The court distinguished between campaigning by seeking to influence public opinion, which is not charitable, and mere discussion of political issues, which can be charitable.

Education and charitable purposes

If the trust is for the advancement of education, or some other charitable purpose, then there will be a valid charitable gift even though there may be some connection with political purposes. In *Re Koeppler's WT* (1986) a gift which was uncertain in its precise terms was construed as being for the purposes of the Wilton Park project which involved conferences on issues of current political debate but which did not involve the propagation of political opinions or any activities of a party political nature. Instead, the object of the project was a genuine attempt to find and disseminate the truth and accordingly the gift was held to be for the advancement of education.

> **Take note**
>
> The Transparency of Lobbying, Non-party Campaigning and Trade Union Administration Act 2014 will have an impact on any campaigning by charities.

Reasons why political purposes are not held to be charitable

As we have seen, there is a theoretically sharp dividing line between charitable and political activity and in addition political activity has a specific meaning. In fact, as we have seen, the boundary between charities and politics is difficult to draw where the charity engages in campaigning activities in support of its activities.

Could it be said that the traditional view that charities and politics should be separate reflects an outmoded view of charities as simply relieving need and ignores the role now played by charities in working with government agencies and thus inevitably being involved in the political arena?

In a letter to the *Daily Telegraph* (8 August 2013) Sir Stephen Bubb, the CEO of the Association of Chief Executives of Voluntary Organisations, pointed out the long history of political campaigning by charities from the presentation of a petition to Parliament in 1787 advocating the abolition of the slave trade to the establishment of societies for the prevention of cruelty to animals in the Victorian era.

It is worth noting that the High Court of Australia has recently held that there is no longer any prohibition in Australia on charities having political purposes (*Aid/Watch Incorporated* v. *Commissioner of Taxation* (2010)). The court specifically recognised the public benefit in charities campaigning for both changes in the law and in government policy.

THE OBJECTS OF THE TRUST MUST BE EXCLUSIVELY CHARITABLE

CORNERSTONE

The trust must be exclusively charitable

If the objects of the body are not exclusively charitable then it cannot meet the requirements for charitable status.

Take note

This point is often forgotten by students as it appears after the two long topics of charitable purposes and public benefit.

This is the third requirement of charitable status and is the one area of the law on charitable status to be unaffected by the Charities Act 2011.

In order to qualify as a charity the trust must be exclusively charitable so that a gift to it will inevitably be used for charitable purposes. Where there are two objects, one undoubtedly charitable, the other not necessarily so, then the trust will not be charitable. In *IRC* v. *Baddeley* (1955) (see above), where property was to be used 'for the promotion of the religious, social and physical well-being of persons', the inclusion of the word 'social' prevented the purposes from being charitable.

Where a gift is given for 'charitable and benevolent' purposes (*Re Best* (1904)) then the gift is charitable because charity is an essential qualification. But if the word 'or' is used instead of 'and' there is an alternative, and all of the funds could be used for non-charitable purposes. Thus in *Chichester Diocesan Fund and Board of Finance* v. *Simpson* (1944) the words 'charitable or benevolent' meant that the gift was not charitable. The point can be summed up by saying that 'and' in these cases means that the words are to be construed conjunctively whereas 'or' means that they are to be construed disjunctively.

Severance

Where trustees are obliged to apply part of the property for a charitable purpose and part for a non-charitable purpose then the court can sever the two parts and allow the charitable part to stand on its own. In *Salusbury* v. *Denton* (1857) a fund was to be used partly towards the foundation of a charity school and partly for the benefit of the testator's relatives. The court severed the two parts and, as the size of each part had not been specified, it was held, on the principle that 'equality is equity', that they would be divided equally. Severance would not, of course, be possible if the gift could, at the discretion of the trustees, be applied wholly for non-charitable purposes.

FAILURE OF CHARITABLE GIFTS

CORNERSTONE

Failure of charitable gifts

A charitable gift will fail if the body to which it was given has either ceased to exist or has never existed.

Introduction

A charitable gift may fail where the charity to which it was made has ceased to exist, or indeed has never existed. Failure of objects in the case of a private trust brings into operation a resulting trust for the settlor or his estate (see Chapter 4). However, where the gift is charitable it may be possible to apply the money for other objects *cy-près* (so near) to the original ones.

APPLICATION

Imagine that Sue has set up a trust fund for the benefit of three people but by the time of her death they have died. This is not a charitable trust as there is no public benefit and so the money in the fund will go on a resulting trust for Sue's estate.

Now imagine that Sue has set up another fund in her will for the benefit of a particular local hospice. However, by the time of her death this has ceased to exist. This gift would have been charitable under s. 3(1)(d) and so, although the actual gift has failed and cannot be carried out, the money can still be devoted to its charitable purposes by the doctrine of *cy-près*.

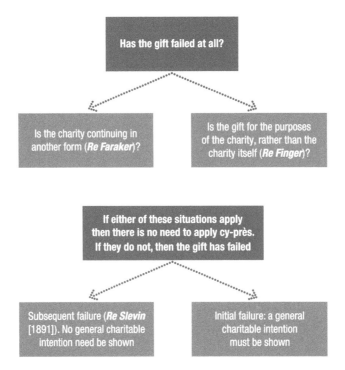

Figure 6.1 Summary of the position where there is a possible failure of a charitable gift

Situations where the courts have held that the gift has not failed at all

Continuation of the charity in another form

If the charity no longer exists as a separate entity but instead has been amalgamated with other charities, it may be possible to say that the particular charity to which the gift was made is continuing. In *Re Faraker* (1912) a testatrix bequeathed a legacy to 'Mrs Bailey's Charity, Rotherhithe', the object of which was to benefit poor widows. However, the charity had been amalgamated with others with the object of benefiting the poor in general of Rotherhithe. The court held that the amalgamated charities were entitled to the gift.

Gift for the purposes of an unincorporated association

An unincorporated association has no legal existence as such. This principle causes much difficulty in the case of non-charitable gifts (see Chapter 5). However, with charitable gifts the fact that the gift was to an unincorporated association can be a positive advantage because, as the gift could not have been to the association due to its lack of a legal existence, it must be instead for its purposes, and provided that these are still continuing the gift has not failed. The point was taken in *Re Finger's WT* (1972) where a testatrix left shares of her residuary estate to various charities, two of which had ceased to exist at the date of her death. One of these was an unincorporated association and as it was held that as the gift was for charitable purposes, and these purposes were still being carried on, a scheme would be ordered to give effect to the gift. The other charity was a corporation and so, as the gift was to the corporation itself and not for its purposes, the gift failed. However, it was possible to apply it *cy-près*.

Incorrect description of the institution

Provided that it is still possible to identify the institution the gift will not fail. In *Re Spence* (1978) the gift was to 'The Blind Home Keighley' instead of 'Keighley and District Home for the Blind', but the gift here failed on other grounds (see below).

Cy-près doctrine

CORNERSTONE

Cy-près doctrine

The *cy-près* doctrine enables gifts which have been made to charities but which have failed within the meaning of s. 62 of the Charities Act 2011 to be used for another charitable purpose *cy-près* (so near) to the original purpose provided that there was a general charitable intention.

Assuming that neither the *Re Faraker* (1912) nor the *Re Finger* (1972) solution is possible and so the gift has failed, *cy-près* application can be ordered. This doctrine enables the court (or the Charity Commissioners) to make a scheme to apply the gift for purposes as near as possible (*cy-près*) to the donor's original intention.

Cy-près application is possible provided that:

(a) the donor showed a general charitable intention;

(b) the gift failed within the meaning of s. 62 of the Charities Act 2011.

General charitable intention

Subsequent failure of the gift

The requirement of a general charitable intention need not be satisfied where the charity ceases to exist *after* the testator's death (a case of subsequent failure), because the property would already have vested in the recipient and so it can be applied *cy-près*. In *Re Slevin* (1891) money was left to an orphanage which existed at the testator's death but ceased to exist before the money was paid over. Cy-près application was ordered. In practice, the principle in *Re Slevin* will only be of use if the charity ceases to exist between the date of the testator's death and the time when his/her estate is to be distributed.

Initial failure of the gift

Most situations, however, concern initial failure of the gift, i.e. the institution was not in existence at the date of the testator's death. In such cases a general charitable intention must be found. In *Re Lysaght* (1966) Buckley J said that such an intention would exist where there was 'a paramount intention on the part of the donor to effect some charitable purpose', as distinct from a situation where 'the donor means his charitable intention to take effect but only if it can be carried into effect in a particular specified way'. This he called a particular (often called a specific) charitable intention.

(a) ***Gift is only for the purposes of a particular institution***. If that institution has ceased to exist before the testator's death then *cy-près* application is not possible because there is no general charitable intention. Thus, in *Kings* v. *Bultitude* (2010) a gift was left by will to the trustee of the

Ancient Catholic Church 'for the general purposes of the said Church'. This church had ceased to exist at the date of the testator's death. *Cy-près* application was not possible as there was an intention to benefit only that church and thus no general charitable intention.

(b) ***Gift is for a purpose represented by a particular institution***. In *Re Roberts* (1963) the gift to the Sheffield Boys' Home could be applied *cy-près* because the gift was not so connected with the Home as such that it ended when the Home did. Whether a case falls into this category or (a) above is a question of fact. In *Re Finger* (1972) (see above) the gift to the corporation, the National Council for Maternity and Child Welfare, was held to show a general charitable intention partly because the Council co-ordinated the activities of other bodies over a fairly wide field.

(c) ***Gift to an institution which has never existed***. In *Re Harwood* (1936) a gift to the Belfast Peace Society, which had never existed, was applied *cy-près* because the testator showed a general intention to benefit societies whose object was the promotion of peace. However, the mere fact that an institution has never existed is not always evidence of a general charitable intention and in *Re Koeppler's WT* (1986) *Re Harwood* was doubted on the ground that promotion of peace was political and not charitable.

(d) ***Gift to several institutions***. A gift to several charitable institutions with similar objects may show a general charitable intention so that if one of them either does not exist, or no longer exists, this gift may be applied *cy-près*; see Megarry V-C in *Re Spence* (1978) where he described this as 'charity by association'. However, where there are several charitable gifts together with a non-charitable gift which has failed, the inclusion of the non-charitable gift may negate the presumption of general charitable intention. In *Re Jenkins' Will Trusts* (1966) the testatrix bequeathed her residuary estate to six charitable institutions together with the British Union for the Abolition of Vivisection, which was not charitable. The court held that the mere inclusion of a non-charitable gift among charitable gifts did not imply that the non-charitable gift was intended to take effect as a charitable gift. In *Re Satterthwaite's Will Trusts* (1966) the testatrix left her residuary estate to a number of animal welfare organisations, which were charitable, an anti-vivisection society, which was not charitable, and also to the London Animal Hospital, which had never existed. It was held that this last gift could be applied *cy-près* as there was a general charitable intention. *Re Satterthwaite* was decided 12 days earlier than *Re Jenkins*, in which it was not cited and with which it is difficult to reconcile. A possible explanation is that the London Animal Hospital had never existed as a charity and so the principle in *Re Harwood* (1936) (see above) applied.

(e) ***Gift for purposes***. A gift for purposes rather than an institution can be applied *cy-près* if there is a general charitable intention. In *Biscoe* v. *Jackson* (1887) a gift to provide a soup kitchen and cottage hospital 'for the parish of Shoreditch' was held to show such an intention to provide for the sick and poor of the parish.

Removal of conditions

Where a particular condition attached to a trust is preventing the carrying out of the main purpose of the trust, the *cy-près* doctrine may be used to remove the condition on the ground that its existence makes the carrying out of the trust impossible. In *Re Lysaght* (1966) a gift to the Royal College of Surgeons (RCS) to hold on trust to found medical studentships contained a condition stating, inter alia, that the students should not be of the Jewish or Roman Catholic faith. The RCS refused to act as trustee unless this condition was removed, which it was.

A general charitable intention must, of course, also be found in these cases. In *Re Lysaght* (1966) it was held that the general charitable intention was the foundation of medical studentships.

Impossibility

This is dealt with in s. 62(1) of the Charities Act 2011 which sets out the occasions when property can be applied *cy-près*, provided of course that there is a general charitable intention:

(a) where the original purposes, in whole or in part –

    (i) have been as far as may be fulfilled, or

    (ii) cannot be carried out, or not according to the directions given and to the spirit of the gift, and the social and economic circumstances prevailing at the time of the proposed alteration of the original purposes.

In *Re Lepton's Charity* (1972) a gift was made by will in 1715 of land to be held on trust to pay out of the rents £3 a year to the minister of a chapel and the 'overplus of the profits' to the poor of the town. In 1715 the total income was £5 a year. The land had been sold and the resulting investments yielded £791 a year. The court held that the basic intention could no longer be carried out and so a scheme was ordered whereby the minister received £100 a year.

(b) where the original purposes provide a use for part only of the property available by virtue of the gift,

(c) where –

    (i) the property available by virtue of the gift, and

    (ii) other property applicable for similar purposes,

    can be more effectively used in conjunction, and to that end can suitably, regard being had to the appropriate considerations, be made applicable to common purposes,

(d) where the original purposes were laid down by reference to –

    (i) an area which then was but has since ceased to be a unit for some other purpose, or

    (ii) a class of persons or an area which has for any reason since ceased to be suitable, regard being had to the appropriate considerations, or to be practical in administering the gift,

In *Peggs and others* v *Lamb and others* (1993) the court applied this rule so as to enlarge a class of beneficiaries from the freemen and their widows of the Borough of Huntingdon to all the inhabitants of the Borough. It was still possible to ascertain the spirit of the gift because although there was no founding document, the spirit could be inferred.

(e) where the original purposes, in whole or in part, have, since they were laid down –

    (i) been adequately provided for by other means,

    (ii) ceased, as being useless or harmful to the community or for other reasons, to be in law charitable, or

    (iii) ceased in any other way to provide a suitable and effective method of using the property available by virtue of the gift, regard being had to the appropriate considerations.

Anonymous donors

Suppose that funds are raised in aid of a school which is threatened with closure. However, the campaign to save the school fails and a large amount of the campaign funds are unspent. Some of the donors can be traced and so their donations are returned to them. However, there were many anonymous donations made through, for example, collecting boxes. What is to happen to these?

Section 63(1) of the Charities Act 2011 provides that property given for specific charitable purposes which fail is applicable *cy-près* as if given for charitable purposes generally, if it belongs –

(a) to a donor who after –

(i) the prescribed advertisements and inquiries have been published and made, and

(ii) the prescribed period beginning with the publication of those advertisements has ended,

cannot be identified or cannot be found, or

(b) to a donor who has executed a disclaimer in the prescribed form of the right to have the property returned

Note the advantage of charitable status here and compare these detailed statutory provisions with the complex and unsatisfactory case law where there are anonymous donations to a non-charitable fund as in the *Gillingham Bus Disaster Fund* discussed in Chapter 11.

As a last thought on charities, it is interesting to reflect on the role of charities in the light of David Cameron's pledge to bring more charities into the public sector through his 'big society' initiative. In fact, *Guardian* research reveals the total number of registered charities operating in the UK fell by more than 1,600 in the coalition's first year. More than 8,000 charities have been removed from the official register, held by the Charity Commission, since May 2010, and only 6,400 new charities have been founded in their place.

Charity bosses fear the reduction in the total number of charities is a portent of a contraction in the sector, which is only just beginning to be felt as billions of pounds in statutory support are cut. The number of charities fell by more than 700 in March 2011 alone, just before the first round of grant reductions resulting from drastic local authority budget cuts. Bringing in charities to provide public services to 'tackle our most deep-rooted social problems' is a cornerstone of David Cameron's big society project, but charity leaders have warned cuts in charitable grants could kill off the proposals. 'The big society doesn't come for free,' said Emily Holzhausen, Director of Policy and Public Affairs at Carers UK.

A Charity Commission spokeswoman said the number of charities on the register generally remained constant each year. The commission has seen a 150% increase in the number of cases its mergers until has dealt with since 2009, driven in part by charities adapting to straitened economic circumstances.

KEY POINTS

- To be registered as a charity a body must satisfy three requirements: it must exist for charitable purposes as defined by the Charities Act 2011; there must be an element of public benefit; it must be exclusively charitable.

- Public benefit must be proved in all cases and regard must be had to the Charity Commissioners' Guidance on what constitutes public benefit.

- Trusts for political purposes cannot be charitable but a charity can engage in political activities if they are ancillary to their main (charitable) purposes.

- Where a gift to charity has failed within the meaning of s. 62 of the Charities Act 2011 then it may be possible to apply it *cy-près* – for purposes so near to the original charitable intention.

CORE CASES AND STATUTES

Case	About	Importance
Re Coulthurst	Was a trust charitable as being for the relief of poverty?	Evershed MR's remark that poverty does not mean destitution but can include persons who have to 'go short'.
Re Shaw	Gift in a will for research into a new phonetic alphabet was not charitable partly because one object was to persuade the public that a phonetic alphabet would be a good thing.	Propaganda, rather than education, will not be charitable.
Thornton v. *Howe* (1862)	A trust for the publication of the works of Joanna Southcote, who styled herself as the mother of the second Messiah, was charitable.	Charitable status on the ground of advancement of religion is accorded to sects which are small and the beliefs of which may be considered eccentric.
Attorney General's Reference v. *Charity Commission* (2012)	Requirement of public benefit.	It clarified the law by holding that public benefit is part of the nature of each charitable purpose.
Dingle v. *Turner* (1972)	Public benefit in trusts for the relief of poverty.	In trusts for the relief of poverty there is a requirement of public benefit but the line is drawn differently than on other cases.
Oppenheim v. *Tobacco Securities Trust Co. Ltd* (1951)	A trust to provide for the education of children of employees or former employees of a particular company held not to be charitable.	Requirement of public benefit in cases of charities for the advancement of education.

→

Case	About	Importance
Gilmour v. *Coats* (1949)	A gift to a community of enclosed nuns was not charitable because any benefit conferred on the public by their prayers was not capable of proof.	Requirement of public benefit in cases of charities for the advancement of religion.
McGovern v. *Attorney-General* (1981)	A trust was established by Amnesty International with various purposes, some of which were held political.	Political purposes are not charitable. The court in this case provided a list of purposes which would be political. The case also illustrates the point that to be charitable, a trust must be exclusively charitable.
Kings v. *Bultitude* (2010)	Gift to a particular church that had ceased to exist at the date of the testator's death.	Modern instance of where the *cy-près* doctrine cannot apply because of lack of a general charitable intention.

Statute	About	Importance
Charities Act 2011	Consolidates virtually all existing statutes on charities.	Now the first point of reference for anyone seeking information about the legal basis of charity law.
Charities Act 2006	Modernised charity law but its provisions are now in the Charities Act 2011.	This Act marked a watershed in charity law and so it is essential to know that it was this statute that actually made the major recent changes to charity law even though its provisions are now in the Charities Act 2011.

FURTHER READING

Chesterman, M. (1979) *Charities, Trusts and Social Welfare* (Weidenfeld and Nicolson).
As the title indicates, this sets the law of charities in its social context. It is still interesting, especially in view of the Charities Act 2011.

Cranmer, F. (2009) 'Religion and public benefit' 11 *Ecc. LJ* 203.
This article considers in detail the guidance on public benefit in advancement of religion issued by the Charity Commission. Look also at Iwobi (2009).

Dunn, A. (2008) 'Demanding service or servicing demand? Charities, regulation and the policy process' 71(2) *MLR* 247.
This article looks at the role of charities in promoting social reform and the increasing role of the state in promoting social welfare. It then looks at the rules which restrict the political activities of charities.

Garton, J. (2007) 'Justifying the cy-pres doctrine' 21(3) *Tru.LI* 134.
This is a really interesting account of the history of the doctrine and its present day role.

Hackney, J. (2008) 'Charities and public benefit' 124 *LQR* 347.
This is an essential article especially in view of the debate on the extent to which public benefit is required. Its main points are summarised in the text.

Iwobi, A. (2009) 'Out with the old, in with the new: religion, charitable status and the Charities Act 2006' 29 *LS* 619.

Luxton, P. and Evans, N. (2011) 'Cogent and cohesive? Two recent Charity Commission decisions on the advancement of religion' 75 *Conv.* 144.
This article analyses two recent decisions of the Charity Commission on the advancement of religion.

McInnes, M. (2008) 'Charity and sport: a Canadian perspective' 124 *LQR* 202.
This article looks at recent Canadian case law – this could give any answer on sport and charity law a good comparative perspective.

The *Preston Down Trust* case has been raised in Parliament.
See www.lawandreligionuk.com/2012/11/07/charitable-status-public-benefit-and-closed-congregations-update/

Warburton, J. (1997) 'Charities, members, accountability and control' 61 *Conv.* 372.
This is a very valuable article on some contemporary issues.

CHAPTER 7

Completely and incompletely constituted trusts

BLUEPRINT

Completely and incompletely constituted trusts

KEY QUESTIONS

LEGISLATION

- Law of Property Act 1925, s. 52(1)
- Contracts (Rights of Third Parties) Act 1999

CONTEXT

- Position of women in society: equity recognised marriage consideration to enable them to enforce pre-nuptial agreements.

CONCEPTS

- What is meant by constitution
- Methods of constitution
- Rules apply to gifts and trusts
- Cases where equity may perfect an imperfect gift

- Have cases e.g. *Pagarani* and *Pennington* relaxed the constitution rules? Is this justifiable?

- How is the trust property transferred to the trustees? What are the consequences if this does not happen?

CASES

- *Milroy* v. *Lord*
- *Jones* v. *Lock*
- *Re Rose*
- *Pennington* v. *Waine*
- *Re Ralli*
- *Cannon* v. *Hartley*
- *Re Kay*
- *Strong* v. *Bird*
- *Re Craven*

REFORM

- Abolition of the law on donatio mortis causa?

SPECIAL CHARACTERISTICS

- Contrast between rules of equity and common law in what constitutes consideration in contract and in the remedies they award

CRITICAL ISSUES

Setting the scene

You have been promised by your friend Pam that, to celebrate her 21st birthday, she will take you with her on a trip to Paris. You are naturally very excited about this but then Pam suddenly tells you that she has changed her mind and will not be going after all. Relations between you and Pam deteriorate as you not unnaturally feel that Pam should have kept her promise.

Let's change the scenario a bit. Pam has now told you that she intends to set up a trust fund with £50,000 which she has won on the lottery and that Sheila will be the trustee and that you will be one of the beneficiaries. Sheila confirms that this is true and Pam has told her that this is what she will do.

You then wait . . . and wait . . . and wait . . . and nothing happens. Once again Pam has not kept her word. Pam, as the settlor, has failed to constitute the trust as she has not transferred the £50,000 to Sheila. In a nutshell the situation is exactly the same as with the promised trip to Paris: Pam has not kept her word.

What, if anything, can you do about this? You could do nothing about the promised trip to Paris as there was clearly no contract between you and Pam. However, here the situation is different: we have a promise to create a trust and so we are in the province of equity.

Keep this basic point in mind throughout this chapter: Pam as settlor has not kept her promise as she has failed to constitute the trust. *She did not do what she promised to do.* Do you – and/or Sheila for that matter – have any remedies against her? Read on to find out the answer!

When you study this chapter you will find that there is some mixing of equitable and common law principles, for example, in the area of consideration, and also some classic equity, for example, the focus on unconscionability (see e.g. *Pennington* v. *Waine*) and the setting aside of statutory requirements in the interests of equitable principle as in the doctrine of *donatio mortis causa*.

INTRODUCTION

In Chapter 4 we looked at the need for certainty in the creation of the trust and the formal requirements needed to create a trust. Here we are concerned with what can be considered the third vital requirement: that the property to be held on trust is actually vested in the trustees.

WHAT DOES THE TERM 'COMPLETELY CONSTITUTED' MEAN?

A completely constituted trust is one where the trust property is actually vested in the trustee(s). It is not sufficient for a settlor merely to intend to create a trust.

The constitution of a trust has important consequences for all parties:

(a) The settlor cannot change her mind and reclaim the property.

(b) The trustees must hold the property in accordance with the terms of the trust.

(c) The beneficiaries can enforce the trust against the trustees (*Paul* v. *Paul* (1882)).

APPLICATION

Constitution of a trust is illustrated by the following example: Mary transfers Blackacre to Charles to hold on trust for Hubert. The trust is now constituted and so Charles cannot claim that Blackacre belongs to him. Charles is obliged to hold it on trust for Hubert and Hubert can enforce the trust against Charles.

WHEN IS A TRUST COMPLETELY CONSTITUTED?

CORNERSTONE

Methods of constitution

The fundamental rules for how a trust can be constituted were set out by Turner LJ in *Milroy* v. *Lord*. Note that this leads to two methods of constitution of a trust:

(a) the settlor has vested the legal title to the trust property in the trustee(s) (Method One); *or*

(b) the settlor has declared that he now holds the property as trustee (Method Two).

In *Milroy* v. *Lord* (1862) Turner LJ held that:

the settlor must have done everything which, according to the nature of the property comprised in the settlement, was necessary to be done in order to transfer the property and render the settlement binding upon him. He may, of course, do this by actually transferring the property to the persons for whom he intends to provide, and the provision will then be effectual, and it will be equally effectual if he transfers the property to a trustee for the purposes of the settlement, or declares that he himself holds it in trust for those purposes; . . . in order to render the settlement binding, one or other of these modes must, as I understand the law of this court, be resorted to, for there is no equity in this court to perfect an imperfect gift.

CORNERSTONE

Imperfect gift

The term 'imperfect gift' can cover two cases:

(a) Where a person promises an outright gift of property rather than promises to create a trust of it.

(b) Where a person promises to give property to others for them to hold as trustees.

→

The same principle will apply to imperfect gifts in situation (a) as will apply to what are incompletely constituted trusts in situation (b) because generally a trust is created by the settlor without consideration being promised by the beneficiaries. If so, the beneficiaries under a trust have also been promised a gift. Thus whether it is a straight gift as in (a) or a gift in the form of a trust as in (b) equity will not assist a person to obtain it unless any of the rules outlined in this chapter apply.

In the most recent case on this area, *Pennington* v. *Waine* (2002) (below), Arden LJ considered this whole area and pointed out that the general principles governing the constitution of trusts are, in fact, really an instance of equity following the law (e.g. Methods One and Two) and it is in the recognition of exceptions to these rather rigid rules that we can see the influence of equity. Her judgment is well worth reading as it casts light on what can be a dark area.

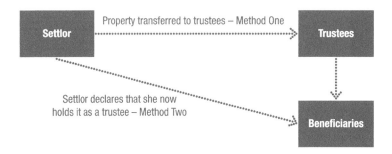

Figure 7.1 Property transferred to trustees

In addition, as Turner LJ said, the property can be actually transferred to those who are to benefit. In this situation there is an outright gift to them and not a trust. As we shall see, some of the principles in this chapter can apply to gifts as well as trusts (see below).

NOTE: We are only concerned here with *inter vivos* transfers because where the trust is created by will, it is constituted by the trust property vesting on the death of the testator in his personal representatives who are then under a duty to vest the property in trustees appointed by the testator.

Method One: transferring the trust property to trustees

CORNERSTONE

Methods of effecting the actual transfer of the property

The method by which trust property is to be transferred to trustees will depend on the type of property in question. One important point is that legal estates in land must be transferred by deed: s. 52(1) of the LPA 1925.

Accordingly:

(a) *Legal estates in land* must be transferred by deed (s. 52(1) of the LPA 1925) and, if title is registrable, then the requirements of the Land Registration Act 2002 must be observed.

(b) *A disposition of an equitable interest* must be in writing (s. 53(1)(c) of the LPA 1925).

(c) *Shares* must be transferred by the appropriate form of transfer followed by registration (see ss. 770–772 of the Companies Act 2006 and s.1 of the Stock Transfer Act 1963 as amended by the Stock Exchange (Completion of Bargains) Act 1976).

(d) *Copyright* must be transferred by writing (s. 90(3) of the Copyright, Designs and Patents Act 1988).

(e) *Bills of exchange* must be transferred by endorsement (s. 31 of the Bills of Exchange Act 1882 and see *Jones* v. *Lock* (1865) below).

(f) *Choses in possession* can be transferred either by:

  (i) delivery to the trustee, coupled with the intention to make a gift; *or*

  (ii) by a deed of gift – this will immediately vest the property in the trustee, even though delivery is later; *or*

  (iii) by contract.

Method Two: settlor declares that he holds the property as a trustee

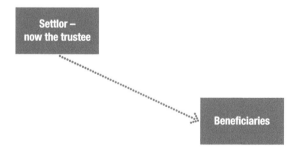

Figure 7.2 Settlor declares that he no longer holds the property as absolute owner but as trustee – Method Two

Take note

In this case there is no transfer of the legal ownership but what does change is the capacity in which the settlor holds the property. Previously he was the absolute and beneficial owner; now he holds as trustee. The clearest way in which this can happen is for the settlor to execute a declaration of trust that he now holds as trustee for particular beneficiaries.

The courts have, however, held a less formal declaration of trust to be effective as in *Paul* v. *Constance* (1977). Here Mr Constance and the claimant lived together, although they were not married. An account was opened in Mr Constance's name only because they would have been embarrassed by having a joint account in different names, and £950 awarded to Constance following an injury at work together with three small joint bingo winnings were paid into it. One withdrawal was made which was for their mutual benefit. At various times Constance said to the claimant: 'the money is as much yours as mine'.

The court held that these words, supported by the evidence of the transactions in the account, established that Constance intended to declare himself a trustee of the money in it for himself and the plaintiff jointly.

INTERSECTION

The case has been criticised on the ground that it is difficult to see an intention to create an express trust (see Chapter 4 here). Could it have been better construed as a gift by Constance to himself and Paul jointly? In addition, the case was argued on the basis that there was an express trust. Surely it would have been better considered as an implied or constructive trust?

CORNERSTONE

Jones v. Lock

Where a gift is imperfect because the donor has not complied with the requisite formalities the courts will not save it by holding that the donor has instead constituted himself trustee of the gift for the donee by making a declaration of trust. The starting point is *Jones* v. *Lock*.

Both these principles are illustrated by *Jones* v. *Lock* (1865). A father, on returning from a business trip, was scolded by his family for his failure to bring a present for his baby son. He therefore produced a cheque made out in his name for £900 and said 'Look you here, I give this to baby', and placed the cheque in the baby's hand. He then took the cheque back but apparently intended to see his solicitor to make provision for the baby. However, he died before he could do this.

The court held that:

(a) there was no gift to the baby because the cheque had not been endorsed (this is no longer necessary: s. 2 of the Cheques Act 1957);

(b) nor was there a declaration by Jones that he now held the cheque on trust for the baby. The court said that it would not impose the onerous duties of a trustee on a person unless it was clear that a declaration of trust was intended. Here the father's giving of the cheque to the baby was only symbolical of intention to make proper provision for him.

The baby therefore received nothing.

A similar decision that there was a lack of evidence that the settlor intended to declare himself a trustee was reached in *Richards* v. *Delbridge* (1874).

Where there is more than one trustee and the trust property has been vested in only one trustee

This point arose in *T Choithram International SA* v. *Pagarani* (2001) where the Privy Council, on appeal from the Caribbean Court of Appeal, held that the trust would be constituted. Mr Pagarani, in his last illness, executed a trust deed establishing a foundation which would act as an umbrella for four charities which he had established. Immediately after he had signed, he stated that all his wealth, including shares in a number of companies, would now belong to the trust. He himself was one of the trustees. He then told his accountant to transfer all his money to the trust but he failed to sign the necessary forms. Apparently he disliked signing these types of documents and had been told that it was not necessary. The companies in which he held shares acted in accordance with the deed by registering the trustees of the foundation as shareholders. After Pagarani died, his family claimed that he had not effectively transferred his wealth to the foundation, which accordingly belonged to them.

The Privy Council's decision that the trust was constituted rested on two points:

(a) Pagarani had made an effective declaration of trust. The context of the words clearly indicated a trust: he intended to give to the foundation and this body was a trust.

(b) Assuming that Pagarani had declared himself a trustee (Method Two above), did it matter that the trust property was not vested in the other trustees? The Privy Council held that it did not. Pagarani had executed a solemn declaration of trust and it would be unconscionable to allow him to resile (i.e. go back) from this promise.

Whilst the decision can be supported as an application of *Milroy* v. *Lord*, the more liberal view taken of the requirements for constitution, and the use of the notion of unconscionability, are in line with the approach in *Pennington* v. *Waine* (below) and may signal a more relaxed view of the constitution rules. One could say that the decision in *Pagarani* represents a kind of 'third way' between Methods One and Two of constitution of a trust.

REFLECTION

TWO SITUATIONS WHERE EQUITY RELAXES THE RULES ON CONSTITUTION OF A TRUST

(a) Settlor constituting a trust by doing all in his power to do so

CORNERSTONE

Principle in *Re Rose*

The leading case here is *Re Rose* although this decision must now be read subject to *Pennington* v. *Waine*.

Method One (see above) of completely constituting a trust, under which the settlor must transfer the trust property to the trustee, appears to be subject to an exception in certain cases where a trust has been held to be completely constituted when the settlor has done everything which it is in his power to do to transfer the property even though the transfer is not complete until some other person has done a particular act.

APPLICATION

Sally wishes to transfer shares in the Midland Optical Illusion Co. to her friend Sue. Sally executes the transfer and sends it off to the company. What more can she do? Nothing. However, the transfer may not take effect as the directors of the private company may refuse to register the transfer because the articles of a private company can give directors power to do this. Thus equity will require Sally to hold the shares on trust for Sue.

A typical example of such a clause in Articles of Association would be: 'The directors at any time in their absolute and uncontrolled discretion refuse to register any transfer of shares and shall not be bound to give any reason for such refusal.'

The decision in *Re Rose*

In *Re Rose* (1952) the directors of a private company did in fact register the transfer. The issue here was the time at which the transfer was complete. If this was when Rose executed the transfer then there would be no liability to estate duty because Rose died more than five years after the transfer. If the effective date was the date of registration by the directors then as Rose had died within five years of this, estate duty would be payable. The court held that the effective date was when Rose executed the transfer as by then he had done everything in his power to transfer the property. It should be noted, however, that this case did not deal with whether a *trust of shares* had been completely constituted but the principle in it has applied to this type of situation.

Implications of the decision in *Re Rose*

What is the position if the directors refuse to register? Evershed MR in *Re Rose* said that the settlor would hold as trustee for the beneficiaries. But this seems to conflict with Turner LJ's statement in *Milroy* v. *Lord* (1862) that if a gift 'is intended to take effect by transfer, the court will not hold the intended transfer to operate as a declaration of trust.' However, in *Re Rose* (1952), Evershed MR held that this principle only applied where the transfer was incomplete because of failure to comply with the appropriate formalities, as had indeed happened in *Milroy* v. *Lord* itself, where a transfer of bank shares was incomplete because the entry in the books of the bank, which was necessary to transfer the legal title, was never made. In the *Re Rose* situation, however, the problem lies not with the transferor but with some third party.

In *Re Fry* (1946) an intended transfer of shares fell through because the donor had not obtained Treasury consent to the transfer, although it had been applied for. The court held that as the donor had not done all in his power the gift remained imperfect. Yet it is difficult to distinguish this case from *Re Rose*. What could the donor do?

Applications of the *Re Rose* principle

The principle was applied to land registration in *Mascall* v. *Mascall* (1985). Here a gift of land by a father to his son was held to be complete when the father handed over the transfer and the land certificate to the son even though the son had not sent the documents to the Land Registry and had not therefore acquired title (s. 19 of the Land Registration Act 1925). It is assumed that the trust pending acquisition by the son here of title was constructive and so no written declaration of trust would be needed (s. 53(1)(b) and s. 53(2) of the LPA 1925).

> **Take note**
>
> Although the estate duty provisions dealt with in *Re Rose* no longer exist, the principle remains important because the Finance Act 1986 imposes an Inheritance Tax on gifts made within seven years of death. The tax is chargeable on death but it can also apply to some lifetime gifts.

> **Take note**
>
> It is not clear whether the principle in *Re Rose* applies whenever some act needs to be done by a third party, over which the settlor has no control, or whether it is restricted to certain types of property. Is there any reason why it should not apply to shares in public companies, given that the act of registration of a person as a shareholder is done by the company?

CORNERSTONE

Pennington v. *Waine*

Pennington v. *Waine* is an important modern application of the principle in *Re Rose*. In particular the judgment of Arden LJ widens the *Re Rose* principle and her judgment rests on the principle of unconscionability.

Another application of the *Re Rose* principle was in *Pennington* v. *Waine* (2002), which did, in fact, involve shares in a private company. It broke new ground as, unlike in *Re Rose* itself, the question involved the constitution of a trust. Mrs Crampton, a shareholder in a private company, told

Pennington, a partner in a firm who acted for the company, that she wished to transfer some of her shares to her nephew and she later signed a share transfer form to this effect and gave it to Pennington. He took no further action and the question was whether, on her death, the shares had been transferred to the nephew.

The Court of Appeal held that they had, although the reasoning in each of the two main judgments differs. Arden LJ upheld *Re Rose* but also held that the fact that there was clear evidence that Mrs Crampton intended an immediate gift of the shares amounted to an assignment of them to the nephew anyway. She held that on the facts it would be unconscionable to allow Mrs Crampton, in view of all that she had done to transfer the shares to the nephew, to then turn round and change her mind and say that they were not his. Clarke LJ's reasoning was more straightforward: there was in fact a perfect gift of the shares as actual delivery of the transfer form was not needed.

Pennington v. *Waine* is also interesting in that it had previously been thought that *Re Rose* itself could be explained on the basis that it was a taxation case and it would be wrong that liability to estate duty might depend on the tardiness of directors in registering a transfer. Now we have a decision which is not concerned with taxation and which upholds *Re Rose*. (There are several articles on this decision: see e.g. Doggett (2003) and Garton (2003).)

REFLECTION

In *Zeital* v. *Kaye* (2010), agents held shares in a company on trust for Zeital, who gave Stefka the transfer form relating to a share without adding her name as transferee. However, it was in his power, even though he only had an equitable interest in the shares, to procure the actual share certificate which she would require to be registered. He did not do this and so could not be said to have done all in his power to make Stefka the owner (see Griffiths 2010). It could be argued that this decision represents a return to a stricter approach than was the case in *Pennington* v. *Waine* and restores the position which was taken in *Re Rose*.

INTERSECTION

Check your knowledge of formality requirements and make sure that you are clear about the difference between:

(a) the formality requirements; and

(b) the constitution requirements (this chapter).

The point arose again in *Curtis* v. *Pulbrook* (2011), where a Mr Pulbrook attempted to transfer shares in a company, Farnham Royal Nurseries, to his daughter and his wife. He issued them with new share certificates, although he had no authority to do so, and they never received stock transfer forms. In these circumstances the court had no difficulty in holding that the *Re Rose* principle did not apply.

You could now reflect on the extent to which the rules on constitution set out in *Milroy* v. *Lord* at the start of this chapter have in fact been modified by the three decisions in *Re Rose*, *Choithram International SA* v. *Pagarani* and *Pennington* v. *Waine*.

Is a new rule on constitution developing?

INTERSECTION

Had the claim based on *Re Rose* succeeded the court would have set the transfers aside under s. 423(3) of the Insolvency Act 1986 as a transaction to defraud creditors. This was because the reason for the purported transfers of shares was Pulbrook's belief that he was going to be subject to a major claim arising out of his misuse of a bank account of a deceased party.

(b) Indirect constitution of a trust

CORNERSTONE

Indirect constitution of a trust

Suppose that the settlor fails to transfer the property directly to the intended trustee but it reaches him by a different, less direct, route. This principle is shown by *Re Ralli's Will Trusts* where the trust was constituted by the same person being trustee of two trusts.

Another instance of this principle is where the trustee becomes the settlor's executor (or possibly administrator).

In *Re Ralli's Will Trusts* (1964) a testator left his residuary estate on trust for his widow for life and then for his daughters, Helen and Irene. Helen had entered into a marriage settlement in which she covenanted to settle future property on volunteers. There was therefore an incompletely constituted trust. However, the trust was constituted by the accident that the claimant was the sole surviving trustee of both Helen's settlement and the testator's will. Accordingly her share of the residuary estate was vested in him, as both the testator's widow and Helen were dead.

The court held that the claimant held Helen's share on the trusts of the marriage settlement, and not for those entitled under the will. Buckley J said that the claimant 'is at law the owner of the fund and the means by which he became so have no effect upon the quality of his legal ownership'.

Figure 7.3 The effect of *Re Ralli*

REFLECTION

The basis of the decision in *Re Ralli* is not entirely clear. One argument is that it is an extension of the rule in *Strong* v. *Bird* (this is discussed below – and note especially the link with *Re Stewart*), but the other is that provided the trust property reaches the trustees equity is not concerned about the exact route.

Be that as it may, *Re Ralli* presents two main difficulties:

(i) Although Buckley J said that he was following the decision in *Strong* v. *Bird* (1874), this decision is based on the intention *of* the donor. Yet the principle in *Re Ralli* (1964) can operate independently of the donor's intention and, indeed, allow a gift to be perfected by mere chance.

(ii) In addition, reliance was placed on *Re James* (1935) (see below), which is of doubtful authority. The decision subjects a person in the position of the claimant here to competing claims of loyalties: to both those entitled to the property under Helen's marriage settlement and those entitled to it under the will as forming Helen's residuary estate. The court failed to give clear guidance on the position where someone in the claimant's position chooses to favour those entitled under the will.

INCOMPLETELY CONSTITUTED TRUSTS: WHAT IS AN INCOMPLETELY CONSTITUTED TRUST?

CORNERSTONE

What is meant by the term 'incompletely constituted'?

A trust is incompletely constituted when it has not been constituted by any of the above methods.

APPLICATION

Josephine is the owner of a house, 155 High Street Downstairs. She executes a declaration of trust under which Eileen is now to hold the house on trust for Anne. However, Josephine fails to convey the house to Eileen. In this case the trust is not constituted and the beneficiary, Anne, has no rights unless she gives consideration to Josephine. The reason is that 'equity will not assist a *volunteer*' (Lord Eldon in *Ellison* v. *Ellison* (1802)). If Anne does not provide consideration she is a volunteer.

REFLECTION

However, as Gardner (2011) points out, it is wrong to think of this as a general principle: equity, for example, assists volunteers to obtain injunctions although not specific performance. Even so, in this situation, it has chosen not to do so.

CONTRACTS (RIGHTS OF THIRD PARTIES) ACT 1999

CORNERSTONE

Contracts (Rights of Third Parties) Act 1999

The law in this area, already complex, now requires us to distinguish between the position where any covenant to settle property was made before the Contracts (Rights of Third Parties) Act came into force on 11 May 2000 and the position thereafter. The position will first be considered on the basis that the Act does not apply, and then on the basis that it does.

INTERSECTION

You will almost certainly have studied this Act before in your contract studies and now is a good time to revise your memory of it. Remember that it effected a relaxation in the doctrine of privity of contract so that in some cases third parties to a contract can sue on the contract. The question here now is the extent to which this Act applies to beneficiaries under trusts. They are likely to be third parties as the parties to the covenant to settle property will be the settlor and the trustee.

Contracts (Rights of Third Parties) Act 1999 does not apply

CORNERSTONE

Equity and common law positions

The contrast between equity and the common law is seen in these cases both in the different remedies which they grant and in their differing attitudes to what constitutes consideration.

(a) If the intended beneficiaries have given valuable consideration other than marriage consideration to the settlor they can sue either at common law for damages or in equity to compel the settlor to constitute the trust.

(b) If the intended beneficiaries are within marriage consideration they can sue in equity but not at common law.

(c) If the intended beneficiaries are parties to a deed of covenant with the settlor they may sue upon the covenant at common law and claim damages.

(d) If neither (a) nor (b) nor (c) applies, the intended beneficiaries have no remedies as they are volunteers, no assistance will be given by the common law nor by equity for 'there is no equity in this court to perfect an imperfect gift' (Turner LJ in *Milroy* v. *Lord* (1862)).

> **Take note**
>
> Note that once the trust has been completely constituted the above rules do not apply. The beneficiaries, whether volunteers or not, have full rights.

The following examples illustrate the rights of the beneficiary in three different situations.

APPLICATION

Sam promises Ted that he will transfer £20,000 to him to hold on trust for Bert, a volunteer. Sam fails to do so. The trust is incompletely constituted and as Bert is a volunteer he cannot either seek damages from Sam or sue in equity to compel Sam to transfer the £20,000 to Ted.

APPLICATION

Let us now assume that Sam has entered into a deed of covenant to which Bert is a party to transfer £20,000 to Ted on trust for Bert. Here, although Bert, as a volunteer, cannot sue in equity to compel Sam to constitute the trust, he can sue at common law for damages for breach of covenant.

APPLICATION

Assume now that in the above example Bert has provided consideration for Sam's promise. Again Bert can sue Sam to compel him to constitute the trust, although if the consideration is only marriage consideration then only equitable remedies will be available.

It will be seen from the above examples that:

(a) Equity recognises marriage consideration. The common law does not.

(b) The common law enforces promises made in a deed, without valuable consideration. Equity does not.

(c) The common law remedy is damages whereas equity can compel a transfer of property by the remedy of specific performance.

Consideration

Equity follows the common law rules on consideration and thus good consideration (such as natural love and affection) is not valuable. Nor is past consideration. (See *Re McArdle* (1951), which illustrates not only past consideration but also failure to constitute a trust.) Equity alone, however, recognises marriage consideration.

The doctrine of privity of contract (see e.g. *Tweddle* v. *Atkinson* (1861)) is recognised by equity as well as the common law but this has been affected by the Contracts (Rights of Third Parties) Act 1999, which is dealt with below.

> **Take note**
>
> The equitable notion of consideration is, in this context, wider than that of the common law.

CONTEXT

The fact that equity recognised marriage consideration as valid led to marriage settlements, of which an example is given below. These settlements took effect behind a trust. This may seem an old fashioned area but it does tell us something about both equity and the common law. The issue was the subservient status of women because until the Married Women's Property Act 1870 women were treated by the common law as having no right to own property. Instead their husbands were the owners of all the property and, as their guardians, were supposed to protect their wives' property.

Equity, however, tried to get round the rule that married women could own no property by allowing settlements to be made either on marriage or in contemplation of marriage. This meant that property could, on her marriage, be settled on the wife for her use so that she became a beneficiary under a trust with a trustee who was responsible to the Court of Chancery. If equity had not recognised marriage consideration as valid then the woman could not have enforced the settlement. As it was, although on marriage she no longer had any legal rights of ownership of property, she did have separate property rights in equity.

Marriage consideration

(a) In order for marriage consideration to be valuable, it must be contained in a settlement made either:

(i) before and in contemplation of marriage; *or*

(ii) after marriage but in pursuance of an ante-nuptial agreement. If it is not made in pursuance of such an agreement then the consideration (i.e. the marriage) is past. Therefore the issue of the marriage are volunteers. There may be other consideration between the husband and wife but under the doctrine of privity of contract, their issue will not be parties to this.

(b) Who is within marriage consideration?

  (i)   the husband, wife and issue of the marriage;

  (ii) more remote issue, e.g. grandchildren (*McDonald* v. *Scott* (1893)).

Illegitimate children, children by a former marriage, children by a possible second marriage or children to which one or both parties stands *in loco parentis* will only be within marriage consideration if their interests are so interwoven with those of the natural children of the marriage that it would be unjust that only the latter should benefit (see *A-G* v. *Jacobs-Smith* (1895)). Next-of-kin are certainly volunteers (see *Re Plumptre's Settlement* (1910) below).

The way in which marriage consideration works in the constitution of a trust is shown by the following example.

APPLICATION

Bob and Sue, on their engagement, covenant with the trustees of the marriage settlement that:

(a) Bob will transfer Blackacre to the trustees.

(b) Sue will transfer to the trustees any property she receives on the death of her father to be held on the following trusts:

  (i)   for Bob and Sue for their joint lives;

  (ii) remainder to any children of the marriage;

  (iii) in default of issue, to Bob's next-of-kin.

If Bob and Sue have issue, then as they are within marriage consideration they can apply to the court which can either order Sue to settle the property in accordance with the covenant (i.e. transfer it to the trustees) or, if appropriate, simply declare that the property is subject to the trusts of the settlement (as in *Pullan* v. *Koe* (1913)). If Bob and Sue do not have issue, then their next-of-kin (e.g. brother, sister, cousins) are volunteers and cannot take any action to compel Y to carry out her undertaking (see *Re Plumptre's Settlement*). If Bob has an illegitimate child, Sid, and Bob and Sue have issue, then Sid, in order to claim a share in the property which Sue undertook to transfer, must prove that his interests are interwoven with those of the issue of the marriage (*A-G* v. *Jacobs-Smith* (1895)). If Bob and Sue have no issue, Sid might be able to claim if Bob and Sue were *in loco parentis* to him.

Beneficiary a party to a deed of covenant

CORNERSTONE

Cannon v. *Hartley*

Where a person is a party to a deed of covenant then they can sue at common law to enforce it (*Cannon* v. *Hartley*).

If one of the intended beneficiaries is a party to a deed of covenant then although equity will give him no assistance he may still bring an action for damages at common law and the fact that he is a volunteer is immaterial. Equity will not intervene to frustrate such an action unless fraud or undue influence (see Chapter 2) is involved.

In *Cannon* v. *Hartley* (1949) a father covenanted on the breakdown of his marriage to make provision for a daughter by settling certain property on her. The daughter was a party to the deed and was thus held able to obtain damages at common law when the father refused to settle the property.

Action by trustees

⊕ CORNERSTONE

Re Kay

Where trustees seek to enforce an unconstituted trust then the court may direct them not to do so (*Re Kay*).

As *Cannon* v. *Hartley* (1949) illustrates, a party to a deed of covenant may sue on it at common law. If the beneficiaries are not volunteers, the trustees can sue on a covenant to which the trustees are parties and ensure that the property is settled (*Pullan* v. *Koe* (1913)).

What if the beneficiaries are volunteers? In many cases of incompletely constituted trusts, trustees have been parties to covenants (see *Re Plumptre's Settlement*). Can trustees then sue and obtain damages at common law even though the intended beneficiaries, as volunteers, cannot do so? Any damages could then be held in trust for the beneficiaries.

NOTE: An action in equity would of course not be possible (*Re Plumptre* (1910) above).

However, the courts have discouraged such actions. In *Re Pryce* (1917) there was a marriage settlement where the ultimate beneficiaries were the next-of-kin of the wife, who were volunteers. The husband had died and the wife did not want the covenant to be enforced. It was held that the trustees ought not to take steps to enforce the covenant by bringing an action for damages. In *Re Kay* (1939) the court went further by directing them not to do so. *Re Cook* (1965) is a slightly weaker authority as the decision was simply that the intended beneficiaries could not compel the trustees to take proceedings. It should be said, though, that these are all decisions at first instance and in none of them did the trustees actually attempt to sue: they simply sought the directions of the court on what they should do.

One problem, if trustees were allowed to sue, is the measure of damages which they would be awarded. It is the beneficiaries, not the trustees, who need to be compensated and on this basis damages awarded to the trustees should be nominal. Yet in *Re Cavendish Browne's Settlement Trust* (1916), trustees were awarded a sum which was equivalent to the value of the property which had been covenanted to settle. However, the case pre-dates *Re Pryce* (1917) and the other cases above.

If substantial damages are awarded, then for whom should they be held? One argument is that instead of being held for the beneficiaries they should be held on a resulting trust for the settlor because as the settlor has not yet fully constituted the trust he considers the trustee as holding on a resulting trust for him meanwhile.

The Contracts (Rights of Third Parties) Act 1999 does apply

This Act was, as is well known, passed to reduce the effect of the doctrine of privity of contract, which prevented a third party from enforcing a contract. The object of the Act is to allow a third party to enforce it when that contract was made for his benefit. Section 1 provides that a third party may, in his own right, enforce a term of a contract if that contract expressly provides that he may, or if the term purports to confer a benefit on him. This will not, however, apply if it appears on a proper construction of the contract that it was not intended that the third party should benefit. The third party must be identified by name in the contract, or as a member of a class, or as answering a particular description, but need not be in existence when the contract is made. Finally, and most importantly for our purposes, it is clear from s. 7(3) that the word 'contract' includes both simple contracts and also special contracts, i.e. those entered into by deed. Thus, it will apply where there is a covenant to settle.

If the third party does have a right of action, then he may have any remedy which would be available had he been a party to the contract and was bringing an action for breach. Thus, both common law and equitable remedies may be claimed. There is doubt as to whether a third party could obtain specific performance as he is a volunteer and in *Cannon* v. *Hartley* a volunteer who was a party to a deed was unable to do so. However, why should a third party claiming under the Act be in a better position than an actual *party* to a deed? The probability is, therefore, that a third party cannot obtain specific performance.

Leaving this issue aside, the Act changes the position as in *Re Pryce*, where, it will be recalled, the next-of-kin were unable to compel the trustees to bring an action for damages. Under the Contracts (Rights of Third Parties) Act the next-of-kin would be able in their own right to sue for damages provided that the conditions in the Act are satisfied. If a trustee does sue and obtains damages on behalf of the beneficiaries, then, if those beneficiaries also sue under this Act, s. 5 provides that the court will reduce the damages awarded to them to take into account the sum already awarded to the trustees.

EXCEPTIONS TO THE RULE THAT EQUITY WILL NOT PERFECT AN IMPERFECT GIFT

CORNERSTONE

Cases where equity may perfect an imperfect gift

There are three cases where equity may perfect an imperfect gift: where the rule in *Strong* v. *Bird* applies; where there is a *donatio mortis causa*, and proprietary estoppel.

The rule in *Strong* v. *Bird* (1874)

The rule states that if an incomplete gift is made during the donor's lifetime and the donor has appointed the donee his executor, then the vesting of the property in the donee completes the gift.

The rule in *Strong* v. *Bird* may be said to rest upon the donor's intention, unlike that in *Re Ralli* (1964) (see above) and also upon convenience because, as the whole of the estate has vested in the donee as executor, there would be no point in the donee suing himself (see Walton J in *Re Gonin* (1979)).

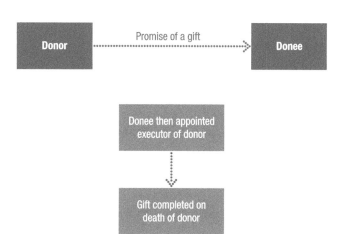

Figure 7.4 Application of the rule in *Strong* v. *Bird*

In *Strong* v. *Bird* X borrowed £1,100 from Y, his stepmother, who lived in his house, and who paid £212 10s a quarter for board. It was agreed that the debt should be paid off by X reducing Y's rent by £100 a quarter until the debt was repaid. This happened for two quarters but Y then generously said that in future she would pay the full rent, which she did until her death. X was her executor and it was held that this appointment of X extinguished the remainder of the debt which X owed to Y.

Common law and equitable rules in this area

The common law regarded the appointment of a debtor as executor as extinguishing the debt because it assumed that the creditor, by making the appointment, intended this to be so. Equity took a different view: it required the debtor to account to the estate for the debt so that the money was available to pay off creditors or be available for the beneficiaries. The significance of *Strong* v. *Bird* was that here equity followed the common law and allowed the appointment of the debtor to extinguish the debt. The reason for this was the stepmother's continuing intention to release the debt.

However, equity struck out on its own in *Re Stewart* (1908) when the rule in *Strong* v. *Bird* was extended from cases of forgiveness of debts to those where there has been an incomplete transfer of property to a person who is also appointed executor under the will of the transferee. The effect is that the transfer may now be valid. It is here that the rule is one of equity alone. The deceased handed his wife an envelope containing a letter from his brokers saying that notes had been bought together with a bought note (i.e. evidence of the purchase). The envelope did not, however, contain the actual notes and so there was an incomplete transfer. The wife was one of the executors and it was held that she was entitled to the bonds.

Conditions for the rule to apply

(a) The rule will apply even though there are other executors, because the entire legal estate vests in each executor (*Re Stewart* (1908)).

(b) In *Re James* (1935) the rule was extended to administrators. The difficulty is that this decision makes the perfection of a gift rest upon the mere fortuitous chance that the donee was appointed **administrator** and has nothing to do with the donor's intention. In *Strong* v. *Bird* (1874) itself the rule was said to apply only to an executor and in *Re Gonin* (see below) Walton J would only have followed *Re James* with the greatest reluctance. As *Re James* is a decision at first instance the point remains open in the higher courts.

(c) The donor must intend to make an immediate *inter vivos* gift. An intention to make a testamentary gift is not enough (*Re Stewart* (1908)).

(d) There must be a *continuing* intention to make the gift. In *Re Gonin* (1979) a mother wished to leave her house to her daughter but thought that she could not do so because the daughter was illegitimate. Instead she wrote a cheque for £33,000 in the daughter's favour which was found after her death. The cheque could not be cashed as the mother's death terminated the bank's authority to pay it but the daughter, as administratrix, claimed the house under the rule in *Strong* v. *Bird*. The court held that even if the rule applied to administratrices, there was no continuing intention on the mother's part that the daughter should have the house. Instead, the giving of the cheque indicated that she should have the money instead.

The requirement of a continuing intention will likewise not be met if the donor, having intended to give property to X, later gives or lends it to Y (*Re Freeland* (1952)) or, indeed, once again treats the property as his (*Re Wale* (1956)). In neither case will X's appointment as executor or administrator perfect the gift.

See Kodilinye (1982) for a survey of the rule in *Strong* v. *Bird*.

> ### Take note
>
> Do remember that you only need to consider if there was a valid *donatio* if the required formalities for transfer of the property were not observed. If they were, there is a valid gift anyway. It is arguable that the Singapore High Court in *Koh Cheong Heng* v. *Ho Yee Fong* (2011) (see below) failed to appreciate this point. Purely because a person makes a gift when in contemplation of death does not necessarily mean that there is a case of a *donatio*.

Donatio mortis causa (gifts in contemplation of death)

This doctrine allows gifts which satisfy certain requirements to be made informally on death without satisfying the requirements of the Wills Act.

Figure 7.5 How a DMC operates

The relationship between a will and a *donatio* (DMC) is shown by the following example:

John has left his car by will to Jack. On his deathbed John gives it to Alice under a valid DMC. The car does not belong to Alice until John's death but immediately on John's death the car does belong to Alice and so it does not form part of John's estate which is left by will. Accordingly Alice gets the car and not Jack.

CORNERSTONE

Re Craven's Estate

In *Re Craven's Estate* (1937) Farwell J laid down three conditions for an effective *donatio*, to which a fourth must be added: that the property is capable of passing by *donatio*. In practice, one would consider the fourth condition first of all. Note in particular *Sen* v. *Headley* where it was held that there can be a *donatio* of land.

The conditions for a valid *donatio mortis causa*

(a) There must be a clear intention to make a gift which will automatically be complete on death. This is often expressed briefly by saying that the gift must not be absolute but only conditional on death.

However, the fact that the gift is conditional on death need not be expressly stated but may be inferred from the circumstances (*Re Lillingston* (1952)). Thus in *Northcott* v. *Public Trustee* (1955) the donor handed over her Post Office Savings Bank Book to her aunt and said 'I want you to have it now'. At the time she was dangerously ill and indeed she died the next day. It was held that there was a valid *donatio*, despite the use of the word 'now', which, by itself, indicated an absolute gift.

The gift may be revoked should the donor recover. If the gift is revoked, then the donee holds the gift as trustee for the donor. A gift will also be revoked by the donor recovering dominion over it (*Bunn* v. *Markham* (1816)) or by the donee predeceasing the donor (*Tate* v. *Hilbert* (1793)) but not where the donor takes the property back for safe custody (*Re Hawkins* (1924)).

(b) The gift must be made 'in contemplation of the conceived approach of death' (Lord Eldon in *Duffield* v. *Elwes* (1827)).

The words 'conceived approach of death' mean that death is contemplated as an actual possibility in the relatively near future. Therefore the donor must have been doing more than merely contemplating the fact that he is not immortal but, on the other hand, he need not be *in extremis* or in his last illness. What seems to be required is that the donor should believe his death to be impending for some reason (Farwell J in *Re Craven's Estate* (1937)). However, in *Thompson* v. *Mechan* (1958) death from the ordinary risks of air travel was held to be insufficient. If this requirement is satisfied then it is immaterial that death occurs from some other cause. In *Wilkes* v. *Allington* (1931) the donor was suffering from incurable cancer but in fact died in an even shorter time from pneumonia. A gift made was held valid.

(c) The donor must part with dominion over the subject matter of the gift.

This is the vital feature of a *donatio*; the law will not accept mere words: there must be some act of handing over the goods or, where this is not possible, some other delivery such as the keys to a car (*Woodard* v. *Woodard* (1991) – below). In older cases it was often said that 'dominion' over the goods must be transferred but this concept was never clearly explained and now in *Sen* v. *Headley* (1991) Nourse LJ helpfully said that the test was whether the 'ability to control' had been transferred. This covers not only keys to a car but also the keys to a box where the deeds of house are kept (*Sen* v. *Headley* – below). However, as Borkowski (1999) points out, it would be better to use the word 'right to control'.

The case law can be divided as follows:

- *Chattels.* The donor must hand over the chattel itself or the means of obtaining control of it, such as the key to the box where it is. On the other hand, in *Re Craven's Estate* (1937) Farwell J said that this would not be sufficient if the donor retained a duplicate key; nor will it be enough if the donor parts with the box but not the key to it (*Re Johnson* (1905)). In *Woodard* v. *Woodard* (1991) the deceased, having already allowed his son to use his car and given him the keys, said to him on his deathbed in hospital, 'You can keep the keys, I won't be driving it [the car] any more'. It was held that this was a valid *donatio*. The parting with the keys was enough and there was no need to have parted with the car's log book as this is not a document of title. The fact that the deceased may have had a second set of keys at home was irrelevant because he could not use them unless he made a miraculous recovery which would, in any case, revoke the gift, and it did not matter either that the son was already in possession of the car as a **bailee**.

- *Choses in action.* As physical delivery is not possible the donor must part with a document which would have to be produced in any action on the chose, even though the document does not pass the legal ownership. (If it does, the gift is perfect and there is no need to worry about whether there is an effective *donatio*.) Instances of where a particular document has been held to be sufficient are: a bank deposit pass-book; a Post Office Savings Bank Book (both in *Birch* v. *Treasury Solicitor* (1951)); National Savings Certificates (*Darlow* v. *Sparks* (1938)); and a building society pass-book (*Griffiths* v. *The Abbey National BS* (1947)).

(d) The property must be capable of passing by *donatio*.

For various reasons, certain types of property have been held to be incapable of passing by *donatio*. The main instances are:

- *The donor's own cheque or promissory note.* The reason for the exclusion of cheques is that the donor's death terminates the bank's authority to pay on it (*Re Beaumont* (1902)). A holder for value may sue, but in this case there will, by definition, have been a contract and the rules on *donatio* will be inapplicable. A possible exception to this rule is where a cheque is paid immediately after death before the banker has been told of the death and closed the account (*Tate* v. *Hilbert* (1793)). In this case there would be a *donatio* of the money represented by the cheque and not of the cheque itself. A promissory note is only a gratuitous promise to pay. There seems, however, no reason why a cheque drawn on another's account, but negotiated to the donor, cannot be the subject of a valid *donatio*.

- *Stocks and shares.* In *Re Weston* (1902) the court held that a certificate of building society shares could not be the subject of a valid *donatio* and in *Moore* v. *Moore* (1874) the same principle was applied to railway stock. This latter decision was based on *Ward* v. *Turner* (1752), which appeared to decide that South Sea Annuities could not be the subject of a valid *donatio* although it is probable that the decision turned upon the manner of the transfer and so *Moore*

v. *Moore* is of doubtful authority. In *Staniland* v. *Willott* (1852) shares in a public company were held to be capable of being the subject of a valid *donatio*. There seems to be no authority on shares in private companies. This particular area is in need of clarification: there seems no good reason why a certificate of building society shares cannot be the subject of a valid *donatio* (*Re Weston* above) and yet a building society passbook can be (*Griffiths* v. *The Abbey National BS* above).

If there has been a complete transfer of the subject matter of the *donatio*, such as the handing over of a chattel, then the *donatio* will be complete on death. If some further action is necessary to complete the transfer, as where a bank deposit book has been handed over, then prior to the completion of formalities the personal representatives of the donor will hold the legal title on trust for the donee.

REFLECTION

Can land be the subject of a valid *donatio*?

In *Sen* v. *Headley* (1991) the Court of Appeal held that land can be the subject of a valid *donatio* and that in such a case the land will be held on a constructive trust for the donee pending the actual transfer. The deceased had lived with the plaintiff as man and wife for some years and on his deathbed he managed to put the keys to his house into the plaintiff's handbag and later said: 'The house is yours, Margaret. You have the keys. They are in your bag. The deeds are in the steel box.' The court held that as all the other requirements for a valid *donatio* were satisfied, there was a valid *donatio* of the house. Parting with dominion over the deeds could amount, in principle, to parting with dominion over the land itself and here this was so, especially as there was no practical possibility of the deceased ever returning home. It was possible for land to pass by *donatio* because on a *donatio* a constructive trust arose.

INTERSECTION

Lord Eldon in *Duffield* v. *Elwes* (1827) had recognised that such a constructive trust could arise by operation of law and thus the formalities requirements of what is now s. 53(1)(b) of the LPA 1925 do not apply because a constructive trust of land can arise without the need for written evidence (s. 53(2) of the LPA 1925). A close parallel can be observed here with secret trusts (see Chapter 8), which also take effect under a constructive trust and which are also ways of making a transfer without complying with the formalities prescribed for the making of wills.

What would have been the position though if the land had been registered? Would the handing over of the Land Certificate have been sufficient? In *Koh Cheong Heng* v. *Ho Yee Fong* (2011) the Singapore High Court held that there could be a *donatio* of registered land. However, it is difficult to understand this decision as there seems no need for a *donatio*. In England there is now no longer a Land Certificate to hand over and so how could condition (c) above be satisfied?

REFLECTION

Proving a *donatio*

There are no clear rules of evidence as to how a *donatio* must be proved. This might seem surprising given that there is the obvious temptation on the part of an unscrupulous person who is present at the bedside of a dying person to allege that a *donatio* was made to them. The courts do look very carefully at the evidence but there have been cases (e.g. *Sen* v. *Headley*) where the court accepted the uncorroborated evidence of the donee that there had been a *donatio* to them.

The future of *donatio mortis causa*

The future of *donatio mortis causa*

Nourse LJ in *Sen* v. *Headley* observed: 'Let it be agreed that the doctrine [of *donatio mortis causa*] is anomalous'. Moreover, he later said: 'Every such gift [by *donatio*] is a circumvention of the Wills Act 1837'. Here are the issues in a nutshell: the doctrine of *donatio* is undoubtedly anomalous and, moreover, it operates in direct contradiction to a statutory provision. This latter point has never bothered equity much and indeed the same objection could be made to the doctrine of secret and half secret trusts (Chapter 8). It has been suggested that the doctrine could be confined to property below a certain value. However, the fixing of an arbitrary upper limit seems wrong in principle and a better idea could be to have a presumption against a *donatio* unless it could be shown that the donor had no reasonable alternative means of disposing of the gift.

REFLECTION

Many people try to dispose of property by a *donatio*. The painter J.W.M. Turner (1775–1851) tried unsuccessfully to dispose of Austrian bonds which were found, after his death, in a box. The bonds were in packets, one of which was endorsed: 'The first five numbers of the Austrian bonds belong to and are Hannah Darby's property.' Turner had signed this and Hannah Darby, who had been Turner's housekeeper, had the key to the box. However, the gift failed as there had been no delivery of the bonds. The case was reported as *Trimmer* v. *Danby* (1856).

Turner's paintings remain famous, especially through their depictions of battling elements such as 'Frosty Morning' (1813) and 'The Burning of the Houses of Parliament' (1835).

CONTEXT

Proprietary estoppel

APPLICATION

Bob owns a piece of land and says to Jake 'You can have it as a market garden'. Jake takes over the land and develops it as a market garden but the land is never conveyed to him. Bob later attempts to turn Jake out.

Here the gift is imperfect because of the lack of a conveyance but the injustice of allowing a person in X's position to rely on this may be remedied by the doctrine of proprietary estoppel.

INTERSECTION..

See Chapter 9 for details of proprietary estoppel.

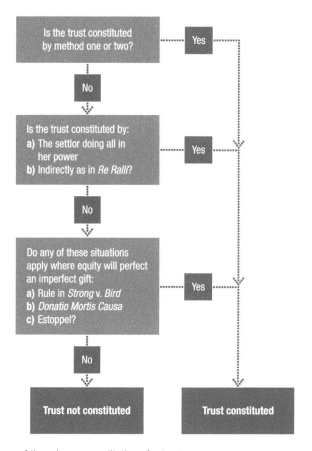

Figure 7.6 Summary of the rules on constitution of a trust

KEY POINTS

- There are two methods of constituting a trust: Method One: Transfer of trust property by settlor to trustee(s); Method Two: Settlor declares himself a trustee.
- A trust may, in some cases, be constituted by the settlor doing all in his power to transfer the property.
- Where the trust is not constituted the beneficiaries cannot enforce it unless they have promised consideration or are parties to a deed of covenant.
- Equity recognises marriage consideration; the common law does not.
- A trust may be constituted indirectly (*Re Ralli*).
- There are three cases where equity will perfect an imperfect gift: rule in *Strong* v. *Bird*; *donatio mortis causa*; and proprietary estoppel.

CORE CASES AND STATUTES

Case	About	Importance
Milroy v. *Lord* (1862)	Constitution of a trust.	Sets out basic rules on constitution.
Jones v. *Lock* (1865)	Method Two of constitution.	No constitution as no declaration of trust.
Re Rose (1952)	Constitution by the settlor doing all in their power.	Relaxation of strict rules on constitution set out in *Milroy* v. *Lord* but only in specific situations.
Pennington v. *Waine* (2002)	Principle in *Re Rose* (above).	Emphasis on unconscionability as the basis for the application of the principle.
Re Ralli's Will Trusts (1964)	Indirect constitution of a trust.	Another example of a relaxation of the strict rules on constitution.
Pullan v. *Koe* (1913)	Enforcement of a trust by those within marriage consideration.	What is meant by 'marriage consideration'.
Cannon v. *Hartley* (1949)	Position where a beneficiary is a party to a deed of covenant.	Beneficiary as a party to the deed may be able to obtain damages for its breach.
Re Kay (1939)	Can a trustee sue on behalf of beneficiaries to seek to enforce a covenant to settle property and so constitute a trust?	The courts directed the trustees not to do so.
Strong v. *Bird* (1874)	Exception to the rule that equity will not perfect an imperfect gift.	Where the donor has made an incomplete gift then appointment of the donee as executor can perfect it.
Sen v. *Headley* (1991)	*Donatio mortis causa* of land.	This is possible.

Statute	About	Importance
Section 52(1) of the Law of Property Act 1925	Legal estates in land must be transferred by deed.	Where land is the property of an express trust then this method must be used to transfer the property to the trustees.
Contracts (Rights of Third Parties) Act 1999	Rights of beneficiaries under a trust.	Beneficiaries may be able to compel constitution of a trust or seek damages for a failure by the settlor to do so.

FURTHER READING

Borkowski, A. (1999) *Deathbed Gifts* (Blackstone Press).
Contains a summary of every significant case on this area as well as being a fascinating account of this branch of the law.

Doggett, S. (2003) 'Explaining *Re Rose*; the search goes on' 62 *CLJ* 263.
Looks at recent cases in this area, especially *Pennington* v. *Waine*.

Gardner, S. (2011) *An Introduction to the Law of Trusts*, 3rd ed. (Oxford University Press).
Chapter 4 has some useful ideas on this area, especially on the policy considerations.

Garton, J. (2003) 'The role of the trust mechanism in the rule in *Re Rose*' 67 *Conv*. 364.
Another look at recent cases here.

Griffiths, G. (2010) 'Doing everything necessary: a recent manifestation of an ongoing issue' 4 *Conv*. 321.
This is a comment on the recent decision in *Zeital* v. *Kaye*.

Halliwell, M. (2003) 'Perfecting imperfect gifts and trusts: have we reached the end of the Chancellor's foot?' 67 *Conv*. 192.
Yet another look at the recent cases here.

Kodilinye, G. (1982) 'A fresh look at the rule in *Strong* v. *Bird*' *Conv*. 14.
A useful account of the origin and development of this rule.

CHAPTER 8

Creating the trust: secret and half secret trusts; mutual wills

BLUEPRINT

Creating the trust: secret and half secret trusts; mutual wills

LEGISLATION

- Wills Act 1837
- Law of Property Act 1925, s. 53(1)(b)

CONTEXT

- Why should I want to keep the contents of a trust that I have set up secret?

CONCEPTS

- Secret and half secret trusts
- Mutual wills
- Example of how equity works 'to prevent a statute being used as an engine of frand'

- Is there a place for secret and/or half secret trusts at all?

- How and why can what is in a will be altered by a trust?

CASES

- *Ottaway* v. *Norman*
- *Re Stead*
- *Re Keen*
- *Goodchild* v. *Goodchild*

REFORM

- Simplify the rule in *Re Stead* and have the same rules for secret and half secret trusts.

SPECIAL CHARACTERISTICS

- Different rules on communication of secret and half secret trusts
- Secret and half secret trusts avoiding the formalities required by the Wills Act
- Relationship between secret and half secret trusts and wills

CRITICAL ISSUES

Setting the scene

Did you know that, once a will has been admitted to probate, then it is a public document and anyone can see it? The procedure is to complete and send Form PA1S, known as an Application for a Probate Search, to the Leeds Probate Registry.

Why is this information relevant to a chapter on trusts and testamentary formalities though? Take this situation. John is married with a wife, Anne, but unknown to Anne John also has a mistress, Fifi. John wishes to leave Fifi £10,000 in his will but knowing that Anne will be able to see the will he does not want his liaison with Fifi to be discovered, even after his death. So he finds a trustworthy friend, Sue, lets her into his secret, and asks her if she will agree to be left £10,000 in his will but only on condition that she agrees to hold it on trust for Fifi. Sue agrees.

The result is that when John dies a gift of £10,000 to Sue appears in his will but there is no mention of Fifi. The trust under which Sue holds the £10,000 for Fifi is a secret trust in the sense that it does not appear on the will. It may not be literally secret at all; for example, John may have told many people of it (but not, one assumes, his wife!).

This is only one reason why a trust may be secret from the will and we will see others as we go through this chapter, but, from the cases, it does seem to be a fairly common reason. First, however, as wills form the background to much of this chapter, we need to be clear about what a will is.

INTRODUCTION: AN OUTLINE OF THE LAW OF WILLS

The theme of this chapter is trusts and wills. As we saw in the above situation, secret and half secret trusts operate against the background of wills and later in this chapter we will look at mutual wills, which involve the imposition of a trust.

However, wills are important throughout trusts law because, as we saw in Chapter 4, many trusts are created by will. This means that terms such as 'residuary legatee' keep popping up and so this chapter begins with some basic information on what a will is and the law of wills.

CORNERSTONE

Wills Act 1837

The formal requirements for the execution of wills are contained in the Wills Act 1837.

Here, to start with, is a specimen will. The notes at the side explain what certain terms and clauses mean.

This is the last will and testament of me **John Smith** of 25 Barset Street Barset whereby **I revoke** all previous wills and declare this to be my last will.

John Smith is the **testator** (females used to be referred to as the testatrix but now it is common for them both to be called testators). The basic rule is that an earlier will is revoked by a later one but it is best to make this clear by a **revocation clause**, as here.

I **bequeath** the sum of **£10,000** to my godson James.

Bequeath is the technical term for leaving personal property by will although today one often just says 'leave'. A bequest of money, as here, is a pecuniary bequest. It is common to use the term **legacy** rather than bequest. The person who receives the legacy is the **legatee**.

I **devise** my freehold house 25 Barset Street Barset to my sister Margaret Baxter of 38 Downstairs Road Barset.

Devise is the technical term for leaving real property (freehold land) by will, although again 'leave' is perfectly acceptable.

I bequeath all my property not otherwise disposed of by this my will to the League of Friends of Sick Cats (Reg. Charity No: 1234567).

This is a gift of **residue** which leaves property not otherwise disposed of by the will. You will have come across it in Chapter 4 where, for example, there is a lack of certainty of objects and so the gift goes to the residuary legatee. It is worthwhile checking that an organisation which is to receive property is either a company or a registered charity because, as noted in Chapter 3 and discussed in more detail in Chapter 5, gifts to other bodies may not be valid.

I appoint my sister Margaret Baxter and my brother in law Harold Baxter both of 38 Downstairs Road Barset to be executors of this my will.

An **executor** may also be a trustee. An executor can be a beneficiary under the will.

As witness my hand this . . . day of . . . 20 . . .

Strangely there is no actual requirement for wills to be dated but it is of course very sound practice to do this as if a testator has left more than one will we need to know which came last.

Signed by the testator JOHN SMITH in our presence and then by us in his.

This is the attestation clause where the witnesses sign below the testator. A minimum of two witnesses is required. Section 15 of the Wills Act 1837 (as amended) provides that a witness cannot take a benefit under a will which either the witness or his/her spouse or civil partner attested. However, where there are more than two witnesses then the signature of the witness who is a beneficiary is ignored.

Checklist:

Terms used in the law of wills

You may find it helpful to refer to this in the course of your studies.

CODICIL: A document that amends a previously executed will. It can be used where, for example, an executor dies and is replaced by another. A codicil must be executed with the same formalities as a will.

EXECUTOR: Person(s) appointed to administer a will.

PROBATE: Grant of probate authorises the executor(s) to deal with the estate.

ADMINISTRATOR: Person(s) appointed by the court to administer an estate where there is an intestacy. They correspond to executors where there is a will. The major difference is that an executor derives her powers from the will but an administrator derives her powers from the court.

ESTATE: Property owned by a person on death.

INTESTACY: Where a person dies without leaving a valid will.

LEGACY: Gift under a will.

LEGATEE: Person who receives a gift under a will.

PERSONAL REPRESENTATIVES: Executors and administrators are both classed as personal representatives (PRs). The fundamental distinction is that the function of a PR is to wind up the estate but a trustee's function is to hold property on trust. However, there is a considerable overlap.

RESIDUARY LEGACY: Gift by will of any property not specifically disposed of by the will.

RESIDUARY LEGATEE: Person who receives a residuary legacy.

LAPSE: Where a gift fails because the beneficiary predeceases the testator. There is an exception to this rule in s. 33 of the Wills Act 1837 which applies where property is left to issue (i.e. children, grandchildren etc.). If they predecease the testator then the gift goes to their issue. An example of lapse is where the beneficiary has witnessed the will. Here the gift to that beneficiary lapses unless there are two other witnesses.

SECRET AND HALF SECRET TRUSTS

CORNERSTONE

Secret and half secret trusts

Secret and half secret trusts are ways in which property can be left on death without all or some of the details of who it is left to and the amount appearing on the will. The effect is that they can allow a testator to supplement and, in effect, change the wording of his or her will.

A secret trust arises where a will (or other document) states that property is left to a beneficiary as an absolute gift but in fact the testator (or donor if it is not in a will) has agreed with the beneficiary that the beneficiary is to hold the property as a trustee. Therefore there is no mention in the will or other document of a trust.

APPLICATION

The above example given in 'Setting the scene' was a secret trust.

REQUIREMENTS FOR THE VALIDITY OF A SECRET TRUST

CORNERSTONE

Ottaway v. Norman

In *Ottaway* v. *Norman* (1972) Brightman J held that the following requirements must be proved:

(a) The **intention** of the testator to subject the primary donee (i.e. the intended trustee) to an obligation in favour of the secondary donee (i.e. the intended beneficiary). In *Kasperbauer* v. *Griffith* (2000) Peter Gibson J emphasised that all three certainties must be satisfied.

(b) **Communication** of that intention to the primary donee.

(c) **Acceptance** of the obligation by the primary donee either expressly or by acquiescence.

The three requirements in detail

The intention of the testator

The principle here is the same as with any form of trust: there must be certainty of intention although the actual word 'trust' is not needed.

APPLICATION

Ted says to his friend Peter: 'I am going to leave you £5,000 in my will and I very much hope that you will consider the needs of my children.' This may look like a secret trust but in fact Ted has not shown any intention to create a trust and so is it likely that Peter can treat the £5,000 as an absolute gift.

INTERSECTION

Look back to Chapter 4 and revise your knowledge of the three certainties as you will need this information in this chapter.

Communication of the testator's intention

The fact that he is to hold the property on trust, and the details of the trust, must be communicated to the legatee before the testator's death (*Wallgrave* v. *Tebbs* (1855)). It does not matter whether communication is before or after the will and it can be made through the testator's authorised agent (*Moss* v. *Cooper* (1861)). If the existence of the trust is not communicated to the intended trustee until after the testator's death then he will take beneficially, as happened in *Wallgrave* v. *Tebbs* (1855), unless he had accepted the position of a trustee, in which case it would be fraudulent for him to take beneficially, and he will hold on a resulting trust for the testator's estate.

What is the position where the existence but not the detail of the trust is communicated before the testator's death? In *Re Boyes* (1884) it was held that the legatee held on a resulting trust for the testator's estate. However, it appears that the secret trust can be enforced if the legatee is not actually told its details *before* the testator's death but is told where to find them *after* his death, for example, by the testator giving him a sealed envelope with the details. In *Re Keen* (1937) Lord Wright drew an analogy with the case of a ship 'which sails under sealed orders', and is therefore 'sailing under orders though the exact terms are not ascertained by the captain till later'. However, *Re Keen* did not in the end turn on this precise point which can still, to some degree, be considered open.

Position where the testator intends to impose a secret trust on more than one person, but does not communicate the trust to all persons

CORNERSTONE

Re Stead

Re Stead lays down the rules for deciding on the validity of communication of a secret or half secret trust where the details are communicated to some but not all the trustees.

In *Re Stead* (1900) Farwell J distinguished between where a gift is made to joint tenants and to tenants in common. He held that:

(i) If the gift is made to tenants in common then any secret trust imposed will only be binding on those to whom it is communicated. The rest take beneficially.

(ii) If the gift is made to joint tenants and the secret trust is communicated and accepted by some joint tenants before the will is made then all are bound. If, however, the communication and acceptance take place after the will but before the testator's death then only those joint tenants to whom the trust was communicated and accepted are bound. The others take beneficially. This is what happened in *Re Stead* (1900).

APPLICATION

Graham leaves property by will to Tim and Tom in equal shares and tells Tim (but not Tom) that both Tim and Tom are to hold in trust for Kate. Tim and Tom are tenants in common because the words 'in equal shares' are words of severance (*Payne* v. *Webb* (1874)). Thus Tim is bound by the trust but Tom is not.

APPLICATION

Graham leaves property by will to Tim and Tom and again tells Tim, but not Tom, that Tim and Tom are to hold the property on trust for Kate. Tim and Tom are joint tenants because there are no words of severance. Thus whether Tom is bound depends on whether Graham communicated the secret trust in favour of Kate to Tim before he made his will. If he did, then Tom is bound. If he did not, Tom is not bound and takes beneficially.

Figure 8.1 The rules in *Re Stead* on communication of a secret trust where there is more than one trustee

These rules in *Re Stead* (1900) do not seem to rest on any clear principle and Perrins (1972) has persuasively argued that the decision is not supported by the cases upon which Farwell J relied. Instead, the correct rule is that enunciated in *Huguenin* v. *Baseley* (1807) that 'no man may profit by the fault of another'. The question to be asked is whether the gift (as in the above example) to Tom was **induced** by Tim's promise that both he and Tom would hold the property in trust for Kate. The practical significance of this, according to Perrins (1972), is that if the secret trust is communicated to and accepted by Tim **after the will is made** then it will become very difficult to show that the gift to Tom (and Tim) in the will already made was induced by Tim's subsequent promise. Thus Tom is likely to take beneficially.

REFLECTION

Position where the trust is communicated but a later addition or alteration to it is not

In *Re Colin Cooper* (1939) a testator communicated a secret trust in respect of £5,000 which he had left to trustees but failed to tell them of a later codicil increasing the sum to £10,000. The extra £5,000 was held to go on a resulting trust for the testator's estate. Greene MR observed that it might have been different had the later codicil stipulated a lesser sum or if there had been a trifling difference. In each case the trustees would probably be bound by the sum in the codicil.

Where the secret trustee predeceases the testator the position is probably is as stated in *Re Maddock* (1902), where Cozens-Hardy LJ said *obiter* that the trust would fail because the existence of the trust depends on the personal obligation imposed on the trustee. The same may apply if the trustee disclaims.

Acceptance of the trust

In *Wallgrave* v. *Tebbs* (1855) it was held that the testator could accept the trust if he either 'expressly promises, or by silence implies, that he will carry the testator's intention into effect'.

REQUIREMENTS FOR THE VALIDITY OF A HALF SECRET TRUST

A half secret trust arises where a will or other document states that property is left to a beneficiary not as an absolute gift as with secret trusts, but on trust. However, it does not state what the terms of the trust are. Instead the terms of the trust are agreed between the trustee and the beneficiary. Thus the will mentions the existence but not the terms of the trust.

.... **APPLICATION**

Take the example in 'Setting the scene' and suppose that John had actually put in the will 'I leave £10,000 to Sue on trust'. It is the use of the words 'on trust' which distinguishes a half secret trust from a secret trust.

You will probably have realised that if John uses a half secret trust then this is much less satisfactory than a secret trust as he immediately invites questions about why he is doing this whereas the secret trust gave nothing away. So why bother with a half secret trust at all? There are also other problems with the recognition of half secret trusts and there is an argument that they should not be upheld, as we shall see.

CORNERSTONE

Rules on communication of half secret trusts – *Re Keen*

The rules on the testator's intention and on acceptance of the trust which apply to secret trusts (see above) also apply to half secret trusts. However, the rules on communication differ. The leading case is *Re Keen* where unfortunately the exact ratio is not entirely clear.

Communication of a half secret trust

Here the position is different from that in secret trusts and, to make matters worse, the law here is confused.

There are three possible rules:

Rule 1. Communication must be in accordance with the terms of the will so that if the will says 'on trusts the details of which **have been** communicated by me' then a communication **after** the will would be invalid.

Rule 2. The will itself must not refer to the possibility of a future communication.

Rule 3. Communication must, irrespective of what the terms of the will are, occur before or at the time of the making of the will.

Thus, if Rule 1 applies, communication can be before or after the will, provided that it is in accordance with the terms of the will, whereas, if Rule 2 applies, communication must be at or before the making of the will and in addition the will itself must not allow for the possibility of a later communication. Thus, even if communication was before the will, if Rule 2 applied it would not be valid if the will itself allowed for the possibility of communication after the will.

In *Johnson* v. *Ball* (1851) the will referred to a letter which had been signed containing trusts and yet in fact communication was after the will. It was held that, in accordance with Rule 1, communication was invalid as being inconsistent with the terms of the will. In *Blackwell* v. *Blackwell* (1929) the trusts had been communicated before the will and the will itself referred to a previous communication by the use of the words 'indicated by me to them'. Thus on Rules 1, 2 and 3 above, communication was valid. The main source of confusion is *Re Keen* (1937). A testator gave £10,000 to trustees to hold on trust and to be 'disposed of by them among such person, persons or charities as may be notified by me to them . . . during my lifetime'. One of the trustees had previously been given a sealed envelope containing the name of the beneficiary, which he did not open until after the testator's death, although he was aware that it contained the beneficiary's name. The Court of Appeal held that, had the rules on communication been complied with in other ways, the fact that the envelope was not opened until after the testator's death would not have made communication of the trust invalid. However, communication was invalid and Wright MR gave the following reasons for this:

(a) The words 'to be notified by me' indicated a future communication and this was invalid because the testator would be giving himself power to make dispositions after he had made his will which were informal rather than by a duly attested codicil. (This was an application of Rule 2 above.)

(b) The actual communication was before the will and was thus inconsistent with its terms which indicated a future communication (application of Rule 1 above).

Re Spence (1949) and *Re Bateman's WT* (1970) are both useful illustrations of the rules on communication of half secret trusts.

It is often said that the correct rule is Rule 3, that communication must be at or before the making of the will, although none of the cases were decided on this point alone. The true rule is still an open question in the House of Lords and possibly in the Court of Appeal also in view of the uncertainty of the precise ratio of *Re Keen* (1937). Rule 3 itself rests on an observation in *Blackwell* v. *Blackwell* (1929) by Viscount Sumner who said that 'A testator cannot reserve to himself a power of making future unwitnessed dispositions by merely naming a trustee and leaving the purposes of the trust to be supplied afterwards'. This was, however, *obiter* because, as we saw above, communication here was before the will. There was *dicta* to the same effect by Parker V-C in *Johnson* v. *Ball* (1851).

Rule 3 seems to depend on the probate doctrine of incorporation by reference under which a testator can incorporate a document into his will that has not been duly executed. This is, however, subject to the requirement that the document must already be in existence at the date of the will and also be referred to in the will as being already in existence (in *The Goods of Smart* (1902)).

> **Take note**
>
> The problem is that both Rules 1 and 2 are concerned with the relationship between the communication of the trust and the terms of the will. The justification which Wright MR gave for Rule 1, which was that the testator should not give himself a power to make future unwitnessed dispositions, is questionable in view of the clear rule that secret trusts operate *dehors* the will.

It is difficult to see why the rules for secret and half secret trusts should be different and one reason in favour of having the same rule is that, as a will can be revoked at any time until death and thus does not take effect until then, why should any other document, such as one containing details of a secret or half secret trust, be subject to rules which insist that validity is to be decided at an earlier date?

On the assumption, which represents the majority view today, that the correct rule is Rule 3, then the communication requirements for a valid secret and half secret trust can be summarised as shown in Figure 8.2.

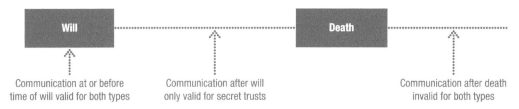

Figure 8.2 Different rules on communication of secret and half secret trusts

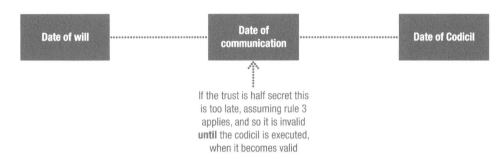

Figure 8.3 Effect of a later codicil on the time of communication

<table>
</table>

> ### Take note
>
> A codicil to a will, in the absence of any contrary intention on the part of the testator, has the effect of republishing that will. Accordingly the date of the will is now the date of the codicil with the result that, at the date of the codicil, the testator will have made a new will together with the alterations in the codicil (*Re Champion* (1893)).

If a testator executes a will where there is a half secret trust and subsequently communicates the details of that trust to the trustee, then communication may be invalid as being after the will. If, however, that testator executed a codicil to his will then communication would automatically have now been made before the will and so communication would be valid. There is no rational principle here and it is suggested that this is another reason for applying the same rules on communication of a secret trust to half secret trusts also.

BASIS ON WHICH EQUITY ENFORCES SECRET AND HALF SECRET TRUSTS

(a) Prevention of fraud

This appears to have been the original justification. The courts felt that, if they were to allow devices such as these, which disregarded statutory provisions, a compelling reason was needed which could only be found in the need to prevent fraud. Lord Westbury in *McCormick* v. *Grogan* (1869) said: 'the jurisdiction which is involved here is founded altogether on personal fraud'.

APPLICATION

Jane leaves £50,000 absolutely by will to Teresa but tells Teresa that Teresa is to hold it as trustee for Richard. If Teresa is able to disregard Jane's wishes because Jane has not complied with the formalities in the Wills Act and keep the £50,000 herself then Teresa is using a statute as an 'engine of fraud', i.e. to enable her to commit a fraud.

INTERSECTION

The principle that a statute must not be used as an 'engine of fraud' so that a failure to comply with a statute allows a fraud to be committed is one of the main reasons why equity developed the idea of the constructive trust. Chapter 9 gives further detail on this and on constructive trusts generally.

(b) Valid declaration of *inter vivos* trust

The modern view is that secret and half secret trusts are enforced simply because the testator validly declared an *inter vivos* trust and on the testator's death this trust became completely constituted by the property vesting in the trustee. Their essence is therefore the acceptance by the legatee of a personal obligation. This theory does account for not imposing a resulting trust because the effect of this would usually be that the testator's family received the property which, if the testator had intended to benefit a mistress or an illegitimate child, would run counter to the obligations imposed on the legatee.

(c) Remedial constructive trust

In the New Zealand case of *Brown* v. *Pourau* (1995) Hammond J held that the old fraud theory should no longer be used as a justification for secret trusts. Instead it should be based on the remedial constructive trust with the result that the legatee will hold the property on a remedial constructive trust to give effect to the (secret) trust placed on him.

(d) Estoppel

It has been argued by Brown and Pawlowski (2004) that where it is the testator (as opposed to the secret trustee) who seeks to go back on his promise to benefit the secret beneficiary then the correct basis for preventing this is the doctrine of estoppel.

INTERSECTION

The remedial constructive trust and estoppel are considered in Chapter 9.

The whole basis on which secret trusts are enforced has most recently been examined by Critchley (1999), who concludes that the fraud theory is still a possible justification for their enforcement but only if certain conditions are met.

Why are secret and half secret trusts used?

(a) A will is a public document and a testator may not wish a particular bequest to be known. An obvious example is a bequest to a mistress of whose existence his family was unaware.

(b) In the case of a secret trust the testator, having made his will, can then alter its terms at any time before his death simply by communicating with the trustee. This advantage does not apply to half secret trusts (see *Re Keen* (1937) below).

SECRET AND HALF SECRET TRUSTS AND THE FORMALITIES REQUIRED FOR THE MAKING OF WILLS

CORNERSTONE

Avoiding the formalities in the Wills Act

The effect of a secret or half secret trust is to avoid the formalities required by the Wills Act 1837.

The effect of these trusts is to enable a testator to avoid the formalities required by the Wills Act 1837 (as amended by s. 17 of the Administration of Justice Act 1982). An instruction to a trustee of a secret or half secret trust can, on the other hand, be oral or, even if it is in writing, there is no need to comply with the requirements of the Wills Act. Thus in *Re Young* (1951) the beneficiary under a half secret trust had witnessed the will in which the existence of the trust was declared. The rule that a witness to a will cannot normally take a legacy (Wills Act 1837, s. 15) was held not to apply here because the beneficiary did not take by virtue of the gift in the will but by virtue of the half secret trust. The result would of course have been the same had the trust been secret. This point is often expressed by saying that secret and half secret trusts take effect '*dehors*' (outside) the will.

Attestation of a will by a trustee of a half secret trust should not affect the validity of the legacy and therefore of the trust because he is not a beneficiary on the face of the will (*Cresswell* v. *Cresswell* (1868)). However, a trustee of a fully secret trust does take beneficially on the face of the will and the position where he attests is uncertain. The principle in *Re Young* (1951) may apply so that the legacy and therefore the trust are saved or it may be held that the legacy is ineffective and so the trust fails through lack of subject matter.

In *Re Gardner (No. 2)* (1923) one of the beneficiaries under a secret trust predeceased the testatrix but it was held that the share of the deceased beneficiary did not lapse but passed to her personal representative. However, had the gift been made by will her share would have lapsed and fallen into residue.

Although this decision clearly illustrates the point that secret and half secret trusts operate '*dehors* the will' it has been doubted in most of the leading textbooks and may well be wrong. Romer J explained his decision on the basis that the beneficiary acquired an interest as soon as the trustee had accepted the secret trust, but this conflicts with the principle that a beneficiary acquires no interest under a trust until it has been completely constituted (see *Milroy* v. *Lord* (1862) and Chapter 7). It is impossible to reconcile these two propositions and thus it is doubtful if *Re Gardner* would be followed.

REFLECTION

SECRET AND HALF SECRET TRUSTS IN SITUATIONS OTHER THAN WILLS

(a) Intestacy

Although the case law is concerned with secret trusts arising under wills, there is no reason why they cannot arise under intestacy.

APPLICATION

Amanda says to her sister, Dawn: 'I am thinking of making a will but I really haven't the time or money to see a solicitor about it. As you are my only relative you will get everything on my death but I want you to hold my property on trust for the following friends of mine, each of whom is to have an equal share.' Amanda then tells Dawn the names of the friends who are to benefit. Dawn agrees to this. On Amanda's death her estate will vest in Dawn as administrator.

There seems no reason why a secret trust should not arise in these circumstances (see *Sellack* v. *Harris* (1708)).

(b) On an *inter vivos* transfer of property

Can a secret or a half secret trust arise on an *inter vivos* transfer of property? There is no reason why this should not be so. One example is *Gold* v. *Hill* (1999) where the doctrine of secret trusts was applied to a nomination under which the deceased nominated Gold to receive benefits payable on his death under an insurance policy.

Standard of proof required

In *Re Snowden* (1979) Megarry V-C indicated that there were two possible standards of proof required to establish the existence of a secret or half secret trust:

(i) If fraud is alleged then a high standard is required. In *McCormick* v. *Grogan* (1869) Lord Westbury had referred to the need 'to show clearly and most distinctly' that the intended trustee acted *in malo anima* (in bad faith).

(ii) If there is no fraud then the standard is the ordinary civil standard of proof required to establish the existence of a trust, i.e. a balance of probabilities.

OTHER RULES APPLICABLE ONLY TO HALF SECRET TRUSTS

(a) The trustee cannot take beneficially if the intended trust fails. Unlike secret trusts (see *Wallgrave* v. *Tebbs* (1855) above) the trustee of a half secret trust cannot take beneficially if the trust fails because of lack of compliance with the communication requirements. As he has been named as trustee he will hold on a resulting trust for the testator's estate. An interesting but as yet unresolved issue is the position where he is himself the residuary legatee.

APPLICATION

Jack by will leaves £10,000 to Arnold 'for the purposes which I shall communicate to him'. On Jack's death a letter is found from him to Arnold telling him to hold the £10,000 for various charities. The trust will fail as it was not communicated to Arnold under the rules set out above. Thus Arnold will hold the £10,000 on a resulting trust for Jack's estate and so Jack's residuary legatee will inherit. If there is no residuary legatee then it will go to those entitled on Jack's intestacy. What if there is a residuary legatee but that person is Arnold? If he can inherit this gives him an incentive to say that he did not receive the letter!

(b) Where the trustee under a half secret trust predeceases the testator the probability is that the trust will not fail (*Re Smirthwaite's Trusts* (1871)), the basis of this rule probably being the maxim that a trust does not fail for want of a trustee. The trustee's personal representatives would then become trustees.

QUESTIONS APPLICABLE TO BOTH SECRET AND HALF SECRET TRUSTS

(a) Can the trustee take beneficially under the trust?

(i) The will may make it clear that the trust does not apply to the whole of the legacy and that therefore a person is a trustee of only part and a legatee of another part. It may be, however, that the legacy is conditional on the person performing his obligations as a trustee (see *Irvine* v. *Sullivan* (1869)).

(ii) The will may not refer to a beneficial gift to the trustee, who may however seek to prove such a gift by reference to extrinsic evidence. In *Re Rees' Will Trusts* (1950) the court refused to allow evidence to be admitted that the trustees were intended, after certain payments had been made, to hold any surplus for themselves. In *Re Tyler's Fund Trusts* (1967), while finding on the facts that no beneficial gift was intended in this case, Pennycuick J confessed that he found difficulty with *Re Rees* and it seems that in principle extrinsic evidence is admissible unless it is clear from the will that the *whole property* is to be held on trust, as in *Re Rees*.

(b) Are secret and half secret trusts express or constructive?

CORNERSTONE

Section 53(1)(b) of the LPA 1925

If s. 53(1)(b) of the LPA 1925 applies then a secret or half secret trust of land will require written evidence.

If these trusts are express, then do the requirements of s. 53(1)(b) of the LPA 1925 apply so that written evidence is required? If they are constructive, then such evidence is not required (s. 53(2) of the LPA 1925).

If the rationale of these trusts is the prevention of fraud then it follows that they are constructive. However, as they are created by the express declaration of the trustee, they may also be express although presumably not subject to the requirements of the Wills Act. In the New Zealand case of *Brown* v. *Pourau* (1995) (see above) it was held that these are constructive trusts.

> Now that we have looked at the law on secret and half secret trusts we should put this in context by looking at some research by Rowena Meager (2003) on how they actually arise in practice and when they arise. Her article is based on a postal survey in 2001 of solicitors specialising in wills and probate. The article quotes a number of statistics of which perhaps the most notable is that 35% of respondents had clients who had asked them about what the article calls 'a secret testamentary bequest'. Thus the argument that this topic is not of any practical value is clearly wrong. The article lists a number of reasons why these trusts are made, one striking example being where a secret trust was advocated 'to make a gift for the benefit of a handicapped child on state-funded support so as not to break the personal asset threshold'. This brings us back to the fundamental question: should secret trusts be allowed as the element of secrecy can allow a beneficiary to profit in a way which would not be possible were the gift made publicly. Is this right?

CONTEXT

MUTUAL WILLS

Mutual wills

Mutual wills exist where two people, having mutually agreed that the same person(s) should inherit their property after they are both dead, make separate wills, usually in which they leave property to each other but which has the essential characteristic that there is a gift to the same agreed beneficiary. However, the doctrine only applies where the wills are indeed mutual (*Goodchild* v. *Goodchild*).

In practice those who have agreed to make mutual wills have been married or are civil partners but this is not a requirement (*Walpole* v. *Orford* (1797)).

Each party's will is often in similar terms but there seems no reason why this should always be so.

A husband, George, and his wife, Mary, agree that George will make a will in which he will leave his estate to Mary for life with remainder to their children, Tim and Tom. They also agree that Mary will make a will in identical terms so that if she dies first her estate will be left to George for life with remainder to Tim and Tom.

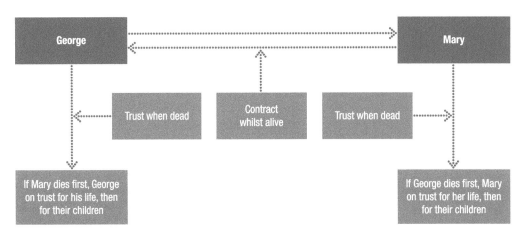

Figure 8.4 Property left to each other

In *Re Dale* (1993) Morritt J held that the doctrine of mutual wills could also apply where the second testator (Mary in the above example) receives no personal benefit under the will of the first testator (i.e. George). The first testator has performed his part of the agreement by making his will in the manner promised in it and so it would be a fraud on him to allow the second testator to ignore that agreement.

The contract stage

CORNERSTONE

Goodchild v. *Goodchild*

The doctrine of mutual wills only applies where the wills are indeed mutual.

If the wills are not mutual then the doctrine will not apply, as in *Goodchild* v. *Goodchild* (1997), where, although the husband and wife had executed identical wills, there was no evidence that this was as a result of an agreement not to revoke them. However, the court felt that as the mother had left the estate to the father in the, albeit mistaken, belief that he would be legally bound by their agreement that the property would ultimately go to their son, this created a moral obligation on the father. Thus the court could award the son maintenance out of the estate under the Inheritance (Provision for Family and Dependants Act) 1975. As the son, this was an adult and able to look after himself this would not normally have been ordered but the existence of the mother's belief tipped the scales in his favour. There have been two recent cases on this point: *Charles* v. *Fraser* (2010) and *Fry* v. *Densham-Smith* (2010) where again despite any express agreement not to revoke wills it was held on the facts that the wills were mutual.

While George and Mary are still alive the situation is one of contract: the revocation by either of them without notice to the other of a will made in pursuance of the agreement will be a breach of contract and damages will be payable by the party in breach. Thus in *Healey* v. *Brown* (2002) it was emphasised that when there is a lifetime disposition in breach of the agreement then the duty crystallises. An action for breach can be brought by the survivor, as a party, and possibly also by a beneficiary if the Contracts (Rights of Third Parties) Act 1999 applies and if the agreement was entered into on or after 11 May 2000, as the Act does not apply to contracts entered into before this date. (The Act is dealt with in more detail in Chapter 7 but, briefly, the agreement must be capable of being construed as conferring a benefit on the third party.) The same applies if the breach consists of a refusal by a party to make a will. If the breach only becomes apparent after the death of a party, when it is found that he has not left a will in accordance with the agreement, then damages can be recovered from his estate as in *Robinson* v. *Ommanney* (1883). However, it is not clear how damages would be calculated in these cases. In *Re Parkin* (1892) Stirling J referred to the possibility also of an action for specific performance to complete the transfer of the property. However, no action can be brought to restrain the actual revocation of the will because wills are always revocable (*Re Hey's Estate* (1914)).

The trust stage: liability of the survivor

The law of trusts is involved at a slightly later stage when the first testator has died, leaving an unrevoked will made in pursuance of the agreement. Here, then, the survivor will be treated as holding the property on trust to apply it so as to carry out the effect of the mutual will. Thus in the above example if George dies first, then Mary holds his £10,000 in a bank account on trust for Tim and Tom. If, however, George has broken the agreement by executing a new will revoking the one made under the agreement, then on George's death no trust was in existence, although, as explained above, there may be contractual remedies. Suppose that Mary, after George's death, herself makes a new will in different terms? Although, as mentioned above, she cannot be restrained from making a new will, her personal representatives will still hold her property that was the subject of the agreement on trust for the intended beneficiary. It should finally be noted that there is some authority for saying that the trust arises at a later stage only when the survivor receives the benefit under the first will, which would accord with the notion of these trusts being constructive (see below). Yet even if this is so, the trust will relate back to the death of the first to die.

Proof of an agreement

An agreement must be proved on the ordinary civil standard of a balance of probabilities. In *Re Cleaver* (1981) an elderly couple made wills in each other's favour and in default of survival to the testator's three children in equal shares. They then each reduced the interest of one child to a life interest after the testator's death. The testatrix made a will in similar terms. Although the testatrix made two later wills in different terms it was held that evidence of mutual wills was established by the similarity of the original wills, the fact that both then reduced the interest of one child, and the conformity of the testatrix's will made after her husband's death with the previous one.

Which property is included in the trust?

The express terms of the will may clarify which property is included in the trust but if they do not then:

(a) The trust undoubtedly includes property received by the survivor from the estate of the first to die.

(b) It must also include all property owned by the survivor at the time of the first death (*Re Hagger* (1930)).

(c) Does it include property acquired by the survivor after the first death? The position is doubtful but in *Re Cleaver* (1981) Nourse J said that the survivor could enjoy the property as absolute owner, unless, of course, the will only gave him a life interest.

(d) A trust arising from mutual wills cannot be express but there is a difference of opinion among textbook writers as to whether it is either a resulting (or implied) trust or a constructive trust. In *Re Cleaver* (1981) the court held that the trust is constructive.

Mutual wills and joint wills

Although a will jointly made by two parties is obviously different from mutual wills the same principles apply in that the survivor of joint testators will also be bound by a trust. Joint wills are rare in practice.

KEY POINTS

- The existence of a secret trust does not appear on the will or other document.
- By contrast, where the trust is half secret the fact of the trust does appear on the will or other document but not the terms of the trust.
- There are different rules on the communication of secret and half secret trusts.
- A mutual will is one where the two testators make wills, usually but not necessarily leaving property to each other, but always where there is a gift to the same beneficiary.

CORE CASES AND STATUTES

Case	About	Importance
Wallgrave v. *Tebbs* (1855)	Communication of a secret trust.	Holds that the fact that the intended trustee is to hold the property on trust, and the details of the trust, must be communicated to that person before the testator's death.
Re Keen (1937)	Communication of details of a secret trust by means of an envelope.	The secret trust can be enforced if the intended trustee is not actually told its details *before* the testator's death but is told where to find them *after* his death, for example, by the testator giving him a sealed envelope with the details.
Re Stead (1900)	Where a gift is made to two persons but the secret trust is only communicated to one of them.	You need to decide if the legatees under the will are joint tenants or tenants in common as different rules apply.
Re Keen (1937)	Communication of a half secret trust.	Rule is probably that it must be communicated before the will (note difference between this and secret trusts).
Goodchild v. *Goodchild* (1997)	Mutual wills.	The doctrine of mutual wills only applies where the wills are mutual in the sense that there is an agreement not to revoke them. The fact that the wills are identical is not enough.

Statute	About	Importance
Wills Act 1837	Formalities required for the making of a will.	These provisions do not apply to secret and half secret trusts.
Section 53(1)(b) of the Law of Property Act 1925	Formalities for a declaration of a trust of land.	These only apply to express trusts and so will not apply if a secret trust is held to be a constructive trust (s. 53(2) of the LPA). However, half secret trusts are likely to be express and so will be caught by s. 53(1)(b).

FURTHER READING

Brown, J. and Pawlowski, M. (2004) 'Constituting a secret trust by estoppel' 68 *Conv*. 388.
This article considers the situation where the testator himself tries to go back on his promise by revoking the instructions that he has given to the secret trustee so in effect ending the trust. Can he be estopped from doing so?

Critchley, P. (1999) 'Instruments of fraud: testamentary dispositions and secret trusts' 115 *LQR* 631.
A useful look at the whole area.

Davis, C. (2003) 'Mutual wills; formalities; constructive trusts' 67 *Conv*. 238.
This is a comment on *Healey* v. *Brown*.

Griffiths, G. (2011) 'At best inconvenient and at worst little short of disastrous? Recent considerations on mutual wills' 75 *Conv*. 511.
This case comment looks critically at the two recent cases of *Charles* v. *Fraser* and *Fry* v. *Densham-Smith*.

Meager, R. (2003) 'Secret trusts: do they have a future?' 67 *Conv*. 203.
Interesting research, of which some was cited above, showing that secret trusts are important in practice and giving some fascinating and at times unexpected reasons why they are used.

Perrins, B. (1972) 'Can you keep half a secret?' 88 *LQR* 225.
This article demonstrates that the principles in *Re Stead* rest on a tenuous historical basis.

PART 3

Resulting trusts, constructive trusts, trusts of the home

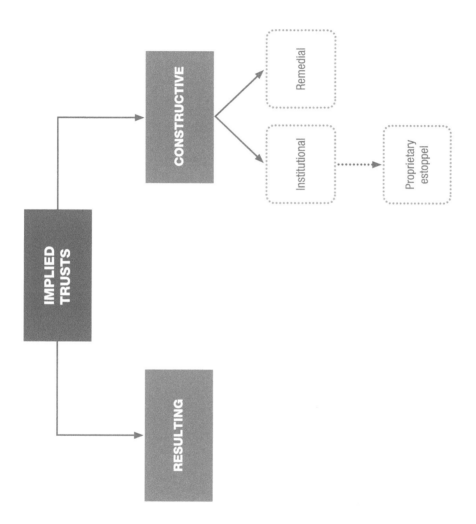

PART 3 INTRODUCTION

The common feature of both resulting and constructive trusts is that, unlike express trusts, they are not created by the express agreement of the parties as evidenced in a trust deed, or some other writing or, except in the case of trusts of land or an interest in land (LPA 1925, s. 53(1)(b)), orally. Although this much is clear, the exact nature of both these trusts and their relationship to each other has been the subject of considerable debate. Both types of trusts have been used by the courts in the last 50 years in creative ways which have added much to the influence of equity on the regulation of everyday life, but, as often in English law, the exact foundations on which these trusts operate is still uncertain, although they have the common feature that they are both implied by the courts.

A most useful indication to the differences between express trusts, on the one hand, and both resulting and constructive (which he calls imputed) trusts on the other, is provided by Moffat (2009, pp. 606–607), who observes that there are three distinctions between them:

(a) Functional. Express trusts are often employed as a planning device but imputed trusts are ways of resolving disputes over ownership or entitlement to property.

(b) Formal. Express trusts must comply with certain formalities such as s. 53(1)(c) of the LPA. Imputed trusts are not affected by these (LPA 1925, s. 53(2)).

(c) Substantive. Express trusts arise because of some expression of intention by a property owner but imputed trusts arise by operation of some legal rule. As Moffat points out, this particular distinction breaks down in cases of disputes over the family home where intention plays a significant role.

CHAPTER 9

Constructive trusts; proprietary estoppel

BLUEPRINT

Constructive trusts;
proprietary estoppel

LEGISLATION

- Land Registration Act 2002, s. 116
- Law of Property (Miscellaneous) Provisions Act 1989, s. 2

CONTEXT

- When we agree to act as a trustee and become a fiduciary, what does this mean?

CONCEPTS

- Nature of a constructive trust
- Fiduciaries
- Statute as an engine of fraud
- Remedial constructive trusts
- Promissory and proprietary estoppel
- Unjust enrichment

- Relationship between ' no conflict' and 'no profit' rule.
- Distinction between institutional and remedial constructive trusts.
- Use of proprietary estoppel to enforce future promises, e.g. to leave by will.

- What do we mean by constructive trusts and proprietary estoppel and why are they important?

CASES

- *Keech* v. *Sandford*
- *Boardman* v. *Phipps*
- *Sinclair Investments Ltd* v. *Versailles*
- *Rochefoucauld* v. *Boustead*
- *Halifax Building Society* v. *Thomas*
- *Yeoman's Row Management Ltd* v. *Cobbe*

REFORM

- Recognition of the remedial constructive trust?

SPECIAL CHARACTERISTICS

- Position of company directors as fiduciaries
- Receipt of bribes

CRITICAL ISSUES

Setting the scene

Suppose that you were a member of a local cricket club. You were getting ready for the season when you discovered that your Treasurer, Osbert, had suddenly disappeared. You and other members then found out that he had taken £15,000 from the club account. Osbert was traced to an address abroad and was eventually convicted of fraud. It was found that he had bought a yacht with the £15,000 but then sold it to Fred. The club wishes to recover the yacht from Fred.

The first question is whether Osbert can be regarded as being in a fiduciary position. If he can, and it seems that this is so, then he will be liable to the obligations of a constructive trustee and there will be a constructive trust with the club and its members as beneficiaries. This is important as it means that the beneficiaries will have remedies against the trust property, which in this case is the £15,000 that then became the yacht. The end result is that they may be able to recover the yacht and sell it so that the money can then be put back into the club funds.

From this you will see that:

(a) Constructive trusts often arise when there has been wrongdoing.

(b) Where there is no express trust then it is crucial to identify a fiduciary relationship.

(c) The existence of a constructive trust then results in equitable remedies becoming available.

All of these points are dealt with in this chapter although you will find the details of equitable remedies for breach of trust in Chapter 10.

INTRODUCTION

This chapter first links two examples of equitable intervention which have much in common: the constructive trust and estoppel. Although generalisations are notoriously risky in this area it can be said that in both cases equity is reacting to a set of circumstances, and whilst in one the solution is the imposition of a trust, in the other it is the granting of a broad-based remedy. However, it will be seen that constructive trusts can themselves be seen as a remedy and the interplay between constructive trusts and estoppel as performing a remedial function has led to much debate. This theme will also be explored in the next chapter (Trusts of the home).

CONSTRUCTIVE TRUSTS

CORNERSTONE

Constructive trusts

A precise definition is difficult but the wording of Lord Millett (below) seems to capture their essence.

These have been defined by Millett (1998, p. 400) as arising 'whenever the circumstances are such that it would be unconscionable for the owner of the legal title to assert his own beneficial interest and deny the beneficial interest of another'. The difficulty has always been in going further and giving a clearer indication of when a constructive trust may arise. One problem is that, in cases involving the family home, a constructive trust has been said to rest on the common intention of the parties and secret trusts (Chapter 8) can also rest on intention, in this case that of the testator. If this is so then it is very difficult to find any clear conceptual basis for constructive trusts as intention plays a part in result trusts and obviously express trusts arise from the intention of the settlor.

INTERSECTION

Look at Chapter 11 on resulting trusts and note the arguments about the basis of a resulting trust. One point is clear: that the intentions of the parties play a much more significant part in resulting trusts than they do in the case of constructive trusts.

If trusts of the family home and secret trusts are left out of the equation then some ideas become clearer. It then is true that a constructive trust has nothing to do with intention, whether express or implied, and such a trust is imposed by law. The other clear point which can be made is that a constructive trust will be imposed when the conscience of the owner of property is affected in such a way that equity insists that he/she should hold it for the benefit of another.

It has often been said that it would be wrong to go beyond this type of statement. This is because, as Edmund Davies LJ put it in *Carl Zeiss Siftung* v. *Herbert Smith & Co.* (1969): 'Its boundaries [i.e. of the constructive trust] have been left perhaps deliberately vague so as not to restrict the court by technicalities in deciding what the justice of a particular case may demand.' Similarly Lord Scott in *Yeoman's Row Management Ltd* v. *Cobbe* (2008) said: 'It is impossible to prescribe exhaustively the circumstances sufficient to create a constructive trust but it is possible to recognise particular factual circumstances that will do so and also to recognise other factual circumstances that will not.'

FIDUCIARIES AND CONSTRUCTIVE TRUSTS

It is essential to have an appreciation of the concept of a fiduciary given that it is precisely because a person has been identified as a fiduciary that they have been held to be constructive trustees.

Meaning of fiduciary

CORNERSTONE

Fiduciary

There is no definition of fiduciary. A useful description often quoted is that a fiduciary 'is, simply, someone who undertakes to act for or on behalf of another in some particular matter or matters' (Finn 1977, p. 1).

A fiduciary need not be an express trustee. Various relationships have been held to be fiduciary such as those between a company director and a company, employer and employee, solicitor and client and principal and agent. The search for a wide-ranging principle has, as Mason (1985, p. 246) points out, been inhibited by the fact that labelling a relationship as fiduciary 'unleashes equitable remedies'. The result is that, for example, in the *Quistclose* case (see Chapters 3 and 11), the imposition of a fiduciary relationship, on what had appeared to be one of lender and borrower, led to the lender having an equitable proprietary interest in the subject matter of the loan (i.e. the money lent) and the ability to have a prior claim over the borrower's creditors.

A good working definition of a fiduciary was given by Millett LJ in *Bristol and West Building Society* v. *Mothew* (1998): 'A fiduciary is someone who has undertaken to act for or on behalf of another in a particular matter in circumstances which give rise to a relationship of trust and confidence. The distinguishing obligation of a fiduciary is the obligation of loyalty.'

Mason (1977) has, in a well-known phrase, described the fiduciary relationship as a 'concept in search of a principle'. As Tan (1995, p. 19) puts it: 'The fiduciary concept is like an accordion . . . it may be expanded, or compressed, to maintain the integrity of relationships perceived to be of importance to contemporary society.'

> ### Take note
>
> The term 'principal' is used to indicate a person who employs a fiduciary.

The core liability of a fiduciary has several facets. A fiduciary must act in good faith; he must not make a profit out of his trust; he must not place himself in a position where his duty and interest may conflict; he may not act for his own benefit or the benefit of a third person without the informed consent of his principal.

English law has traditionally restricted the relationship to the types of categories set out above. However, in Canada the courts have been more adventurous. In *Norbert* v. *Wynrib* (1992) the doctor–patient relationship was categorised as fiduciary so that when a doctor prescribed a drug in return for sexual favours the courts held that he was liable not only for assault and battery but also for equitable compensation (see Chapters 2 and 10). In *M(K)* v. *M(H)* (1992) the relationship between child abuser and his daughter, who was his victim, was also fiduciary.

Profits made by a person in a fiduciary position

CORNERSTONE

Profits made by a fiduciary

Fiduciaries must not make a profit out of their position.

In *Bray* v. *Ford* (1896) Lord Herschell stated that: 'It is an inflexible rule of a court of equity that a person in a fiduciary position . . . is not allowed to make a profit; he is not allowed to put himself in a position where his duty and interest conflict.'

Where they do so, fiduciaries can be liable as constructive trustees to account for those profits. However, the distinction between the 'no conflict of interest rule' and the 'no profit rule' has not always been drawn clearly – see the Reflection box 'Conflicts of interest and profits' on *Boardman* v. *Phipps*.

CORNERSTONE

Keech v. *Sandford*

Keech v. *Sandford* applies the fundamental principle that a fiduciary must not profit from his position.

In *Keech* v. *Sandford* (1726) a trustee (X) of a lease of a market was granted a renewal of the lease in his own name because the landlord did not wish to renew it on trust as the beneficiary was a minor who could not be bound by the usual covenants. It was held that X held the renewed lease on trust for the minor even though the trustee had not intended to benefit from the transaction.

REFLECTION

In *Motivex Ltd* v. *Bulfield* (1988) Vinelott J observed that: 'I do not think that it is strictly accurate to say that a director owes a fiduciary duty to the company not to put himself in a position where his duty to the company may conflict with his personal interest or with his duty to another.' Thus Lord Herschell's words should perhaps be rephrased to say that where there is a conflict between personal interests and duty as a trustee then the duty is not to take advantage of that conflict and to consider only the interests of the trust (see Koh 2003).

CONTEXT

Oakley (1996) contends that the decision in *Keech* v. *Sandford* should be viewed very much as a creature of its own time and place. He observes (at p. 235) that at that time charitable and other public bodies were restricted in the length of leases which they could grant and so leases were often renewed as a matter of right. Accordingly, a failure to renew was depriving the trust of a grant of a lease which it had a right to expect. Moreover, this was a time of 'extravagant financial speculation and even more extravagant financial collapses' (one example being the well-known South Sea Bubble of 1720).

Thus the judges may well have been influenced by a concern to protect trust beneficiaries from having their assets dissipated in these ways and as a result have been keen to impose very strict duties on trustees. The obvious question to ask is then: should we regard *Keech* v. *Sandford* as a valuable precedent for today?

The rule also applies where a person making the profit is not a trustee but is in a fiduciary position (see *Boardman* v. *Phipps* (1967) and *Industrial Development Consultants Ltd* v. *Cooley* (1972) below)) but will not apply if no such relationship can be found.

CORNERSTONE

Boardman v. *Phipps*

Boardman v. *Phipps* is a modern and controversial application of the principle set out in *Keech* v. *Sandford*.

The principle in *Keech* v. *Sandford* and *Bray* v. *Ford* was applied in *Boardman* v. *Phipps* (1967), where the appellants were a solicitor to a trust (Boardman) and one of the beneficiaries (Phipps). The trust owned a substantial holding of shares in a company and the appellants were dissatisfied with its performance. They obtained information, acting as agents of the trust, about the company's affairs and as a result they decided to obtain control of the company by purchasing the remainder of its shares. Having done this they reorganised it and made considerable profits for themselves. The trust could not have bought the shares without seeking the sanction of the court and it did not consider doing this. The appellants were held liable to account to the trust for the profits made because they had acted as agents of the trustees to acquire the necessary information about the company and in addition the respondent beneficiary had not been kept fully informed of the situation. However, the appellants had acted in good faith throughout and so should be allowed 'liberal payment' for their skill in the negotiations which had resulted in the trust acquiring a considerable benefit.

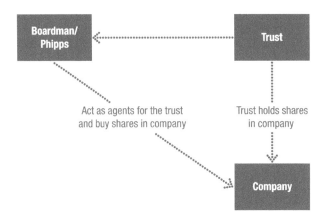

Figure 9.1 *Boardman* v. *Phipps*

Conflicts of interest and profits

There was no doubt that the appellants in *Boardman* v. *Phipps* were in a fiduciary relationship towards the trust, out of which they obtained the opportunity to make a profit. Thus we could say that they broke the 'no profit rule'. However, the 'no profit rule' does not stand on its own: there is no law against a person making a profit. The 'no profit rule' applies where a person is, as a result of their fiduciary position, in a position where their duty and interest conflict (see *Bray* v. *Ford* above).

Were they in a position where their duty as fiduciaries and their personal interest might conflict? Lord Upjohn, who forcefully dissented in *Boardman* v. *Phipps*, said that they were not and observed that 'the appellants have bought for themselves and with their own money shares which the trustees never contemplated buying and they did so in circumstances fully known and approved of by the trustees'. Moreover, their actions benefited the trust as the trust's own shares increased in value.

In *Murad* v. *Al-Saraj* (2005) the Court of Appeal suggested *obiter* that the rule as applied in *Keech* v. *Sandford* and *Boardman* v. *Phipps* might be looked at again where the fiduciary has acted in good faith with no concealment.

You could also look at *Bhullar* v. *Bhullar* (2003), another decision involving the 'no conflict of interest' and 'no profit' rules in the context of company directors.

REFLECTION

INTERSECTION

When you come to look at remedies for breach of trust in Chapter 10 do bear *Boardman* v. *Phipps* in mind and ask what remedy was used in *Boardman* v. *Phipps*. Was it liability to account or was it a personal remedy? It is arguable that the courts did not make this clear.

Company directors as fiduciaries

CORNERSTONE

Company directors

Company directors must not make a profit from their position. If they do, they will be held liable to account for the profit to the company.

In *Regal (Hastings) Ltd* v. *Gulliver* (1967) Regal Ltd (R) set up a subsidiary (X Ltd) to acquire the leases of two cinemas. The owner of the cinemas was only prepared to lease them if the share capital of X Ltd was fully subscribed and, because the resources of R only permitted it to subscribe for part of the share capital, the directors of R then subscribed for the rest. The directors subsequently made a profit from their shares and were held liable to account for this to the company. As in *Boardman* v. *Phipps* (1967) they had acted in good faith and here the company, as with the trust in *Boardman*, did not intend to buy the shares. The result in both cases was to provide a windfall: for the company in this case and for the trust in *Boardman*.

In *Industrial Development Consultants Ltd* v. *Cooley* (1972) the defendant was a director and general manager of the claimant company. He attempted, on the company's behalf, to interest a Gas Board in a project but the Gas Board, having declined to deal with the company, offered the project to the defendant personally. He was held liable to account to the company for the profit he had made and unlike the parties in the two above cases he had not acted in good faith: he had obtained his release from the claimants so as to take up the contract by falsely stating that he was ill.

A less rigorous view was taken in *Queensland Mines Ltd* v. *Hudson* (1978) where the defendant, the managing director of the claimant company, had obtained licences for the claimant to develop some mines. When the claimant found itself unable to do so the defendant, with the claimant's full knowledge, took the licences himself and developed them. He was not held liable to account for profits made because he had not deprived the claimant of any opportunity and had kept the claimant fully informed. It is difficult to reconcile this decision with *Boardman* and *Regal* but it is worth noting that Australian judges tend to take a different approach and to follow the minority view of the judges in the House of Lords in *Boardman* v. *Phipps*.

The imposition of fiduciary duties on company directors raises the question of the extent to which fiduciary duties are an appropriate mechanism for controlling business activities. This then brings in another issue: is the standard imposed by *Boardman* v. *Phipps* an appropriate one? Information constantly comes into commercial enterprises and so do opportunities. It is argued that the strict *Boardman* standard is right, especially in view of recent scandals in the financial world. On the other hand, it is argued that it is important not to discourage business enterprise.

REFLECTION

INTERSECTION

Company law

Although company law is a specialist area which you may not study it is important to be aware of what company law says about situations where a director has an interest which conflicts, or possibly may conflict, with the interests of the company.

Section 175(4)(b) of the Companies Act 2006 now provides that a director must avoid acting in situations where he has an interest which conflicts, or possibly may conflict, with the interests of the company. Section 175(4)(b) provides that this duty is not infringed if the matter has been authorised by the directors. This seems to reflect the dissenting speech of Lord Upjohn in *Boardman*.

Receipt of bribes by a person in a fiduciary position

CORNERSTONE

Receipt of bribes by fiduciaries – *Sinclair Investments* v. *Versailles Trade Investments*

Where a person receives a bribe in the course of acting as a fiduciary the proceeds are not held on a constructive trust for the principal (*Sinclair Investments* v. *Versailles Trade Investments*).

In *Lister & Co.* v. *Stubbs* (1890) it was held that a bribe received by a fiduciary from a third party was not held on trust for the principal. The reasoning was that proprietary claims (i.e. those founded on trust) were only available where the principal seeks to recover property which belonged to him *before* the breach of fiduciary duty. A bribe, by contrast, is not the property of the principal but is property held by the fiduciary in breach of fiduciary obligation.

APPLICATION

John acts as a scout for a large and famous football club, Melchester United. He is paid a secret commission of £30,000 by a small club (Hanbury Rovers) for recommending a player, George Worst, to Melchester United because Melchester have promised Hanbury Rovers to pay them a large transfer fee.

In fact, Worst is unable to hold down a place in the Melchester side and their manager says that he is 'absolutely hopeless'.

Melchester dismiss John as a scout and, when they find that he was bribed by Hanbury Rovers, they seek to recover the bribe from him. In fact John has filed for bankruptcy and has substantial debts.

This is why the label of constructive trustee is so important: if John was a constructive trustee of the proceeds of the bribes then Melchester would have priority over those of his creditors to whom he simply owed money.

The principle in *Lister* v. *Stubbs* was reversed in *Attorney-General for Hong Kong* v. *Reid* (1994), which held that benefits obtained from a third party in breach of fiduciary obligation, such as bribes, belong in equity to the principal from the moment of receipt. A Crown prosecutor took bribes and then used them to buy land. It was held that, when he took the bribes, he came under an immediate duty to pay them over to his principal (i.e. his employer) and so the bribes were the property of his employer in equity. Thus the employer was entitled to claim the profits from the bribes when they were invested.

This was in itself reversed in the latest case, *Sinclair Investments (UK) Ltd* v. *Versailles Trade Finance (in administration)* (2011), which has changed the position back to what it was before *Reid* and so *Lister* v. *Stubbs* is once again good law. Here traders advanced their money to a company to be held on trust on the understanding that it was to be used as trade finance. Further finance was raised from banks but in fact the money was never used for this. Instead one of the fraudsters, X, sold some of his shares in the company for £28 million and used £9.9 million to acquire a house in central London. Y was an investor who took an assignment of the company's claims against X and he claimed a proprietary interest in the traceable proceeds of the gains made by X.

The Court of Appeal held that Y's claim failed as he had no proprietary interest in the money as it had never been the property of the principal (the company). The reasoning in *Lister* v. *Stubbs* (above) was approved. The effect was that Y only had the personal remedy of an account which would not override the payments already made to the banks.

> Hicks (2011), commenting on the High Court decision, approved by the Court of Appeal, points out that one unresolved issue is what is meant by 'property' and says: 'Opportunity, or information used to exploit an opportunity, has been treated as the intangible property of the principal in many cases' (e.g. *Boardman* v. *Phipps*). Hayton (2011), commenting on the Court of Appeal decision, says that in consequence many trust deeds will now provide that any bribe or other secret profit received by the fiduciary will be held on trust for the relevant beneficiaries or the other contracting party.
>
> **REFLECTION**

WHERE A STATUTE HAS BEEN USED AS AN ENGINE OF FRAUD

CORNERSTONE

Statute as an engine of fraud

Equity may set aside statutory requirements where insistence on observance of the precise formalities required by statute for a particular transaction to be valid may be the cause of fraud.

A constructive trust can be imposed to enforce an oral agreement in a case where written formalities are required by the LPA 1925 if to insist on those formalities would amount to fraud.

INTERSECTION ....

A classic illustration of the maxim is found in the doctrine of secret trusts dealt with in Chapter 8. If I promise to leave James by will £1,000 on the strength of an oral promise by him that he will hold it on trust for Jill then James can argue that the promise is not binding on him as it does not comply with the requirements of the Wills Act. So equity holds that James is bound by a secret trust in favour of Jill which it will enforce despite the failure to comply with the formalities. A secret trust is an example of a constructive trust.

CORNERSTONE

Rochefoucauld v. *Boustead*

Statutory requirements were set aside as they could have resulted in fraud.

In *Rochefoucauld* v. *Boustead* (1897) the claimant had mortgaged land but was having difficulty in repaying the mortgage. The defendant bought the land and orally agreed to hold it as trustee for the claimant. However, he treated the land as his own. The court held that the claimant was entitled to an account of profits made on the land because although the trust in the claimant's favour, not being in writing, did not satisfy the requirements of what is now s. 53(1)(b) of the LPA 1925, it would be a fraud on the defendant's part to take the profits for himself.

This principle was followed in *Bannister* v. *Bannister* (1948) and in *Hodgson* v. *Marks* (1971). Here the owner of a house sold it to her lodger (Evans) on the oral understanding that the house would continue to be hers. Evans then sold the house to Marks, who took without notice of the agreement. The court held that the house was held on trust for Mrs Hodgson who thus remained the beneficial owner in equity and so had an overriding interest under what was s. 70(1)(g) of the Land Registration Act 1925 (now the Land Registration Act 2002), which bound Marks.

A difficulty here is deciding which type of trust was created. In *Rochefoucauld* the court appeared to be simply enforcing the express trust which existed in the claimant's favour and to be saying that the formalities provisions (here s. 53(1)(b) of the LPA) can be disregarded where to do otherwise would lead to fraud. In *Hodgson* the trust was categorised as a resulting trust, which by s. 53(2) is exempted from the formalities requirements, and only in *Bannister* was it held to be a constructive trust, to which s. 53(2) also applies. It is suggested that the exact category in which the trust is fitted does not greatly matter as it is the principle which is important.

Rochefoucauld v. *Boustead* is considered in relation to the formality requirements.

REFLECTION

The courts do not always, however, impose a trust where a failure to comply with a statutory requirement can lead to injustice. In *Midland Bank Trust Co. Ltd* v. *Green (No. 1)* (1981) an option granted by a father to his son to purchase a farm had not been registered as required by the Land Charges Act 1972 and the father, having changed his mind about the sale, then carried out a 'sham' sale to his wife so that the son's option was then defeated. The son's claim failed, Lord Wilberforce observing that 'it is not fraud to rely on legal rights conferred by an Act of Parliament'.

THE REMEDIAL CONSTRUCTIVE TRUST

CORNERSTONE

Remedial constructive trust

The remedial constructive trust is a broad-based equitable remedy, not tied to concepts such as the existence of a fiduciary duty.

English courts have imposed a constructive trust in circumstances where a fiduciary duty can be identified as, for example, in *Keech* v. *Sandford* and *Boardman* v. *Phipps*. However, in a series of cases in the 1970s Denning MR sought to develop what he called 'a constructive trust of a new model', generally known as a remedial constructive trust. The existence of a fiduciary relationship was not required to found such a trust: instead one would be imposed 'whenever justice and good conscience require it . . . it is an equitable remedy by which the court can enable an aggrieved party to obtain restitution' (*Hussey* v. *Palmer* (1972)).

The classic example of this approach is found in *Binions* v. *Evans* (1972) where Mrs Evans was given a licence to occupy a house for life by the Tredegar estate in South Wales for which her late husband worked. However, the estate then sold the house. The purchasers were aware of Mrs Evans' right to occupy when they purchased and indeed paid a reduced price for the house because of her licence but having purchased they then sought to evict her on the ground that a licence does not bind third parties.

A licence does not give a proprietary interest in land and indeed the decision was not that she had one: the subject matter of the trust was the licence as such. The Binions had not actually taken the house on trust for Mrs Evans but a trust of the licence was imposed to give Mrs Evans a remedy in the event of eviction proceedings being brought against her.

INTERSECTION

Contractual licences form part of a land law syllabus but note that licences do not bind third parties (*King* v. *David Allen Ltd* (1916)).

There are two objections to the new model constructive trust:

(a) To look at a constructive trust as a remedy and not as a substantive institution is wrong because, even though constructive trusts have always been remedies in one sense (see the cases above), they have also been substantive trusts because the property is trust property and therefore if the trustee becomes bankrupt the beneficiaries take priority over the trustee's creditors.

(b) The idea of imposing a constructive trust whenever justice requires leads to uncertainty. Mahon J memorably observed in the New Zealand case of *Carly* v. *Farrelly* (1975): 'No stable system of jurisprudence can permit a litigant's claim to justice to be consigned to the formless void of individual moral opinion.'

A distinction is often drawn between a remedial constructive trust and an institutional one, the basis of this being that an institutional constructive trust is a trust in itself with identifiable trust property giving rise to fiduciary duties on the part of the trustee. A remedial constructive trust, by contrast, exists purely to give a remedy or to operate as a defence to some action brought by another as in *Binions* v. *Evans*. However, Bryan (2012a) and others have pointed out that in fact all constructive trusts are in essence remedial. If you look again at cases such as *Keech* v. *Sandford* and *Boardman* v. *Phipps* you will see that the action was brought to obtain a remedy. Where there is a difference is that 'institutional' (for want of a better term) constructive trusts belong to recognised categories and the function of the court is merely to declare that a trust already exists. With a remedial constructive trust the trust only exists from the date of the court order when it is granted as a remedy.

The notion of the remedial constructive trust enjoyed a certain vogue with decisions such as *Lyus* v. *Prowsa Developments Ltd* (1982) but then fell out of favour in English law.

CORNERSTONE

Halifax Building Society v. *Thomas*

The Court of Appeal rejected the idea of a remedial constructive trust.

It was firmly rejected by the Court of Appeal in *Halifax Building Society* v. *Thomas* (1995). The defendant obtained a loan to buy a flat by a fraudulent misrepresentation and, when he fell into arrears, the mortgagee sold it. After it was sold there was a surplus and the mortgagee claimed this on the ground that there was constructive trust in its favour as the defendant should not gain from his fraud. The court held that this was wrong. A constructive trust could only be imposed where there was a fiduciary relationship between the parties and here there was none. In effect the court declined to impose a trust simply because it seemed that this was necessary to prevent what might be considered unconscionable behaviour.

In *Re Polly Peck International plc (in administration) (No. 2)* (1998) the Court of Appeal also firmly rejected the idea of imposing a remedial constructive trust. Here the applicants, who owned land in Cyprus, claimed that they were entitled to a remedial constructive trust of the profits which subsidiaries of Polly Peck had made from their land after it had initially been wrongfully appropriated by the Government of Northern Cyprus. The object of the claim was to give them a proprietary remedy which would give them priority over the creditors of Polly Peck. The Court of Appeal, in rejecting their claim, pointed to the difficulty in imposing a remedial constructive trust. As Nourse LJ pointed out, you cannot grant a proprietary right to A, who has not had one before, without taking one away from B.

This debate is fundamentally about whether a constructive trust should be tied to equitable principles, albeit functioning as a remedy in one sense as in *Boardman* v. *Phipps* (1967) or if it should simply be a general remedy, taking its place alongside damages and injunctions (see Gardner 2011, Chapter 11).

However, although the idea of the remedial constructive trust is strictly not recognised in English law, somehow the idea refuses to die. Indeed in *Westdeutsche Landesbank Girozentrale* v. *Islington LBC* (1996) Lord Browne-Wilkinson appeared to leave the door open for its development in English law. Here are three examples of the continuing vitality of the idea:

(a) The notion of a board-based remedial constructive trust may have been given a new lease of life by the speech of Lord Scott in *Thorner* v. *Major* (see below).

(b) The High Court of Australia in *John Alexander's Clubs Pty Ltd* v. *White City Tennis Club Ltd* (2010), whilst holding that on the facts there was no room for the imposition of a remedial constructive trust, still held that the concept existed and could be applied in future cases.

(c) The remedial constructive trust is well recognised in the USA: the Restatement (Third) of the Law of Restitution and Unjust Enrichment (2010) provides that a remedial constructive trust may be imposed in situations where there has been unjust enrichment.

INTERSECTION

See later in this chapter for the concept of unjust enrichment in English law.

PROPRIETARY ESTOPPEL

CORNERSTONE

Proprietary estoppel

Proprietary estoppel will prevent one party (X), usually an owner of land, who has made an imperfect gift of some estate or interest in it to another (Y), from then asserting his (X's) rights in the land as against Y. It must be distinguished from promissory estoppel (see below).

In *Thorner* v. *Major* (2009) Lord Walker identified the three main elements needed for a claim based on proprietary estoppel:

(a) a representation made or assurance given to the claimant;

(b) reliance by the claimant on the representation or assurance;

(c) some detriment incurred by the claimant as a consequence of that reliance.

APPLICATION

Mark owns a piece of land and says to Teresa: 'You can have it as a market garden.' Teresa takes over the land and develops it as a market garden but the land is never conveyed to her. Mark later attempts to turn Teresa out.

Here there is no deed of conveyance but equity provides that it could be unjust to allow a person in Mark's position to rely on this fact, so it may be remedied by the doctrine of proprietary estoppel.

Take note

Proprietary estoppel and promissory estoppel

Promissory estoppel applies in contractual relationships and essentially prevents a party from going back on a promise. It operates in a defensive mode.

Proprietary estoppel applies in property as well as contractual situations and can, unlike promissory estoppel, give rights where none existed before.

A good example of proprietary estoppel is *Dillwyn* v. *Llewellyn* (1862) where a father's encouragement to his son to build a house on the father's land meant that on the father's death the land built on was ordered to be conveyed to the son.

Another is *Inwards* v. *Baker* (1965). A father suggested to his son that he should build a bungalow on land owned by the father. The son did so, although there was no formal conveyance to him, and on the father's death it was held that the son could remain in the bungalow for as long as he wished.

The idea of detriment

This generally means that the person seeking to rely on an estoppel must have altered his position in some way in reliance on the encouragement of the other, as occurred in the above two cases.

The requirement of a representation

APPLICATION

Sue says to Deb, her carer: 'You have looked after me for many years with very little payment. After I have gone I will see that you are all right.' In fact Sue's will does not leave Deb anything. Deb claims a half share in Sue's estate.

One problem is that Sue never made any specific representation to Deb that she would leave anything to Deb. The most that Sue said was that 'I will see that you are all right'.

Is this a sufficiently clear representation?

Take note

Lord Scott in effect proposed that where a future property right (as in *Thorner* v. *Major*) was the subject of a representation then the claim should be on the basis of a remedial constructive trust (see above) instead of estoppel as when the promise was made there was no specific property to which it could apply. The other judges, however, applied proprietary estoppel.

However, in *Thorner* v. *Major* (2009) D had worked at P's farm for no payment from 1976 onwards and, by the 1980s, hoped that he might inherit the farm. No express representation had ever been made, but D relied on various hints and remarks made by P over the years. The House of Lords held that these amounted to an estoppel. Lord Walker, in this case, held that it was sufficient if the representations were sufficiently clear and unambiguous in all the circumstances.

Furthermore, the idea of Lord Walker in *Yeoman's Row* v. *Cobbe* (below) that the claimant must believe that they have been made an irrevocable promise was not accepted. This would inevitably have meant that promises to leave by will would not be covered by proprietary estoppel as a will can be revoked. However, in *Thorner* v. *Major* it was held that the question is whether a party has reasonably relied on an assurance by the other as that person's conduct.

Proprietary estoppel does not apply simply to provide a remedy for unconscionable conduct

CORNERSTONE

Yeoman's Row Management Ltd v. Cobbe

In *Yeoman's Row Management Ltd* v. *Cobbe* the House of Lords refused to use proprietary estoppel simply to provide a remedy for unconscionable conduct.

Estoppel is a classic equitable doctrine where flexibility is an essential element. Thus in *Taylor Fashions* v. *Liverpool Victoria Trustees Co. Ltd* (1982) Oliver J emphasised that the basis of the doctrine is whether the assertion of strict legal rights would be unconscionable.

However, this does not mean that the essential elements of proprietary estoppel can be ignored. In *Yeoman's Row Management Ltd* v. *Cobbe* (2008) an oral agreement between the company and Cobbe provided that a block of flats owned by the company would be demolished and Cobbe would apply for planning permission to erect houses in their place with any excess of the proceeds over £24 million shared equally with the company. After planning permission had been obtained the company went back on the oral agreement and demanded more money as it now realised that the land was worth much more. Cobbe claimed that the company was estopped from going back on the agreement.

Lord Scott in the House of Lords asked: What is the fact that the company is estopped from asserting? There was no question that the oral agreement was unenforceable and Cobbe did not claim a specific property right, merely a hope of entering a contract. Thus the situation was not the same as in *Dillwyn* v. *Llewelyn*, for example, where there was the definite expectation of a property right: the farm. He held that the Court of Appeal, which held in Cobbe's favour, had been influenced too much by the fact that it regarded the behaviour of the company as unconscionable without requiring the essential elements of proprietary estoppel to be present. In fact both parties were commercial entities and were independently advised and so as a matter of fact there was no reliance by one party on the other.

> Another way to look at this decision is that although there was unconscionable conduct by the company it was disappointing that equity would not award a remedy. This is the view of Piska (2009, p. 1015), who remarks that the 'hopes that equity may be able to provide some form of moral compass in the commercial context' have been defeated. This reference to 'the commercial context' is significant as equity is increasingly active in commerce through such devices as the constructive trust.

REFLECTION

How should the rights be given effect to?

CORNERSTONE

Section 116 of the Land Registration Act 2002

It is important to note the effect of s. 116 of the Land Registration Act 2002 in enabling rights acquired by proprietary estoppel to bind third parties in some cases.

The tendency in earlier cases was to award a remedy based on fulfilling the expectations of the party that had relied on the promise. An example is *Dillwyn* v. *Llewelyn* (above) where the promisee had been led to expect that he would receive a farm and was indeed awarded a farm.

More recent cases have asked: what would be fair to satisfy the equity created? This may lead to the promisee receiving less than he had expected. In *Jennings* v. *Rice* (2003) X worked for nearly 30 years as a gardener and odd-job man for Y. He was initially paid but then Y promised him that she would leave him her house and that he would be 'all right one day'. After this he was no longer paid. Y died intestate. X claimed either Y's whole estate (value: £1,285,000) or the value of the house (£435,000). It was, however, held that X would be awarded £200,000 as a larger sum would have been out of all proportion to what X might have charged for his services.

Proprietary estoppel and third parties

A right by proprietary estoppel may bind a purchaser where title to the land is registered. Section 116 of the Land Registration Act 2002 provides that, in registered land, an equity by estoppel and a mere equity have effect from the moment they arise as an interest capable of binding successors in title. Therefore, it can be protected by a notice against the title. In addition, if the person claiming the estoppel is in occupation, under it he or she may have an overriding interest under LRA 2002, Sch. 3, para. 2.

In *Inwards* v. *Baker* (1965) the son was given a licence to remain but problems with the enforceability of licences against third parties (see above) may have been the reason why in *Pascoe* v. *Turner* (1979) conveyance of the legal estate was ordered.

Proprietary estoppel and constructive trusts

CORNERSTONE

Law of Property (Miscellaneous) Provisions Act 1989

One debated area is whether proprietary estoppel can be used to enforce an agreement which does not satisfy s. 2(1) of the Law of Property (Miscellaneous) Provisions Act 1989.

Estoppel has been linked to the concept of the constructive trust in cases involving the family home and so the obvious question is whether they are distinct areas of equity or if it is, as it were, just a case of two labels for the same contents.

A fundamental distinction is that an institutional constructive trust as a substantive institution pre-dates any court order and the court simply declares that there is a trust in existence. By contrast, a proprietary estoppel exists from the date of the court order. Moreover, although generalisations are dangerous, a constructive trust, and indeed all trusts, are fundamentally different in their nature from proprietary estoppel in that the idea behind a trust is that titles (legal and equitable) are split but in proprietary estoppel, as Matthews (2009) points out, either the representee is left with the interest that he thought he had (i.e. the bungalow in *Inwards* v. *Baker*) or at least the representor is prevented from asserting the interest he thought he had.

INTERSECTION

Note that the remedial constructive trust also comes into existence from the date of the court order, as with proprietary estoppel.

In *Stack* v. *Dowden* (2007) Lord Walker said that

> Proprietary estoppel typically consists of asserting an equitable claim against the conscience of the 'true' owner . . . It is to be satisfied by the minimum award necessary to do justice . . . which may sometimes lead to no more than a monetary award. A 'common intention' constructive trust, by contrast, is identifying the true beneficial owner or owners, and the size of their beneficial interests.

REFLECTION

Can proprietary estoppel be used to rely on an agreement for the sale of land which is itself unenforceable as it is not in writing and so does not satisfy s. 2(1) of the Law of Property (Miscellaneous) Provisions Act 1989? If it can, then equity is in effect overriding a statutory provision.

Take the facts of *Whitaker* v. *Kinnear* (2011) where Mrs Whitaker alleged that she entered into an agreement with a developer, Mr Kinnear, for the sale of her house for £750,000, plus a potential 30% share in any development gains. Mr Kinnear assured her that she could live in the house for as long as she wanted. However, this agreement was not in the contract of sale.

Mrs Whitaker could claim a constructive trust but this looks like estoppel. Does s. 2(1) of the Law of Property (Miscellaneous) Provisions Act 1989 prevent estoppel from being relied on? See below for the decision.

Take note

Although s. 2(1) of the Law of Property (Miscellaneous Provisions) Act 1989 really belongs more to land law you may find it helpful to know its provisions. It provides that contracts for the sale or other disposition of an interest in land made on or after 27 September 1989 must: be in writing; contain all the terms agreed by the parties; be signed by all the parties.

Note also s. 2(5) '. . . nothing in this section affects the creation or operation of resulting, implied or constructive trusts'.

In *Herbert* v. *Doyle* (2010) owners of two adjoining properties, X and Y, had verbally agreed on transfers of parking spaces on their land, provided a number of conditions were satisfied. It was held that the agreement did not satisfy s. 2(1) of the Law of Property (Miscellaneous) Provisions Act 1989. However, the parties had come to a sufficiently certain agreement, made orally, which created a constructive trust over their respective parts of the property. The language used by the Court of Appeal was that of proprietary estoppel but the actual decision was that there was a constructive trust as Lord Scott in *Yeoman's Row* v. *Cobbe* had held that: 'proprietary estoppel cannot be prayed in aid in order to render enforceable an agreement that statute has declared to be void . . . Equity can surely not contradict the statute.'

However, in *Whitaker* v. *Kinnear* (2011) (above) the court held that proprietary estoppel in a case involving the sale of land *had* survived the enactment of s. 2 of the Law of Property (Miscellaneous) Provisions Act 1989 and drew a distinction between domestic cases (where the party will seek an interest) and commercial cases (where the party is expecting to get a contract). An estoppel is more likely to succeed in the domestic context, which is to be gauged according to the nature of the parties' dealings and not the nature of the property. *Yeoman's Row* v. *Cobbe* was, of course, a commercial case.

Take note

Whitaker v. *Kinnear* came before the High Court on a preliminary point and so the facts were not actually found.

UNJUST ENRICHMENT

CORNERSTONE

Unjust enrichment

Unjust enrichment operates separately from the law of trusts but it does touch trusts law at some points.

Although not strictly part of equity, the topic of unjust enrichment needs a mention here. It has appeared in Commonwealth cases on the family home, and it now forms a distinct part of the law whereby a defendant who is enriched at the expense of the claimant where there is no juristic basis for this enrichment can claim redress on the basis of unjust enrichment. One example is where a person receives money paid to her on the basis of a mistake of fact. Here there may be a claim to restore it. The link with equity, if any, arises when it sought to establish a proprietary right to the money.

Can unjust enrichment operate to give proprietary remedies as well as personal ones? Birks (2005) argued strongly that it should, with the result that there would be one single law of restitution based on unjust enrichment. The result would be that where, for example, a person received property in circumstances making them at present a constructive trustee the remedy would instead be on the basis of unjust enrichment. In *Westdeutsche Landesbank Girozentrale* v. *Islington BC* (1996) Lord Browne-Wilkinson saw no reason for this development and felt that the 'perceived need' to allow such a remedy involved a 'distortion of trust principles'. Bryan (2012b, p. 605) sees constructive and resulting trusts as being the law's 'principal vindicatory remedy' and thus there is no need for a separate law on unjust enrichment in property cases.

KEY POINTS

- There is no exhaustive list of circumstances in which a constructive trust can be imposed.
- A fiduciary need not be an express trustee.
- Persons in a fiduciary position must not use that position to make an unauthorised benefit out of their fiduciary position.
- A bribe received by a fiduciary from a third party is not held on trust for the principal.
- A remedial constructive trust can be imposed even though there is no pre-existing fiduciary relationship: it is an equitable remedy by which the court can enable an aggrieved party to obtain restitution. However, such a trust is not recognised in English law.
- Proprietary estoppel will prevent a party who has made an imperfect gift of some estate or interest in it to another from then asserting his own rights in the land.

CORE CASES AND STATUTES

Case	About	Importance
Keech v. *Sandford* (1726)	A trustee (X) of a lease of a market was granted a renewal of the lease in his own name. It was held that X held the renewed lease on trust for the minor even though X had not intended to benefit from the transaction.	A person in a fiduciary position is not, unless expressly authorised, entitled to make a profit.
Boardman v. *Phipps* (1967)	A solicitor to a trust who was in a fiduciary position made a profit out of shares acquired through knowledge gained whilst acting as a fiduciary.	The principle established in *Keech* v. *Sandford* applies even in the absence of fraud on the part of the fiduciary.
Lister & Co. v. *Stubbs* (1890)	A bribe received by a fiduciary from a third party was not held on trust for the principal.	Proprietary claims (i.e. those founded on trust) are only available where the principal seeks to recover property which belonged to him *before* the breach of fiduciary duty – the bribe is acquired *through* a breach of fiduciary duty.
Sinclair Investments (UK) Ltd v. *Versailles Trade Finance Ltd* (2011)	When a proprietary interest in property can exist, especially in the context of bribes.	Constructive trusts and remedies for breach of trust.
Rochefoucauld v. *Boustead* (1897)	Trust of land did not comply with the statutory formalities.	A trust was still imposed as to do otherwise would be to allow a statute to be an engine of fraud.
Halifax Building Society v. *Thomas* (1995)	The defendant obtained a loan to buy a flat by a fraudulent misrepresentation and when he fell into arrears the mortgagee sold it. The mortgagee claimed the resulting surplus on the ground that there was a constructive trust in its favour.	A trust would not be imposed simply because the conduct of the defendant was unconscionable.
Inwards v. *Baker* (1965)	A son built a bungalow on land owned by his father at his father's suggestion, although there was no formal conveyance to him.	Proprietary estoppel applied and the son was granted a licence to occupy the bungalow for his life.
Yeoman's Row Management Ltd v. *Cobbe* (2008)	Applicability of proprietary estoppel in a commercial context.	Proprietary estoppel cannot be invoked simply because a person's conduct has been unconscionable.

Statutes	About	Importance
Section 116 of the Land Registration Act 2002	In registered land, equity by estoppel and a mere equity have effect from the moment they arise as an interest capable of binding successors in title.	Can make an interest in land acquired by proprietary estoppel binding on third parties.
Section 2 of the Law of Property (Miscellaneous) Provisions Act 1989	Imposes formal requirements on contracts for the sale or other disposition of an interest in land.	Oral contracts which do not comply with these requirements may be enforced if there is evidence of either a constructive trust or proprietary estoppel.

FURTHER READING

Birks, P. (2005) *Unjust Enrichment*, **2nd ed. (Oxford University Press)**

Bryan, M. (2012a) 'Constructive trusts: understanding remedialism' **in Jamie Glister and Pauline Ridge (eds)** *Fault Lines in Equity* **(Hart Publishing).**
This is a very valuable up-to-date account of the place of the remedial constructive trust today and also clarifies our thinking on the distinction between institutional and remedial constructive trusts.

Bryan, M. (2012b) '*Boardman* **v.** *Phipps'* **in** *Leading Cases in Equity* **(Hart Publishing).**
This really clarifies exactly what the issues were in this case and emphasises the agency relationship between Boardman and the trust.

Conaglen, M. (2005) 'The nature and function of fiduciary loyalty' **121** *LQR* **452.**
This article asks if in fact there is only one fiduciary duty, that of loyalty, and suggests that the concept of fiduciary loyalty is not an end in itself but a means of ensuring that non-fiduciary duties are carried out. Look then at the view of Smith (2003) (below) who suggests that the istinguishing characteristic

of a breach of fiduciary obligations is disloyalty by the fiduciary.

Finn, P. (1977) *Fiduciary Obligations* **(Sydney Law Book Company).**
This has a most valuable discussion of the fiduciary principle which can be read in conjunction with other more recent articles.

Gardner, S. (2010) 'Reliance-based constructive trusts' in C. Mitchell (ed.) *Constructive and Resulting Trusts* **(Hart Publishing).**
This considers arguments about the true basis of the constructive trust and in particular the argument that certain types of constructive trust can be analysed as correcting a loss suffered in reliance on the undertaking of another.

Gardner, S. (2011) *The Law of Trusts*, **3rd ed. (Oxford University Press).**
See especially Chapter 8 'Instances of Constructive Trusts'.

Hayton, D. (2011) 'Proprietary liability for secret profits' 127 *LQR* **487.**
Hicks, A. (2011) 'Constructive trusts of fiduciary gain: Lister revived?' **1** *Conv.* **62.**
Both these articles (Hayton 2011 and Hicks 2011), which are referred to in the text,

consider the decision in *Sinclair Investments* v. *Versailles Trade Finance*.

Koh, J. (2003) 'Once a director, always a fiduciary?' 62 *CLJ* 403.
A useful discussion of fiduciary duties of directors. Students with no prior knowledge of company law will find this an accessible account.

Mason, A.F. (1977) Foreword to Finn, *Fiduciary Obligation* (Sydney, Law Book Company).

Mason, A.F. (1985) 'Themes and prospects' in P.D. Finn (ed.) *Essays in Equity* (Law Book Co.).

Matthews, P. (2009) 'The words which are not there: a partial history of the constructive trust' in C. Mitchell (ed.) *Constructive and Resulting Trusts* (Hart Publishing).
This article covers the history and development of constructive trusts in a most enjoyable and stimulating way and is full of ideas, not all of which you may agree with but that is not a bad thing!

McFarlane, B. (2009) 'Apocalypse averted: proprietary estoppel in the House of Lords' 125 *LQR* 535.
This article analyses the decisions in *Yeoman's Row* v. *Cobbe* and *Thorner* v. *Major* and concludes that Lord Scott's view of estoppel in *Yeoman's Row* was wrong.

Millett, P. (1998) 'Equity's place in the law of commerce' 114 *LQR* at 400.
This is one of the most stimulating accounts of the law and is still worth reading. The author was, of course, a noted Chancery judge.

Oakley, A.J. (1996) 'Liberalising remedies for breach of trust' in A.J. Oakley (ed.) *Trends in Contemporary Trust Law* (Oxford University Press).

Piska, N. (2009) 'Hopes, expectations and revocable promises in proprietary estoppel' 72 *MLR* 998.

Smith, P. (2003) 'The motive. Not the deed' in J. Getzler (ed.) *Rationalising Property, Equity and Trusts* (Lexis Nexis).

Tan, D. (1995) 'The fiduciary as an accordion term: can the Crown play a different tune?' 69 *ALJ* 440.
This article is a valuable account of the search for a meaning of the elusive term 'fiduciary'. Read it and then go on to Finn (1977).

CHAPTER 10
Breach of trust and remedies

BLUEPRINT

*Breach of trust
and remedies*

KEY
QUESTIONS

LEGISLATION

- Trustee Act 1925
- Limitation Act 1980

CONTEXT

- Trusts are not always used as a vehicle for long-term planning but as a means to an end.

CONCEPTS

- Actions *in rem* and actions *in personam*
- Tracing as a procedure and not a remedy

- Is the term 'equitable compensation' satisfactory?
- Should there be separate rules for tracing at common law and in equity?
- Relationship between unjust enrichment and remedies for breach of trust.

- What is a breach of trust and how is it remedied?

CASES

- *Target Holdings* v. *Redferns* (1996)
- *Bank of Credit and Commerce International Ltd* v. *Akindele* (2001)
- *Royal Brunei Airlines Sdn Bhd* v. *Tan Kok Ming* (1995)
- *Foskett* v. *McKeown* (2001)

REFORM

- Further control of trustee exemption clauses?

SPECIAL CHARACTERISTICS

- Different tests applied to cases of receipt of trust property and assistance in a breach of trust
- Distinction between tracing at common law and in equity
- Trustee exemption clauses
- Protection of trustees from liability

CRITICAL ISSUES

Setting the scene

Remedies for breach of contract

Jim made a contract with Alec, a car salesman, to buy a new 'Cougar' car. The cost is £30,000. However, the car soon develops problems and after two short journeys it completely breaks down. Jim was intending to use the car to take him and his wife Anne on a holiday of a lifetime touring all the capitals of Europe. Alec had been told of this. When Jim contacts Alec he is told that there was nothing at all wrong with the car when delivered and he is under no liability at all to Jim.

What legal avenue should Jim pursue? Obviously he should claim damages for breach of contract not only for the cost of the car but also for the disappointment of the lost holiday. A complication is that Alec is now insolvent. The result is that unfortunately Jim has much less chance of getting his money back because he has only a *personal* remedy against Alec.

Remedies for breach of trust

Suppose that Alec is also a trustee of a trust fund established for the benefit of his two children, Sophie and Terry. When Alec is adjudged insolvent it is found that he wrongly took £50,000 from the trust fund and used it to pay off business debts. Sophie and Terry want to know what to do. Here Alec has committed a breach of trust, not a breach of contract as with Jim.

The crucial difference that you must remember is that although Sophie and Terry do have a personal remedy against Alec they also have a *proprietary* one because, as there was a trust, the trust money that Alec wrongly parted with was theirs in equity as beneficiaries under the trust. So when they bring a claim for the recovery of their money they are, in a real sense, claiming *their* money. When Jim, by contrast, claimed damages for breach of contract he was in effect claiming that money that presently belonged to Alec should now belong to him as damages.

In any answer to a question on remedies for breach of trust you must never lose sight of this distinction. Its importance can be seen in the fact that Alec is insolvent. When there is insolvency then if the beneficiaries have a proprietary remedy they will have priority over other creditors.

Suppose, in this example, that Alec has only £20,000 left and debts of £1 million. Sophie and Terry claim the return of the £50,000 wrongly taken from the trust fund. All the other claimants, such as Jim, have personal claims only. The result is that Sophie and Terry will have priority over all the other creditors and so they will be first in the queue for repayment. Their claim for £50,000 will exhaust the whole fund and the others, including Jim, will get nothing.

One more point. You will have noted that Jim had a claim for the disappointment of the lost holiday. When claims are brought for breach of trust there can be similarities to a claim like this. Suppose that, for example, there is a claim that trustees have been negligent in making investments and so the trust fund is less than it should be. In both cases the court has to assess the loss and in this type of case there can be some similarities between claims at common law for damages and for breach of trust, as we shall see.

INTRODUCTION

CORNERSTONE

What is meant by a breach of trust?

The term 'breach of trust' means that trustees have failed to observe the duties laid on them by equity and by the trust instrument.

What is a breach of trust? Trustees are in breach of trust if they fail to observe the duties laid on them by equity and by the trust instrument. Various examples of breaches of trust can be found in the previous chapters, e.g. purchasing trust property without authority, investing in unauthorised investments. A good working definition is that by Millett LJ in *Armitage* v. *Nurse* (1998):

> Breaches of trust are of many different kinds. A breach of trust may be deliberate or inadvertent; it may consist of an actual misappropriation or misapplication of the trust property or merely of an investment or other dealing which is outside the trustees' powers; it may consist of a failure to carry out a positive obligation of the trustees or merely of a want of skill and care on their part in the management of the trust property; it may be injurious to the interests of the beneficiaries or be actually to their benefit.

REMEDIES OF THE BENEFICIARY: A SUMMARY

The various remedies which we are about to consider may seem complex but this is because they are designed to cover different situations.

Take note

When discussing equitable remedies, always start from the point that the beneficiary is asserting his proprietary interest in the trust property. All the rest flows from this.

APPLICATION

Paul, a trustee of money in a bank account in the name of the trust, wrongfully withdraws that money and puts it in his own bank account. The beneficiaries have a straightforward remedy: the return of the money. This is a remedy *in rem*, i.e. against the thing itself, here the restitution of the money. The right to bring an action *in rem* is important where the trustee is insolvent as the beneficiary can claim the property in preference to other creditors.

Frank, a trustee of £5m, without taking advice, invests all of it in a small company on the advice of an inexperienced financial adviser that the company will do well. In fact all of the money is lost when it goes into liquidation. The beneficiaries are, of course, entitled to a remedy but the position is not straightforward as they may not be entitled to all of the money back. It may be that there was a reason for investing some of the money in that company but not all of it or it may be that, on the facts, there was no liability at all as the advice was not negligent. Whatever the outcome, the point is that the remedy is for money compensation and is against the trustee personally (*in personam*).

CORNERSTONE

Types of remedies

There are two types of remedies available for a breach of trust: personal (*in personam*) and proprietary (*in rem*).

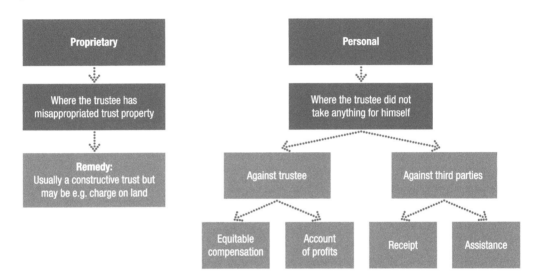

Figure 10.1 Remedies for breach of trust

PERSONAL REMEDIES

Against the trustee

Equitable compensation

There has been much debate in this area and in particular the term 'equitable compensation' is often used to describe money payments by trustees where there has been a breach of trust. The difficulty is that the term 'compensation' seems the same as damages and then it is easy to make a link with damages at common law and think that damages in equity are the same. If this is the case then what about such issues as foreseeability and remoteness? Do the same rules apply in equity as at common law? It is clear that they do not as the nature of equitable remedies is different, as we saw above, being based on the proprietary rights of the beneficiaries.

   The other problem with the term 'equitable compensation' is that in order to decide the principles on which it should be awarded one has to use the term 'account'. This can lead to confusion with where the term 'account' is used to describe the remedy of an account of profits. However, the term 'equitable compensation' is in such general use that it must be used here.

It is vital to distinguish between different types of breaches of trust and, at a more basic level, to note the distinctive character of remedies for breach of trust. This rests on the proprietary interest in the trust property held by the beneficiaries and is entirely different from an action at common law for compensation for, for instance, personal injury where there is no pre-existing legal relationship between the parties. Here there is: that of trustee and beneficiary, and the remedy sought is proprietary. In common law actions for damages the remedy sought is personal.

The two types of breaches of trust are:

(a) *Where the trustee misapplies trust money by, for instance, distributing it to the wrong person*. The essence is that the trustee has done something which she must not do. We will call the first **Breach A**.

> *Take note*
>
> When considering remedies in this area, start with the breach. Identifying the type of breach will lead you to the appropriate remedy.

(b) *Where the trustee, for instance, makes unauthorised investments and, in doing so, fails to show the necessary standard of care*. Here the trustee has done something that she is entitled to do – make the investments – but has done it negligently. As Millett LJ said in *Armitage* v. *Nurse* (1998) 'a breach of trust may be deliberate or inadvertent'. We will call this **Breach B**. There is an obvious parallel between Breach B cases and those for the tort of negligence at common law and this has caused confusion.

The fundamental duty of the trustee is to produce accounts for the beneficiary to examine. This flows from the beneficiaries' proprietary interests in the trust property. As the trust assets are the beneficiary's in equity then she has the right to know in what state they are. In *Ultraframe (UK) Ltd* v. *Fielding* (2007) Lewison J said 'The taking of an account is the process by which a beneficiary requires a trustee to justify his stewardship of trust property.' Where a breach of trust has occurred then the beneficiaries can require the taking of an account which will show that a sum has been misapplied.

There are then two possibilities.

(a) Falsification of the account

This means that the sum misapplied is disallowed. Lewison J in the above case instanced where trustees have made an unauthorised investment (Breach A) that falls in value. The account is taken as if the expenditure had not been made and thus as if the unauthorised investment has not formed part of the trust assets. In this sense the account is falsified. The trustee is then required to account to the trust for the unauthorised disbursement, i.e. the full amount of what he had taken out of the trust account wrongly and so the trustee is restoring the trust property and the claim is for performance of the trustee's obligation to deliver the assets of the trust (substitutive performance). Thus the term 'compensation' is misleading in this context as the beneficiaries are not compensated for harm suffered and so questions of foreseeability and remoteness have no place. Thus Blackburne J in *Re Lehman Brothers International (Europe) (in administration) (No. 2)* (2009) said that a beneficiary's remedy for breach of trust 'is principally directed to securing performance of the trust, rather than to the recovery of compensation or damages'.

APPLICATION

Trustees of a trust for two children invest £100,000 in overseas companies although the trust specifically prohibits this. The amount is now £80,000. Technically this £80,000 is in the account but as the investment was in breach of trust this sum is ignored and the investment is treated as having been bought with the trustees' own money and on their behalf. Thus, what is really a trust asset (the £80,000), as it was bought with trust money, is treated as having been bought with the trustees' own money and so is not a trust asset and that is why we say that the account is falsified.

The reason for this is that the court then requires the trustees to account to the trust for the full sum of £100,000 which was lost to the estate, i.e. to replace the £100,000.

Incidentally, if the unauthorised investment has gained in value then the beneficiary may choose not to falsify the account and so the investment, although unauthorised, will stay as a trust asset.

(b) Surcharging the account

CORNERSTONE

Target Holdings v. Redferns

The leading case here is *Target Holdings* v. *Redferns*. The decision has, however, been subject to much debate and you need to be aware of this.

The account is surcharged where there is a type B breach where, for example, the beneficiary alleges that the trustee has not exercised due care and diligence in making an investment. The account is taken as if the trust had received what it would have received if the trustee had exercised due diligence. This is sometimes known as a reparation claim.

APPLICATION

Trustees make an investment of £100,000 which is not strictly prohibited to them but applying the standard investment criteria in s. 4 of the Trustee Act 2000 appears to have been negligent. The investment is now worth £80,000 but had the money been properly invested it would have been worth £120,000. The account produced by the trustees is surcharged so that the trustees are liable for the difference between the two sums: £40,000.

It is here that there has been some confusion as this looks like common law damages for negligence and the decision in *Target Holdings Ltd* v. *Redferns* (1996) illustrates this. Money was lent by a finance company (X) to developers(Y) on the security of two properties which were fraudulently overvalued. Redferns acted for both parties and received the mortgage advance on a bare trust for the claimant to release it to Y when the transfers of the properties were executed. However, in breach of trust they released it early. This was a type A breach as the trustees had misapplied trust money. Y subsequently went into liquidation, and X sold the properties for much less than their value. X claimed against Redferns for the loss on the transaction but failed.

The House of Lords held that the rule in assessing compensation for breach of trust in commercial dealings such as this, especially as the solicitor was only a bare trustee, is that a trustee is only liable for losses caused by the breach and not for losses which would have occurred anyway. Thus although the solicitors, the trustees, acted in breach of trust by releasing the funds early, the claimants obtained the mortgage securities later anyway. The early release of the funds did not decide if the mortgage would go through, and it was this which caused the loss.

The decision itself seems correct but the remarks of Lord Browne-Wilkinson have caused debate. He felt that X should have to prove a causal link between its loss and the breach of duty by the solicitors, which does not accord with the principles set out above, and he distinguished between commercial-type trusts, such as the bare trust, and family trusts. He seemed to feel that in commercial-type trusts it should not be possible for a claimant to recover all loss flowing from the breach so that the trust fund is reconstituted regardless of causation whereas in family-type trusts the rules on causation might not apply.

Lord Millett (1998b) disagrees. He argues that even if the trust in *Target Holdings* had been a family-type trust it would have been wrong for the solicitors to have been held liable to repay the whole loss as it did not actually result from the breach of trust and that Lord Browne-Wilkinson failed to distinguish between substitutive performance (for a type A breach) and reparation claims (for a type B breach). *Target Holdings* was an instance of the first type as the trustees performed their duty eventually by obtaining the mortgage securities and it is only in the second type that issues of causation are relevant.

INTERSECTION

Do not confuse equitable compensation in this context with the power of the court to order damages in addition to or in substitution for an injunction or specific performance. This is a different topic and is dealt with in Chapter 2.

Account of profits

This is an alternative personal remedy against a trustee but of course is only applicable where the trustee has profits made by the wrongful use of trust property. The consequence of this remedy can actually be proprietary as the court may order that these profits are held on a constructive trust for the beneficiary.

In *Keech* v. *Sandford* (see Chapter 9) the lessor who had the lease renewed to himself in breach of trust was ordered to account to the infant beneficiary for any profits made from it.

> **Take note**
> Have a look at *Swindle* v. *Harrison* (1997) where the decision in *Target Holdings* v. *Redferns* was applied.

REMEDIES AGAINST THIRD PARTIES

CORNERSTONE

When third parties may be involved in a breach of trust

Third parties may be involved in a breach of trust in two ways: by actually receiving trust property or by assisting the trustee to commit a breach of trust. The tests for establishing liability in these cases are different.

Dishonest receipt of trust property

The courts have found difficulty in establishing an all-embracing principle for determining when a stranger who has received trust property can be liable. In *Baden Delvaux Lecuit* v. *Société Générale* (1983) Peter Gibson J proposed five categories which stretched to 'knowledge of circumstances which would put an honest and reasonable man on enquiry'. There was then a move away from this. Megarry V-C in *Re Montagu's ST* (1987) held that there were three situations where liability could be imposed:

(a) actual knowledge;

(b) wilfully shutting one's eyes to the obvious;

(c) wilfully and recklessly failing to make enquiries which an honest person would have made.

CORNERSTONE

Test for liability for dishonest receipt of trust property

The test for establishing liability for dishonest receipt of trust property is set out in *BCCI Ltd* v. *Akindele* (2001).

Take note

Keep in mind that there are three possibilities here:

(a) that there is strict liability – i.e. liability arises automatically on the receipt of trust property or the giving of assistance;

(b) that there is no liability;

(c) that liability depends on knowledge of some kind.

In fact the courts have adopted (c) but there have been debates on how to measure the standard of knowledge required.

The present law is in the decision in *Bank of Credit and Commerce International (Overseas) Ltd* v. *Akindele* (2001) where Nourse LJ held that there should be a single test of knowledge: did 'the recipient's state of knowledge . . . make it unconscionable for him to retain the benefit of the receipt?' This, he felt, would enable there to be common-sense decisions in the context of commercial transactions. It remains open to doubt whether this is so.

In *Charter plc* v. *City Index plc* (2007) Carnwarth J suggested that, in deciding if conduct is unconscionable, a court should ask first if the conduct came within any of the three categories in *Re Montagu* (above). If so then this may demonstrate unconscionability. Alternatively the court should consider if there was something unconscionable about the circumstances of the case.

This is a notoriously awkward for the law to pin down but one simple test may be helpful: in *Polly Peck* v. *Nadir (No. 2)* (1992) Scott LJ said that whatever test is applied the judge must ultimately ask if the defendant ought to have been suspicious as to where the property came from.

REFLECTION

Lord Millett in *Twinsectra* v. *Yardley* (2002, pp. 81–85) held that 'liability for "knowing receipt" is receipt based. It does not depend on fault.' He went on to say that 'there is no basis for requiring actual knowledge of the breach of trust, let alone dishonesty, as a condition of liability. Constructive notice is sufficient, and may not even be necessary.' The action was, he held, restitutionary. Writing extra-judicially, Millett J (as he then was) wrote in 1991 that to label a person in these circumstances a constructive trustee is 'profoundly mistaken'. He considers that whether or not 'a recipient has retained or parted with the property his liability remains the same, i.e. the receipt of trust property to which he is not entitled' and he views this liability as arising under a resulting, rather than a constructive, trust. If this view is correct then the term 'knowing receipt' is a misnomer.

Note how many of these cases were where the trust was not used in the traditional sense of a vehicle for long-term planning but very much as a means to an end. For instance in *Target Holdings* v. *Redferns* the solicitors were only trustees in the context of a mortgage transaction. In itself this is not problematical but there are dangers where trusts are used in this way and the fundamental equitable principles are ignored. You can see an instance of this in *Schmidt* v. *Rosewood*. In the longer term is this leading to a division in the law of trusts between the traditional type of trust and commercial ones where the traditional fiduciary relationship is not significant? Another echo of this is in the increasing use of trustee exclusion clauses considered below.

Liability of a person who has assisted in a breach of trust

Here there is no acquisition of trust property and so it is incorrect to speak of such a person as a constructive trustee. The remedy is a personal one against the wrongdoer and is called liability for 'dishonest assistance' in a breach of trust. Where the dishonest accessory has made a profit he can be required to account for it or there is the possibility of a reparation claim surcharging the account (see above).

APPLICATION

It may help you to understand what the law is trying to achieve here if you look at this example from the judgment of Lord Nicholls in *Royal Brunei Airlines Sdn Bhd* v. *Tan Kok Ming* (1995):

> A trustee is proposing to make a payment out of the trust fund to a particular person. He honestly believes he is authorised to do so by the terms of the trust deed. He asks a solicitor to carry through the transaction. The solicitor well knows that the proposed payment would be a plain breach of trust. He also well knows that the trustee mistakenly believes otherwise. Dishonestly he leaves the trustee under his misapprehension and prepares the necessary documentation.

Remember that the trustee is liable anyway as the liability of trustees is strict, unless she is able to claim that an exclusion clause (see below) protects her. The question for us is to establish the principle of law on which those who assist in breaches of trust, such as the solicitor here, should be liable.

CORNERSTONE

Test for liability for dishonest assistance in a breach of trust

The test for establishing liability for dishonest assistance in a breach of trust is set out in *Royal Brunei Airlines Sdn Bhd* v. *Tan Kok Ming*.

In *Royal Brunei Airlines Sdn Bhd* v. *Tan Kok Ming* (1995) Lord Nicholls held that the accessory's liability should depend on whether he had been dishonest. He held that the liability of the person who assisted in the breach of trust did not depend on the trustee's own state of mind as a person should

Take note

You will see that there is much discussion in the cases below of the terms 'objective' and 'subjective'. Do keep in mind that objective means a general standard whilst subjective means a standard which relates to some extent to that person.

not be allowed to set his own standard of what is dishonest. Instead they must be judged by the standards of right-thinking members of society. The standard was, he said, an objective one. However, he did suggest some subjective elements by stating that 'a court will look at all the circumstances known to the third party at the time. The court will also have regard to personal attributes of the third party, such as his experience and intelligence, and the reason why he acted as he did'.

The matter then became confused as a result of speeches by members of the House of Lords in *Twinsectra Ltd* v. *Yardley* (2002). Lord Hutton, whose speech was supported by Lord Hoffmann, held that a person will not be dishonest unless it is established that his conduct had been dishonest by the ordinary standards of reasonable and honest people *and that he realised that by those standards his conduct was dishonest*. This amounted to saying that self-conscious dishonesty is required which is subjective and was exactly what Lord Nicholls in *Royal Brunei Airlines* had said was not the test.

The matter was clarified in *Barlow Clowes International Ltd (in liquidation)* v. *Eurotrust International Ltd and others* (2005), where Lord Hoffmann, who delivered the unanimous judgment of the Privy Council, held that objective dishonesty is required so that although the defendant must have known that he was acting contrary to normal standards of honesty he need not have been actually conscious that he was doing wrong. Thus Lord Hoffmann seemed to backtrack from his views and those of Lord Hutton in *Twinsectra* v. *Yardley* and indeed admitted that there was 'an element of ambiguity' in what Lord Hutton said in that case about subjective dishonesty. In the subsequent decision, *Abou-Rahmah* v. *Abacha* (2006), Arden LJ in the Court of Appeal considered that the decision in *Barlow Clowes* should be followed in England although the other two judges did not consider it necessary to examine the conflict between the two cases, because they held that the conduct of a bank in this case was not even objectively dishonest.

APPLICATION

The above discussion may seem at first sight to be just a matter of words but a look at the facts of the cases shows that it is not. For example, in *Barlow Clowes* v. *Eurotrust* (above) a fraudster had laundered money through various bank accounts and one director of Eurotrust, a Mr Henwood, suspected that money passing through his hands was stolen but had not made enquiries as to what was going on. This was partly because, as the trial judge found, Mr Henwood 'may well have lived by different standards and seen nothing wrong in what he was doing'. He had, the judge said, an 'exaggerated notion of dutiful service to clients, which produced a warped moral approach that it was not improper to treat carrying out clients' instructions as being all important. Mr Henwood may well have thought this to be an honest attitude, but, if so, he was wrong.'

If we applied the test of self-conscious dishonesty put forward by Lord Hutton in *Twinsectra* v. *Yardley* then Mr Henwood might not have been found liable as he did not realise that his conduct was dishonest by the standards of the reasonable and honest person. However, on the basis of the test applied in *Royal Brunei* and followed in *Barlow Clowes* v. *Eurotrust* he was liable. Surely this was right? A person should not be able to set his own standards of what is right and wrong.

INTERSECTION

Note the test for dishonesty in the criminal law established in *R* v. *Ghosh* (1982): must a defendant have done something that right-thinking people would regard as dishonest and have been aware that they would regard his actions as dishonest? This test seems to have influenced Lord Hutton in *Twinsectra* v. *Yardley*. As you can see, the law on knowing assistance now uses a different test. Why do you think that different branches of the law should use different tests?

Starglade Properties Ltd v. *Nash* (2010) is a good example of the present application of the rules on dishonest assistance.

Position where land is sold in breach of trust

The position where land is sold in breach of trust is complex and detailed consideration really belongs to land law.

INTERSECTION

Look at the land law rules on overreaching (see ss. 2(1) and 27 of the LPA 1925) and at the rights of occupiers of land held on trust. Note the impact of the Land Registration Act 2002 where title to land is registered and in particular Schedules 1 and 3.

TRUSTEE DE SON TORT

This is where a person acts as a trustee but is not authorised to do so. They will be liable in the same way as any other trustee.

Proprietary remedies for breach of trust

The idea here is that the claimant (usually the beneficiary) is claiming a right against the trust property itself rather than a remedy against a trustee personally and so here we see the advantage of a proprietary remedy as it will give the claimant priority over the ordinary creditors of the defaulting trustee.

    The usual remedy here is the imposition of a constructive trust (see Chapter 9) but it may be that, for example, a charge over land is appropriate.

APPLICATION

John is a trustee and in breach of trust he acquires land. Bert, the beneficiary, can seek an order that this land is held by John on a constructive trust for him.

    Alf is a trustee and in breach of trust spends trust money on the improvement of land owned by him personally. Here the proprietary remedy will be a charge over that land.

You can find the details of when there can be a constructive trust in Chapter 9 but here we need to look at the process of tracing which is used to identify property which can be subject to a proprietary remedy.

TRACING

CORNERSTONE

Tracing

Tracing is not a remedy as such but a means to obtain a remedy. There are different rules at common law and equity but the essential point is that equity permits tracing in wider circumstances than the common law.

Remember that the term tracing, as with restitution, is often misunderstood. It is not a remedy as such but a process giving the right to trace (i.e. follow) trust property into the hands of a person who then becomes a constructive trustee of it or where a charge can be imposed on it. Tracing leads to a proprietary remedy and it is the imposition of a trust which gives rise to the remedy, as this gives rise to the equitable right.

APPLICATION

Maria is treasurer of the Hanbury Begonia Society. She is allowed to sign cheques on behalf of the society and she wrongly pays £1,000 of the society's money into her own bank account and uses another £5,000 to buy herself a new suite of furniture. The fraud is discovered and Maria is imprisoned. However, the members want their funds back. Tracing is the process by which they follow their money both into the bank account and into the property which was bought with trust funds.

It is important to establish the persons against whom there is a right to trace. These are anyone except a bona fide purchaser of the trust property for value without notice that it was trust property. The term 'notice' means either actual knowledge that it was trust property (actual notice) or constructive notice.

Tracing at common law

> **Take note**
>
> Where you are dealing with a claim arising out of a trust then you must apply the equitable tracing rules. The common law ones are included to give a complete picture.

Tracing is allowed but is limited in the following ways:

(a) It probably does not allow tracing where the money representing the proceeds of sale has been mixed with other money (see *Agip (Africa) Ltd* v. *Jackson* (1989)).

(b) It does not allow a beneficiary under a trust to trace as no one with an equitable interest can trace at common law.

This means that for our purposes we are concerned with the right to trace in equity.

Tracing in equity

The following are the requirements for tracing in equity.

(a) *Fiduciary relationship*. Clearly a beneficiary under an existing trust can trace but the courts have extended the concept of a fiduciary relationship further than this. In *Elders Pastoral* v. *Bank of New Zealand* (1989), the court held that a fiduciary relationship was not necessary and unconscionability was the key requirement. In practice the requirement of a fiduciary relationship is easily satisfied in cases of commercial fraud because whenever an employee of a company ·wrongfully takes property it will be in breach of a fiduciary duty.

In *Aluminium Industrie Vaassen BV* v. *Romalpa Aluminium Ltd* (1976), it was held that the incorporation of a reservation of title clause in a contract for the sale of goods, providing that the goods should remain the property of the seller until the purchase price had been paid, enabled the seller to trace the proceeds of sale of those goods and recover this money in priority to the buyer's other creditors when the buyer became insolvent. The reservation of title clause meant that when the buyer resold the goods he did so as the seller's agent and this created a fiduciary relationship.

In *Re Diplock* (1948), the defendant by will gave the residue of his property on trust for charitable benevolent objects. This was held not to be charitable in *Chichester Diocesan Fund* v. *Simpson* (see Chapter 6) but the executors previously thought that it was and so had distributed the money to various charities. The next-of-kin were allowed to trace the money into the hands of the charities. The court held that provided there is an initial fiduciary relationship the beneficial owner of an equitable interest in property can trace it into the hands of anyone except a bona fide purchaser for value without notice. Here the initial fiduciary relationship was between the next-of-kin and the executors. One case where there is no fiduciary relationship and thus no right to trace is where money is stolen by a thief.

(b) *Equitable proprietary interest*. A beneficiary under a trust clearly has such an interest and, as with fiduciary relationships, this concept too has been extended as in the above cases. It is not clear whether a legal, as distinct from an equitable, owner can trace in equity. In principle there seems no reason why not and in the *Aluminium Industrie* v. *Romalpa* case (above) tracing by a legal owner was accepted although without any argument on the point. In *Foskett* v. *McKeown* (2000) Lord Millett doubted the need for an equitable proprietary interest where it is sought to trace in equity.

(c) *Tracing would not be inequitable*. In *Re Diplock* money had been spent on alterations to buildings and the erection of new buildings. It was held that it would be inequitable to allow tracing here as the result would be a charge on the land and an innocent volunteer might have to sell his own land.

(d) *The property must be in a traceable form*. If the trustee has sold trust property and still has the proceeds of sale then the beneficiary can take them if they are identifiable. If the trustee has used the proceeds to buy other property then the beneficiary can follow this and either take the property bought or have a charge on it for the amount of trust money used to buy it (Jessel MR in *Re Hallett's Estate* (1880)). If, however, the money has been spent, e.g. on a holiday, then it is no longer identifiable and equity can give no remedy.

Take note

Where the trustee has mixed trust money with other money, often his own, is where the tracing rules are really significant.

Mixed funds

Position between trustee and beneficiary

Beneficiaries have a first charge over the mixed fund or any property bought with it. It is for the trustee to show that a particular part of the trust fund is his own.

Position as between two or more trusts or a trust and an innocent volunteer

Where a trustee has mixed funds belonging to two or more trusts, or has transferred funds to an innocent volunteer, then the trusts, or the trust and the volunteer, share *in pari passu* (in proportion to the amount contributed by each) in both the mixed funds and property bought with them.

Bank accounts

Mixing is most likely to take place in bank accounts and the following rules apply:

(i) Position between a trustee and a beneficiary. In *Re Hallett's Estate* (1880) the rule was established that when making withdrawals from an account a trustee is presumed to spend his own money first. Once the amount in the account falls below the amount of trust funds then it is assumed that part of the trust funds must have been spent. Any later payments in are not treated as repayments of the trust money unless the trustee has shown an intention to do this (*Roscoe* v. *Winder* (1915)).

APPLICATION

Chris, a trustee, puts £10,000 of trust money and £3,000 of his own money into the trust account. He takes out £11,000 and spends it. £3,000 of this is presumed to be his own money, but the remainder must be trust money. Therefore there is now £2,000 of trust money left. He then puts £3,000 into the account. This is presumed to be his own money unless Chris shows an intention to repay the trust money. If he does not then, although the beneficiaries claim the £2,000 in the account, they will have to take their place along with Chris's other creditors in a claim for the balance.

In *Re Oatway* (1903) it was held that if a trustee mixes his own and trust money in an account and then takes all the money and spends it on identifiable property the beneficiaries have a first charge on this property for the recovery of the trust money. If the rule in *Re Hallett* applied to this situation the trustee, being presumed to have spent his own money first, would be treated as owner of the property as it was bought with his own money. Thus *Re Oatway* (1903) establishes a different principle here.

CORNERSTONE

Foskett v. *McKeown*

Foskett v. *McKeown* is the leading modern case on tracing and in particular deals with the position where it is sought to trace into assets which have now increased in value.

In *Foskett* v. *McKeown* (2000) Lord Millett has clarified the position as against the defaulting trustee. He held that where trust money is mixed with the trustee's own money then the beneficiary is 'entitled to locate his contribution in any part of the mixture' and to subordinate the claims of the defaulting trustee and their successors to those of the beneficiary.

Suppose that the property bought has increased in value. Is the charge limited to the amount of trust money spent on the purchase? In *Re Hallett* Jessel MR indicated that this was so but in *Re Tilley's WT* (1967) it was said, *obiter*, that beneficiaries would be entitled to any profit to the extent that it resulted from the use of trust money. Any other rule would allow a dishonest trustee to profit from his breach of trust. It has now been confirmed by the House of Lords in *Foskett* v. *McKeown* (2000) that where the trust fund has increased in value then the beneficiary may claim either:

(a) a share in the fund in proportion to that which the original trust fund bore to the mixed fund at the date when it was mixed; or

(b) they may have a lien on the fund to secure a personal claim against the fund for the return of the money (per Lord Millett).

Thus any increase in value can be claimed under option (a) but if the fund has decreased in value then the beneficiaries can have a lien under option (b) for the amount that they are owed. In *Foskett*, trust money was wrongly used to pay for two life insurance premiums which were paid just before the death of the trustee. The amount wrongly paid in was just over £20,000 and the value of the policy was just over £1 million. The beneficiaries were entitled to 40% of this, which was the amount which their trust fund bore to the total fund.

(ii) Position where mixed funds in an account represent the funds of two or more trusts or the funds of a trust and an innocent volunteer. We are concerned here with two types of competing claim:

(a) between two or more persons with a right to trace;

(b) between a person with a right to trace and an innocent volunteer.

The rule in *Clayton's Case* (1816) provides that in the case of an active continuing bank account the trustee is regarded as having taken out of the fund whatever had been first put in. 'First in, first out.'

The position where funds are mixed is illustrated by the following example.

APPLICATION

Jane, a trustee, puts £1,000 of trust A money into a bank account on 1 June and £500 of trust B money into the same account on 2 June. There is now a total of £1,500 trust money in the account. Jane then takes out £1,200, and, in breach of trust, spends this. As the trust A money was put in first she is presumed to have taken all of this out together with £200 of trust B money. The remaining £300 belongs to trust B.

In *Barlow Clowes International* v. *Vaughan* (1992) the rule in *Clayton's Case* (1816) was not applied to claims by investors to share in the assets of a company which had managed investment plans for them. The investments were in a collective scheme by which investors' money was mixed together and invested in a common fund and it was held to be wrong that those who invested first could expect least. In fact, the date when investments were actually received often depended on agents combining the investments of a number of clients and forwarding a lump sum to the company. The court held that the rule in *Clayton's Case* is only one of convenience and would therefore be displaced here and instead investors would share rateably in the company's assets in proportion to the amounts due to them.

In *Russell-Cooke Trust Co.* v. *Prentis (No. 1)* (2002) many hundreds of investors paid money to a firm of solicitors run by Prentis to be invested in short-term high-interest mortgages. The Law Society intervened and Prentis was struck off. How were the funds remaining in the client account of Prentis to be distributed? Here there was the extra problem which did not apply in the *Barlow Clowes* case (above) that how much of each investor's money had been used in particular investments was unknown. Thus it was held inappropriate to apply *Clayton's Case* and instead the mortgage investments were held rateably for each investor according to the proportion to which they had contributed capital.

> Why should there be separate rules for tracing at common law and in equity? The requirement in equity of a fiduciary relationship was described by Millett J (1991, p. 76) as 'difficult to understand and impossible to defend' and he also suggested that in this situation the thief could be liable on a resulting trust. In *Foskett* v. *McKeown* (2000) Lord Millett (as he had then become) returned to this theme by observing that there was no logical justification for insisting on this requirement and that, in addition, there should be the same rules for tracing both in common law and in equity.

REFLECTION

Note that it is possible to bring a personal action against recipients of trust property (action *in personam*) in claims arising out of the administration of an estate as in *Re Diplock*.

LIABILITY OF INDIVIDUAL TRUSTEES

CORNERSTONE

Liability of individual trustees

When we have decided that trustees are liable then we need to decide if they are all liable equally and if they are liable for breaches by other trustees. It is possible that some trustees may be more blameworthy than others.

A trustee is liable for breaches of trust committed by him, but is not vicariously liable for breaches committed by other trustees. Thus in *Re Lucking* (1968), the fact that one trustee was liable for failing to supervise the managing director of the company did not mean that his co-trustee was liable. However, a trustee can be personally liable if he stands by while his co-trustee commits a breach of trust, or if he leaves funds under the control of a co-trustee without making proper enquiry as to what he is doing with them (*Bahin* v. *Hughes* (1886)).

Liability for breaches before and after appointment

A trustee is not liable for breaches committed before his appointment. However, if there is evidence that breaches have been committed, then a new trustee can be liable if he fails to take steps against those responsible. A trustee remains liable after retirement for breaches committed by him during his time as trustee. However, it is possible for the trustee, when he retires, to be released from liability by either the trustees or by all the beneficiaries, so long as they are of full age and capacity and in possession of all the material facts.

A trustee will not be liable for breaches committed after his retirement unless he retired in order to assist in a breach of trust taking place (*Head* v. *Gould* (1898)).

Liability between trustees

The general principle is that one trustee is not liable for the acts of another trustee (*Townley* v. *Sherborne* (1634)). However, although all are individually liable for their own actual breaches, when it comes to paying compensation for breaches to the beneficiaries, they are jointly and severally liable and the fundamental equitable rule is that no regard is taken of fault. Therefore a trustee who was actively involved in the breach and a completely passive trustee are equally liable. However, one who has paid compensation for the breach of a fraudulent trustee can then claim a contribution against the fraudulent trustee for the compensation that he has paid.

This rule is modified by the Civil Liability (Contribution) Act 1978, which provides that the amount recoverable from any defendant shall be such as may be found by the court just and equitable, having regard to the extent of that person's responsibility for the damage in question

APPLICATION

Tim and Tom are trustees. Tom claims to be a financial expert and, acting on his advice, Tim agrees to the lending of £100,000 to a company which in fact, and unknown to Tim, is controlled by Edith, Tom's wife. Tom and Edith then abscond with the money.

Tim may have been negligent but even if he was not he can be sued by the beneficiaries for the loss. Under general equitable principles Tim is liable for the whole £100,000 but under the Civil Liability (Contribution) Act 1978 his liability may be reduced. Whatever Tim has paid to the beneficiaries he may seek to recover from Tom. On the other hand he may not be able to find him!

The Act does not, however, apply to cases where one trustee is liable to **indemnify** his fellow trustees and this applies in the following cases:

(a) A trustee who is also a beneficiary must indemnify his co-trustee to the extent of his beneficial interest (*Chillingworth* v. *Chambers* (1896)). After that property has been used to meet the claim, liability can be shared according to the Act.

(b) Where one trustee is a solicitor and the breach was committed solely as a result of his advice, then he must indemnify his co-trustee against any damages which they have had to pay as a result of the breach of trust (*Re Partington* (1887)).

(c) Where the trustee has obtained trust property and used it for his own fraudulent purposes (*Bahin* v. *Hughes*).

Criminal liability of trustees

A breach of trust is not a crime at common law precisely because the common law regarded the trustee as the owner of the trust property. However, s. 1 of the Theft Act 1968 defines theft as the dishonest appropriation of property belonging to another with the intention of permanently depriving the other of it, and under s. 5(2), any person with a right to enforce the trust (e.g. a beneficiary) is regarded as a person to whom the trust property belongs. Thus, in this slightly roundabout way, where trustees take trust property and treat it as their own this is theft from the beneficiaries.

EXEMPTION CLAUSES AND TRUSTEES

CORNERSTONE

Exemption clauses and trustees

Trustees can, in some cases, be exempted from liability for a breach of trust. The question which we have to answer is: which breaches?

The use of exemption clauses has become common in trusts, especially where the trustees are professional trustees. The Trustee Act 2000 does not restrict the scope of these, nor does it lay down any conditions on their use. However, it does provide (Sch. 1, para. 7) that the statutory duty of care is inapplicable 'if and so far as it appears from the trust instrument that the duty is not meant to apply'. Thus it is possible to restrict the scope of the statutory duty, although almost certainly not for fraud.

INTERSECTION

Look at the law on exemption clauses in contract and tort. Why should equity take a different attitude to their validity?

Take note

If you are faced with a trustee exemption clause then do first check that there appears to be some liability for which the trustees might be exempt – deal with this first and when you have decided that there could be liability then deal with the validity of the clause.

The leading case is *Armitage* v. *Nurse* (1998), which concerned property including agricultural land and the beneficiaries' alleged negligence in its management. Millett LJ, who gave the leading judgment, held that 'there is an irreducible core of obligations owed by the trustees to the beneficiaries and enforceable by them which is fundamental to the concept of a trust' and liability for this could not be excluded. As he pointed out: 'If the beneficiaries have no rights enforceable against the trustees there are no trusts.' Thus liability for actual frauds could not be excluded but a clause could 'exclude liability for breach of trust in the absence of a dishonest intention on the part of the trustee whose conduct is impugned'. He did not accept that there is a distinction between negligence, for which liability can be excluded, and gross negligence, for which it cannot.

In *Spread Trustee Co. Ltd* v. *Hutcheson* (2011) the beneficiaries claimed that the trustee had been grossly negligent in failing to identify and investigate breaches of trust on the part of previous trustees. A clause in the trust instrument exempted the trustee from liability for breaches of trust arising from his own gross negligence. It was held that the parties could lawfully agree to exclude a trustee's liability for breaches arising from negligence or gross negligence. Lord Clarke in effect agreed with Millett LJ in *Armitage* v. Nurse and said that 'To describe negligence as gross does not change its nature so as to make it fraudulent or wilful misconduct.'

REFLECTION

Should it be possible for trustees to exclude their liability at all? Given the very high standard which equity expects trustees to observe, the idea can seem wrong in principle but a distinction may need to be drawn between family trusts (where an exemption of liability may be unacceptable) and large commercial ones (where it may be right). If so, the current battleground is just what liability such a clause can exclude.

Have a look at the dissenting judgment of Lady Hale in *Spread Trustee* v. *Hutcheson*, who felt that trustee exclusion clauses should not be able to cover liability for gross negligence. She pointed to the Law Commission's Consultation paper No. 124 on '"Fiduciary duties and regulatory rules" (1992) which said that "it seems that a trustee may not exclude liability for 'wilful default'". There is however uncertainty as to whether liability for gross negligence can be excluded' (para. 3.3.6). She also gave the example of a case where the guardian of the estate of a minor might seek to rely on a clause exempting him from liability for gross negligence which she felt any English lawyer would regard as unacceptable.

INTERSECTION

The operation of the so-called rule in *Re Hastings-Bass* has been curtailed. As trustees are now far less likely to have the option of asking the court to undo a transaction where trustees acted on incorrect advice (leading to the possibility of more claims against the trustees by the beneficiaries) will this lead to an increase in the use of trustee exclusion clauses?

PROTECTION OF TRUSTEES

CORNERSTONE

Protection of trustees

The rules on protection of trustees are set out in the Trustee Act 1925 and case law.

(a) Section 61 of the Trustee Act 1925

Section 61 provides that the court may relieve a trustee from liability if he has acted honestly and reasonably and ought fairly to be excused both for the breach and for omitting to obtain the directions of the court.

Thus a trustee must show not only that he acted honestly, but also that he acted reasonably. The standard here has been held to be that of the 'prudent man of business' but it seems logical now to apply the statutory duty of care in s. 1 of the Trustee Act 2000 and other criteria, such as the standard investment criteria in s. 4. What s. 61 is not, in the words of Evershed MR in *Marsden* v. *Regan* (1954), is a 'passport to relief'.

In *Re Evans* (1999) a father died intestate leaving a son and daughter, who would each be entitled to a 50% share. The daughter was appointed administratrix, having been estranged from the brother for 30 years. She advertised for him to come forward, but with no result, and was then advised that, rather than obtaining a *Benjamin* Order (below), she should take out an insurance policy to cover herself if the brother reappeared. She then transferred all the assets to herself. In fact the insurance policy was inadequate, as it did not take account of interest which was due to the brother from the date when he should have received his share. The brother then finally reappeared and it was held that the daughter was covered by s. 61 so that, despite the inadequate policy of insurance, she was not liable to compensate her brother to the full extent of his entitlement, but only to the extent that she still had estate property in her hands.

INTERSECTION

Compare s. 61 of the Trustee Act 1925 which contains similar defences available to company directors under s. 1157 of the Companies Act 2006 and the case of *Bairstow* v. *Queens Moat Houses plc* (2001) which applied its predecessor, s. 727 of the Companies Act 1985.

It is also worth noting that the relief from trustees' personal liability provided by s. 61 was not available in *Boardman* v. *Phipps* (see Chapter 9) as it applies to trustees and here the parties were agents of trustees.

(b) Where a beneficiary participates in, or consents to, a breach of trust

The court can impound the beneficiary's interest, so that it is available to replace any loss to the trust and the trustees are therefore given an indemnity to this extent from actions by beneficiaries in respect of the breach. The following conditions must be satisfied:

(i) The beneficiary had full knowledge of all relevant facts. In *Re Somerset* (1894), trustees had wrongly invested trust funds on a mortgage of particular property at the instigation of a beneficiary, but the beneficiary had left it to them to decide how much to lend. The court refused to impound the beneficiary's interest.

(ii) The beneficiary was of full age and sound mind.

(iii) The beneficiary freely consented to the breach of trust. Thus in *Re Pauling* (1964) it was held that consent by a beneficiary to advances of capital which she knew would be used to benefit her parents was not free consent because the presumption of undue influence by a parent over a child continues to exist, as in this case, for a period after the child attains its majority.

INTERSECTION

Re Pauling is concerned the power of advancement. Look at the details of this case and see how the law on advancements and this area of the law are linked.

(iv) The beneficiary must have intended to derive a personal benefit from the breach, even though he may not have actually received one.

(c) Power under section 62 of the Trustee Act 1925 to impound a beneficiary's interest

This also allows the court to impound a beneficiary's interest where he has instigated or requested the breach of trust or has consented in writing to it. The principles on which the court exercises its jurisdiction here are similar to those under its inherent equitable jurisdiction (b) (above) but the main difference is that, for s. 62 to apply, there is no requirement that the beneficiary should have intended to obtain a benefit. In addition, s. 62 only applies to a written consent to a breach, whereas the equitable power to impound can be exercised even if the consent was oral.

The way in which the above rules work is illustrated by the following example.

·· APPLICATION

Jane is a trustee. There are three beneficiaries: Sarah aged 17, Michael aged 25 and Denis aged 30. Denis persuades Jane to invest all the trust property in a speculative property venture and Sarah agrees to this. The venture turns out to be a complete failure and all the trust property is lost. Quite clearly Denis cannot sue Jane, as the idea was his and she merely acted on it. Can Michael and Sarah sue? Yes. Although Sarah consented, she was not of full age (see (b)(ii) above). Michael did not consent, so he obviously can. If they succeed, and this will depend on whether the investment was in breach of the standard investment criteria in the Trustee Act 2000, then Denis's beneficial interest under the trust can be taken to satisfy their claims.

Benjamin Orders

If beneficiaries cannot be traced then the money can be paid into court or the court may make a *Benjamin* Order (from *Re Benjamin* (1902)). This will authorise a trustee to distribute the property as if the beneficiary is dead. This will protect the trustees but if the beneficiaries do come forward within the limitation period they may proceed either against the trust property or against those wrongly paid.

Limitation of actions against trustees

CORNERSTONE

Limitation Act 1980

If you have decided that an action against trustees should be brought then you must check that the possible action is not time barred, i.e. that it is not too late to bring it. The rules are set out in the Limitation Act 1980.

(a) *Under the Limitation Act 1980.* Section 21(3) lays down a general rule that a beneficiary has six years from the date when the breach was committed to bring the action, i.e. in which to issue the claim or other originating process. This applies to actions for breach of trust in relation to trust property. In certain cases the limitation period does not apply:

(i) Time does not begin to run against those beneficiaries who were under a disability at the date of the breach until their disability ends (s. 28).

(ii) A right of action in respect of future interests is not treated as having accrued until the interest falls into possession: only then does time begin to run (s. 21(3)).

(iii) No limitation period applies where the action is in respect of any fraud to which the trustee was a party, or privy, or where the action is to recover from the trustee either trust property which is still in his possession, or the proceeds of a sale of it (s. 21(1)). Nor is there any limitation period if the action is against defendants who claim through a fraudulent trustee, unless they are bona fide purchasers for value without notice (*Re Dixon* (1900)).

(iv) No limitation period applies to an action *in rem* (for a proprietary remedy) against those who have received trust property, other than purchasers in good faith and without notice.

INTERSECTION

Refer to Chapter 3 for an explanation of what is meant by notice in equity.

(v) Where a right of action has been concealed by fraud or where the action is for relief from the consequence of a mistake, then time does not begin to run until the claimant has discovered the fraud, concealment or mistake or ought with reasonable diligence to have done so (s. 32). In this case, the actual breach of trust will not have been fraudulent, as if it was there would have been no period of limitation (see (iii) above). It is the concealment of the breach which is fraudulent.

(b) *Under the doctrine of laches.* Where the Act does not apply, e.g. (iii) and (iv) above, a claim can still be barred by laches under which delay by a claimant in bringing a claim may prevent them from obtaining an equitable remedy. The court will look at any hardship caused to the claimant by the delay and decide whether, on balance, the interests of justice would still be served by granting relief. An example of laches is *Allcard* v. *Skinner*.

KEY POINTS

- Remedies for breach of trust are different in nature from common law remedies in contract/tort as they are proprietary.
- A beneficiary's remedy for breach of trust is principally directed to securing performance of the trust, rather than to the recovery of compensation or damages.
- The fundamental duty of the trustee is to produce accounts for the beneficiary to examine.
- There are different tests for liability depending on whether it is a knowing receipt case or a knowing assistance one, so make sure that you are clear on the distinction between these.
- Tracing is not a remedy in itself but is a means to establishing a remedy.
- Trustees may escape liability if the conditions in s. 61 of the Trustee Act 1925 apply.
- Section 21(3) of the Limitation Act 1980 lays down a general rule that a beneficiary has six years from the date when the breach of trust was committed to bring the action but there are exceptions.

CORE CASES AND STATUTES

Case	About	Importance
Target Holdings v. *Redferns* (1996)	The principles to be applied when assessing the amount that the trustee should restore to the trust estate when there has been a breach of trust.	Relationship between equitable and common law principles in assessing amounts to be paid on a breach of trust (equity) or breach of contract or tort (common law).
Bank of Credit and Commerce International (Overseas) Ltd v. *Akindele* (2001)	Sets out the test for liability in cases of knowing receipt of trust property.	Compare this with the test for knowing assistance set out in *Twinsectra Ltd* v. *Yardley* (2002) (above).
Royal Brunei Airlines Sdn Bhd v. *Tan Kok Ming* (1995)	Sets out the test for liability in cases of dishonest assistance in a breach of trust.	Compare this with the test for knowing receipt set out in *Bank of Credit and Commerce International (Overseas) Ltd* v. *Akindele* (2001).
Barlow Clowes International Ltd (in liquidation) v. *Eurotrust International Ltd and others* (2005)	Clarified the test for dishonest assistance in a breach of trust following the decision in *Twinsectra* v. *Yardley* (2002).	Emphasises that the test is not self-conscious dishonesty: a person cannot set his own standards of what is dishonest.
Re Hallett's Estate (1880)	To explain that when making withdrawals from an account a trustee is presumed to spend his own money first.	Illustrates how tracing works.
Foskett v. *McKeown* (2000)	The principles which apply where it is sought to trace into a fund that has increased in value.	Illustrates how tracing works.
Clayton's Case (1816)	Where there is an active continuing bank account the trustee is regarded as having taken out of the fund whatever has been put in first.	The position where mixed funds in an account represent the funds of two or more trusts or the funds of a trust and an innocent volunteer.
Armitage v. *Nurse* (1998)	To explain the circumstances when trustees can exclude liability.	Determines the extent to which the courts have discretion in the grant of equitable remedies.

Statute	About	Importance
Section 61 of the Trustee Act 1925	Sets out the circumstances where a court may relieve a trustee from liability.	This is important where it is established that there has been a breach of trust.
Section 62 of the Trustee Act 1925	Power of the court to impound the interest of a beneficiary where he/she has instigated/requested the breach of trust or consented to it.	This is also important where there has been a breach of trust but this time the focus is on a beneficiary who has been involved in the breach.
Section 21(1) of the Limitation Act 1980	Limitation periods for actions against trustees for breach of trust.	This is important where there has been a breach of trust and the question is the time limit for commencing proceedings.

FURTHER READING

Birks, P. (2005) *Unjust Enrichment*, 2nd ed. (Oxford University Press).
This area is a developing one and you should be aware of its importance to any discussion of equitable remedies.

Conaglen, M. (2003) 'Equitable compensation for breach of fiduciary dealing rules' 119 *LQR* 246.
This has an interesting angle on compensation in equity.

Fox, D. (1998) 'Constructive notice and knowing receipt: an economic analysis' 57 *CLJ* 391.
This is another slightly different perspective and a most useful one.

Gardner, S. (2009) 'Moment of truth for knowing receipt' 125 *LQR* 30.
This looks at the decision in *City Index Ltd* v. *Gawler* (2007) and argues that knowing receipt should be the usual liability for failure to preserve trust property.

Getzler, J. (2008) 'Excluding fiduciary duties: the problem of investment banks' 124 *LQR* 15.

This article looks at the decision in *Australian Securities and Investments Commission* v. *Citigroup Global Markets Australia Pty Ltd* (2007).

McCormack, C. (1998) 'The liabilities of trustees for gross negligence' *Conv*. 100.
This useful article argues that trustee exclusion clauses have gone too far. Follow this with looking at what the Law Commission said on this subject: 'Trustee Exemption Clauses' (LC No. 301) (2006).

Millett, P. (1991) 'Tracing the proceeds of fraud' 107 *LQR* 76.

Millett, P. (1998a) 'Restitution and constructive trusts' 114 *LQR* 399.
Both of these articles by Millett are of central importance in this area as the author was one of the leading Chancery judges of his time. Lord Millett delivered a significant speech in *Twinsectra* v. *Yardley* which you should then read.

Millett, P. (1998b) 'Equity's place in the law of commerce' 114 *LQR* 214.

CHAPTER 11
Resulting trusts

BLUEPRINT

Resulting trusts

LEGISLATION

- Equality Act 2010, s. 199

CONTEXT

- Is it right that a resulting trust should be imposed when I make a gift?

CONCEPTS

- Nature of a resulting trust
- When a resulting trust can arise: purchase in another's name
- Failure to specify the beneficial interests
- Resulting trusts in commercial contexts

- What is the true basis of resulting trusts? Is it right that *Quistclose* trusts give an advantage to beneficiaries over creditors?

- What do we mean by a resulting trust and where are such trusts found?

CASES

- *Re Vinogradoff*
- *Gascoigne* v. *Gascoigne*
- *Tinsley* v. *Milligan*
- *Re Gillingham Bus Disaster Fund*
- *Quistclose Investments* v. *Barclays Bank*

REFORM

- Change in the law on surplus gifts to non-charitable associations. Reversal of a *Tinsley* v. *Millgan* situation?

SPECIAL CHARACTERISTICS

- Presumptions of a resulting trust
- Presumption of advancement

CRITICAL ISSUES

Setting the scene

You have already met the term 'resulting trust'. For instance we came across it in Chapter 4 when we learnt that where there was a lack of certainty of objects in a private trust but the other certainties were present then the property would be held on a resulting trust for the settlor or, if the trust was created by will, for the testator's estate.

In this chapter we are going to look at other instances of where resulting trusts can operate and also at the theory behind them. Here is another example dealing with a situation which we will meet later on.

Teresa tells John that he is to be the trustee of the sum of £1,000 belonging to her. John agrees but then Teresa dies. She leaves a will where all of her property is left to her son Sam. What happens to the £1,000? It cannot go on trust as we do not know who the beneficiaries under the trust are. John cannot keep the £1,000 as he is a trustee and, as you know, a trustee cannot benefit from the trust unless expressly named as a beneficiary. The obvious answer is that Sam is to have the £1,000 but how do we move the property from John, who is presently the owner, to Sam? The answer is that as John cannot be a trustee of the first trust, which has failed through lack of certainty of objects, John becomes a trustee of the £1,000 for Sam under a resulting trust. Therefore Sam, as the sole beneficiary under this trust, can simply require John to transfer the £1,000 to him.

WHAT IS MEANT BY A RESULTING TRUST?

CORNERSTONE

Nature of a resulting trust

A resulting trust gets its name from the Latin verb *resalire* (to jump back) and this identifies the essential feature of the trust: that the beneficial interest results to, or jumps back to, the settlor who created the trust.

The idea is strange: a person, Alf, gives property to another, Mike, and then Mike ends up holding it on trust for Alf and so the property comes back to Alf. Note that 'resulting' does not describe the reason the trust arises but only the identity of the beneficiary (viz, the transferor of the rights in question).

INTERSECTION

It is important at this stage not to confuse this situation with that where there is an express trust and the settlor under that trust (Alf in the above example) is one of the beneficiaries. What we are concerned with in this chapter is a situation where equity needs to *impose* a trust to get the property back to Alf.

CORNERSTONE

Presumptions and resulting trusts

There are certain situations where equity presumes that there will be a resulting trust but they will only operate where the intentions of the settlor/testator as evidenced by the words setting up the trust are not clear.

SITUATIONS WHERE A RESULTING TRUST CAN ARISE

There are certain situations where equity presumes that there will be a resulting trust but they will only operate where the intentions of the settlor/testator as evidenced by the words setting up the trust are not clear. If they are clear, then we have an express trust, which is what normally happens. Thus in *Vandervell* v. *IRC* (1967) Lord Upjohn said: 'in reality the so-called presumption of a resulting trust is no more than a long stop to provide the answer when the facts and circumstances fail to yield a solution'. The message is that in any situation you should see if the actual trust provides sufficient certainty. Only if it does not do you need to look at a possible resulting trust.

BASIS OF THE RESULTING TRUST

(a) Automatic and presumed resulting trusts

> **Take note**
>
> You may find it helpful to note these three situations where there can be a presumption of a resulting trust:
>
> (a) Purchase of property in another's name or where there is a voluntary transfer.
> (b) Where the settlor has failed to specify the beneficial interests or where the settlor's intentions with regard to the disposal of the trust property cannot be carried out, either fully or at all.
> (c) In a commercial context as in *Barclays Bank* v. *Quistclose*.

REFLECTION

The prevailing orthodoxy used to be that there were two types of resulting trust:

(i)   Automatic resulting trusts, where there was a resulting trust independent of the intentions of the settlor, as where the settlor has failed to specify the beneficial interests and so there is either a lack of certainty of objects or no objects at all (see Chapter 4).

(ii) Presumed resulting trusts, as where a person transferred property to another without consideration but where no words of gift were used. These, which are dealt with in this chapter, were considered to arise from the presumed intention of the transferor. One example is *Re Vinogradoff* – see below.

This division was proposed by Megarry J in *Re Vandervell's Trusts (No. 2)* (1974) but this was disapproved of by Lord Browne-Wilkinson in *Westdeutsche Landesbank Girozentrale* v. *Islington BC* (1996) who saw resulting trusts as arising from the common intention of the parties. However, the use of the phrase 'common intention' has also been the source of confusion. Nor is it felt by many (e.g. Chambers 1997) that it is justified from the facts of cases which often show that the transferee is unaware of the actual transfer, as in *Re Vinogradoff* (1935). Here the testatrix had transferred an £800 War Loan which was in her own name into the joint names of herself and her four-year-old daughter. It was held that the daughter held it on a resulting trust for the testatrix, on principles dealt with more fully below. As Mee (2012) points out, in cases where one party (X) has provided the purchase money for a purchase in another's name (Y) the resulting trust does not rest on any common intention of the parties but on the presumption that X intended to retain the beneficial interest (see e.g. *Dyer* v. *Dyer* (1788)).

In cases of beneficial entitlement to the family home the leading case of *Lloyds Bank* v. *Rosset* (1991) did identify a common intention as a necessary requirement and rested this case on the notion of a constructive trust, but this has now been overtaken by later decisions.

(b) Resulting trust based on the conscience of the transferee being affected

Lord Browne-Wilkinson in *Westdeutsche* then argued that a resulting trust only came into existence when the conscience of the transferee was affected by notice that he had received property from which he was not intended to benefit. This has been forcefully criticised by Chambers (1997), who gives this example: suppose that Alf gives money to Bert by mistake and Bert gives it to Chris, who has no notice of Alf's mistake. Alf's right to recover the money from Chris would depend on whether Bert had notice of the mistake before he gave it to Chris. Why should notice matter? Surely, Chambers argues, the trust should respond to Alf's lack of intention to benefit the recipient and does not depend on notice. Accordingly the resulting trust comes into existence as soon as the property is transferred.

At present the two theories which are advanced as possible explanations for resulting trusts are:

(i) Resulting trust arising from the lack of intention to pass a beneficial interest to the transferee

This is suggested by Chambers (1997), who proposes that all resulting trusts should be considered as arising from the presumption of the lack of any intention by the transferor to pass any beneficial interest to the transferee when the transferee has not provided the entire consideration for the property. Thus, as Chambers points out, the resulting trust operates to return specific property to the transferor because he/she did not intend to benefit the transferee. The effect is that, unless this presumption is rebutted, a resulting trust arises by operation of law. Chambers would then see resulting trusts as being the major vehicle by which equity contributes to the law of unjust enrichment, a concept which is touched on in this book in connection with a breach of trust (see Chapter 10). This presumption arises, Chambers suggests, when the transfer is made on trust but the transferor did not intend to benefit the transferee.

(ii) Resulting trusts imposed to give effect to the transferor's intention to create a trust for himself

The problem with this basis is that it simply does not explain cases where clearly the transferor does not intend this. For example in *Re Vinogradoff* (above) there is no evidence that the testatrix intended a trust for herself. What happened is that, doubtless unknown to the testatrix, equity decided that this was a situation where a resulting trust would be imposed.

Does it explain a case like *Hodgson* v. *Marks* (1971)? The claimant had transferred her house into the name of her lodger with the intention that he should hold it on trust for her. This express trust was unenforceable as it did not comply with s. 53(1)(c) of the LPA 1925 and so it was held that the lodger should hold it on a resulting trust for the claimant. Chambers argues that this is a case where clearly the claimant (the transferor) did intend to create a trust for herself but it was a case of an intention to create an *express* trust with the resulting trust only being imposed on the failure of this. It is highly doubtful that the transferor ever considered the possibility of a resulting trust.

The debate on the nature of resulting trusts shows no sign of ending and you should try to keep up to date with it. Swadling (2008) argues that there is a distinction between 'presumed' and 'automatic' resulting trusts but cannot find any satisfactory basis for automatic resulting trusts.

REFLECTION

INTERSECTION

You will find a section on 'unjust enrichment' in Chapter 10 which tries to show how this idea has affected the law of trusts. It is also referred to in the following chapter (Chapter 9).

What happens to the beneficial interest?

Lord Reid in *Vandervell* v. *IRC* (1967) argued that this remains with the transferor (or donor) throughout and so equity is simply recognising a fact. This view is now no longer generally held and instead it is considered that on any transfer only the legal interest passes to the transferee and where the resulting trust arises from that transfer then a new equitable interest arises which is held for the original transferor (see Chambers 1997).

Take note

Another issue is the extent to which a resulting trustee is subject to any of the duties of a trustee. A resulting trustee does not assume office as a result of voluntarily agreeing to do so and, of course, there is no trust instrument. Even so, in some cases a resulting trustee will owe fiduciary duties.

APPLICATION

Property is transferred to John to hold on trust for 'all my drinking pals'. This is invalid as there is no certainty of objects (see Chapter 4) and so John is a trustee with a fiduciary duty to hold the property for the settlor, or, if they are dead, their estate.

INTERSECTION ....

The concept of fiduciary duties is central to the law of trusts and is dealt with in full in Chapter 9. The concept is met throughout this book and can be stated briefly as the rule that a trustee is not allowed to make a profit or put himself in a position where his duty and interest conflict.

PURCHASE OF PROPERTY IN THE NAME OF ANOTHER OR IN THE JOINT NAMES OF THE PURCHASER AND ANOTHER

CORNERSTONE

Purchase of property in the name of another

Where property is actually purchased in the name of one person but is paid for by another then a resulting trust can arise for the purchaser.

Where a person pays the purchase money for property and has it put into another's name then it is presumed that the other intends to hold the property on trust for the person who paid for it (*Dyer* v. *Dyer* (1788)).

Where more than one person contributes to the purchase price of the property there is a presumption that the beneficial interest is to be held in the proportions to which each contributed and a resulting trust gives effect to this (*Wray* v. *Steele* (1814)). The principle of 'he who pays, owns' is important in questions arising as to ownership of the family home. However, it is important to note that the idea of common intention, which played such an important part in the development of the law on the family home, was entirely absent in these earlier cases where the emphasis was on the intention of each contributor.

Voluntary transfers

(a) Where there is a voluntary transfer (i.e. a gift) of personalty to another or into the joint names of the transferor and another, there is a presumption of a resulting trust for the transferor. See *Re Vinogradoff* (1935) (page 170).

(b) Where there is a voluntary conveyance of land then s. 60(3) of the LPA 1925 provides that a resulting trust for the grantor (i.e. the transferor) is not to be implied merely because the land is not expressed to be conveyed on trust for him. The effect of this has been debated but in *Lohia* v. *Lohia* (2001) the High Court held that in effect it means what it says: where land is conveyed as a gift then there is no presumption of a resulting trust. This was the argument of Chambers (1997, pp. 18–19).

Presumption of advancement

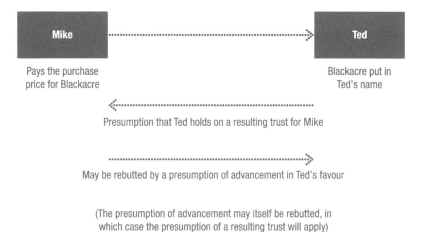

Figure 11.1 Resulting trusts and presumptions of advancement

The above rules are only presumptions. They can be rebutted by evidence of a contrary intention on the part of the transferor, as in *Standing* v. *Bowring* (1885) where the claimant transferred consols (a type of government stock) into the joint names of herself and her godson with the express intention that the godson should have them absolutely if he survived her.

CORNERSTONE

Presumption of advancement

In certain situations equity goes further and holds that there is a presumption of advancement (or gift) which displaces the presumption of resulting trust.

APPLICATION

Jason, by deed of gift, transfers his house into the name of his son Giles. The first point to mention is that, as a deed of gift was used, equity as a general rule will presume that Giles will hold the house on a resulting trust for Jason. Thus although equity recognises that in law the ownership of the house has been transferred, it is able to impose a trust so that Jason still has the beneficial interest.

However, you will note that Giles is Jason's son and so here equity will apply another presumption: that of advancement. This means that there will be no presumption that Giles holds the house on trust for Jason and that instead it is presumed that Jason intended a gift of the house for Giles.

You do need to be careful not to be dogmatic here. These are only presumptions and it may be that on the evidence they will not apply. For example, the evidence may show that Jason did not intend a gift of the house to Giles and so there will be no presumption of advancement and instead the presumption of resulting trust will apply.

Glister (2009, p. 808) remarks that 'The presumption of advancement operates to allocate the burden of proof in disputes over the voluntary transfer of property'.

The effect of the Equality Act 2010

CORNERSTONE

Section 199(1) of the Equality Act 2010

Section 199(1) of the Equality Act 2010 provides that 'The presumption of advancement (by which, for example, a husband is presumed to be making a gift to his wife if he transfers property to her, or purchases property in her name) is abolished.'

The reason for the passage of s. 199 into law was the then Government's belief that the presumption of advancement prevented the UK from acceding to Protocol 7 of the European Convention on Human Rights because the relevant part of Article 5 provides that 'Spouses shall enjoy equality of rights and responsibilities of a private law character between them, and in their relations with their children, during marriage and in the event of its dissolution.' Glister (2010) has argued that the Government misunderstood the effect of Article 5 as it applies in the context of marriage and the presumption of advancement applies in the context of parenthood. Thus there was no need to abolish it at all.

REFLECTION

You might assume from this that there would be no need to study this topic but you would be wrong as s. 199(2) provides that the

'abolition . . . of the presumption of advancement does not have effect in relation to:

(a) anything done before the commencement of this section, or

(b) anything done pursuant to any obligation incurred before the commencement of this section.'

APPLICATION

Take the above application where Jason transferred his house by deed of gift into the name of his son Giles. Suppose that this was in 2009 and it is only in 2059 that some question of ownership arises. As s. 199 was not in force in 2009 the presumption of advancement will still apply as the actual date of the dispute was 50 years later. In *Lohia* v. *Lohia* (2001) a purchase in 1955 was only the subject of litigation on these issues in 2010.

At the time of writing (August 2013) s. 199 is not in force but when it is and you are faced with a question on presumptions of advancement you will need to check when the actions giving rise to a possible presumption happened.

Situations where there is a presumption of advancement

There is a presumption of advancement where a transfer is made from a father to a child and from a husband to a wife. In addition the presumption probably applies where a transfer is made to a child by a person standing *in loco parentis* to it, i.e. a person who has taken on the duty of father of a child to make provision for that child (Jessel MR in *Bennett* v. *Bennett* (1879)). In *Pecore* v. *Pecore* (2007) it was held by the Supreme Court of Canada that the presumption did not apply to transfers by parents to their adult children.

However, the presumption can apply to any relative or other person who, because the parents are unable or unwilling to do so, has taken on the duty of looking after a child and can also apply to the father of an illegitimate child (*Beckford* v. *Beckford* (1774)). There is statutory presumption of gift in relation to an engagement ring, even though no marriage takes place (s. 3(2) of the Law Reform (Miscellaneous Provisions) Act 1970).

There is no presumption of advancement where a transfer is made from a wife to a husband, or where she pays the purchase money for property and has it put in his name, and thus a resulting trust will arise. Nor is there a presumption between a mother and a legitimate child because, according to *Re De Visme* (1863), a woman is under no obligation to maintain her children. However, in the Australian case of *Nelson* v. *Nelson* (1995) a presumption of advancement did apply when a mother transferred property into the names of her children.

APPLICATION

Alf is the father of Jack. He opens a bank account in Jack's name and Alf puts £1,000 into it. There is a presumption of advancement here. However, Alf may bring evidence to show that he still regarded himself as owner of the money and so try to establish that Jack holds the £1,000 on a resulting trust for him.

If, however, the bank account was opened by Mary, Jack's mother, then the presumption of advancement will not apply and there will be a presumption that Jack holds the £1,000 on trust for Mary. However, the presumption can be rebutted by evidence that a gift was intended.

REBUTTING THE PRESUMPTION OF ADVANCEMENT

As mentioned above, the presumption can be rebutted by evidence of a contrary intention which can now (*Lavelle* v. *Lavelle* (2004)) even be evidence of statements and conduct made after the gift.

Presumptions of advancement and evidence of fraudulent conduct

CORNERSTONE

Evidence of fraudulent conduct

In some cases evidence that is used to support a claim that there is a resulting trust in a party's favour is based on evidence which itself discloses some illegality and thus may not be admissible.

In a number of cases a party's claim, either to a share in property under a resulting (or constructive) trust or a claim to rebut a presumption of advancement, has been based on evidence which itself discloses some illegality. To what extent is this evidence admissible? If it is not admissible, the other party may obtain an absolute right to property purchased, at least in part, with money belonging to the party who is relying on the evidence of illegality. If it is admissible, what then of the maxim that 'he who comes into equity shall come with clean hands'?

⊕ CORNERSTONE

Gasciogne v. Gasciogne

A claim that there was a resulting trust was based on fraudulent conduct and so was not admissible.

In *Gascoigne* v. *Gascoigne* (1918) a husband who was in debt to moneylenders took a lease of land on which he built a house with his own money but he put the lease into his wife's name with the object of protecting the property from his creditors. His later claim that the wife held as trustee for him was dismissed because he was not allowed to rebut the presumption of advancement in his wife's favour by bringing evidence of his fraudulent conduct. In *Tinker* v. *Tinker* (1970) the conduct involved was not in fact fraudulent at all. A husband put the matrimonial home into his wife's name in case a business venture which he was considering might fail. The court held that he could not claim that his wife held as trustee for him because he was an honest man and must be taken to have intended that the house should belong to his wife so that he could truthfully say that it was her property.

⊕ CORNERSTONE

Tinsley v. Milligan

A claim that there was a resulting trust was not based on fraudulent conduct, even though the conduct of the party claiming to benefit under the trust had been fraudulent, and so the claim succeeded.

In *Tinsley* v. *Milligan* (1992) the issue was not a possible claim by creditors but a claim to a beneficial share in a house because of contributions made to its purchase. The parties were lesbian lovers and the house was in the claimant's name only in order to facilitate a fraudulent claim to housing benefit by the defendant. The court held that the claimant held the house on a constructive trust for both her and the defendant in equal shares. In the Court of Appeal it was held, by a majority, that there was no rigid rule that whenever property was put into another name for an illegal or immoral purpose this always prevented the owner from recovering it. The 'public conscience' test was applied under which the court must weigh the consequences of granting, or not granting, relief. In the House of Lords, the majority held that the issue of illegality was irrelevant: the defendant's claim was made out by proving the existence of a common understanding concerning ownership and she had no need to refer to the reason why the house was conveyed into the claimant's name alone.

The reasoning of the House of Lords has been much criticised but has been followed, although without much enthusiasm, by the Court of Appeal in *Silverwood* v. *Silverwood* (1997). The High Court of Australia declined to follow *Tinsley* v. *Milligan* in *Nelson* v. *Nelson* (see also above). A mother transferred property into the names of her children so that she would qualify for a defence service loan on a property which she was buying. A presumption of advancement arose between her and the children (see above) and this was not rebutted. The court favoured a broader approach to the question of whether the fraudulent purpose was relevant and held here that the mother would be sufficiently penalised under the penalties imposed under the Act which she had sought to circumvent. To prevent her from enforcing a resulting trust would not, on the facts, be justified.

In 2010 the Law Commission published another report (*The Illegality Defence* LC 320) recommending that where a trust has been set up to conceal the beneficiary's interest in order to commit a criminal offence, legislation should provide the judges with a discretion to deprive the beneficiary of their interest in limited circumstances. As yet there has been no sign of legislation on this.

Failure by the settlor to specify the beneficial interests

Where a trust fails for lack of certainty of objects (beneficiaries) there is a resulting trust (see Chapter 4). Again in *Vandervell* v. *IRC* (1967) Vandervell had given Vandervell Trustees Ltd an option to purchase shares which he had transferred to the Royal College of Surgeons but had failed to specify the trusts on which the shares were then to be held. There was thus a resulting, or what Lord Wilberforce called an automatic, trust, for Vandervell. The beneficial interest, he said, could not 'remain in the air' therefore 'it remains in the settlor'.

Failure to dispose of the beneficial interest

CORNERSTONE

Failure to dispose of the beneficial interest

Where the trust does not dispose of the beneficial interest then a resulting trust can arise. An example is *Re Gillingham Bus Disaster Fund*.

There are two possible consequences:

(a) *Resulting trust for the settlor. In Re Gillingham Bus Disaster Fund* (1958) money left over from a fund to care for those disabled in an accident was held on a resulting trust even though a good deal of the fund came from street collections and thus the subscribers were untraceable (this case and others on this topic are dealt with in greater detail in Chapter 5).

This case resulted from a dreadful accident in Dock Road, leading to Chatham Dockyard, on the night of Tuesday 4 December 1951 when a bus came upon a column of Royal Marine Sea Cadets who were marching to a boxing tournament and ploughed into them. Twenty-six of them, aged 9–15, lost their lives and many others were injured. The cause of the accident was found to be a combination of inadequate street lighting, a lack of proper safeguards for the cadets and the failure of the bus driver to use his headlights. The sum of £7,300 was subscribed to the fund and the result of the decision that there was a resulting trust for the subscribers was that this money remained in the Treasury as the contributors could not be found. This unhappy situation lasted until 1994 when, after publicity in the *Guardian* newspaper, the money was distributed to the 17 survivors of the accident who each received £400. If you go to the scene today you will see a lovely memorial unveiled by Prince Philip on 2 December 2001 'in everlasting memory' of those who died that night. Had the trust been charitable then this problem would not have happened as the Charity Commission could have ordered a scheme.

(b) *Absolute gifts to the beneficiaries.* In *Re Osaba* (1979) it was held that where a trust had been created for the maintenance of two women and the education of the third then on the death of the first two and the completion of the third's education the property belonged absolutely to the third.

THE *QUISTCLOSE* TRUST

CORNERSTONE

Resulting trusts in commercial contexts: *Barclays Bank* v. *Quistclose Investments*

In *Barclays Bank* v. *Quistclose Investments* it was held that where money has been contributed for a specific purpose which then fails the money may then be held on trust for the lender.

This recognition of the existence of this type of trust has been one of the major extensions of equitable jurisdiction into the area of commerce. The case of *Barclays Bank* v. *Quistclose Investments Ltd* (1970) was referred to in Chapter 3 to illustrate the idea of an equitable proprietary interest but it merits more detailed consideration here.

Rolls Razor was in financial difficulties and declared a dividend on its shares but did not have the money to pay it and so Quistclose made a contract to make it a loan for the express purpose of enabling it to pay this dividend. The money was paid into a separate account at Barclays Bank and it was agreed with the bank that the account would 'only be used to meet the dividend due on July 24th 1964'. Before the dividend was paid Rolls Razor went into liquidation and the question was whether Barclays Bank could set the sum in the account off against Rolls Razor's overdraft or whether they held it on trust for Quistclose.

The House of Lords held that there was a trust for Quistclose as the letter clearly indicated that the money was to be used to pay the dividend and for no other purpose. It followed that if for any reason the money could not be used for this purpose then it had to be returned to Quistclose. Accordingly it was held by Rolls Razor on trust for Quistclose.

As Watt (2004) has observed: 'there is something beguiling about the *Quistclose* trust. It has the seemingly magical ability to turn a lender's personal rights under a loan for a specific purpose into proprietary rights under a trust'.

Norris J pointed out in *Bieber and others* v. *Teathers Ltd (in liquidation)* (2012) that 'the mere fact that the payer has paid the money to the recipient for the recipient to use it in a particular way is not of itself enough' to bring the *Quistclose* principle into play. Instead, as he pointed out, it must be clear from the terms of the transaction 'that the funds transferred should not be part of the general assets of the recipient but should be used *exclusively* to effect particular identified payments, so that if the money cannot be so used then it is to be returned to the payer'. Lord Millett put it thus in *Twinsectra* v. *Yardley* (2002): 'The question in every case is whether the parties intended the money to be at the free disposal of the recipient.' If so, there will be no *Quistclose* trust.

The application of this principle is seen in *Templeton Insurance Ltd* v. *Penningtons* (2006) where an insurance company (X) deposited £500,000 with solicitors (Y) 'for the express purpose of completion' of a property to be acquired by a client. Y used some of the money for other purposes as the actual price was only around £236,000. It was held that Y was liable to return to X that part of the £500,000 not used for the purchase as it was held for X on a resulting trust under the *Quistclose* principle.

The lending of money to purchase equipment can create a *Quistclose* trust. In *Re EVTR* (1987) the appellant lent £60,000 to a company to assist it in purchasing new equipment. The company made an agreement to purchase this and temporary equipment was delivered but it went into liquidation before the actual new equipment was due for delivery. The court held that the *Quistclose* principle applied and that the £60,000, less agreed deductions, should be held on a resulting trust for the appellant. Had the contract for the purchase of the equipment been completed and the money entirely spent then, as Dillon LJ observed, no trust would have arisen and the appellant would have merely been an unsecured creditor.

A well-known instance of where the *Quistclose* principle did not apply is *Re Farepak Food and Gifts Ltd (in administration)* (2006) where under a Christmas hamper scheme operated by Farepak customers placed orders for hampers with Farepak's agents who then passed them on to Farepak. In October 2006 Farepak decided to cease trading. Before it went into administration the directors attempted to 'ring fence' money which was received by Farepak so that it could be returned to customers. They did this by a declaration of trust but it was held that the *Quistclose* principle could not apply because the money had been received by the Farepak agents (not Farepak) and when it was received there was no suggestion that it was to be kept separate from other money. Thus there could be no *Quistclose* trust as there was, in effect, no trust property. There could only have been such a trust had the money from customers been kept in a separate fund so that it could not be touched until the customers had received their hampers.

INTERSECTION ....

The problem in cases where there has been held not to be a *Quistclose* trust is that, first, there may not be an intention to create a trust and, even if there is, as in the Farepak case, there is no certainty of subject matter – (see Chapter 4 for the three certainties).

What type of trust is the *Quistclose* trust?

In *Barclays Bank* v. *Quistclose* Lord Wilberforce analysed the trust as a primary trust in favour of the creditors and a secondary one in favour of the lender if, in that case, the purpose failed and the dividend could not be paid. It is difficult to find a primary trust on the *Quistclose* trust and indeed there have been doubts expressed as to whether a primary trust exists at all in this type of case, but in *Re EVTR* Dillon LJ held that the trust for the lender could be 'a resulting or constructive trust'. It is suggested that the better view is that of Chambers (1997), that it is a resulting trust and not a constructive trust which is imposed. Chambers suggests that the resulting trust arises when the purpose of the loan fails. However, in *Twinsectra* v. *Yardley* Lord Millett analysed the position differently as one where an express trust arises for the lender *as soon as* the money is transferred to the borrower, but subject to the right of the borrower to apply it for the purpose for which it was lent. In this case if it was not applied for that purpose then the express trust takes over.

REFLECTION

The fact is that in most of the cases involving the *Quistclose* principle there is a contest between different lenders and if a lender is able to establish the existence of a *Quistclose* trust then he will gain a beneficial interest in the subject matter of what he lent and will have priority over the ordinary creditors. Is this the kind of area with which equity, with its concern for justice and conscience, should be involved?

Moreover, the fact that say X has lent money to Y can give a false impression to others that Y's business is successful as they will not know that the money lent by X to Y is held on a *Quistclose*-type trust. Thus others may be induced to trade with Y when in fact Y is in grave financial difficulties and, as unsecured creditors, they will not get their money back, if Y does become insolvent, until X is repaid.

KEY POINTS

- Resulting trusts return the beneficial interest in the property to the settlor who created the trust.
- Resulting trusts can arise where property is purchased in another's name.
- The presumption of a resulting trust could be rebutted by a presumption of advancement but this has been abolished by s. 199 of the Equality Act 2010.
- Where the transfer giving rise to the alleged trust is made for a fraudulent purpose then the court in its discretion may not impose a resulting trust for the lender.
- Resulting trusts arise where the settlor fails to specify the beneficial interests.
- A '*Quistclose* trust' can result where money is lent for a particular purpose and does not form part of the general assets of the borrower. The effect is that the lender has a beneficial interest in the money.

CORE CASES AND STATUTES

Case	About	Importance
Re Vinogradoff (1935)	Presumptions of resulting trusts on a voluntary transfer of property.	This is also important in the debate on the nature of resulting trusts and when they may be imposed.
Pecore v. *Pecore* (2007)	Presumptions of advancement.	Do not apply to transfers from parents to adult children.
Gascoigne v. *Gascoigne* (1918)	Rebutting the presumption of advancement.	Evidence of fraudulent conduct cannot be used to do this.
Tinsley v. *Milligan* (1992)	Is evidence of fraudulent conduct relevant to a claim to a beneficial share in a house?	This evidence was not relevant as the claim was based on contributions to its purchase.
Re Gillingham Bus Disaster Fund (1958)	Example of where a resulting trust can be imposed.	The trust did not dispose of the beneficial interest.
Barclays Bank v. *Quistclose Investments Ltd* (1970)	Loan of money to be used for a particular purpose and which does not form part of the general funds of the recipient.	Imposition of a trust in favour of the lender to give the lender a beneficial interest in the money.

Statute	About	Importance
Section 199 of the Equality Act 2010	Abolition of the presumption of advancement.	Applies to advancements made after this section comes into force but not before and so the present law is still relevant.

FURTHER READING

Andrews, G. (2007) 'The presumption of advancement: equity, equality and human rights' 71 *Conv*. 340.
This article has to some extent been overtaken by the provisions of s. 199 of the Equality Act 2010 analysed by Glister (2010) – below – but is still worth reading.

Chambers, R. (1997) '*Resulting Trusts*' (Oxford University Press).
Essential reading but the views expressed have not found universal acceptance. It is a good place to start in view of the clarity of the exposition.

Glister, J. (2009) 'The presumption of advancement' in C. Mitchell (ed.) *Constructive and Resulting Trusts* (Hart Publishing), at p. 289.
This looks at the origin of the presumption and at its fate in other jurisdictions.

Glister, J. (2010) 'Section 199 of the Equality Act 2010: how not to abolish the presumption of advancement' 73(5) *MLR* 785.
As the title indicates, the author is critical of the drafting of s. 199 and questions the extent to which it has abolished this presumption.

Mee, J. (2012) '*Pettit* v *Pettit* and *Gissing* v. *Gissing*' in *Leading Cases in Equity* (Hart Publishing).
This analyses these two decisions and looks at the origin of the doctrine of common intention. It also recommends that Lord Diplock's speech in *Gissing* v. *Gissing* deserves a fuller consideration.

Moffat, G. (2009) *The Law of Trusts* (Cambridge University Press).
This book is full of insights and has a useful section (referred to in the text) on the differences between express trusts, on the one hand, and both resulting and constructive (which he calls imputed) trusts.

Swadling, W. (1996) 'A new role for resulting trusts' 16 *LS* 110.
Useful survey of this area.

Swadling, W. (2008) 'Explaining resulting trusts' 124 *LQR* 72.
A further analysis – its views are referred to in the text.

Watt, G. (2004) Publication review 'The Quistclose Trust – Critical Essays ed. Swadling' 68 *Conv*. 418.
It is not a long article and really does give you some useful insights into this area.

12

Introduction to equity

 Equitable maxims

It has already been seen that historically equity developed based not on any formal process of precedent, but rather on the discretion of the Lord Chancellor. However, as time went on, the decisions of the Court of Chancery began to form a set of principles and doctrines, which one can say have become as rigid as the common law. What emerged in the course of the development of equity were a set of maxims which explained the way in which equity would intervene in given situations.

Equity will not suffer a wrong without a remedy

This equitable maxim provides that, where possible, a wrong should be redressed by the courts. It does not suggest that every possible wrong complained of should be addressed, but that where there is a defect in the common law then equity should provide an answer. A good example here is the trust. In the early development of equity, the Court of Chancery readily upheld the rights of the beneficiary of the trust despite the trustee having a legal title to the trust property enforceable at common law. The trustee would be compelled to recognise the rights of the beneficiary and to transfer the property to the beneficiary. Another example of the operation of this maxim is in the context of a contract. A contract may be perfectly recognised at common law in that it has satisfied all the common law requirements as to form. However, if such a contract has been entered into on grounds of fraud, mistake or undue influence, equity will allow the party affected by the fraud, mistake or undue influence to escape contractual liability. Unlike the common law, equity can put the contract to an end by the remedy of recission, the purpose of which is to undo the contract and put the parties in the position they would have been in had the contract not been entered into.

Equity follows the law

Equity developed as a response to the defects of the common law; however, it did not aim to override the common law. Of course, where there was a conflict between law and equity,

equity would prevail. This maxim is particularly relevant in the context of land law where equitable estates and interests in land reflect legal estates and interests in the land. Thus, where a legal estate in the land fails for want of formality such as a deed, the same estate will be recognised in equity.

Equity acts *in personam*

One of the more important maxims of equity is that 'equity acts *in personam*'. This maxim has its origins in the manner in which the Lord Chancellor would seek to redress a legal wrong complained of by a claimant. The Chancellor would not interfere with the common law rule or judgment awarded by the common law courts; instead he would ask the defendant to appear before him personally. A decision would be given and an order would be made personally against the defendant to carry out what was instructed. For example, where a contract was capable of being specifically performed, an order would be made to perform that contract. Similarly, where a trustee refused to recognise the rights of a beneficiary under a trust, an order would be made compelling the trustee to so recognise the rights of the beneficiary and convey the title to the trust property in appropriate circumstances. Failure to comply with the order amounted to a contempt of court, which could lead to imprisonment; thus there was every incentive to comply with such an order. What is clearly apparent from the idea of acting *in personam* is that the Chancellor and, therefore, equity did not interfere as such with the property in the hands of the defendant. For example, in the context of a trust, equity did not have the power to say that the beneficiary was the legal owner of the property, but could compel the trustee to recognise the existence of the trust, and if appropriate to convey the title to the trust property to the beneficiary in the appropriate common law way.

A modern example of this maxim was illustrated in **Webb v Webb**[1] where the Court of Justice of the European Community recognised that equity acting *in personam* was sufficient to give jurisdiction over a person abroad and it made no difference that the order related to property situated abroad. On the facts, a son was ordered to hold a flat on resulting trust for his father on the grounds that his father had paid the purchase price of the flat but did not take legal title to it.[2] Given the fact that the order related to the person and not the property, there was no conflict with the laws of the foreign country regarding ownership of the disputed property.

He who comes to equity must come with clean hands

This maxim is one that students of law become more accustomed to than any other. Unlike the common law, which is based on precedent and looks to questions of form, equitable relief is given on a discretionary basis. Indeed, all equitable remedies are given on a discretionary basis and are not available per se. Thus, even if all matters of form were complied with, the Lord Chancellor could deny the claimant a remedy if there was some impropriety in his conduct leading up to the dispute complained of. A good example is a claim between a landlord and tenant under a lease. Although a lease confers on the tenant an estate in the land, it is also a contractual agreement. Any attempt by the landlord to

---

[1] [1994] QB 696. See also *Richard West and Partners (Inverness) Ltd v Dick* [1969] 2 Ch 424 where an English court had jurisdiction to grant specific performance of a contract for the sale of land in Scotland.

[2] Resulting trusts arising on grounds of contribution to the purchase price of property.

remove the tenant contrary to the terms of the lease agreement amounts to a breach of contract; the tenant can ask equity to decree specific performance of the lease. However, it is quite clear that equity will not decree specific performance where the tenant is at fault, for example, by not observing the covenants in the lease agreement.

An example of the operation of the maxim can be seen in *Lee v Haley*[3] where the claimants sought an injunction to protect their coal business. This was, however, denied by the Court of Appeal on the simple grounds that they had fraudulently sold their customers short.

It is important, however, that the wrongful conduct of the complainant must have a direct nexus with the dispute in question for the maxim to apply. For example, in *Argyll (Duchess) v Argyll*[4] the fact that the wife's adultery was the sole reason for divorce proceedings did not prevent her from obtaining an injunction stopping her former husband from publishing confidential information. Similarly, in *Tinsley v Milligan,*[5] where the House of Lords considered the maxim in detail and the extent to which it was admissible to prevent the court from awarding the claimant a remedy, the House of Lords explained that the wrongful conduct must be causally related to the dispute in question. On the facts of this case, a lesbian partner had joined her co-partner in the purchase of land but did not put herself on the title to the disputed property. This was done in order to make dishonest claims for social security benefits. When her co-partner denied her an interest in the disputed property, she complained that she had an equitable interest under a resulting trust by virtue of her contribution to the property. Her co-partner (the legal owner of the house) argued that her dishonest conduct in claiming social security benefit was sufficient to deny her equitable relief because she was not coming to equity with clean hands. The House of Lords, however, held that the maxim only applied where the wrongful conduct of the claimant had the purpose of setting up her entitlement in the first place. On the facts, although there had been wrongful conduct by the claimant, her right to an interest in the property purchased was not influenced by the wrongful conduct put before the court.[6] In Lord Browne-Wilkinson's opinion the claimant did not need to rely on her dishonest conduct to establish an entitlement to the property: that entitlement arose by virtue of the resulting trust in her favour. In other words, if the dishonest conduct of the claimant was the only basis upon which her entitlement could be established then that would be not entertained by the court. A good example of this is illustrated in *Gascoigne v Gascoigne*[7] where a husband took a lease in the wife's name. This was sufficient to raise a presumption of advancement and infer a donative intent on his part.[8] The husband sought to rebut that presumption of advancement by arguing that the only reason he transferred the lease in his wife's name was to defraud his creditors. The Court of Appeal, however, held that he was not entitled to use evidence of an illegal nature to rebut the presumption of advancement.

More recently in *O'Kelly v Davies*[9] the question arose for the first time as to the role and effect of illegality in the context of a common intention constructive trust of land. In particular, is a claimant barred from enforcing a beneficial interest in land under such a trust

---

[3] (1869) 5 Ch App. 155.
[4] [1967] Ch 302.
[5] [1994] 1 AC 340.
[6] See also *Tribe v Tribe* [1996] Ch 107.
[7] [1918] 1 KB 223.
[8] The equitable presumption of advancement infers a donative intent when a transfer is made from father to child or husband to wife.
[9] [2014] EWCA 1606.

if he or she has been involved in some illegal purpose? The Court of Appeal held that a claimant was entitled to enforce his beneficial interest under a constructive trust of land despite his participation in an illegal purpose. The illegal purpose was not relied upon to set his entitlement to the beneficial interest.

Equity looks to substance as opposed to form

Equity will not be defeated by lack of compliance with form. It has already been observed in *Walsh v Lonsdale*[10] that a long lease which failed for want of formality was nevertheless recognised and upheld in equity on grounds that in substance the landlord had purported to grant a long lease. Sometimes this maxim is also explained by saying that equity looks to intent rather than form. The matter is neatly explained by Romilly MR in *Parkin v Thorold*[11] when he commented that 'courts of equity make a distinction between that which is a matter of substance and that which is a matter of form; and if it finds that by insisting on the form, the substance will be defeated, it holds it inequitable to allow a person to insist on form, and thereby defeat the substance'.[12]

Equity regards that as done which ought to be done

Equity sees that as done which ought to be done at law. Once again the decision in *Walsh v Lonsdale*[13] provides a perfect example of the operation of this maxim. The decision to uphold the long lease in that case was based on the ground that equity regarded that as done which ought to be done, and in doing so, the court regarded the long lease as having been granted even though at common law it failed for formality. The maxim also explains the grounds upon which the equitable remedy of specific performance is decreed in the case of a contract for the sale of land or some other special property. Where a contract is capable of being performed, the vendor becomes a constructive trustee and the equitable interest in the subject matter of the contract passes to the purchaser. The basis for treating the purchaser as owner in equity is simply because equity regards that as done which ought to be done. The decree of specific performance will require the vendor to transfer the legal title to the purchaser.

He who seeks equity must do equity

Where a person seeks equitable relief he must act fairly towards the other party against whom the equitable relief is being sought. For example, where an individual seeks to set aside a contract by asking the court to rescind the contract, he must be prepared to pay over any money received under the contract. Equally where a contract is set aside, for example, on grounds of undue influence, one party will be allowed to retain remuneration for work done despite having to return the profits made under the contract which is now rescinded. Thus, in *O'Sullivan v Management Agency and Music Ltd*[14] a contract between a singer and a music agency was set aside on grounds of undue influence. The Court of Appeal ordered the music company to return any profits made to the singer but also held that the company was entitled to retain some of the profits by way of remuneration for

---

[10] (1882) 21 Ch D 9.
[11] (1852) 16 Beav. 59.
[12] (1852) 16 Beav. 59 at 66.
[13] (1882) 21 Ch D 9.
[14] [1985] QB 428.

their labour and skill. A similar result was achieved in **Boardman v Phipps**[15] where a solicitor who was acting in connection with a trust advised the trustees, who already held shares in a private company, that they should acquire more shares in the same company with a view to exerting greater control in that company. The trustees refused to purchase further shares on the basis that the trust instrument did not authorise them to do so. After consultation with some of the trustees, the solicitor acquired a controlling interest in the company and made a substantial profit for himself as well as restructuring the company and profiting the beneficiaries. The House of Lords held by a bare majority that the solicitor was required to account for those profits made in his capacity as a fiduciary. Despite the absence of dishonesty on his part, those profits had been made in his capacity as a fiduciary and thus belonged to the beneficiaries. The decision illustrates the strict rule of equity that a fiduciary is not entitled to retain any property made in his capacity as a fiduciary. Boardman, however, was authorised to retain some of the profit by way of remuneration on the basis of *quantum meruit*. Both the Court of Appeal and the House of Lords were aware that Boardman was a man of great ability and had expended labour in reorganising the company and increasing the share therein.

Equity imputes an intention to fulfil an obligation

Equity will impute an intention to fulfil an obligation. If a person intends to carry out an obligation and then does something which has the effect of fulfilling that obligation, equity will deem that obligation to be satisfied. This maxim is better explained by what has become known as the rule in **Strong v Bird**.[16] This rule holds that where a person (donor) intends to make a lifetime gift to another (donee) but fails to do so then, provided his intention to make the gift continues up until his death and he appoints the donee as his executor or administrator, the gift is said to be complete. The vesting of the donor's property in the donee as executor or administrator is deemed to impute an intention that he wanted the donee to keep what he was promised during the lifetime of the donor.

Delay defeats equity

Otherwise known as the equitable defence of laches, a person who seeks equitable relief must do so within a reasonable time.[17] If he does not assert his right to bring an action within a reasonable time then his conduct is seen as being acquiescence with the wrong complained of. The equitable defences of laches, which still applies in some cases today, must be seen in light of the Limitation Act 1980.

Where equities are equal, the first in time prevails

Where there are two competing equitable interests in the same property then the first in time will prevail. For example, if A grants an equitable mortgage to B and then subsequently grants an equitable mortgage to C, B's mortgage will take priority.[18]

---

[15] [1967] AC 46.
[16] (1874) LR 18 Eq. 315.
[17] See *Smith* v *Clay* (1767) Amb. 645 and also *Lindsay Petroleum Co* v *Hurd* (1874) LR 5 PC 221.
[18] An equitable mortgage will arise, for example, where the mortgagor only has an equitable interest to mortgage. Thus, a beneficiary under a trust can only grant an equitable mortgage over the equitable interest in the trust property.

Where the equities are equal, the law prevails

Unlike the last maxim, which seeks to address priority between two competing equitable rights, this maxim addresses the priority between an equitable right and a legal right in respect of the same property. The legal right takes priority over the equitable right. It does not matter whether the equitable right pre-existed the legal right.

Where there is a conflict between law and equity, equity prevails

It has already been seen above that where there is a rule of the common law and a rule of equity, equity is said to prevail over and above the common law.

CHAPTER 13

Co-ownership (Part 1)

BLUEPRINT

Co-ownership (Part 1)

LEGISLATION

- Law of Property Act 1925
- Trusts of Land and Appointment of Trustees Act 1996

CONTEXT

- All property bought by more than 1 person is subject to a trust.
- All trusts have trustees and beneficiaries - this can be expressly declared or implied through 'common intention'.
- 2 million unmarried couples living in the UK.

CONCEPTS

- Resulting and constructive trusts
- Equitable interests
- Acquisition
- Quantification
- Common intention – express and implied

- Who was right – Baroness Hale or Lord Neuberger – flexibility or certainty?
- Should the courts 'imply, infer or impute' common intention?
- If there is no express declaration – shouldn't equity always follow the law?

- What is the fundamental difference between a resulting and constructive trust?
- Is there a distinction between a constructive trust and proprietary estoppel?
- Was Baroness Hale right in *Stack* – should we be following a holistic approach?

CASES

- *Stack* v. *Dowden* [2007]
- *Pettitt* v. *Pettitt* [1970]
- *Eves* v. *Eves* [1975]
- *Lloyds Bank* v. *Rossett* [1991]
- *Oxley* v. *Hiscock* [2004]
- *Laskar* v. *Laskar* [2008]
- *Jones* v. *Kernott* [2011]

REFORM

- Should the Law Com Report 307 become law – do we need legislation to clarify the position for unmarried partners?

SPECIAL CHARACTERISTICS

- The 'real' difference between a constructive and resulting trust
- The meaning of 'common intention'

CRITICAL ISSUES

Setting the scene

When a property is owned outright by a sole owner, clearly that person owns the legal title of that property. However, the situation becomes far more complicated, certainly in land law terms, when two or more people buy a property together. This is known as 'concurrent ownership' and land law refers to them as co-owners. Rather confusingly, they are also referred to as 'joint tenants' (see Chapter 14) and they also carry the 'burden' of being trustees of that land – holding the land on trust for each other and any further beneficiaries.

The correct terminology, since the introduction of the Trusts of Land and Appointment of Trustees Act 1996 (TOLATA 1996 – see also Chapter 14), is that whenever there is co-ownership, there is a *trust of land* created – either *expressly* stated in the conveyance or on Land Registry Forms (the Form JO) or *implied* by way of a resulting or constructive trust. This chapter will seek to explain these types of trust – how and when they are created and the implications these trusts of land hold for both trustee and beneficiary.

It is also important to realise that there are a number of different possibilities available in any co-ownership relationship. A married couple, let's say Rebecca and Keith, buy a property together. Both names are on the title, and both contribute equally. It can be said that they are both co-owners at law (as joint tenants) and in equity – as they are holding as trustees for each other, also being, therefore, the beneficiaries. It could also be the case, though, that only Rebecca's name is on the register as legal owner. Is Keith just a lodger? Clearly that would not be the usual scenario in a 'relationship situation'. The couple may have declared a trust expressly setting out each person's 'real value' as Professor Martin Dixon calls the equitable interest. They may have also filled out a Land Registry form (Form JO) which also sets out their 'real' equitable interest. However, they may have not done either of the above – in which case there may be an implied trust in operation – even if the couple have no idea that this is the case.

This is *relatively* unproblematic if indeed Keith and Rebecca are married – we have legislation (see below) to assist us in the event of an unfortunate marital breakdown or a default in mortgage payments and a forced sale. Where the couple is unmarried no such legislation exists, and as such the computation of each person's equitable share becomes even more complex. The purpose of this chapter is to try to explain the effect of a 'trust of land' in any given co-ownership scenario. Since the 'holistic approach' taken by Baroness Hale in *Stack* v. *Dowden* [2007] the acquisition and quantification of the equitable interest behind a trust is perhaps, according to Lord Neuberger's view in *Stack*, 'difficult, subjective and uncertain'. According to Baroness Hale, though, the law in relation to co-owners has rightly 'moved on', with, as Martin Dixon suggests, 'our most senior judges (being) determined to introduce more flexibility'.

THE CONCEPT OF CO-OWNERSHIP – RECOGNITION OF EQUITABLE INTERESTS

CORNERSTONE

Legal and equitable ownership of land

It is one of the key principles of land law, and also one of the key areas of confusion, that there is a fundamental difference between legal and equitable ownership. In a co-ownership scenario, the legal owner (also the trustee) is the person whose name appears in the proprietorship section of the register. However, this is merely the 'title-holder' because, as Professor Martin Dixon points out (see Further Reading), it is the equitable interest that is the 'real value' in the property. The common law does not recognise an equitable (beneficiary) interest, focusing only on the legal title. This of course allows for certainty and clarity but lacks flexibility and also fails to recognise the 'relevant intentions of the parties' and can at times 'unconscionably frustrate their legitimate expectations' (Gray and Gray – see below).

As such, equity will play a positive role in at least trying to prevent 'unconscionable dealings' between the parties in relation to shared ownership. One way equity 'steps in' is through the doctrine of proprietary estoppel and there is an obvious overlap between estoppel and implied trusts which will be analysed later in this chapter. Other than estoppel, equity may intervene through the equitable imposition of an implied trust – either *resulting* or *constructive* – in order to avoid unconscionable dealings in co-owned property. It is also very pertinent to point out that there is statutory assistance here to avoid the formalities of land transfer – as section 53(2) of the LPA 1925 sets down that land transfer formalities are not necessary when such implied trusts are in operation. The question arises as to whether an implied trust is based on a resulting or a constructive trust – and in order to understand the difference, we need to trace back through the historical case law surrounding these devices to try to understand the basis for such an informal transfer of land. As the court commented in *Springette* v. *Defoe* [1992], the law does not simply 'allow property rights to be affected by telepathy'.

TRUSTS OF LAND

As explained above, whenever there is co-ownership, there is a *trust of land* created – either expressly stated in the conveyance or on Land Registry Forms (the Form JO) or implied by way of a *resulting* or *constructive trust*. Co-ownership is, of course, usually the model when two people purchase property within a relationship (spouses; partners; civil partners) but property can also be co-owned commercially within a business relationship. In either situation, co-ownership will create this trust of land (no longer referred to as a '*trust for sale*' since the Trusts of Land and Appointment of Trustees Act 1996, section 1 – see Chapter 14). As such there will be always be a trustee–beneficiary relationship in existence, and although this has no real meaning whilst the co-owners live in 'perfect harmony', the extent of their legal (trustee) and equitable (beneficiary) interests become vital if the property is repossessed, sold or there is a dispute over ownership.

As suggested above, if the co-owners are married, then legislation such as the Family Law Act 1996 (as amended) and the Matrimonial Causes Act 1973 set down basic rules for the division of property on divorce. However, if there is no divorce or if the co-owners are not married in the first place, then the situation as to the quantification (and in some cases the acquisition itself) of the equitable interest in the property is far more complex. Baroness Hale in the key case of *Stack* v. *Dowden* [2007] and the Law Commission in its 2007 report on *Cohabitation: The Final Consequences of Relationship Breakdown* (Law Com. No. 307), both seem to state quite categorically that the common law in relation to property and trusts can only go so far. The law on resulting and constructive trusts, especially in relation to quantification of an equitable interest, has been, as Lord Walker suggested in *Stack*, 'potentially productive of injustice' and needs to be 'recast'.

Express trusts

The most straightforward way to ensure clarity when two or more parties take ownership of a property together is to declare a trust in writing, either before the purchase in the conveyance deed itself, or after the purchase following the requirements of the Law of Property Act 1925, section 53 (emphasis added):

CORNERSTONE

LPA 1925, section 53

53   Instruments required to be in writing

(1)   Subject to the provision hereinafter contained with respect to the creation of interests in land by parol—
   (a)   no interest in land can be created or disposed of except by writing signed by the person creating or conveying the same, or by his agent thereunto lawfully authorised in writing, or by will, or by operation of law;
   (b)   *a declaration of trust respecting any land or any interest therein must be manifested and proved by some writing signed by some person who is able to declare such trust or by his will;*
   (c)   a disposition of an equitable interest or trust subsisting at the time of the disposition, must be in writing signed by the person disposing of the same, or by his agent thereunto lawfully authorised in writing or by will.

(2)   *This section does not affect the creation or operation of resulting, implied or constructive trusts.*

The parties are free to set down the extent of their equitable ownership in a declaration of trust deed: once 'witnessed, signed and delivered' as a deed, an express private trust of land will have been created. If the express trust has been validly created (without any fraud or mistake) then it is conclusive (*Goodman* v. *Gallant* [1986]).

Alternatively, since 1 November 2012, the co-owners are now able to lodge a Form JO (see Figure 13.1) with the Land Registry, in order to declare the beneficial interest in a property. However, there is a very brief window of opportunity here – the form must be lodged between exchange of contracts and completion of the transfer. According to Macdonald (see Further Reading below), the Form JO – put in place by the Registry following Baroness Hale's 'heavy hint' in *Stack* – is especially useful 'if one of the joint purchasers is not on the title', describing the Form JO as 'an important opportunity for those who do not intend equity to follow the law, or who have unusual arrangements about the equity'.

Land Registry
Trust Information

This form may accompany an application in Form AP1, FR1 or ADV1 where:
- panel 9 of Form FR1 or ADV1 has not been completed and the applicant is more than one person, or
- the Form AP1 relates to a transfer (in Form AS1, AS3, TP1, TP2, TR1, TR2 or TR5) or a prescribed clauses lease (within rule 58A of the Land Registration Rules 2003) of a registered estate to more than one person (the Joint Owners), and
  - the declaration of trust panel in the transfer or lease has not been completed and/or the transfer has not been executed by the Joint Owners, and the estate transferred or leased is not a rentcharge, franchise, profit or manor.

Enter the same information as either in the transfer or lease to the Joint Owners or in panel 6 of Form ADV1. Leave blank if this form accompanies a Form FR1.	1 Title number(s) of the property:
Insert address including postcode (if any) or other description of the property as it appears either in the transfer or lease to the Joint Owners, in panel 3 of Form ADV1 or in panel 2 of Form FR1.	2 Property:
	3 Date:
Give full name(s) and address(es), as in either the transfer or lease to the Joint Owners, panels 6 and 7 of Forms ADV1 or panels 6 and 8 of Form FR1.	4 Joint Owners:

Complete either this or panel 6.

Place an 'X' in the appropriate box.

If completing the fourth box, insert details either of the trust or of the trust instrument under which the Joint Owners hold the property.

The registrar will enter a Form A restriction in the register if an 'X' is placed:
- in the second or third box, or
- in the fourth box, unless it is clear that the Joint Owners hold on trust for themselves alone as joint tenants.

5 ☐ The Joint Owners declare that they are to hold the property on trust for themselves alone as joint tenants

☐ The Joint Owners declare that they are to hold the property on trust for themselves alone as tenants in common in equal shares

☐ The Joint Owners declare that they hold the property on trust for themselves alone as tenants in common in the following unequal shares: (*complete*)

☐ The Joint Owners are to hold the property (*complete*):

If this panel is completed, each Joint Owner must sign.

Please refer to Land Registry's *Public Guide 18 – Joint property ownership* and *Practice Guide 24 – Private trusts of land* for further guidance. These guides are available on the website www.landregistry.gov.uk

Signature of each
of the Joint Owners   _____

_____

Date:

Figure 13.1 The Form JO
Source: from Land Registry, Crown copyright

6	Under the term of a written declaration of trust dated (*complete*) the Joint Owners

☐   hold the property on trust as joint tenants for themselves alone

☐   do not hold the property on trust as joint tenants for themselves alone

If this panel is completed, a conveyancer must sign.

Signature of conveyancer   _____

Date:

WARNING
If you dishonestly enter information or make a statement that you know is, or might be, untrue or misleading, and intend by doing so to make a gain for yourself or another person, or to cause loss or the risk of loss to another person, you may commit the offence of fraud under section 1 of the Fraud Act 2006, the maximum penalty for which is 10 years' imprisonment or an unlimited fine, or both.

Failure to complete this form with proper care may result in a loss of protection under the Land Registration Act 2002 if, as a result, a mistake is made in the register.

Under section 66 of the Land Registration Act 2002 most documents (including this form) kept by the registrar relating to an application to the registrar or referred to in the register are open to public inspection and copying. If you believe a document contains prejudicial information, you may apply for that part of the document to be made exempt using Form EX1, under rule 136 of the Land Registration Rules 2003.

© Crown copyright (ref: LR/HO) 10/12

Figure 13.1 (*continued*)

However, case law suggests that for whatever reason, express trusts, especially between couples, are far from the norm.

Resulting trusts

As stated above, where there is a lack of any express written agreement, equity intervenes to potentially impose an implied trust of land, historically, either a resulting or a constructive trust. The presumption of a resulting trust dates back to 1788 and *Dyer* v. *Dyer*: if a property is purchased by A with money solely from B, then a '*trust of the legal estate . . . results to the man who advances the purchase money*'. What happens in a scenario such as *Dyer* is that A holds the legal title, but on trust for B who is the beneficial owner. If A and B contribute equally, then traditionally at the time of acquisition, equity will find a 'presumed intention' that the co-owners have a 50/50 beneficial interest, based solely on contribution to purchase price *at the time of purchase. Curley* v. *Parkes* [2004] clarifies that it must be by way of contribution to the purchase at the time of transfer, contributions to mortgage payments will not generate a resulting trust (though they may generate a constructive trust). In order for the resulting trust to operate, there must be evidence of the 'common intention' of both parties at the time of purchase that 'B' should take a beneficial share of the property and that evidence will be based on contributions to the purchase where there is a lack of words.

.... **APPLICATION**

Springette v. *Defoe* [1992]

The common intention must be founded on evidence such as would support a finding that there is an implied or constructive trust for the parties in proportions to the purchase price. The court does not as yet sit, as under a palm tree, to exercise a general discretion to do what the man in the street, on a general overview of the case, might regard as fair . . . (Dillon LJ)

However, since the case of *Stack* v. *Dowden* it seems that other than in purchases for investment reasons rather than as a home (see *Laskar* v. *Laskar* later), as Baroness Hale suggests, 'it is now clear that the constructive trust is generally the more appropriate tool of analysis in most matrimonial cases'.

Constructive trusts

Even though the 'policy' behind a constructive trust is still to prevent unconscionable dealing, seminal cases such as *Lloyds Bank* v. *Rosset* [1991] and more recently *Stack* v. *Dowden* [2007] set down that for a constructive trust to arise there must be evidence of common intention and detrimental reliance by the 'injured' party. The key difference between a resulting and a constructive trust, however, is that the common intention can be evidenced *at any time*, not just at the time of purchase.

INTERSECTION

The equitable doctrine of proprietary estoppel is explained in full. It is obvious that there is an overlap between a constructive trust and a claim for proprietary estoppel. Estoppel requires the claimant to show that there has been a clear promise made in relation to land ownership; reliance on that promise; some detriment suffered; and overall that it would be unconscionable for the person making the promise to go back on their word and deny the proprietary interest promised (see *Gillett* v. *Holt* [2000]). If a constructive trust is to be imposed there must also have been detrimental reliance and unconscionability is still of course the central pillar – the subtle difference being that constructive trusts need evidence of common intention rather than evidence of what really can be described as a unilateral promise. The usual 'wording' of a promise in estoppel is along the lines of 'when I die all of this will be yours' whereas in a constructive trust, if words are used those words suggest current co-ownership rather than subsequent ('this house is yours as well as mine'). If words are not used, the 'common intention' is evidenced by contributions given and accepted by both parties. Post-*Stack*, due to the infinitely wider definition of 'contributions' it may of course now be possible to choose your route when claiming an equitable interest – either estoppel or constructive trust. It should be noted, however, that estoppel is usually viewed as the last resort, as the role of the court in estoppel claims is to 'do the minimum necessary to achieve justice' whereas, with a constructive trust, the role of the court is to provide a remedy based on contributions – Baroness Hale would argue that this 'holistic approach' is far more likely to bring about a proportionate remedy.

In *Lloyds Bank* v. *Rosset* [1991], Lord Bridge identified two categories of constructive trust – the first based on express discussion, the second based on implied intention through conduct.

(i) Evidence – 'the express common intention constructive trust'

For the requirement of common intention to be satisfied, if the party claiming the interest can point to clear words promising co-ownership rights, then this should suffice. In *McKenzie* v. *McKenzie* [2003] it was stated that where such 'common intention can be proved or imputed . . . the technique of equity is to impose a constructive trust'. For the 'express common intention' trust to be successfully argued, there must be evidence of some 'agreement, arrangement or understanding reached' between the two parties that the 'property is to be shared beneficially' (Lord Bridge in *Lloyds Bank* v. *Rossett* [1991]). In *Springette* v. *Defoe* [1993] the court used precisely the same definition but added that this 'agreement, arrangement or understanding' must be based on 'evidence of express discussions . . . however imperfectly remembered and however imprecise their terms may have been'. However, the court added that there must be evidence of such a discussion, as 'trust law does not allow property rights to be affected by telepathy'. What is clear, however, is that this express intention may assist in arguing that an equitable interest has been *acquired* but may not assist greatly in terms of *quantification*. In *Oxley* v. *Hiscock* [2004] it was held that the parties do not need to have agreed the size of their beneficial interest. This can be done through the second 'category' of constructive trust – the 'implied or inferred [or maybe even imputed] common intention constructive trust'.

(ii) Evidence – 'the implied or inferred common intention constructive trust'

In the early 1970s, the implied 'common intention constructive trust' could only really be said to succeed if there had been substantial contributions to the purchase price or at least mortgage payments after purchase. Two cases affirmed this rather stringent approach. In *Pettitt* v. *Pettitt* [1970], a rare case where the husband was claiming an equitable share of a property solely owned by his wife, Lord Diplock ruled that it would be an 'abuse of legal technique' to allow the husband to succeed as contributing by way of minor decorations to the property did not give rise to a constructive trust. Similarly, in *Gissing* v. *Gissing* [1971] the wife's contribution of £220 towards furnishings and mowing the lawn did also not evidence common intention of a trust. Once again, Lord Diplock stated that where there was 'no initial contribution' to the purchase deposit and no other 'direct contribution to the mortgage instalments' the inference is that there was a common intention only to 'share the day-to-day expenses' and no more.

However, in 1975, Lord Denning 'created' the 'new model constructive trust', allowing such a trust to be based on broader contributions. In *Eves* v. *Eves* [1975] Mr Eves bought a property solely in his name. His reason was such that his girlfriend Janet was not yet 21 years of age. However, Janet worked 'extensively on the dirty and dilapidated house', as Lord Denning put it, whilst breaking up a patio 'wielding a 14lb sledgehammer'. This, Lord Denning stated, gave rise to a 25 per cent share in the property under the 'new model' constructive trust. Less than ten years later, however, the Court of Appeal returned to a more 'orthodox' approach in *Burns* v. *Burns* [1984]. The claimant had lived with Patrick Burns, unmarried, for 19 years, but had made no initial contribution or payments towards the mortgage. She had, however, brought up their children, acted as 'homemaker' and also paid towards household bills. Lord Justice Fox stated that 'the mere fact that the parties live together and do ordinary domestic tasks is . . . no indication . . . that they thereby intended to alter the existing property rights of either of them'.

This high threshold was followed by Lord Bridge in *Lloyds Bank* v. *Rosset* [1991] where, once again, the property was in the sole name of Mr Rosset. Mrs Rosset spent six months supervising the renovation of the property, managing the project and the builders. Mr Rosset then defaulted on a mortgage and the bank came seeking possession. At that point Mrs Rosset claimed an overriding interest as a person in actual occupation under the provisions of section 70(1)(g) of the Land Registration Act 1925.

Even though Lord Bridge did concede that Mrs Rosset, either in her own right or through her builders, was in actual occupation, he held that she did not have a proprietary right to begin with and was therefore unable to claim such an overriding interest against the bank. He stated that, without an express agreement evidencing common intention, there needed to be evidence of clear common intention implied or inferred through conduct. He said that Mrs Rosset's efforts were 'the most natural thing in the world for any wife . . . irrespective of any expectation she might have of enjoying a beneficial interest in the property'. He went on to state quite categorically that 'direct contributions to purchase price . . . or . . . payment of mortgage instalments, will readily justify the inference necessary to the creation of a constructive trust . . . it is at least extremely doubtful *whether anything less will do*' (emphasis added).

In 1995, in *Midland Bank* v. *Cooke*, the Court of Appeal took a slightly broader approach in relation to quantification at least. Even though Mrs Cooke's direct contribution equated to just under 7 per cent, the Court of Appeal decided that the whole 'course of dealing' between the parties can be analysed and as such, using equitable principles, they found an implied common intention through her conduct (substantial financial contribution to bills, an earlier mortgage and evidence of sharing everything equally) that Mrs Cooke was entitled to a 50 per cent share in the property. However, it was not until 2004 that the *Rosset* 'narrow view' began to change more dramatically – especially in terms of quantification rather than acquisition of the equitable interest.

Recent developments – *Stack* v. *Dowden* [2007] to *Jones* v. *Kernott* [2011]

Generally speaking, much of the early case law was based on acquisition arguments as there was only one name on the register as legal owner – this was true in *Pettitt*, *Gissing* and *Rosset*. In *Oxley* v. *Hiscock* [2004] Mrs Oxley and Mr Hiscock bought a property together using just over 70 per cent of Hiscock's money and 30 per cent from Oxley. The legal title was in the sole name of Mr Hiscock. Both parties contributed to the maintenance and improvement of the property. When the relationship broke down, the Court of Appeal was asked to determine their equitable shares – hence the real question here was one of quantification. Chadwick LJ decided that it was equitable, where there is no evidence of actual discussion, to have 'regard to the whole course of dealing between them in relation to the property' and this includes 'the arrangements they make from time to time in order to meet the outgoings'. The result was a 60/40 split in favour of Mr Hiscock. He argued that a resulting trust mathematical approach should be avoided where possible in such cases as this. This seemed to pave the way for the 'holistic approach' that was about to be taken by Baroness Hale in *Stack* v. *Dowden* – a case where this time *both parties* were on the register as legal owners.

CORNERSTONE

The Case of *Stack* v. *Dowden*

The facts of the case are as follows:

Mr Stack and Ms Dowden began a relationship in 1975 and lived together as man and wife raising four children. They bought a property together, in joint names, with 65 per cent of the purchase price being paid from Dowden's building society account and with proceeds from the sale of a previous house owned solely by Dowden. The remaining 35 per cent came from a joint mortgage and two endowment policies – one of which was in Dowden's sole name. Over the years the parties kept separate bank accounts and saved and invested separately. The mortgage was eventually paid off with Dowden contributing around 60 per cent of the lump sum payments. On the breakdown of the relationship, Mr Stack argued that where there was no evidence of express discussion between the parties as to their equitable share, then 'equity follows the law' where there is a legal joint tenancy (see Chapter 14) and the share should be 50/50. The House of Lords imposed a constructive trust based on 'holisitic approach' and found in favour of Ms Dowden to the tune of 65/35.

The House of Lords did agree that the start point for quantification in a case where there are two or more legal owners is that 'equity follows the law' and the equitable interest should be shared equally. However, Lord Hoffmann suggested that a relationship such as the one in *Stack* is 'ambulatory', with the parties' intentions capable of changing and developing over time. Lord Walker 'respectfully doubted' the stringent approach taken in *Rosset*, stating that the 'law has moved on, and your Lordships should move it a little more in the same direction'. Lord Walker, along with Baroness Hale, was also keen to point out that the Law Commission was, in 2007, 'soon to come forward with proposals' for legislation in relation to the financial regulation of the breakdown of unmarried couples' relationships. This did come to fruition in the Law Commission Report *Cohabitation: The Financial Consequences of Relationship Breakdown* (No. 307, 31 July 2007) (see Further Reading below) where the Law Commission proposed a scheme for 'property adjustment' for unmarried partners. Recently, David Cameron's Alliance government announced that there were no plans to legislate. This has been heavily criticised, with the head of family law at the law firm Mishcon de Reya, Sandra Davis, commenting that 'the continued failure of Parliament to introduce legislation which protects the property interests of the two million cohabiting couples in this country is a disgrace' (see Further Reading below).

As such, it was left to Baroness Hale to state in *Stack* that in 'exceptional circumstances', where there are joint legal owners and no express declaration, equity does not need to 'follow the law' at all, but can rather find a way to justify awarding an 'equitable share' that falls either side of the 50/50 'default line'. Baroness Hale, at what is now referred to simply as 'paragraph 69', goes on to list the factors which may be taken into account:

CORNERSTONE

Stack v. *Dowden*, paragraph 69

69. In law, 'context is everything' and the domestic context is very different from the commercial world. Each case will turn on its own facts. Many more factors than financial contributions may be relevant to divining the parties' true intentions. These include: any advice or discussions at the time of the transfer which cast light upon their intentions then; the reasons why the home was acquired in their joint names; the reasons why (if it be the case) the survivor was authorised to give a receipt for the capital moneys; the purpose for which the home was acquired; the nature of the parties' relationship; whether they had children for whom they both had responsibility to provide a home; how the purchase was financed, both initially and subsequently; how the parties arranged their finances, whether separately or together or a bit of both; how they discharged the outgoings on the property and their other household expenses. When a couple are joint owners of the home and jointly liable for the mortgage, the inferences to be drawn from who pays for what may be very different from the inferences to be drawn when only one is owner of the home. The arithmetical calculation of how much was paid by each is also likely to be less important. It will be easier to draw the inference that they intended that each should contribute as much to the household as they reasonably could and that they would share the eventual benefit or burden equally. The parties' individual characters and personalities may also be a factor in deciding where their true intentions lay. In the cohabitation context, mercenary considerations may be more to the fore than they would be in marriage, but it should not be assumed that they always take pride of place over natural love and affection. At the end of the day, having taken all this into account, cases in which the joint legal owners are to be taken to have intended that their beneficial interests should be different from their legal interests will be very unusual.

Baroness Hale also states, at paragraph 70, that the list is 'not exhaustive'. She also stated that due to this 'holistic approach' there is no longer a place for a resulting trust application in marital or relationship situations. It should be noted that Lord Neuberger dissented vociferously, first disputing that the courts should be asked to 'impute' common intention, especially from a 'course of dealing'. He also disputed that the role of the resulting trust is consigned to history, and successfully proved in a later Court of Appeal case that there is still a place for the resulting trust, albeit in an 'investment' purchase by a couple rather than as a family home (*Laskar* v. *Laskar* [2008]). However, it seems that the 'holistic approach' hit a judicial nerve, as the '*Stack* approach' was followed in the Privy Council case of *Abbott* v. *Abbott* [2007] (also presided over by Baroness Hale) and in the 2008 Court of Appeal case of *Fowler* v. *Barron*. 'Exceptional facts' were also found in *Ritchie* v. *Ritchie* [2007] but not so in *Segal* v. *Pasram* [2007] where a 50/50 split was ordered. It is perhaps not surprising that Professor Dixon refers to the real legacy of *Stack* as being uncertainty – a case is 'exceptional' he states '. . . or not, as the judge chooses' (see Further Reading below).

The question of quantification where there are two legal owners arose again in what is now a leading case on the subject – *Jones* v. *Kernott* [2011] (see Further Reading below).

APPLICATION

Jones v. *Kernott* [2011]

Leonard Kernott and Patricia Jones separated in 1993 after living together in their property in Thundersley, Essex, for eight years. The Supreme Court was asked whether the assets should be shared 50/50 or predominantly allocated to Ms Jones, who paid all of the mortgage for the past 13 years. Kernott moved out after the break-up, leaving Jones to pay the mortgage, maintain the house and raise the couple's two children. The court was told Kernott waited until his children were grown before making a claim on his old home in 2006. In 2008, a county court judge sitting in Southend ruled that Jones should get 90 per cent of the value of the house and her former partner 10 per cent. That decision was upheld by the High Court in London in 2009. In 2010 the Court of Appeal overturned the lower courts' rulings, deciding that Kernott was entitled to half the value of the house because the couple owned equal shares when they separated and neither had since done anything to change the situation.

The case then went on appeal to the Supreme Court in late 2011.

The judgment in the lower courts found in favour of Ms Jones 90 per cent to Mr Jones 10 per cent, following the 'exceptional circumstances' ratio set down in *Stack*. They found that this was a clear exception to the rule that 'equity follows the law' and found it relatively straightforward to depart from the presumption of 50/50 – even though Ms Jones gave evidence that she conceded that if the property had been sold when the relationship first broke down, Mr Kernott would, in her view, have been entitled to 50 per cent. The question for the Court of Appeal, therefore, was whether the 'common intention' had shifted away from 50/50 as a result of him leaving the marital home and not contributing to the mortgage or upkeep from 1993 when the relationship ended to 2008 at the start of the litigation. Wall LJ began the judgment in the Court of Appeal with a warning: 'This is a cautionary tale, which all unmarried couples who are contemplating the purchase of residential property as their home . . . should study.'

Wall LJ went on to find that the conduct of Mr Kernott did not amount to justification of a movement away from the common intention at the breakdown of the relationship that the equitable interests were equal. The result was that Wall LJ decided that a 50/50 split was fair, as there seemed to be a clear common intention that 'equity should follow the law'. He stated that 'the critical question is whether or not I can properly infer from the parties' conduct since separation a joint intention that, over time, the 50–50 split would be varied . . . Presumably, if the beneficial interests are "ambulatory" and the ambulation continues in the same direction, the appellant's interest in the property will at some point be extinguished.'

However, the case went on final appeal to the Supreme Court in May 2011 with the eagerly awaited judgment given in November 2011. The leading judges were Lord Walker and, of course, Baroness Hale. It perhaps goes without saying that the Court of Appeal judgment was reversed and the 90/10 split reinstated.

> *Take note*
> The judgment is well worth reading in full as, apart from giving a clear insight into the case itself, it also gives a very detailed overview of the entire development of the constructive trust (see Further Reading below).

It seems that unless and until the Law Commission's recommendations are taken up by Parliament, the *implied common intention constructive trust* will continue to be, as Lord Neuberger put it in *Stack*, 'difficult, subjective and uncertain'. It is perhaps true to suggest, as Baroness Hale has done in *Stack*, that the law should move on to respond to 'changing social and economic conditions . . . to ascertain the parties' shared intentions, actual, inferred or imputed'. However Neuberger's dissent suggests that 'fairness is not the appropriate yardstick' when dealing with property transactions, and to analyse 'the whole course of dealing . . . in relation to property is too imprecise'. It is also unclear as to whether the nature of common intention is indeed 'ambulatory'. In the recent Court of Appeal case of *Pankhania* v. *Chandegra* [2012], Mummery LJ in the Court of Appeal ruled that where there is an express declaration of trust between the parties, then the courts should only go behind the express declaration where there are 'valid legal reasons' to do so.

It still remains unclear, however, as to what these *valid legal reasons* might be, and when they may be applied. Perhaps, as Dixon suggests, these difficulties are exactly what '*Lord Bridge sought to avoid*' in **Rosset**. Perhaps we are torn between a judicial desire to 'move the law on' and the need for conveyancing clarity. As the Law Lords and many other key players in the realm of family law have suggested, maybe the only real answer for unmarried couples will be found in future legislation.

REFLECTION

KEY POINTS

- When two or more people own a property together, there is always a trust of land in existence. The legal owners with their names on the title are the trustees and may be holding on trust just for each other as beneficiaries, or for beneficiaries outside the legal title.

- This trust of land can be express, or implied through a resulting or constructive trust.

- The express trust can be written in the conveyance or expressly declared by deed after purchase. It can also be expressly stated on the Land Registry Form JO.

- If it is not express, then a trust can be implied: this can be by way of a resulting or a constructive trust. This falls outside section 53(1)(b) of the LPA 1925, and as such there is no need for formalities (s. 53(2)).

- A resulting trust was traditionally used in all co-ownership situations where there was a direct contribution to the purchase price at the time of purchase.

- Traditionally, a constructive trust could be imposed by the court when there were contributions to purchase price or mortgage payments – but the contributions needed to be substantial (*Pettitt*; *Gissing*; *Rosset*). However, these could be made at any time, including after purchase.

- The case of *Stack* v. *Dowden*, especially in relation to joint legal owners ascertaining the quantification of their equitable interest, set down that almost any contribution may allow the imposition of a constructive trust – using the 'holisitic approach' given by Baroness Hale. The 'common intention' of the parties can be implied, inferred or imputed from their 'holistic' conduct and may even be 'ambulatory' (changing over time). There was strong dissent by Neuberger L who disagreed that the courts can 'impute' and that there is no place for a resulting trust in a 'relationship purchase' (*Laskar*).

- *Stack* was effectively followed in *Abbott* and *Fowler* and importantly in *Jones* v. *Kernott* [2011].

- In the Court of Appeal in *Pankhania* a warning was given that the court should only look behind an express declaration to imply or infer that common intention has changed – if the intention was that 'equity follows the law' and it was 50/50 then it should generally remain so over the passing years.

- The Law Commission Report No. 307 (from July 2007) proposes a statutory framework for unmarried partners on the break-up of property. Perhaps only legislation will create the certainty that is lacking in the current common law.

CORE CASES AND STATUTES

Case	About	Importance
Pettitt v. *Pettitt* [1970] AC 777	Husband carries out minor improvements.	No constructive trust – there needs to be substantial contribution to purchase price or mortgage payments.
Gissing v. *Gissing* [1971] AC 886	Wife pays for furnishings and minor decorations.	As above.
Eves v. *Eves* [1975] 1 WLR 1338	Girlfriend 'wields a 14lb sledgehammer'.	A 'new model' constructive trust – according to Lord Denning.
Lloyds Bank v. *Rosset* [1991] 1 AC 107	Wife oversees building work.	No constructive trust – only doing what is 'natural for any wife' – Lord Bridge.
Oxley v. *Hiscock* [2005] Fam 211	Mrs Oxley contributed 30% – Hiscock 70%.	Chadwick LJ awarded 60/40 in favour of Hiscock – broader application of 'contributions' took into account the 'whole course of dealing'.
Stack v. *Dowden* [2007] 2 AC 432	Joint legal owners – equity should follow the law, 50/50 argued.	Baroness Hale – the law has moved on. Based on a holistic analysis, all and any contributions count towards the quantification of a constructive trust: 65/35 to Ms Dowden.
Abbott v. *Abbott* [2007] UKPC 53	Privy Council case on quantification.	Follows *Stack*.
Laskar v. *Laskar* [2008] 1 WLR 2695	Neuberger's dissent from *Stack* put to effect.	There is still a place for the resulting trust – in relationship investment purchases, however.
Jones v. *Kernott* [2011] UKSC 53	50/50 at the time of the relationship breakdown.	The reasons for moving behind an agreement must be 'exceptional' – but, following *Stack*, 90/10 to Ms Jones.
Pankhania v. *Chandegra* [2012] EWCA Civ 1438	50/50 at the start – can the court look behind an express declaration?	No – not unless there are 'valid legal reasons'.

Statute	About	Importance
LPA 1925, s. 53(1)(b)	Declarations of a trust of land.	Must be evidenced in writing.
LPA 1925, s. 53(2)	Constructive and resulting trusts.	No need for formalities.
TOLATA 1996, s. 1	This defines the relationship between co-owners.	Any co-owned land will be held as a 'trust of land', no longer a 'trust for sale'.

FURTHER READING

Bowcott, O. 'Supreme court rules on property rights for unmarried couples', *The Guardian*, Wednesday 9 November 2011 http://www.guardian.co.uk/law/2011/nov/09/court-rules-property-rights-unmarried
This gives an excellent overview of the judgment in *Jones* v. *Kernott* – explains why the Supreme Court awarded 90 per cent to Ms Jones.

Jones v. *Kernott* [2011] UKSC 53 http://www.supremecourt.gov.uk/docs/uksc_2010_0130_judgment.pdf
The entire judgment is a valuable read from beginning to end – a superb explanation of the development of the law in this area.

Land Registry 'Public Guide 18: Joint property ownership'

http://www.landregistry.gov.uk/public/guides/public-guide-18
This useful practice guide sets down the rules and relevant practice forms available for declaring a trust of land.

Law Commission Report *Cohabitation: The Financial Consequences of Relationship Breakdown* (No 307, 31 July 2007) www.parliament.uk/briefing-papers/sn03372.pdf

MacDonald, S. 'Form JO – A Potentially Important Development' http://familyproperty.org.uk/form-jo-a-potentially-important-development/
This gives an excellent overview of the new JO form available for joint owners – written by a family law barrister from private practice in the Midlands.

CHAPTER 14

Co-ownership (Part 2)

BLUEPRINT

Co-ownership (Part 2)

KEY QUESTIONS

LEGISLATION

- Law of Property Act 1925
- Trusts of Land and Appointment of Trustees Act 1996

CONTEXT

- All property bought by more than 1 person is subject to a trust.
- All trusts have trustees and beneficiaries.
- Not all beneficiaries are also trustees – the context of the '5th' owner.

CONCEPTS

- Legal and equitable ownership
- Joint tenancy and tenancy in common
- Survivorship
- Severance
- The workings of TOLATA, ss.14 and 15

- Should co-ownership always be a joint tenancy – tenancy in common is always possible through severance after all?
- Is it correct that the last surviving joint tenant takes the property?
- Should beneficiaries have more power?

- What is the fundamental difference between a joint tenancy and a tenancy in common?
- Is there a distinction between severance by mutual conduct and by mutual agreement?
- Does TOLATA 1996 go far enough to protect the rights of a beneficiary?

CASES

- *AG Securities* v. *Vaughan* [1990]
- *Goodman* v. *Gallant* [1986]
- *Williams* v. *Hensman* [1861]
- *Burgess* v. *Rawnsley* [1975]
- *Kinch* v. *Bullard* [1999]
- *First National* v. *Achampong* [2003]
- Re Citro [1991]

REFORM

- Does TOLATA go far enough – banks will nearly always win over the 'consequences of debt'.

SPECIAL CHARACTERISTICS

- The 'real' difference between joint tenancy and tenancy in common
- The doctrine of survivorship
- Severance by common law and by LPA, s. 36(2)

CRITICAL ISSUES

Setting the scene

When one person owns a property, generally that person owns the legal title of that property. In relation to land law, the only other people that are 'relevant' are any others who may have a claim on or over that property – such as adjacent landowners with possible easements or covenants or lenders who may have provided the money by way of a mortgage. However, what if Jim and Zoe buy a property together? If there is concurrent ownership by two or more people then land law refers to them as co-owners. Rather confusingly, they are referred to as 'tenants' – not because they have a lease, but because the term 'tenant' is derived from the 14th-century word 'tenaunt', which was in itself derived from the verb 'tenere' – 'to hold' (Chapter 13).

It is also true to say that whenever there is co-ownership, there is a *trust of land* created – either expressly stated in the conveyance or on Land Registry Forms (the Form JO); or implied by way of a resulting or constructive trust (see Chapter 13). Co-ownership is of course usually the norm when two people purchase property within a relationship (spouses; partners; civil partners) but it can also be by way of a business relationship in a commercial sense. In either situation, co-ownership will create this trust of land (no longer referred to as a *'trust for sale'* since the Trusts of Land and Appointment of Trustees Act 1996 (TOLATA 1996)). As such there will be a trustee–beneficiary relationship in existence, and although this has no real meaning whilst the co-owners live 'happily-ever-after', the existence of their legal (trustee) and equitable (beneficiary) interests become vital if the property is repossessed, sold or there is a dispute over ownership. This chapter will seek to explain the different types of co-ownership available – that of the **joint tenancy** and the *tenancy in common* – and illustrate the ramifications of such types of co-ownership. It will also explain the rules of severance and how TOLATA 1996 plays a vital role in the event of a dispute.

JOINT TENANCY AND TENANCY IN COMMON

CORNERSTONE

Legal and equitable ownership

It is absolutely vital to understand from the outset that there is a difference between legal and equitable ownership. The 'paper owner' (legal owner and as such also the trustee) is the person whose name appears in the proprietorship section of the register – but this is really no more than the 'nominal' title. As Professor Martin Dixon points out (see Further Reading), it is the equitable interest that is the 'real value' in the property. The equitable interest, by way of the express or implied trust that is in existence, is the extent of the right the beneficiary has to enjoy and/or use the land. So, if Jim and Zoe buy a property together, and both names appear on the title, then they are said to be joint legal owners (or joint tenants at law) but are also holding the property on trust for each other as beneficiaries – and as such their equitable interest will be either as joint tenants or tenants in common. It should be noted that the legal title can only be held as *joint tenants* under section 1(6) of the LPA 1925 but as this legal co-ownership is only really nominal, it is the equitable interest that is the key – and that can be held as joint tenants or tenants in common. Once again, whilst the co-owners are in a state of harmony, and are still alive, the distinction is of minimal importance. However, on separation, sale, bankruptcy, repossession or death, the distinction becomes vitally important as the status of a joint tenancy or a tenancy in common will lead to a very different outcome in relation to each person's equitable interest. It should also be noted that there can be an infinite number of equitable owners (in theory), but a maximum of four legal co-owners, and where the property is purchased by more than four people together, the first four will be 'named' as the legal owners under section 34(2) of the Trustee Act 1925. It is also worth remembering that if there is only one legal owner, the beneficiaries' interests cannot be overreached.

It is therefore necessary to establish at the outset whether the co-owners are joint tenants in equity or tenants in common. In practice, a conveyancer will usually (if not always) ask the question to the prospective co-owners as to whether they wish to hold as joint tenants or tenants in common and this will be recorded on the conveyance document. A conveyancer or solicitor should be able to explain the consequences of each type of co-ownership, the key consequence being the operation of the rule of '*ius accrescendi*' or *survivorship* and this will be explained below. Essentially though, this means that if the co-owners are joint tenants in equity, they cannot leave their interest in a will – on death, the interest will automatically vest in the remaining joint tenant. If the co-owners are tenants in common, then survivorship rules do not operate and the parties are free to leave their interest in a will to whomever they choose. This will be explained in full below.

APPLICATION

Jim, Zoe, Ava, Jake and Elsa buy a property together. Their conveyancer fills in the relevant conveyance document and all but Elsa are named as the legal owners. The status of the co-ownership relationship is that all but Elsa are joint tenants at law (LPA 1925, s. 1(6)) and are therefore trustees holding for each other as beneficiaries and also holding as trustees for Elsa who only has a beneficial interest. All five are beneficial co-owners but may hold their equitable interests as joint tenants or tenants in common – there are, of course, rules which need to be applied to establish their equitable status – and these will now be explained (see Figure 14.1).

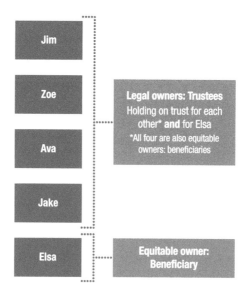

Figure 14.1 Legal and equitable co-ownership

Joint tenancy – the four unities

The defining feature of a joint tenancy is that the joint tenants own the entire property 'as one', with no distinct shares either equal or unequal. As stated by William Blackstone in his *Commentaries on the Laws of England* as far back as 1765, a joint tenancy is an estate which the law recognises as a 'thorough and intimate union of interest and possession' (see Further Reading below). This means that each joint tenant is entitled to the whole of the property. However, for a joint tenancy to exist, as Blackstone put it, the joint tenancy is 'derived from its unity, which is fourfold'. This is commonly known as the 'four unities', namely unity of *possession*, *interest*, *time* and *title* (see Figure 14.2). If a joint tenancy is to be established, these four unities must be present from the outset of the tenancy, as set down in the case of *AG Securities* v. *Vaughan* [1990]:

1. *Possession*: Essentially this means that the co-owners are entitled to possess the entire property. If boundaries or restrictions exist there cannot be a joint tenancy in operation. It is an 'undivided possession' as Blackstone stated.

2. *Interest*: This means that the co-owners have the same interest in the land. For example, if one of the joint tenants has a lease of 10 years, and the other has a lease of eight, it cannot be a joint tenancy. It also stands to reason that no single co-owner can sell the property unilaterally, as they do not own it unilaterally.

3. *Time*: This simply means that the interests of the co-owners vested at the same time – this will of course generally be at the time of the transfer of the property to the joint tenants.

4. *Title*: As above, the co-owners' title must be derived from the same conveyance or transfer of the land.

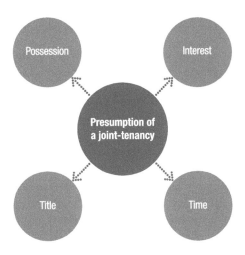

Figure 14.2 The four unities

The effect of the four unities being present is that it creates a *presumption* of a joint tenancy. It is important to understand that the existence of the four unities is only the start point. If there is a clear intention that the parties intended to hold the property in 'shares' – even equal shares – the tenants will be holding their equitable title as 'tenants in common' and not as joint tenants. As explained above, there can be no divisible share; all must own everything.

As such, if there are '*words of severance*' within the conveyance (in other words, any suggestion that the parties hold in shares), the equitable interest will be a tenancy in common regardless of the presence of the four unities. The words 'share and share alike' appeared in *Heathe* v. *Heathe* (1740); 'between' appeared in *Lashbrook* v. *Cock* (1816); and 'in equal shares' appeared in *Martin* v. *Martin* [1987]. These cases were held to be tenancies in common and not joint tenancies. Of course, if there are express words in the conveyance itself to suggest a joint tenancy, and the four unities are present, then generally, according to *Goodman* v. *Gallant* [1986], that will be conclusive. In *Roy* v. *Roy* [1996] the conveyance stated that the property was vested in the co-owners 'as Joint Tenants at law and in equity'. It is also a presumption, that where the four unities exist and there are no words of sever-

> **Take note**
> Remember that co-owners cannot hold the legal title as tenants in common – as the common law does not recognise the latter relationship (LPA 1925, s. 1(6)). It is only the equitable title that can be 'chosen' to be a joint tenancy or a tenancy in common.

ance, then *equity follows the law*, and a joint tenancy at law will also be a joint tenancy in equity.

INTERSECTION

A full discussion of the presumption of 'equity following the law' can be seen in the key case of *Stack* v. *Dowden* [2007] as discussed in Chapter 13.

Tenancy in common – the presumptions

The only 'necessary' unity for a tenancy in common to exist is that of the unity of possession. Each tenant holds a notional, if yet undivided share of the property. As stated above, this can be an equal or unequal share, but the word 'share' should be used here, rather than the word 'interest' which is the more apposite description in a joint tenancy. All tenants in common must still have the right to entitlement of the property – the difference in a tenancy in common is that they hold in this notional fractional share. If there are no 'words of severance' in a conveyance to co-owners, and no express words suggesting a tenancy in common (or a joint tenancy), then equity allows certain presumptions to operate. It is true to say that common law has always favoured the joint tenancy, but in *McDowell* v. *Hirschfield Lipson & Romney* [1992] Stockdale J reminded the court of 'equity's dislike of the joint tenancy and its marked preference for the tenancy in common' for reasons of fairness. The presumptions (albeit rebuttable with appropriate and compelling evidence) operate as follows:

> **Take note**
>
> These presumptions, especially the latter in relation to business partners, clearly demonstrate that the fundamental operational difference between a joint tenancy and a tenancy in common is the application of the doctrine of survivorship.

1. Unequal purchase money contributions: *Bull* v. *Bull* [1955].

2. Joint mortgages: a presumption that each co-owner has an as yet undivided share.

3. Commercial assets in a partnership: due to the rule of survivorship (see below) this is presumed to be a tenancy in common – *Lake* v. *Craddock* (1732).

4. Business tenants: again, mainly due to the presumption that business associates will not want the survivorship rules to apply – *Malayan Credit Ltd* v. *Jack Chia* [1986].

Survivorship

The operation of the rule of survivorship only applies where there is a joint tenancy and *not* a tenancy in common. If a joint tenant dies, then the equitable interest belonging to the deceased joint tenant simply passes to the remaining joint tenants automatically. It was stated above that a joint tenant cannot therefore leave his interest in a will (*Gould* v. *Kemp* (1834)), and neither can it pass to their personal representatives or next of kin if the joint tenant dies intestate. Arguably, this makes conveyancing more straightforward, as there is no need for formal transfer as the property vests automatically in the remaining joint tenants. There is also a rather useful protective element, as if the deceased has creditors, then generally the creditors have no claim on the property. However, there is of course a risk taken by joint tenants, as the 'last man standing', or in legal terms the sole surviving joint tenant, takes the property absolutely! Stockdale J, in the *Romney* case above, likened the risk of survivorship in a joint tenancy to 'the well known gamble of double or quits' pointing out that each joint tenant 'ran the risk of dying first'!

'The Plane Crash Rule?'

Perhaps even more strangely, there is a quaint English law doctrine known as the *commorientes* rule, which states that if joint tenants die simultaneously and the order in which they died cannot therefore be ascertained, the general rule is that the property vests automatically in the estate of the *youngest* of the joint tenants, as 'the deaths are presumed to have occurred in order of age so that the younger is presumed to have survived the elder' (LPA 1925, s. 184).

As such, again as illustrated by Stockdale J, this 'risk' of survivorship has been cited as one of the reasons as to why equity with its inherent belief in fairness, prefers the tenancy in common. It is also one of the reasons why there are rules of *severance* which allow an equitable joint tenancy interest to be *severed* and, as if by magic, 'turned into' a tenancy in common share (see Figure 14.3).

SEVERANCE – COMMON LAW AND STATUTORY METHODS

CORNERSTONE

Severance of the equitable joint tenancy

It is absolutely vital to understand that the legal co-ownership status cannot be severed. Remember that this is really the nominal ownership not the 'real value' of the co-owners' estate. As such, when 'acts of severance' occur, the legal estate remains untouched. There can be no tenancy in common of the legal estate. This can be found at section 36(2) of the LPA 1925: 'No severance of a joint tenancy of a legal estate, so as to create a tenancy in common in land, shall be permissible . . . but this does not affect the right of a joint tenant to . . . sever a joint tenancy in an equitable interest.'

It is also crucial to understand that when the equitable interest is severed by one joint tenant unilaterally, it becomes a tenancy in common interest; the remaining joint tenants maintain their joint tenancy status, as the four unities have not been displaced. Think of it as removing a slice of a pie, that one slice may still be on the plate, but it is now distinct from the rest of the pie that is still intact. All acts of severance create an immediate tenancy in common interest due to the destruction of at least one of the four unities.

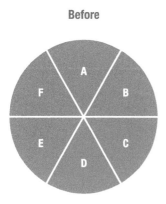

Before	After

- **A, B, C and D** are legal joint tenants
- **A – D** hold on trust for themselves and **E and F**
- All six hold as joint tenants in equity (four unites and no contrary presumptions)

- **F** severs by common law methods in *Williams* v. *Hensman* or by LPA 1925, s. 36(2)
- **F's** share is now a 1/6 tenancy in common share
- **A – E** still have a 5/6 joint tenancy interest in the property

Figure 14.3 Before and after an act of severance

APPLICATION

Andrew, Bharda, Claire, Doda and Elsbeth all buy a property, each contributing 20 per cent. The first four, (A–D), hold the property as joint tenants at law on trust for each other and for Elsbeth, who has just a beneficial interest. All five, due to the four unities being present and a lack of any presumptions to the contrary, hold as joint tenants in equity. Elsbeth decides that she wishes to sell her equitable interest (20 per cent for the sake of simplicity) to Frederica. If the relevant method of severance (see below) has been used then Elsbeth drops out of the picture altogether. As soon as the severance occurs, Elsbeth's interest becomes a tenancy in common interest, and this tenancy in common interest is purchased by Frederica. Due to the fact that she now has a 20 per cent interest in the property along with the other four remaining co-owners, there is still co-ownership between the 'new' five co-owners. However, Frederica's status is as a tenant in common (due to the lack of four unities – time and title especially) whilst A–D still hold as joint tenants with their 20 per cent interests untouched. That of course means that A–D still operate under the survivorship doctrine, whereas Frederica is free to leave her 'share' in a will. It also means that Frederica will not benefit from automatic transfer of A–D's interests if any of them die.

If, however, going back to the original position, A–E all decide to sever 'mutually' (again, following one of the severance methods illustrated below), then all five will have tenancy in common interests – the joint tenancy between all five will be over.

As such, it is necessary to be able to identify the various methods of severance. There are three 'common law' methods (set down in the case of *Williams* v. *Hensman* (1861)) and one statutory method set down at section 36(2) of the LPA 1925.

Williams v. *Hensman* (1861) – the common law methods

(i) An act of any person interested operating upon his own share

This means that one of the joint tenants 'alienates' or transfers his share to another – either someone outside the existing co-owners or one or more of the original joint tenants.

It is also true that partial alienation, such as taking an equitable mortgage of your interest, will also fall under this method of severance, as will being adjudicated bankrupt (as this has the effect of vesting your assets in the 'trustee in bankruptcy'). In *Re Dennis (a bankrupt)* [1995] the Court of Appeal held that bankruptcy severed the joint tenancy between husband and wife, and as such the wife could now leave her share in her will. The husband's creditors were free to claim against his now divided share.

(ii) Mutual agreement

By its very definition, this method requires *all* of the joint tenants to agree to sever the entire joint tenancy, turning it into a tenancy in common for all concerned. Of course, the intention of a common intention to sever must be communicated to all joint tenants and in *Burgess* v. *Rawnsley* [1975] Sir John Pennycuick stated that it is the 'indication of a common intention to sever' that allows severance through mutual agreement; the outcome of any evidenced negotiation is largely irrelevant. This evidence may be implied rather than in a written agreement, or in a simple draft agreement as in *Hunter* v. *Babbage* [1994].

> ### Take note
> Using this first method does not need the agreement of the other joint tenants – it is a unilateral act, but once complete it is final and irrevocable. Hence the serving of a summons at the commencement of litigation on fellow joint tenants, due to its finality and irrevocability, is another example of an act of severance using this first method (*Re Draper's Conveyance* [1967]).

(iii) Mutual conduct

Although on the face of it mutual conduct is not so different from mutual agreement, it is seen by the common law as a distinct method. This involves a 'course of dealing' between the co-owners – again, *all* of the co-owners. In *Burgess* Lord Denning distinguished the two methods by stating that a 'course of dealing' need not amount to an agreement as such; it is sufficient that such a course of dealing which demonstrates an intention to hold the property in shares is an act of severance. In *Hunter* v. *Babbage* John McDonnell QC disputes any real difference between the two methods, but states that the course of dealing must 'intimate that the interests of all were mutually treated as constituting a tenancy in common'.

APPLICATION

> It would seem like the conduct of writing mutual wills leaving the interest to each other may act as severance by mutual conduct, even though technically 'shares' cannot be left in a will when co-owners are joint tenants. It would seem that the act of sitting down and writing the wills is the act of severance, as it demonstrates a common intention to sever (*Re Wilford's Estate* (1879)).

(iv) Murder

It goes without saying (hopefully!) that if one joint tenant murders the other then this does not amount to an act of severance and neither do the rules of survivorship apply (*Cleaver* v. *Mutual Reserve Fund*

Life Association [1892]). There is no authority in a case of manslaughter, however, but section 2(2) of the Forfeiture Act 1982 suggests that the court has discretion in situations such as a suicide pact (*Dunbar* v. *Plant* [1998]).

The statutory method – LPA 1925, section 36(2)

This is the most common and most straightforward way in which to sever a joint tenancy. In conveyancing terms, there is a Land Registry form known as the *Form SEV*: if it, or even a simple letter, is served on all remaining joint tenants, severance will occur. The notice to sever must therefore be in writing, can be a unilateral act and must be served on all remaining joint tenants. It must, however, demonstrate an immediate intention to sever, not a future desire. Wills, therefore, are excluded from the operation of section 36(2). Lawson LJ in *Harris* v. *Goddard* stated that under section 36(2) immediacy is vital. He stated that a 'notice in writing which expresses a desire to bring about the wanted result at some time in the future is not, in my judgment, a notice in writing within section 36(2)'.

It is also true to say that section 36(2) operates in conjunction with sections 196(4) and 196(3) of the LPA 1925, which set down the rules of service for such a notice and illustrate when that notice is deemed to be effective:

CORNERSTONE

LPA 1925, section 196(4)

Any notice . . . shall be sufficiently served, if it is sent by post in a registered letter . . . if that letter is not returned through the post-office undelivered; and that service shall be deemed to be made at the time at which the registered letter would in the ordinary course be delivered.

LPA 1925, section 196(3)

Note also that if the notice is sent by *ordinary post* then section 196(3) applies. This sets down that the notice is deemed to have been served if it is left at the last known address, deemed to be effective in line with normal postage times. As such, posting a notice with a first class stamp would be deemed to be served the next working morning. It is an irrebuttable presumption and the addressee cannot argue that it was never received. Neither does it need to be read by the addressee to be deemed as served.

There are two key cases which illustrate this method and how it operates. In *Re 88 Berkeley Road NW9* [1971], the two co-owners were joint tenants at law and in equity. A notice of severance was sent by one of the joint tenants to the other, and, even though the latter did not receive the notice, as it had been signed for by the severing tenant, it was deemed to have been served.

APPLICATION

The 'tragic case' of *Kinch* v. *Bullard* [1999]

As Neuberger J (as he was then) suggested, this was indeed a 'tragic case' but one which illustrates the operation of section 36(2) perfectly. A man and his wife were living as joint tenants
at law and in equity, but they were en route to a divorce. The wife was also sadly dying from a
terminal illness and believed therefore that she would die before her husband. Her concern was
that as joint tenants the survivorship rule would apply and, on her death, he would automatically
take the entire property. She would be unable to leave any 'share' in a will. So, she decided that
she would go to see her solicitor and send a notice of severance to her husband in order to
convert her interest into a tenancy in common which she could then leave to family members.
The solicitor duly posted a first-class stamped letter to the matrimonial home where they were
both still living. However, just as the letter arrived on the Saturday morning, that very weekend
the husband, before being able to read the notice, suffered a major heart attack and was taken
to hospital. As Neuberger pointedly suggested, any good wife would rush to her husband's
bedside, but the wife rushed home instead to intercept and destroy the letter of severance
because she now, rightly, believed that the husband would die first, and if severance had not
taken place she would take the property entirely!

　　The husband did in fact die 10 days later. The wife, having destroyed the letter, lived for the
next five months believing that the severance had been 'cancelled', at which point she also died
from her illness. The dispute then arose between the two executors (hence Kinch and Bullard)
as to whether there had been valid severance or not.

　　Neuberger J pointed to section 196(3) of the LPA 1925 (as this was ordinary post) and stated
clearly that once such a notice is deemed to have been served – and under section 196(3) this
meant that the notice was served as soon as it 'hit the mat' regardless of the husband not
having read the notice – then it is irrevocable. Once the deed has been done, he said, 'it cannot
be undone' unless the letter is perhaps intercepted by the sender before it arrives or the wife
had informed her husband that, even though the notice had been sent, she had changed her
mind. However, arguably, this 'revocation' would also have needed to take place before the
arrival of the letter.

Once severance has occurred, other than it being possible that an express agreement which states
the contrary may be valid, the tenants in common hold in equal shares, even though they may have
originally contributed unequally to the purchase (*Goodman* v. *Gallant* [1986]).

THE APPLICATION OF THE TRUSTS OF LAND AND APPOINTMENT OF TRUSTEES ACT 1996

Prior to the coming into force of the Trusts of Land and Appointment of Trustees Act 1996 (TOLATA
1996) on 1 January 1997, any land held under co-ownership was said to be held as a 'trust for sale'
– the implication being that the co-owners were holding the property on trust with a duty to sell that
property to realise the cash value, and, once sold, the proceeds of that sale would also be held on
trust for the co-owners. However, as Lord Denning remarked in *Williams* v. *Williams* [1977], the idea

of the 'trust for sale' was in effect a 'legal fiction' as he stated that 'nowadays . . . the house is bought as a home in which the family is to be brought up . . . not treated as property to be sold, nor as an investment to be realised for cash.'

Denning's view did not materialise as legislation until TOLATA 1996, where at section 1, the 'trust for sale' was replaced by a 'trust of land' defined as 'any property which consists of or includes land'. Any existing 'trusts for sale' were instantly 'converted' into 'trusts of land' (ss. 4 and 5) and the trust of land is imposed whether the trust was created expressly or impliedly. Hence the first point to make is that since TOLATA 1996 there is no longer a duty on any trustee/legal owner to sell the property.

The trustees, or joint tenants at law, have a number of key powers under TOLATA:

> ### Take note
>
> Selling to the beneficiaries confirms the old common law in Saunders v. Vautier (1841) (this can be found in the law of equity and trusts where, of course, there is an overlap with land law in this area).

1. Sections 6 and 7: The trustees have the power of an 'absolute owner' – to sell, to lease, or to take a mortgage. They can also sell the land outright to beneficiaries of 'full age and capacity' where they are entitled to full ownership. The trustees can also partition the land under section 7 where the beneficiaries are 'of age and capacity' and are entitled to undivided shares in the land. The powers under sections 6 and 7 may be limited or expressly excluded, however, if the trust was created by a *disposition* (s. 8).

2. Section 9: The trustees may also delegate their powers by 'power of attorney' to any beneficiary of 'age, capacity' and entitled to be in possession of the land.

3. Section 11: This states that the trustees 'so far as practicable' consult the beneficiaries, and where 'consistent with general interest of the trust' give effect to those wishes. This does seem to suggest that TOLATA 1996, section 11 does protect the beneficiaries from an unwanted sale by the trustees, but really, this section is a duty merely to 'consult' – the threshold is set deliberately low to allow trustees to sell relatively freely and, of course, overreaching may always occur where the sale is by at least two trustees. (*City of London Building Society* v. *Flegg* [1988]). It is also true to state that consultation rights can also be expressly excluded (*Waller* v. *Waller* [1967]).

4. Section 12: Allows entitled beneficiaries in possession of the land to occupy the land if the purposes of the trust include 'making the land available for occupation' or the land is already available, but not if the land is 'unavailable or unsuitable' for occupation. What is meant by 'unsuitable' is not clarified, and seems to be case-specific. Jonathan Parker LJ in *Chun* v. *Ho* [2003] stated that it must involve consideration of general situation and the 'personal characteristics, circumstances and requirements of the particular beneficiary'. The right to occupy can also be reasonably restricted or excluded where there are two or more beneficiaries with the right to occupy (see section 13).

5. Section 13: This right to 'occupy' can be reasonably excluded or restricted or the trustees can impose conditions as to occupation. Also, at section 13(6) trustees also have the power to require a beneficiary in occupation to compensate other beneficiaries excluded or restricted under section 12. Under section 13(5) trustees can also impose conditions which compel payment of expenses by beneficiaries to cover the cost of repairs and improvements. This was previously dealt with by the common law in such cases as *Leigh* v. *Dickeson* (1884) and *Re Pavlou* [1993].

Disputes – sections 14 and 15

In any situation where there is a dispute between trustees and beneficiaries, then section 14 gives the power to 'any person who is a trustee or who has an interest in property subject to a trust of land [such as the beneficiaries; mortgagees; trustees in bankruptcy] to make an application to the court for an order under s14(2)'. The court can then make *any order* in relation to the powers of the trustee or make a declaration in relation to the beneficial interests. The factors which are considered by the court are listed at section 15 or, in the case of an application by a 'trustee in bankruptcy', the factors are listed at section 335A of the Insolvency Act 1986. The factors at section 15 are:

(a) the intentions of the person who created the trust;

(b) the purpose of the trust;

(c) the welfare of minors who occupy or might reasonably be expected to occupy;

(d) the interests of any secured creditors of any beneficiaries.

In *TSB* v. *Marshall* [1998], the first case which dealt with section 14, an order for possession and sale was granted as the section 15 factors were not satisfied – there was no evidence to suggest the purpose of the property was to provide a home for the *adult* children. In the key case of *Mortgage Corporation* v. *Shaire* [2001] Neuberger J referred explicitly to the development of the law under section 15 of TOLATA 1996. He stated that section 15 gives far more rights to beneficiaries than the previous 'primary purpose doctrine' under the now repealed section 30 of the LPA 1925. However, he also stated that section 15 allows the court to decide 'what weight to give to each factor' in a particular case. In *Shaire*, Neuberger left the parties to agree terms in a claim by the lender for possession. He made it clear, however, that if Mrs Shaire would not agree to favourable terms which would allow the lender to recover at least some of the debt (caused in no small part by Mrs Shaire's 'forging' partner) then he would order the sale.

> ## Take note
>
> It is normally *not* necessary for legal mortgagees (banks/building societies) to apply under section 14 as there are already relevant statutory provisions under sections 101–105 of the LPA 1925. However, a lender may need to rely on section 14 if one of the co-owners has forged the signature of the other on the mortgage deed – only the forger's interest will then be bound by the mortgage charge (the forgery is in effect an act of severance). The lender may also need to apply section 14 if a mortgage is granted by a sole legal owner where a pre-existing beneficial interest is present and that person is in actual occupation.

It seems quite certain, especially from later cases, that in most situations, banks and lenders will be successful and will be allowed to realise their valuable commercial assets. In *Bank of Ireland* v. *Bell* [2001], another case where section 14 applied due to a forgery by one legal owner, despite the fact that the son of the marriage had great needs and the wife was suffering poor health, the Bank was successful. Peter Gibson LJ stated that, above all, 'powerful consideration is . . . whether the creditor is receiving proper recompense for being kept out of his money, repayment of which is over-due'. This was echoed in *First National Bank* v. *Achampong* [2003] where the Court of Appeal side-stepped the issue of a child with a mental disability and other occupying grandchildren in ordering a sale to prevent the lender 'waiting indefinitely for payment'. In *Pritchard Englefield* v. *Steinberg* [2004], Mrs Steinberg was granted two months' delay to find a buyer, even though this was highly improbable due to the buyer needing to purchase subject to Mrs Steinberg's right to occupy rent-free for life! Peter Smith J did allow this token two-month reprieve, but still ordered the sale should the two months expire without a buyer. A little more leniency was displayed by Park J in *Edwards* v. *Lloyds TSB* [2004] where a five-year postponement of the sale was ordered to account for the relatively small debt, two occupying minors and the proceeds of sale not being sufficient to allow Mrs Edwards to buy elsewhere at the time of the order. In 2010, in the case of *National Westminster* v. *Rushmer* it was decided that section 14 did not contravene Protocol 1 and Article 8 of the European Convention on Human Rights due to the discretion allowed through the application of section 15.

As stated above, where trustees in bankruptcy apply under section 14, the factors listed at section 335A of the Insolvency Act 1986 must be applied. These are similar to those at section 15 but include:

(a) the interests of the creditors;

(b) the residential nature of the property (where it is the home of the bankrupt or their partner);

(c) the conduct of the spouse or partner, so far as it may have contributed to the bankruptcy;

(d) the needs and resources of spouses and partners;

(e) the needs of any children; and

(f) any other circumstances of the case other than the needs of the bankrupt.

However, in *Re Citro* [1991] it was made perfectly clear by Nourse LJ that in cases where a spouse's needs will be weighed against a creditor in a situation of bankruptcy, 'the voice of the creditors will usually prevail . . . and a sale will be ordered within a short period'. Nourse LJ went on to clarify that even where the property is still the marital home, the 'voice of the spouse' will 'only prevail in exceptional circumstances'.

How, then, would you define 'exceptional circumstances'? Nourse LJ in *Re Citro* argues that such factors as young children, schooling issues and a lack of money to buy elsewhere are simply 'melancholy consequences of debt'. He suggests that only perhaps when postponement of the sale does not cause 'any great hardship to any of the creditors' will a delay be ordered, pointing to the judgment in *Re Holliday* [1981], but states that even this 'went against the run of recent authorities'. In *Re Raval* [1998] the spouse's mental illness convinced the court to exercise its discretion, as did the spouse's disability in *Claughton* v. *Charalambous* [1999] but it seems abundantly clear that, as Stuart Isaacs QC stated in *Donohoe* v. *Ingram* [2006], *Re Citro* seems to suggest that 'only circumstances which were inherently unusual qualified as exceptional circumstances'.

REFLECTION

As such, it is unarguable that TOLATA 1996 is useful in relation to a dispute between beneficiaries and trustees or any interested third parties, and if a beneficiary's rights remain intact then at least TOLATA may give them a chance to argue against, as Park J puts it in *Edwards*, 'severe consequences' of an owed debt, but the lender, especially in bankruptcy, will almost certainly prevail.

KEY POINTS

- When two or more people own a property together, there is always a trust of land in existence. The legal owners with their names on the title are the trustees and the equitable owners are beneficiaries under the trust.

- This trust of land can be express, or implied through a resulting or constructive trust – see Chapter 13.

- All co-owners hold the legal title as joint tenants but the equitable co-ownership can be held as joint tenants or tenants in common.

- There can be a maximum of four legal owners but, in theory at least, an indefinite number of beneficiaries. The relationship is also governed by TOLATA 1996.

- A joint tenancy in equity needs the existence of the four unities: possession, interest, time and title. Other presumptions may also apply, including 'equity follows the law', so that a legal joint tenancy points towards an equitable joint tenancy too. Equal purchase price and a 'family/matrimonial' relationship also suggest a joint tenancy.

- Words of severance or a business arrangement may point towards a tenancy in common – this is important due to the lack of survivorship operating in a tenancy in common. Shares may be left in a will or left open to a claim by creditors in a tenancy in common, but not in a joint tenancy.

- Survivorship allows joint tenants' interests to pass automatically to the remaining joint tenants.

- In order to avoid this, joint tenants may sever their equitable joint tenancy by the operation of the three methods in *Williams* v. *Hensman* (1861) or by notice under section 36(2) of the LPA 1925. When a notice of severance is deemed to be delivered it will be effective and irrevocable, converting the interest into a tenancy in common share (*Kinch* v. *Bullard*).

- Trustees and beneficiaries may be able to solve disputes by the application of the key sections of TOLATA 1996, especially sections 14 and 15 (section 335A of the Insolvency Act 1986 in place of section 15 factors in cases of bankruptcy).

- Beneficiaries should be aware that it is usually the bank or lender who will prevail, especially in a case of bankruptcy (*Re Citro*).

CORE CASES AND STATUTES

Case	About	Importance
AG Securities v. *Vaughan* [1990] 1 AC 417	Co-ownership of a property.	This case clarified the four unities needed for a joint tenancy to exist: possession; interest; time; and title.
Martin v. *Martin* [1987] P & CR 238	The words used in a conveyance may be a clear indication of co-ownership status.	Words of severance – 'in equal shares'; indicate a tenancy in common regardless of the four unities.
Goodman v. *Gallant* (1986) Fam 106 *Roy* v. *Roy* [1996] 1 FLR 541	'To X and Y – joint tenants at law and in equity'.	Words in a conveyance will be conclusive – if the interests are as one then the presumption is a joint tenancy.
Malayan Credit v. *Jack Chia* [1986] AC 549	A commercial agreement.	The presumption is that in a business arrangement it will be a tenancy in common as there is a presumption against the operation of survivorship.
Williams v. *Hensman* (1861) 1 John & H 546	Joint tenants wished to sever their co-ownership in equity.	This case sets down the three methods of common law severance – acting on your share/mutual agreement and mutual conduct.
Burgess v. *Rawnsley* [1975] Ch 429	Indication of a common intention to sever through negotiation.	This is an act of severance by mutual agreement – it must include all joint tenants.
Hunter v. *Babbage* (1995) 69 P & CR 548	Draft agreement to sever.	This is severance through mutual conduct.
Kinch v. *Bullard* [1999] 1 WLR 423	The unscrupulous wife who tried to rip up her letter of severance.	Once a letter has been served under section 36(2) of the LPA 1925 (and also LPA 1925, s. 196) it is effective from the moment it is deemed served – not when it is read.
First National Bank v. *Achampong* [2003] EWCA Civ 487	Attempt by a beneficiary to postpone sale by a lender.	Even with a mentally disabled child, the lender prevailed.
Re Citro [1991] Ch 142	Attempt by a bankrupt's family to postpone a sale.	The reasons for postponement must be 'exceptional' – not just the 'consequences of debt'.

Statute	About	Importance
LPA 1925, s. 1(6)	Legal title in co-ownership.	This section sets down that legal title can only be held as a joint tenancy.
Trustee Act 1925, s. 34(2)	Maximum number of legal joint tenants.	Four.
LPA 1925, s. 36(2)	The statutory method of severance – notice in writing.	It must be served on all remaining joint tenants and show an immediate intention to sever.
LPA 1925, s. 196	Once a notice is served it is deemed to be effective on arrival.	Section 196(3) and (4) set down that once a notice is deemed to have arrived through normal postage rules, it is irrevocable.
TOLATA 1996, ss. 12–15 Insolvency Act 1986 s. 335A	This governs the relationship between the trustee and beneficiary and any other interested party.	Sections 14 and 15 in particular allow an interested party to petition the court for a remedy in relation to their trustee power or their beneficial interest. Section 15 sets down the factors the courts will take into account (unless in a case of bankruptcy, where IA 1986, s. 335A factors apply).

FURTHER READING

Blackstone, W. 'Of Estates in Severalty, Joint-Tenancy, Coparcenary, and Common' in *Commentaries on the Laws of England*, Book 2, Chapter 12 http://ebooks.adelaide. edu.au/b/blackstone/william/ comment/book2.12.html
This provides a thorough background to the law on co-ownership – from as far back as 1765!

***Kinch* v. *Bullard* [1998] 4 All ER 650, 47 EG 140**
Examines the nature of severance by notice – a clear explanation of the workings of LPA 1925, ss. 36(2) and 196.

Nicholls, A. 'Joint Tenants or Tenants in Common?' http://www.stephens- scown.co.uk/blog/2012/03/joint- tenants-or-tenants-in-common/ (Stephens Scown Solicitors)
A practical overview of the material differences between a joint tenancy and a tenancy in common and why they matter in conveyancing terms.

Pascoe, S. 'Section 15 of the Trusts of Land and Appointment of Trustees Act 1996 – A Change in the Law?' [2000] Conv 315
This gives a detailed overview of TOLATA 1996 – especially the workings of s. 15 and the changes from LPA 1925, s. 30.